Critical Company Law

Dr Talbot traces the history of the fundamental principles of English company law, including the doctrine of separate corporate personality, directors' duties, minority protection and the doctrine of *ultra vires* from both a black letter and contextual perspective. Relevant aspects of the Companies Act 2006 are thoroughly examined.

Drawing on the influence of American law and American scholarship, the book considers the ideas which have informed corporate governance in England. It includes a case study of mutual building societies' march to the market and corporate identity. The hybrid approach adopted in the text provides a contextual and critical framework in which to understand company law as well as a broad picture in black letter law terms.

The aim is to invigorate what many students and academics consider a dry subject by uncovering the social factors which continue to inform this area of law – and the political nature of the law itself. Dr Talbot maintains that modern company law is shaped by three main factors – economics, ideology and existing law. The state of the law at any one time is determined by the constantly shifting relationship between these factors.

Dr Talbot lectures in company law and comparative company law at London Metropolitan University. Her research interests are in American and English corporate law, business associations and corporate governance from a critical and contextual perspective. She has delivered a number of papers on these areas and has published in the *Company Lawyer*, *Law and Critique* and the *Cambridge Journal of Financial Crime*.

Critical Company Law

LE Talbot

Routledge·Cavendish
Taylor & Francis Group

First published 2008
by Routledge-Cavendish
2 Park Square, Milton Park, Abingdon, Oxon OX14 4RN, UK

Simultaneously published in the USA and Canada
by Routledge-Cavendish
270 Madison Avenue, New York, NY 10016

Routledge-Cavendish is an imprint of the Taylor & Francis Group, an informa business

© 2008 LE Talbot

Typeset in Times and Gill Sans by
RefineCatch Limited, Bungay, Suffolk
Printed and bound in Great Britain by
The Cromwell Press, Trowbridge, Wiltshire

British Library Cataloguing in Publication Data
A catalogue record for this book is available from the British Library

Library of Congress Cataloging-in-Publication Data
Talbot, Lorraine.
   Critical company law / Lorraine Talbot.
      p.   cm.
   ISBN 978–0–415–42542–1 (pbk.: alk. paper)   1. Corporation law – Great Britain.   2. Business enterprises – Law and legislation – Great Britain.   I. Title.
   KD2079.T35   2007
   346.42′066 – dc22

                                                            2007005767

ISBN 10: 0–415–42542–5 (pbk)
ISBN 10: 0–203–94467–4 (ebk)

ISBN 13: 978–0–415–42542–1 (pbk)
ISBN 13: 978–0–203–94467–7 (ebk)

Contents

Introduction

The purpose of this book is to provide a black letter law account of the fundamental principles of company law within a critical and often historical context. By taking this hybrid approach to the study of company law it is hoped that a richer understanding of the subject may be gained. Company law scholarship in Britain is largely composed of highly accomplished black letter technicians and equally accomplished socio-legal scholars with very little dialogue between the two. This book is a small contribution towards bridging the gap.

The theoretical work which is referred to in this book broadly falls into two camps, socio-legal scholarship and contractarianism. Socio-legal scholars understand the law to be an expression of social processes which can include class, culture, ideology politics and the (political) economy. They contend that company law is a reflection of a particular social dynamic, rather than an internally generated legal process. Socio-legal scholarship in its different forms tends to bring a critical and radical approach to the study of law. Many scholars in this tradition would advance as a broad aim the need to change society to serve a social or humanist ends. Accordingly, socio-legal scholarship is a minority perspective today as it is at odds with the current political allegiances to the free market.

Conversely, contractarianism, partly because it does celebrate the free market, is very much in the hegemony. Contractarianism constitutes a huge body of work that has comprehensively reinterpreted all areas of company law. It radically reconsiders the company as being a mass of contractual arrangements between those involved in the business including shareholders, managers, creditors, consumers and employees. Its purported aim is to find mechanisms to enable those arrangements to be cheaply conceived and financially productive. In achieving this, some contractarians argue for a non-interventionist company law which allows the free market to organise exchange, while others argue for regulations which enables efficient bargaining between players. In so doing it reformulates many of the basic tenets of company law and discards the notion of the company being anything other than a profit-maximising vehicle.

Company law scholarship, in both the socio-legal and contractarianism traditions, is largely located within American academies. Throughout this book, reference is made to American scholarship which is applicable to both English companies and American corporations.[1] Historically, the American corporation has been much more politicised than the English company and scholarship has been much more vigorous in both its criticism and praise of corporate law. Thus in order to understand these dynamics and to grasp some of the backdrop to the scholarship which is so widely used in this book, the history of company law set out in Chapter 1 will also include a history of American company law.

It is a further measure of the strength of contractariansm that it did seem to play a role in the construction of the Companies Act 2006. In the company law reform process leading up to the passage of the 2006 Act, there is evidence of this influence. The new Companies Act and its reform process provide a unique opportunity to assess the role of ideology in the formation of law and comprises much of the content of this book.

Reform of company law began with the Law Commission's recommendations on minority shareholder protection and their later work on company directors and Part 10 of the Companies Act 1985. The Commission published its report on company directors in 1999[2] having previously published its report on minority shareholder protection in 1997.[3] This piecemeal approach to reform was superseded by a government initiative to overhaul the entire body of company law. By the time the Commission's report on company directors was published the Government had already announced its intention to commission the Company Law Review (CLR) to critically assess existing company law and to recommend such reforms as would enable British company law to support a competitive economy.[4] Therefore the Commission's work became part of the overall reform process with many of their recommendations being taken up by subsequent CLR Reports, particularly in the area of directors' duties. The CLR itself was an independent group of scholars, practitioners and business people and it was chaired by the Director, Company Law and Investigations at the DTI.

The CLR published its Final Report to the Secretary of State for Trade and Industry in July 2001 having previously published a number of other

---

1 The terms company and corporation will be used interchangeably without them necessarily denoting an English or American business.
2 Company Directors: Regulating Conflicts of Interests and Formulating a Statement of Duties, Law Com No 261.
3 Shareholder Remedies, Law Com No 246.
4 This was announced in the DTI's document of March 1998, 'Modern company law for a competitive economy', the leading title for all subsequent reports from the CLR.

reports.[5] The Government consulted on the recommendations from the CLR that it intended to include in proposed legislation in two white papers, 'Modernising Company Law' (July 2002) and 'Company Law Reform' (March 2005). The Companies Reform Bill was introduced into the House of Lords in November 2004 and received Royal Assent in November 2006. Consultation on implementing most parts of the Act are due to begin in February 2007 and it is the Government's intention to implement all parts of the Act by October 2008.[6] It also intends to implement s 463, Part 28 of the Act and s 1281 by January 2007. Furthermore, it intends to repeal a number of sections with effect from 6 April 2007. These include ss 41, 293 and 294 of the 1985 Act and those parts of the 1985 Act which relate to the disclosure of share dealings by directors and their families. It will also repeal ss 311, 323, 327, 343, 344, 438, 720 and 729.

This book falls into seven chapters. The first chapter sets out the history of English and American company law with some comparative analysis. The purpose of this chapter is to lay down a historical structure within which to better understand legal and intellectual developments in company law. The second chapter assesses the doctrine of separate corporate personality and considers the question of why incorporation led to the notion that the company was a distinct legal person. The third chapter looks at the contractarian notion of the company as a nexus of contracts and at the effect of it on reforms to the company constitution and the statutory contract between shareholder and company. It argues that contrary to contractarian notions, this area of law is guided by regulation rather than contract. The fourth chapter assesses the principle of corporate governance theories of the twentieth and twenty-first centuries within the historical and political context in which they emerged. The purpose of this is to provide an overview of these theories and to understand the contextual dynamics which inform them. The fifth chapter, 'Corporate governance II', assesses the law relating to a director's fiduciary duties and the reforms presented in the 2006 Act. The sixth chapter, 'Corporate governance III', assesses the law and the reforms on

5 These included 'Modern company law for a competitive economy: completing the structure' (November 2000), 'Modern company law for a competitive economy: trading disclosures' (October 2000), 'Modern company law for a competitive economy: registration of company charges' (October 2000), 'Modern company law for a competitive economy: capital maintenance: other issues' (June 2000), 'Modern company law for a competitive economy: developing the framework' (March 2000), 'Modern company law for a competitive economy: company general meetings and shareholder communication' (October 1999), 'Modern company law for a competitive economy: company formation and capital maintenance' (October 1999), 'Modern company law for a competitive economy: reforming the law concerning overseas companies' (October 1999), 'Modern company law for a competitive economy: the strategic framework' (February 1999) and 'Modern company law for a competitive economy' (March 1998).
6 Lord Sainsbury, HL Hansard, 2 November 2006, Col 433.

minority shareholders' protection and considers the ideological influences that have been bought to bear on this area of law. Chapter 7 provides a case study of how a semi-commercial body, the mutual building society, developed into a fully commercialised company, the converted building society and considers how the themes of economy, politics and ideology have affected this transition.

Chapter 1

The history of English and American company law

This chapter gives an historical account of the emergence of modern company law in England[1] and America. In both countries early companies, or corporations as they are called in America, were created by charters and were known as charter companies. Charters were granted by the sovereign power. In England, charters were granted by the Crown, in America they were granted by state legislatures. In both countries they bequeathed and were designed to bequeath privilege. This could be in the form of limited liability for the members or monopoly trading rights, but in both countries this was justified because these corporations formed some quasi-public function such as providing revenue for the state or building public utilities. Later, in the nineteenth century when companies could be formed under general incorporation laws the charter company form in America largely fell into disuse. In England they had already fallen into disuse following the scandalous collapse of the South Sea Company. As companies were incorporated under general incorporation Acts they gradually lost their public character and the privileges and powers inherent in the company form became less apparent.

The companies and company law in England and America are so similar that they are often termed 'Anglo-American companies' governed by 'Anglo-American law'. However, there are some significant differences between the two which may be traced to the different paths companies in the two countries took historically. It is these paths that are followed in this chapter.

PRIVILEGE AND CHARTERS

Early corporations, created by the granting of a charter, were exercises in inequality and an unfree economy. Indeed, inequality was the very virtue of such incorporations, as charters were granted in order to elevate the economic and legal rights of the corporation in question above those of their

---

1 All references in this book to English law are to include the law as it applies to Wales.

actual and potential competitors. For example, in 1600, the East India Company's charter granted it monopoly trading rights,[2] covering the whole of the East Indies.

As charters were prestigious favours granted by sovereign power (originating with monarchical prerogatives), they created privilege rather than equality. Yet despite the desirability of such privilege, in Britain at least, such privilege precipitated the demise of the charter company as a viable business form following the dramatic and fraudulent activities of the most notorious of such entities, the South Sea Company.

The South Sea Company's scheme, to buy government debt and exchange it for its own company shares, depended upon persuading the holders of government bonds and debentures that these shares were highly valuable commodities. In order to do this the directors needed to push up the share price, and, as the company did no real trade, this could only be achieved by legal device, hype and extravagant claims designed to create demand. Problematically, its initial success in raising share prices spawned a general clamour to buy shares in other companies and associations which spurred the government, which was deeply interwoven in the South Sea Company's affairs, to pass the hastily drafted Bubble Act of 1719;[3] an Act which prohibited the sale of shares by associations operating without a charter.[4] It was thereby hoped that the more restricted availability of shares in the market would further enhance the value of South Sea company shares. This further enhanced the status of charter companies. However, the Act could only give a temporary boost to the South Sea Company and after just a few months' trading, its share price collapsed and with it the national economy. Therefore, as a result of this financial catastrophe, the Bubble Act, conceived as a short-term device, stayed on the statute books for 105 years and furthermore the ensuing shock and embarrassment to the English Government made it generally averse to the granting of charters of incorporation *per se*. The raising of joint stock had been described in the Act as 'dangerous and mischievous to trade', and the financial collapse of the South Sea Company seemed to evidence the truth of that statement.[5] Companies with freely transferable shares were not to be desired and in their place business developed under the form

2   Full name the Honourable East India Company, its first charter gave it a 21-year monopoly on all trade in the East Indies.

3   6 Geo 1 c 18.

4   The Act prohibited the raising of *freely transferable* stock without a charter, an emphasis which allowed the later growth of organisations which had some restriction on the transferability of stock.

5   Preamble to the Bubble Act. In contrast, the English judiciary was more sympathetic to those trading in shares. The first prosecution was in 1808 in Rex v Dodd, 9 East 516, and this was unsuccessful.

of partnerships and Deed of Settlement companies[6] so that ironically, an Act that was designed to suppress the use of unincorporated business associations resulted in encouraging their proliferation. In the words of AB DuBois, in his famous account of the 'business company' during the eighteenth century,

> The Bubble Act had decreed a 'new deal' for organised business, but the moral tone of the eighteenth century was not sufficiently advanced to appreciate the benefits of the new dispensation. In consequence, entrepreneurs and their legal advisors turned to the device of the unincorporated association to affect their ends, and in this they were remarkably successful.[7]

The obvious and unjustifiable privileges enjoyed by charter companies, exemplified by the activities of the South Sea Company, had contributed to the hardship of many small investors and general financial collapse. As a result, business in England retreated into a business form that was characterised by an *a priori* equality between members, the partnership. In contrast, America embraced the charter company form as a demonstration of political independence from England. As an English colony, the law relating to business in America originated in English common law; however, the colonialists' use or rejection of this tended to reflect the political relationship between colony and parent state. So, although the Bubble Act was extended to the colonies in 1741 it was for the most part ignored and there was therefore little resort to the burgeoning unincorporated associations of post-Bubble Act England as a vehicle for business.[8] Indeed, after the War of Independence, incorporation by a special Act, passed by individual state legislatures, became the most common method of incorporation.[9]

As in England, American States initially used charters to enhance the privileges of those so granted. In the early part of American economic history, incorporation by charter was first utilised by those dealing with basic utilities, transport (such as canals and later the railroads) and banking, where privilege was sought as a means to override other claims upon land and raw material that might have interfered with the development of these quasi-public services. Later, in the early part of the nineteenth century, charters were sought for, and utilised by, industry, thereby exporting privilege and

---

6 DuBois, AB, *The English Business Company after the Bubble Act 1720–1800*, Oxford: Oxford University Press, 1938.
7 Ibid, p 216.
8 14 Geo 2 c 37.
9 According to Professor Gower, this meant that American law distinguished the corporation as a public body rather than as a creature of contract, earlier than English law. Gower, 'Some contrasts between British and American corporation law' (1956) Harv L Rev Vol 69 No 8, 1372.

inequality into commodity production. The power to grant charters resided in individual state legislatures passing individual pieces of legislation. This effectively gave sovereign power to individual state legislatures to grant privileges for the same kind of benefits enjoyed first by the English monarch, and then by parliament, namely financial reward. However, unlike their reticent English counterparts, American state legislatures granted an enormous number of charters, the majority for general business usage and a few with the most desirable aspects of incorporation such as perpetual succession and limited liability.[10] As Berle and Means showed, State legislators granted less restrictive and more desirable charters to those who were able to influence or bribe them in some way.[11]

Other evidence suggests that the benefits accruing to State legislatures as a result of issuing 'special' charters were such that many States passed general regulating statutes (which set a model corporate form) to free up more time for the legislatures to concentrate on granting even more special customised charters.[12]

However, in the context of the emerging market economy, commercial practices that did not at least *aspire* to fairness were beginning to elicit criticism. The more industrially developed States in particular sought to replace the obvious privileges of the special charters with a generalised law. New York, for example, passed the first general incorporation Act in 1811. But, although a number of other States quickly followed suit passing their own general incorporation Acts, the effect was to further exacerbate inequalities. General incorporation laws tended to create a two-tier market for incorporations based on price; the wealthier capitalists maintaining their economic superiority through the 'purchase' of special charters, whilst the poorer capitalists endured the more restrictive criteria set out in their State's general incorporation Act.[13]

Another response to the inequity of special charters adopted by individual States was to make the practice of granting special charters unconstitutional, and therefore to prohibit their use. Louisiana, in 1845, was first to adopt an absolute prohibition and by 1875, 19 of the then 37 States had followed suit. Yet, despite the widespread practice of absolute prohibition, as late as 1875,

---

10 Butler, HN, 'Nineteenth-Century Jurisdictional Competition in the Granting of Corporate Privileges' (1977) Journal of Legal Studies.

11 Berle, A and Means, G, *The Modern Corporation and Private Property*, London: Macmillan, 1932. Privileges could include such things as perpetual succession and limited liability.

12 Op. cit., Butler, p 141. 'Since the general regulating statutes did not affect the demand for special charters and did not lower the marginal cost of production of many special charters (which did in fact occur after the passage of general regulating statutes) it leads one to speculate that the real purpose of these statutes might have been to enable legislators to capture additional rents from the production of additional charters.'

13 Ibid, p 143.

18 States continued to issue special charters. Indeed, as Butler indicates, so popular were the special charters and so keen were many legislatures to issue them that in those States where *partial* prohibitions in the constitution were ratified the granting and demand for special charters continued unabated. The first of such partial constitutions was ratified in New York in 1846, and contained a provision that became typical of the wording in constitutions subsequently adopted by other States.[14] It restricted the granting of special charters to 'cases where, in the judgement of the legislature, the objects of the corporation cannot be attained under general laws'.[15] This constitution proved a deterrent neither in New York nor in the four other States that adopted such 'qualified constitutional prohibitions against special Corporation Chartering'.[16] So, although Wisconsin adopted constitutional constraints in 1848, between this time and 1871 only 143 business corporations were created under a general incorporation Act whereas 1,130 were created as special charters.[17]

The inequity of the special charter was highly visible because those businesses that sought them were themselves highly visible. The larger the business, the more likely it would be to require a special charter, and to be able to pay for it. So, in the main, it was large manufacturing and mining industries that opted for the special charters. Burgeoning industrialisation meant that incorporators needed a flexible business vehicle that could accommodate commercial requirements and in this context the demand for flexible special charters increased, rather than decreased, and the State legislatures operating without constitutional prohibitions continued to profit. In the States that had some constitutional limitation on the issuing of charters, such as New York, legislators continued to benefit from lobbyists seeking a special charter. They were simultaneously appeasing public anxiety about unfairness and corruption by passing some restrictive legislation on granting special charters but significantly never having an outright ban.

In this context, the economic power that dominated corporate law was highly tangible and highly controversial; the best law was simply for sale and only the richest could afford it. However, this visibility deteriorated with the corresponding historical deterioration of the use of special charters that occurred with the conjunction of a number of developments. These included the expansion of previously state-based markets, the gradual domination of interstate trade and the clarification of a previously hazy area of law.

This 'hazy area of law' was the question of whether or not a corporation could trade in a state other than the one that had issued its charter. If it could,

---

14 Ibid. Illinois and Wisconsin in 1848, Maryland in 1851, North Carolina in 1868.
15 Op. cit., Butler, p 143, citing Poore, BP, Clerk of Printing Records, The Federal and State Constitutions, Colonial Charters, and Other Organic Laws of the United States 1363 (1878).
16 Ibid, p 144.
17 Ibid.

promoters could shop around in other states for the best, special charters thereby creating a national market in special charters. However, the material basis for this competition did not exist in the first part of the nineteenth century, as most industrialists were too small to engage in interstate trade generally and so the question was never tested in court. Thus, in the absence of clear guidance it was generally considered to be impossible.

This question only became significant in the second half of the nineteenth century, when post-Jefferson, America became a highly industrialised, economy. Civil war in the 1860s had accelerated growth, particularly in respect of infrastructure and mass production and, according to Hobsbawn, this propelled the American economy above the more 'quality-based' production of Europe. It was key to success in the war, particularly in respect of weaponry, where over three million rifles were consumed during four years of war.[18] Likewise, infrastructure was essential to the successful pursuit of war. By 1866, a country whose economy was previously characterised by geographical isolation was rapidly possessed of 36,801 miles of railroad.[19] More importantly, argues Hobsbawn, the norms of mass production established during the civil war continued in peacetime and production rocketed. Wool production in the 1870s was double that of the 1840s, and the production of coal and pig iron multiplied by five during the same period. Furthermore, America produced twice the amount of coal per person as was produced in England. In 1859, oil production stood at 2,000 barrels but by 1874, that figure was nearer 11,000,000 barrels. By 1876, the United States had 380 telephones compared to 200 in the whole of Europe.[20] Furthermore, in the post-war years up to 1900, the railroad grew from 36,801 miles to 193,346 miles. The GNP increased twelvefold during those years and the value of exports from American mills and factories grew from $434 m to $1.5 bn.[21]

During this period of rapid development, small local firms gave way to large companies that could and did monopolise whole areas of industry on a national level. Interstate trade provided the impetus to shop around for States with the most liberal charters, and in this context the 1869 decision in *Paul v Virginia*[22] was made. The question in this case was whether the state of Virginia could impose restrictions on a 'foreign' company (one incorporated outside Virginia), selling insurance in Virginia, that were not imposed on 'native' companies. Although the Supreme Court held that it could impose such restrictions, the by-product of the case was the judicial recognition that a state could not prohibit a foreign company from doing interstate business

---

18 Hobsbawn, E, *The Age of Capital 1848–1875*, Weidenfeld & Nicolson 1997.
19 Urofsky, M, 'Proposed federal incorporation in the progressive era' (1982) The American Journal Of Legal History Vol XXVI.
20 Figures from Hobsbawn.
21 Op. cit., Urofsky.
22 75 US (8 Wall) 168 (1869).

per se. This set aside the final barrier to a free market in incorporations, or in Butler's words, 'once the spatial monopolies for corporate privileges had fallen away after *Paul*, legislators faced new challenges and new opportunities in the changed legal environment'.[23]

One such opportunity open to state legislators was to attract incorporators from other States by passing desirable general incorporation laws which would enable that state to enjoy revenue from the sale of incorporations and associated taxes. This opportunity was first taken by New Jersey (a state which already had a history of innovation in respect of incorporations)[24] and in 1875, it passed the first in a number of Acts considered to be the blueprint of modern general incorporation Acts.[25]

The provisions of a cheap alternative to the special charter brought an end to that most lucrative activity. In addition to this, as we shall see, it set in motion a competition between States for incorporations which accelerated a tendency to make corporate law large-investor-friendly.

THE ORIGINS OF MODERN COMPANY LAW IN ENGLAND

In England the origins of *modern* company law derive from unincorporated associations rather than seventeenth-century charter company law. The bursting of the South Sea Bubble shifted the trajectory of English company law, so that instead of legal precedent arising from the seventeenth-century charter company activity, it arises from nineteenth-century partnership law because the modern company emerged in a period when businesses tended to organise as partnerships. So, as early-nineteenth-century companies drew from the normative legal values of the partnership based on contract and agency law, the law of companies could lay claim to contractual notions of choice, equality and consensus. And, although modern company law has since drawn a clear distinction between itself and partnership law, the ideological claims to contractual equality persist.[26]

Historically, the corporate form was not commonly used until the latter half of the nineteenth century. It was facilitated first by the Companies

---

23 Op. cit., Butler, p 156.
24 In 1846, in response to the huge demand for special charters, the Democrat-dominated New Jersey had passed a revised incorporation Act designed to increase the desirability of incorporation by general law and so dampen demand for the special charter.
25 Its procedure was simple: it required a manned office within the state, but there was no necessity for the incorporators to reside in New Jersey.
26 Most notably in the American academies. Exemplifying this contractual approach to company law is Easterbrook and Fischel's *The Economic Structure of Corporate Law*, Harvard University Press, 2001.

Registration Act 1844, which provided for incorporation as of right, and then popularised by the Limited Liability Act 1855, which provided limited liability for company members. Until then, as previously noted, businesses operated as partnerships or Deed of Settlement companies and so the norms and precedents upon which the company was to be understood were to be found in partnership law. In Gower's words, 'The modern English business corporation . . . owes more to partnership principles than to rules based on corporate personality'.[27]

Thus, as might be expected, there are numerous examples of judicial interpretations of the company as a creature of partnership and contract in the nineteenth century and, even today, contractual anomalies exist in English company law. On this point, Gower cites the right of promoters forming a company limited by shares to opt out of or alter Table A. However, these contractual characteristics tend to obfuscate the dominant non-contractual character of company law. For example, in practice, subsequent members of a large company would find the alteration of the articles beyond their voting powers.[28] And, although s 14 of the Companies Act 1985[29] described a contractual relationship between member and company, when s 14 is tested in court, the 'contract' encompassing the memorandum and articles of association seems to be limited to empowering members to enforce their personal membership rights, and not always then.[30]

In England, the development of the company as a distinct business form by the end of the nineteenth century necessitated a corresponding delineation from the partnership form.[31] If the company possessed a particular attribute, the partnership would not; so, for example, while by 1855 a member of a registered company could limit his personal liability, this privilege was explicitly denied to general partners.[32] However, in contrast to English law, American law throughout the States did not make such a sharp delineation between partnership norms and company law norms. For example, most had adopted the European limited partnership form from the 1820s onwards. The

27 Op. cit., Gower, pp 1371–2.
28 Under the Companies Act 1985, s 9, the articles could be altered by special resolution.
29 Section 14(1). Subject to the provisions of the Act, the memorandum and articles, when registered, bind the company and its members to the same extent as if they respectively had been signed and sealed by each member, and contained covenants on the part of each member to observe all the provisions of the memorandum and of the articles. Now the Companies Act 2006, s 33, with some modifications.
30 *Pender v Lushington* [1877] 6 Ch D 70. Gower also cites the just and equitable winding up order as a 'relic of partnership' but this has only been used in companies that are small and originally bound by mutual trust and described as quasi-partnerships such as in *Ebrahimi v Westbourne Galleries* [1973] AC 360.
31 Ireland, P, 'The myth of shareholder ownership', (2001) Modern Law Review.
32 Partnership Act 1890, s 9.

first limited Partnership Act was enacted in New York in 1822,[33] and was soon replicated in other States.[34] In England, sole traders and small partnerships could only enjoy limited liability by registering their business as a limited liability company. It is therefore doubtful that Aron Salomon would have made company law fame if limited partnerships were permitted in England at that time.[35]

Another effect of the legal distinction of company from partnership at the end of the nineteenth century was the judicial unwillingness to allow the company to deviate from the norms of separate corporate personality. Even today, the judiciary is unwilling to pierce the veil unless there is evidence of fraud or it is required by statute to do so.[36] The judiciary in England tenaciously clung to the doctrine of *ultra vires* in early cases despite its unpopularity with business precisely because a company was a separate being from its members and therefore could not change its identity and capacity solely because members wished it.[37]

In contrast, the American courts have been more willing to pierce the veil and may do so if stockholders both own and control the corporation, under the doctrines of 'instrumentality', 'alter ego' or 'identity'. So, in the case of *Zaist v Olsen*, it was held that the veil would be pierced if

> there was such unity of interest and ownership that the independence of the corporation had in effect ceased or had never begun, and adherence to the fiction of separate identity would serve only to defeat justice and equity by permitting the economic entity to escape liability arising out of an operation of one corporation for the benefit of the whole enterprise.[38]

However, the differences are slight, as under both jurisdictions the doctrine of separate corporate personality remains the 'cornerstone' of corporate law. The corporation is always treated as an entity distinct from its members unless there is a very compelling reason not to do so. In so doing, company law reflects the factual separation of shareholder from company in terms of property ownership and in terms of managerial control. To do otherwise

---

33 NY Laws Ch 244 (1822).
34 In 1916 the Uniform Limited Partnership Act was drafted by the Commissioners on Uniform State Laws and this statute was enacted in every state. In 1976, the Commissioners on Uniform State Laws approved a Revised Uniform Limited Partnership Act (RULPA) as a recommended replacement. It is, however, less uniform in its actual enactment than the original ULPA, since a number of States, such as California, adopted the substance of the law but with a number of modifications.
35 The Partnership Act 1907 provided for non-active limited partners.
36 E.g., the Insolvency Act 1986, ss 212–214.
37 *Ashbury Ry Carriage and Iron Company v Riche* (1875) LR 7 HL 653.
38 *Zaist v Olsen* 227 A 2d 552 (1967).

would be to operate a legal doctrine that reflected mere fiction,[39] as we shall see in detail in Chapter 2. In England, the gradual expansion of capitalism altered shareholders' relationship with their company as the growth of industry resulted in a corresponding growth in the numbers of those investing in the company without a controlling interest. Lack of controlling interest coupled with the introduction of limited liability meant that shareholders, on the whole, ceased to attend AGMs, or take part in the management of the company. Thus, their personal relationship and connection to the company in which they held shares diminished, and shares were purchased solely for the purpose of accessing profit.

Furthermore, throughout the nineteenth century, judicial understanding of the share was connected to the size of company involved. Large companies with hundreds of non-involved shareholders were understood to have shares that were a right to dividend but not a right to company assets. In contrast, shares in small companies with involved shareholders were understood to be 'quasi-partnerships'[40] and thus bequeathed the shareholders with rights far in excess of those in larger companies. As the former understanding of the shareholder and share become generalised, the judicial interpretation of the nature of the share in *all* companies was that shares represented rights to revenue, not rights in the company assets. As the tangible assets belonged to the company it became materially and conceptually distinct from its owners – a state of affairs that is expressed in the doctrine of separate legal personality.

THE ORIGINS OF MODERN AMERICAN CORPORATE LAW

In America, as previously noted, the demands of industrialisation came later in the century, but once established, a modern corporate law which reflected English law was accelerated by States competing for incorporations. This state competition for incorporations is a quintessentially American phenomenon emerging at the end of the nineteenth century as an immediate result of New Jersey's amendment to its Incorporation Act 1875[41] in 1889. This amendment, generally attributed to the entrepreneurial activities of New York attorney James B Dill (who lobbied the New Jersey legislature for further liberalisation of the existing law), was proposed as a scheme to pass a general incorporation law that would be so desirable to incorporators that it would allow the incorporating state to make money from incorporation fees and an

---

39 Although the idea of the company as a fiction is precisely the argument put forward by Easterbrook and Fischel, among other economics and law scholars.
40 *Ebrahimi v Westbourne Ltd* [1973] AC 360.
41 1889 NY Laws 265.

annual franchise tax.[42] It was followed by The New Jersey Holding Company Act 1891, which permitted corporations to control or own the stock or assets of other firms. A revised version of this was passed in 1896, which by-passed nearly all the restrictions on corporate structure by removing time limits on a corporation's existence, permitting a wide scope of business activity, facilitating mergers and setting no limit on capitalisation.

The popularity of these liberal corporate laws was overwhelming. In 1896, New Jersey granted 834 charters and received $800,000 in filing fees and franchise charters. By 1903, 2,347 firms had incorporated there, between them paying $2,189,000, an amount that accounted for 60 per cent of the state's revenue. An astonishing 95 per cent of the country's major corporations were incorporated in New Jersey including Standard Oil, US Steel, Amalgamated Copper and the American Sugar Refining Corporation. By 1902, New Jersey had paid off its state debt and abolished property taxes.[43]

Like the preceding practice of granting special charters, New Jersey's liberal corporate law was roundly denounced for its tendency to encourage 'big business', but like the special charters money spoke louder and the success of this legislation led 42 other States to adopt similarly liberal laws. The state of Delaware, in particular, sought to mirror the New Jersey legislation and in 1899 it passed the Delaware Corporation Act, which largely copied the New Jersey Act. So similar were these Acts that a case heard in Delaware in 1900 held that legal precedent in New Jersey could be legal precedent in Delaware, thereby imbuing Delaware corporate law with instant maturity.[44]

However, despite the efforts of Delaware and others, New Jersey remained the incorporator's choice, a mantle that it wore until the passage of a series of anti-trust laws known as the 'Seven Sisters Act', passed at the insistence of Governor Woodrow Wilson[45] and immediately resulting in the abandonment of New Jersey by incorporators in favour of Delaware's incorporation law.[46] To this day Delaware famously remains the preferred state of incorporation and by the end of the twentieth century its incorporations included half of all Fortune 500 companies, more than 40 per cent of all companies listed on the New York Stock Exchange, 82 per cent of publicly traded firms that had reincorporated over the last 30 years and 90 per cent of New York Stock Exchange companies that reincorporated between 1927 and 1977.[47]

---

42 And would allow Dill and his associates to make money from their company that was set up to advertise the benefits of incorporation in New Jersey and to act as agents for interested parties.
43 Op. cit., Urofsky.
44 *Wilmington City Ry Co v People's Ry Co* Del Ch 1900 – cited op. cit., Butler, p 162.
45 Cary, WL, 'Federalism and corporate law: Reflections upon Delaware' (1974) Yale Law Journal Vol 83, No 4, March, 64.
46 New Jersey repealed the Seven Sisters Acts in 1917 but it never regained its lost business in incorporations.
47 Cox, Hazen and O'Neal, *Corporations*, Aspen Law and Business 1997.

The competition for incorporations facilitated the emergence of large financiers who could organise a corporate network that enabled them to control business through stock ownership. Early on in the existence of New Jersey's liberal corporation law, monopolies and trusts rapidly emerged. As Urofsky noted, 'the drive toward consolidation reached a peak between 1898 and 1901, when 2,274 firms disappeared as a result of merger, and merger capitalisation totalled $5.4 bn'.[48]

One of the largest of these monopolies was the United States Steel Corporation, formed in 1901 by the House of Morgan. When John Pierpoint Morgan became sole manager, following the death of his entrepreneurial father, Junius, in 1890, he took over the reorganisation of the railroads by purchasing shares and creating a 'voting trust', by which device he was able to control the activities of numerous railroad companies, and by 1898 he had control of virtually all the important railway lines.[49] Through these 'trusts' , the US Steel Corp became the first billion-dollar corporation in the world, controlling 213 manufacturing plants and transport companies, 41 mines, 1,000 miles of railroads, 112 ore vessels and 78 blast furnaces.[50] In other words, it encompassed finance, industry, fuel and transport. Another classic example of these so-called trusts was Rockefeller's Standard Oil Company, formed in 1870 with $1 m in capital. Rockefeller's strategy was to buy controlling shares in less profitable refineries and to bring them within his business fold. In 1882 he formed the Standard Oil Trust, which became the financial and business centre of the whole of the petroleum industry, controlling Wall Street's City Bank. By 1895, Standard Oil was worth $150 m.

Critics of these kinds of trusts argued that such large corporations were capable of gross abuse of economic power because they connected many sectors of production under the same corporate umbrella. Foremost among these 'anti-big businesses' was Louis D Brandeis, a former corporate lawyer known as the 'people's attorney', who spent much of his long career investigating the relationship between investment banks and industry which large corporations seemed to spawn.[51] In 1914, he published many of his findings in *Other People's Money*, which drew upon much of the testimony given to the Pujo Committee[52] evidencing the rise and dominance of 'finance capital'

48 Op. cit., Urofsky, p 174.
49 This is often cited as a positive development. The railroad's initial construction was under the control of a large number of promoters and had become very unstable and speculative in nature.
50 Op. cit., Urofsky.
51 He was so called because he gave up his practice in order to give free legal representation to the poor.
52 The House Banking and Currency Committee chaired by Arsene Pujo set up to investigate claims that the banking crisis in 1907 had been instigated by a few financiers. The Committee's disclosures helped to create a climate of public opinion that led to the passage of the Federal Reserve Act 1913 and the Clayton Antitrust Act 1914.

(the factual relationship between investment bankers, industry and infrastructure) in American capitalism. In particular, he evidenced the relationship between JP Morgan & Co, National City Bank, First National Bank, the Steel Trust and the railroads. Brandeis showed that JP Morgan & Co and the aforementioned investment bankers, directly or through their trust companies, held hundreds of interlocking directorates in banks, transportation systems, public utilities companies, insurance companies and industrial and trading corporations. The capital value of these arrangements he estimated to be $22 bn.[53]

Brandeis was not alone in his concerns and for many years businessmen and politicians were divided on the issue of federal controls over corporations – legislation which would halt the competition for incorporations which facilitated big business. Ultimately, however, the ability of the national government to impose a federal corporate law was both constrained and complicated. For example, the judiciary tended to take a pro-business position. The first important federal measure to attempt to limit the power of large companies, the Sherman Anti-Trust Act, passed in 1890, provided for the prohibition of trusts that 'unreasonably restrained interstate trade'. However, in the matter of *US v EC Knight Co*[54] the Supreme Court ruled that federal government could not regulate the Knight sugar-refining monopoly because it was a manufacturer and manufacturing was not 'commerce'. Furthermore, in the hands of the judiciary the Sherman Act became an effective piece of anti-trade-union legislation as it became widely accepted that strikes which were organised across state lines did constitute a 'restraint of trade' that was, in the judiciary's view, 'unreasonable'.

As political views clashed on the issue of federal control of incorporations, Bills were proposed and disappeared.[55] President Theodore Roosevelt, famous for 'trust busting' and supportive of federal incorporation, presided over years of debate that saw those who were opposed to federal control (because of its unconstitutional nature) pitted against those in favour. And it was by no means a simple split between politicians and businessmen – opposing groups did not always fall into predictable alliances. For example, those in favour of federal incorporations included the traditional anti-big-businesses, Dill, author of the New Jersey legislation, *and* members of the industrial aristocracy such as John Morgan. Yet, despite the support for federal incorporation in theory, the wording of such legislation often caused considerable dispute. When a major amendment to the Sherman Act was presented to

---

53 As the revelations in respect of the relationship between Citibank, Worldcom, Enron and Salomons reveal, little has changed in the organisation of American capitalism. The Money Programme, BBC2, 9 June 2003.

54 156 US 1 (1895).

55 Op. cit. Urofsky, p 176, notes that between 1901 and 1914 over 20 such measures were introduced into Congress.

congress, it was opposed by many sectors of business because it exempted unions from anti-trust legislation.[56]

By the end of Roosevelt's term, the successful use of the Sherman Act against two major trusts had lessened the support of previously supportive elements of big business for federal legislation and the project was de-prioritised.[57] State competition for incorporations would continue unabated.

Concerns about the abuses inherent in overly large corporations did not dissipate and were finally and dramatically realised in the Wall Street crash of 1929. And so it was not until the presidency of the next Roosevelt, Franklin D, that significant federal legislation was passed to control the activities of corporations. In the wake of the Wall Street crash, it was no longer feasible to a support a laissez-faire policy and in 1933 the Securities Act was passed (designed to assure an informed market of investments) followed by the Securities Exchange Act of 1934 (aimed at correcting trading abuses).[58] The leading political and intellectual architects of these measures were Louis D Brandeis, Adolf Berle and Gardiner Means.

As previously noted, the People's Attorney had long maintained that the interconnection between finance, industry and infrastructure was harmful to competition and industrial development. Furthermore, he argued it gave false information to investors as to the real value of securities. In *Other People's Money* he had argued that interlocking directorates meant conflicts of interests were unavoidable and enabled the few to profit at the expense of many small-time investors, therefore the crash had vindicated many of Brandeis's conclusions.

Brandeis's analysis of the problem of big business led him to conclude that capitalism needed to be more open. He therefore recommended that federal law should emphasise disclosure on securities. Likewise, Berle and Means agreed on the necessity for federal legislation to protect investors that were too powerless and passive to protect themselves. They famously argued that power within large corporations had shifted from investors to managers, which they demonstrated by the empirical studies published in *The Modern Corporation and Private Property*.[59] In this book, written in the wake of the crash, detailed empirical data about stock ownership patterns in large corporations showed that even the largest stockholders held only a tiny percentage of the whole. They concluded that business had undergone an 'evolution

---

56 The Hepburn Bill 1908.
57 In *Standard Oil Co of New Jersey v US* (1911) 221 US 1, the Supreme Court found that the Sherman Act had been violated as it had *unreasonably* restrained interstate trade. It was ordered to dissolve.
58 The Glass-Steagal Act forbade commercial banks to play on the stock market in order to draw a distinction between investment and commercial banking.
59 Op. cit., Berle and Means.

of control', which had resulted in a shift of power from those that owned the corporation, stockholders, to those that controlled it, the managers.

Their analysis led to federal control over that which represented financiers' interests, securities, by promoting a system that protected the interests of passive stockholders. As for areas of corporate law that were unrelated to securities exchange, that was left to individual states engaging in a competition to attract incorporations, making corporate law in America a system of federal control over securities with state control over all other aspects of corporate activities. So in the areas of corporate law which guides management and shareholder control, states compete to provide the law most likely to attract incorporators who are those likely to be majority investors, management or both.

This competition is dominated by the liberal corporate law of Delaware and since the 1980s it has been popular in American academies to view this 'Delaware effect' as a positive attribute of American corporate law because it most accurately reflects the market. Known as the 'race to the top', its exponents agree that market-driven corporation laws most efficiently promote a thriving economy.[60] Notably, Easterbrook and Fischel argue that competition benefits shareholders as it forces states to adopt rules that enhance shareholder value.[61] They argue that the stock market acts as a way of disciplining directors by providing up-to-date information on their competency as facilitators of profit maximisation.[62] Moreover, they assert that states without pro-shareholder and pro-market legislation facilitated uncompetitive companies that were vulnerable to take-over. In another version of the 'top' theory, Roberta Romano argues that it is the stability and predictability that a state can offer that accounts for Delaware's popularity. Dubbed the 'race for predictability and stability', this theory holds that Delaware continues to be very popular despite the fact that many other states have adopted their liberal rules and the fact that the costs associated with incorporation are high. Professor Romano argues that Delaware's dependence on incorporation revenues perpetuates a self-interest in maintaining the predictability and stability in its law. Furthermore, she states that the presence of a small judiciary with corporate expertise together with long-standing precedent on corporate issues reassure incorporators that the law in Delaware will be predictable.

In contrast other theorists assert that state competition for incorporations had led to a 'race to the bottom'.[63] This theory, in a nutshell, says that state

---

60 From early work such as that of Ronald Coase to more recent work by Reiner Kraakman and Henry Hansmann in *The Anatomy of Corporate Law*, Oxford, 2004.
61 Op. cit., Easterbrook and Fischel.
62 Ibid.
63 The free market, 'race to the top' theorists claimed the hegemony from the 'race to the bottom' theories of the post-war period where the political emphasis in both England and America was of community, rebuilding, national industry and socially responsible business.

competition for corporate charters harms smaller shareholders as it encourages the adoption of law that benefits managers and controlling shareholders, the likely incorporators. Foremost of the 'race to the bottom' theorists was Professor William Cary, who spent a substantial part of his career arguing for more federal controls over the activities of corporations, particularly in respect of directors. Cary argued that one of the principal problems with Delaware corporate law was not just the number of corporations it attracts but the extent to which corporate law in other states is defined by Delaware law.[64] This, he argued, had the effect of eroding all state or piecemeal federal attempts to create a more responsible approach to the governing of corporations.

Cary argued that the freedom held by individual states to determine their own corporation laws was an abdication of federal responsibility and maintained that the federal approach to corporate law was lop-sided since, having constructed certain legal norms in respect of securities, it failed to extend these to other areas of corporate law.

According to Cary, faced with competition for incorporation charters, individual states are unable and unwilling to set a different agenda.[65] Furthermore, they do not seem to understand the connection between lax governance and corporate abuse. In Cary's words, 'at a state level there seems to have been a failure to recognise the difference between the goals of industrial capitalism and the abuse of finance capitalism'.[66] In short, he argued, Delaware law leads the way to corporate abuse, first, because decisions lean toward minimal standards of director responsibility[67] and second, because these decisions are constantly cited by other jurisdictions as nearly half of all listed companies are incorporated there. In this way, a legal environment that specialises in fiduciary laxity is sustained.

Although Cary's analysis is based on case law up to the 1970s and not beyond, there has been no substantial shift most areas of corporate law. For example, directors' duties in American states are universally less onerous than those in England and Wales where both judiciary and government are agreed on the need to control directors and to ensure they represent the interests of investors.[68] So, while the American courts have attempted to create an objective standard for a director's duty of care, it is undermined by the infamous business judgement rule which states that no liability will arise for losses

---

64 Op. cit., Cary.
65 In Delaware, in 1971, franchise taxes represented $52 m out of a total of $222 m in state tax collections – one quarter of the total.
66 Op. cit., Cary, p 668.
67 Cary cites a number of examples of the former problem including directors' non-disclosure of share purchases, misleading proxy material, misuse of dividends and abuse of subsidiary company at the expense of shareholders.
68 The 'no cakes and ale' judgment is a classic example of the English approach.

caused by imprudence or honest errors of judgement. And, when the decision of *Smith v Van Gorkom*[69] stated that this rule did not apply to gross errors of judgement, such as the hasty action of an ill-informed board, the Delaware legislator passed a statute eliminating directors' liability for negligence.[70] English law does not allow such protection for directors although, as we shall see in Chapter 5, the Companies Act 2006 has adopted many Americanesque characteristics which allow directors much greater opportunities to expand their business interests.

CONCLUSION

Corporations in America and England have made a historical transition from being organisations that were neither distinct from the members nor distinct from public and governmental interests into organisations that are viewed as arrangements between private contractual individuals. As we shall see in the following chapters, many scholars believe that this has been one of the great ideological victories of the wealthy which has no basis in economic nor legal realities. Furthermore, it will be argued that the notion of the company as a private body is part of an ideological victory that is gaining momentum through the nexus of contract theories that emerged in the 1980s and remain in the hegemony today – these are the intellectual backbone of the Companies Act 2006.[71]

---

69 *Smith v Van Gorkom*, 488 A 2d 858 (Del 1985). In 1980, the trade union senior management became aware that the stock was undervalued. Without consulting the board of directors, Van Gorkom, the owner of 65,000 shares, suggested a $55 per share cash-out merger with a company his friend Jay Pritzker owned. After several meetings, Pritzker agreed. Van Gorkom called a special meeting without informing the directors of its purpose. Despite a negative reaction from the directors, Van Gorkom proceeded with the meeting. In the board meeting he outlined the proposal but failed to mention that it was he that suggested the price. Donald Romans, the corporation's chief financial officer, had opposed the merger at the earlier meeting, but his recommendation was not asked for by the board. After two hours the merger agreement was signed without being read by the directors or Van Gorkom. An action was filed for breach of fiduciary duty and the court held that the directors did not adequately inform themselves as to Van Gorkom's role in forcing the sale of the company and in establishing a sale price, were uninformed as to the intrinsic value of the company and were grossly negligent in approving a sale of the company in such a short space of time.
70 Delaware General Incorporation Law, s 102(b)(7), allows personal liability of directors to be capped.
71 Op. cit., Kraakman *et al.*

Chapter 2

The doctrine of separate corporate personality

The consequence of registering a business as a company is to transform the business into an entity in its own right, with legal rights and responsibilities that are distinct from those of its members. In modern company law registration as an incorporated company bequeaths a company with a separate legal personality; the business becomes a legal entity. This outcome is referred to as the doctrine of separate corporate personality. This doctrine is overwhelmingly important in Anglo-American corporate law and one which the judiciary will defend against huge social pressures. A taste of this assertion may be enjoyed from the American case of the *People's Pleasure Park Co v Rohleder*.[1] In this case a former slave and later major commanding the Virginia Sixth Negro Regiment, Joseph B Johnson, bought land which was subject to a number of covenants restricting transfer to 'colored persons'. Fifty years later such covenants would be declared unconstitutional but at the beginning of the twentieth century they were commonplace. In order to side-step the covenants, Johnson incorporated a company to hold the title. The company, 'People's Pleasure Park Company', was owned entirely by 'colored persons' and the company's stated object was to create an amusement park for the enjoyment of 'colored persons'. The question before the court was whether the company itself could be said to have a colour and thus be restricted from owning the property. The court held that a corporation was incapable of having a colour, the company was a legal being distinct and separate from its owners and incorporators. As the company was not coloured, it was not restricted from holding the property because in law the company and not Johnson was the owner of the property.

This case was heard over 50 years before the civil rights movement and although slavery had been abolished, racial discrimination was still a major feature of American life. Therefore this was a decision which was made in the face of contemporary prejudices. The court might have disguised racial prejudice behind legal reasoning, claiming this was a misuse of the corporate

---

1 61 SE 794 (Va 1908).

form, but the judicial inclination to uphold the doctrine of separate corporate personality overrode all other considerations.

The purpose of this chapter is twofold. The first section will assess the consequences of registration through the black letter law on the doctrine of separate corporate personality, including what the doctrine means in detail and the circumstances in which the courts may deviate from it. From this law it will be seen that the circumstances in which the courts will deviate from the doctrine are extremely limited, eschewing broad considerations such as justice and fairness as a basis on which to set aside the separateness of the company. Indeed, the courts in general have required evidence of fraud before allowing the corporate personality of a company to be dispensed with. The second section will look at explanations of why the company has separate corporate personality, or why incorporation has the consequences it does. In so doing it will assess evidence drawn from the nineteenth century (the century in which the doctrine emerged), in the form of cases and in the form of more contemporary scholarly work about this period. In this section I will assess the role of the economy, law and ideology in creating the doctrine which lies at the heart of modern company law.

THE DOCTRINE OF SEPARATE CORPORATE PERSONALITY

An important consequence of incorporation is that the company may be registered as a limited liability company and the members may enjoy limited liability.[2] This means that the company's liabilities are the legal responsibility of the company and the members will not be liable for the company's debts. No personal liability will arise for the members in addition to the full price of the shares already purchased (in the case of a company limited by shares) or the value of the guarantee pledged (in the case of a company limited by guarantee). Historically, the introduction of limited liability was highly controversial, but now, English company law, more than any other common-law system, is highly protective of the limited liability of company members. In protecting limited liability, company law protects investors and the role of investment in the economy more generally.

Limited liability can pose a problem for the creditors of an insolvent company without sufficient assets to repay its debts. The distinct legal personality of the company means that creditors cannot (as a general rule) turn to the owners of the company for recompense. In this context it is easier to understand the strict rules in respect of the company's name discussed in

---

2 It is important to note that a company may have a separate personality without limited liability and companies may register as with unlimited liability.

this chapter and Chapter 3 as creditors in particular must be sure of whom they are dealing with and the liabilities of that person's members. This is particularly important for small unsecured creditors as more powerful creditors such as banks are likely to require the company's directors to personally guarantee loans made to the company if the company in question is a small private company. This requirement effectively sets aside separate corporate personality as both the director and the company become liable for the company's debts.

The most famous articulation of the doctrine of separate corporate personality was set out by the House of Lords in the case of *Salomon v Salomon Co Ltd*.[3] This case resides at the centre of corporate entity law for two principal reasons. First, it applied the judicial understanding of separate corporate personality, which had previously been applied to large concerns alone, to a small private company which was essentially the business of one man. In so doing it established a general principle in law applicable to all companies. Second, the speeches articulated in detail the nature and consequences of incorporation so that it is a case invariably cited in cases concerning the separateness of an incorporated company. For these reasons *Salomon* will be examined in some detail in the first part of this chapter.

Salomon v Salomon also illustrates how the normative values of modern company law, which emerged from large business organisations, permeated into factual scenarios where, arguably, they were not appropriate. As I shall discuss in the second half of this chapter, treating shareholders as legally distinct from the company when their property (the share) was distinct and separate from the property of the company (the productive assets) and when they have no role in the activities of the company, merely reflects a factual reality. On the other hand, treating all shareholders as separate even if they were factually so close to the company that the business actually runs like a partnership or even like the business of a sole trader, arguably imposes legal norms rather than allowing the law to reflect fact. Thus, in cases where the company was a small concern it could be argued that legal principles determined commercial reality rather than reflecting it. As such, judicial decisions made when strictly applying the doctrine of separate corporate personality could lead to unfairness or absurdity. To counter this, exceptions to the doctrine have been developed through the courts and through statute, which will be examined later in this chapter.

In *Salomon* both Chancery and the Court of Appeal treated Salomon Co Ltd as Mr Salomon's business. Having found that it was factually a sole trader the court concluded that it was a sole trader's business in law, which was incapable of being incorporated and whose owners could not enjoy limited liability. However, this was a position from which the House of Lords roundly recoiled. Notwithstanding the factual reality of Salomon's business

---

3 (1897) AC 52.

it had been legally registered as a company and modern company law declared an incorporated company to be a legal being distinct and separate from its members regardless of its size. As we shall see in the latter part of this chapter, in so doing the House of Lords was espousing the normative values of company law resulting from the economic, ideological and legal developments of the nineteenth century.

This case began as an action by a secured creditor of a small limited company in the case of *Broderip v Salomon* in 1895 and ended with their Lordships setting out the most fundamental principles of a doctrine that underpins all aspects of modern company law.[4] The facts of this case were this. Aron Salomon carried on a business as a boot manufacturer, government contractor and leather merchant. On the 28 July 1892, Mr. Salomon registered his business as a limited company under the 1862 Companies Act. The total purchase money of Salomon's business was £38,782 19s. 7d. and his books were made up by an accountant hired by him. At the time of incorporation the business was solvent although the price that the company was to pay for the business far exceeded the amounts showing in the balance sheet. The nominal capital of the company was £40,000 divided in 40,000 shares of £1 each. The memorandum of association was subscribed to by Aron Salomon, his wife, his daughter and his four sons, who held one share each because this was the minimum requirement under the 1862 Act. After incorporation Aron Salomon afterwards had 20,000 shares allotted to him and no one else ever had a share in the company. The debenture holders (secured creditors) were Aron Salomon and Edward Broderip; the latter had debentures of £10,000 as security for a £5,000 loan. When the company defaulted on payment of interest due on these debentures, Mr Broderip initiated proceedings to enforce the debentures. An official receiver was appointed and an order to wind up the company was made on 25 October 1893.

The judge at first instance held that Salomon Co Ltd was not a legal entity distinct from Aron Salomon and although there was no evidence of fraud, the judge contended that Salomon Co Ltd could not be treated as an independent legal entity distinct from Mr Salomon. He opined that Mr Salomon 'took the whole of the profits, and his intention was to take the whole of the profits without running the risk of the debts and expenses . . . one must consider the position of the unsecured creditor'.[5] Mr Salomon appealed against an order to indemnify the company, Salomon Co Ltd against the unsecured debts and liabilities incurred in the name of the company whilst it carried on business. The Court of Appeal, however, upheld most of the reasoning of the Chancery Division. Lindley LJ held:

4 [1895] 2 Ch 323.
5 Ibid.

There can be no doubt that in this case an attempt had been made to use the machinery of the Companies Act 1862 for the purpose for which it never was intended. The legislature contemplated the encouragement of trade by enabling a comparatively small number of persons – namely, not less than seven – to carry on business with a limited joint stock or capital, and without the risk of liability beyond the loss of such joint stock or capital. But the legislature never contemplated an extension of limited liability to sole traders or to a fewer number than seven.[6]

The case was finally heard in the House of Lords in 1897, wherein the most oft-quoted judgments will be found.[7] The House dismissed the rationale and decisions of the lower courts, finding no reason why Salomon Co Ltd should not be treated as a legal entity, distinct from Aron Salomon and therefore responsible for its own debts. In a direct response to Lindley LJ's statement above, Lord Hershall stated:

How does it concern the creditor whether the capital of the company is owned by seven persons in equal shares, with the right to an equal share of the profit, or whether it is almost entirely owned by one person, who practically takes the whole of the profits? The creditor has notice that he is dealing with a company the liability of the members of which is limited, and the register of shareholders informs him how the shares are held, and that are in the hands of one person, if that be the fact.[8]

And in respect to the notion that the company was an agent of Mr Salomon he stated:

In a popular sense, a company in every case may be said to carry on business for and on behalf of its shareholders; but this certainly does not in point of law constitute the relation of principle and agent between them or render the shareholders liable to indemnify the company against debts it incurs.[9]

The House of Lords was unanimous in upholding Aron Salomon's appeal. The debts of the company remained the responsibility of the company and not its shareholders. Accordingly Aron Salomon was not liable for the company's debts, although he was made a pauper by the court action.

6 Ibid.
7 *Salomon v A Salomon & Co Ltd* (1897) AC 22.
8 Ibid, p 45.
9 Ibid, p 43.

This decision clarified the effect of registration for both large and small companies. A business registered as a company according to the formalities set out in the Companies Acts should be treated in law (in the absence of fraud) as a separate legal personality, notwithstanding that in economic terms it is effectively a one-man company. Thus, henceforth, one-man companies would enjoy separate legal personality. For example, in *Lee v Lee's Air Farming Ltd*[10] the widow of the sole director and shareholder of a limited company was able to claim compensation on the grounds that her husband had been an employee of his company. And, in *Macaura v Northern Assurance Co Ltd*[11] the sole director and shareholder of a limited company was unable to claim for fire damage to the company's property on his own personal insurance. In this case the court held that a claim could only be made on the company's own insurance as a shareholder had no 'insurable interest' in the company's assets.

Macaura raises other related and interesting company law issues. When company law answers the question 'who owns the company' or 'who are the owners of the company', it replies, without exception, that it is the shareholders that own the company. It is not management, who owe a fiduciary duty to the company, or the creditors who have claims against the company, or any other persons with a contract with the company such as employees or contractors. And yet, in *Macaura*, the sole shareholder and therefore the sole owner of the company could not claim for the property he owned (the company) on his own personal insurance although he could claim for all the other things he owned on this insurance.

In deciding the case in this way the court was following the principles laid down in *Salomon* to the letter. The company was a separate legal being which required its own insurance, the company was not something that Macaura could own. This approach is, of course, consistent with *Salomon,* however it directly conflicts with company law's additional insistence that shareholders are indeed the owners of the company. The conjunction of these two perspectives is to say that shareholders own something that cannot be owned because according to the separation doctrine it (the company) is independent and self owning.

Perhaps the simple if not perfect solution to this conundrum would be to say that shareholders are the owners but owners only of title to dividend and residual voting rights – which indeed company law does. However, company law does not stop at this level of ownership and instead promotes the interests of shareholders above all other parties connected with the company on the basis that they, and they alone, are the owners of the company *per se*. In so doing company law extends a shareholder's rights of ownership far beyond

10 [1961] AC 12.
11 [1925] AC 619.

that of a mere dividend owner – a position which may surely only be reached by adopting a layer of ideology which promotes the interests of the investors over and above the logic of black letter company law. *Salomon* states that the company is separate. It is a doctrine which is *the* fundamental principle of company law. And yet, company law also maintains that shareholders own the very thing which the doctrine states cannot be owned. Thus the ideology of shareholder ownership sits uncomfortably with logic of the doctrine of separate legal personality but it does allow company law to both promote investor interests and give them the protection of limited liability.

Exceptions to the doctrine of separate corporate personality

The legal separation between the company and its members and those with whom it deals is often described using the metaphor of a veil, or the veil of incorporation which is drawn between the company and all other legal entities. This separation, following *Salomon*, is recognised in almost all situations; however, a body of law has developed through the courts and through statute that creates exceptions to the doctrine of separate corporate personality. Put another way, in certain circumstances the veil of incorporation may be 'lifted' or 'pierced' in order to reconnect the company with other legal entities such as other companies or people or to impose liabilities which might ordinarily fall to the company upon individuals connected with the company. The cases and the judgments are rarely tidy as veil piercing is not an end in itself but a means to an end. The court is attempting to find a solution to an inequity which may involve entirely disregarding the veil but often involves making an individual other than the company liable for a varied number of reasons. A true veil piercing, that is when the separateness of the company is entirely disregarded, only really occurs when corporate personality is being used to perpetrate a fraud or to sidestep a pre-existing legal obligation. However, many other circumstances have been discussed by the courts under the heading of exceptions to *Salomon*, which do not truly veil pierce but engage some other operation of law. All of these are discussed first in common law and second in statute.

Common law exceptions

- Single economic unit
- Façade or sham companies
- Agency
- National identity
- Tax evasion
- Alter ego for criminal or tortious liability
- Contractual guarantees

Single economic unit

Occasionally, the courts have pierced the veil between companies in a group on the basis that, while legally distinct, economically they exist as one single, interdependent unit. This view was taken in *DHN Food Distributors Ltd v Tower Hamlets LBC*[12] when the veil between the three companies in this group was pierced in order to achieve what the judges considered to be an equitable result. In *DHN*, a firm in the East End of London which imported groceries and provisions and had a cash and carry business had organised its business into three companies. The business was owned by the parent company, DHN Food Distributors Ltd, the land was owned by a subsidiary called Bronze Investment Ltd, and the vehicles were owned by another, DHN Transport Ltd. The parent company held all the shares in both subsidiaries and the directors were the same in all three companies, in other words ownership and control was consistent throughout all three companies. The dispute began when, in 1969, Tower Hamlets London Borough Council made a compulsory purchase order to acquire the company's land. Under the Land Compensation Act 1961 compensation was payable for the cost of the land compulsorily purchased and for any other relevant losses contingent upon the owner's loss of land. DHN Food Distributors Ltd had made business losses as a result of the land purchase, as the three companies were wound up having been unable to find alternative accommodation. However, it had no property interest in the land and so Tower Hamlets refused to pay compensation for its loss of business. Bronze Investment would be compensated for loss of land but not for business, as its only business was holding the title to the land. Compensation for disturbance of business could only be granted within the terms of the Act if the veil between each company was removed and the business was viewed as one single economic unit that possessed both land that was being compulsorily purchased and business that was being disturbed.

The Court of Appeal held that the veil would be pierced, stating: 'This group is virtually the same as a partnership in which all three companies are partners. They should not be treated separately so as to be defeated on a technical point. They should not be deprived of the compensation which should be justly payable for disturbance.'[13]

According to Goff LJ the veil could be pierced between companies in a group if the companies were wholly owned subsidiaries which had no separate business operations and when the owners of all the businesses in question had been disturbed in their possession and enjoyment of it. This case represents a fairly radical departure from the *Salomon* doctrine. Instead of the legal principles being applied to all companies *per se*, it suggests instead that the courts should assess the economic and factual reality of individual com-

12 *DHN Food Distributors v Tower Hamlets London Borough Council* [1976] 1 WLR 852.
13 Lord Denning, ibid, p 860.

panies to decide whether or not they should be treated as companies, or, as in this case, partnerships. An application of such a perspective in the *Salomon* case might well have left Mr Salomon liable for all the businesses debts with costs. Unusually, *DHN* takes a micro-economic perspective, suggesting that a company's separateness should be assessed on a case-by-case basis. As we shall see, it is a perspective that entirely disregards the macro-economic perspective generally adopted, where the domination of the large company over the economy largely determines the normative values of all companies regardless of size. To suggest that the corporate veil, which has important functions such as protecting investors (when accompanied by limited liability), could be set aside through judicial examination of the factual nature of individual companies, or as Lord Denning put it 'whenever it was just and equitable to do so', would be to undermine the very foundation of the economy. Therefore, it was not surprising that after a brief post-*DHN* flurry of speculation on the integrity of the corporate veil, the judiciary resumed its protection of the *Salomon* doctrine. This was first evidenced in a Scottish case, *Woolfson v Strathclyde Regional Council*,[14] heard soon after the decision in *DHN*. This case involved a compulsory purchase order made in relation to shop premises in St George's Street, Glasgow by Glasgow Corporation where although the facts of the case were very similar to those in *DHN*, the veil was not pierced. It was distinguished on the basis that the ownership of the companies was divided between Mr Woolfson and his wife and the court refused to see ownership as embodied in the one person of Mr Woolfson. The decision in *DHN* was to be confined to the exact facts of *DHN* and enjoy no general application.

An overview of judgments in respect to groups of companies was proffered in the case of *Adams v Cape Industries plc*.[15] Here, the plaintiffs were persons and the personal representatives of persons to whom an award was made in a Texan court in respect of claims for damages for personal injuries and consequential loss suffered as a result of exposure to asbestos fibres. These fibres were emitted from an asbestos insulation factory called Unarco Industries from 1954 to 1962, and then by Pittsburg Corning Corporation (PCC) until 1972.

The defendants were Cape Industries plc and Capasco Ltd, companies registered in England. Cape owned the shares in subsidiary companies in South Africa (which had mined the asbestos) and in its subsidiary Capasco, which organised the sale of the asbestos worldwide. Damages were awarded as it was successfully contended that the defendants had been responsible for the supply of asbestos to Unarco and PCC without giving proper warnings of the dangers. Default judgments were made against the defendants and this case related to the enforcement of these judgments in the UK. Cape argued

14 [1979] JPL 169.
15 [1990] Ch 433.

that it should not be liable for the activities of its subsidiary companies in the mining and marketing of asbestos. The House of Lords held that there was no basis upon which the veil could be pierced in order to make Cape liable for the activities of its subsidiaries.

In examining the criteria upon which the veil could be pierced, Lord Keith stated that the economic unit argument was only applicable in cases 'where legal technicalities would produce injustice in cases involving members of a group of companies'. That is, when the courts were attempting to give effect to an outside legal document or statute and could only achieve this end by piercing the veil. He demonstrated this approach with reference to the case of *Revlon Inc v Cripps and Lee*,[16] where the question arose as to whether the goods in question (a trade mark held by Revlon Suisse SA (a subsidiary of Revlon Inc)) were connected in the course of trade with Revlon Inc. In judgment Buckly LJ stated:

> Revlon is neither the registered proprietor nor a registered user of the REVLON FLEX mark. Since, however, all the relevant companies are wholly owned subsidiaries of Revlon, it is undoubted that the mark is, albeit remotely, an asset of Revlon and its exploitation is for the ultimate benefit of no one but Revlon. It therefore seems to me to be realistic and wholly justifiable to regard Suisse as holding the mark at the disposal of Revlon and for Revlon's benefit. The mark is an asset of the Revlon Group of companies regarded as a whole, which all belongs to Revlon. This view does not, in my opinion, constitute what is sometimes called 'piercing the corporate veil'; it recognizes the legal and factual position resulting from the mutual relationship of the various companies.[17]

Although the Salomon principle should mean that a company's assets belonged to the company alone, to apply that in this case would have undermined the purpose and *raison d'être* of a legal document such as a trade mark. The courts took the view that to give legal effect to the trade mark, the veil between the companies should be pierced to the extent that all companies in the group could use the trade mark to identify their products and activities as part of the Revlon Group.

Lord Keith went on to state that the court could only lift the veil if a defendant was using the corporate structure in an attempt to evade limitations imposed on his conduct by law, or such rights or relief against him as third parties *already* possessed. Importantly, he held, the veil would not be pierced to set aside limited liability, if the rights or grievances of third parties were gained after the legitimate incorporation of a business. The veil would not

16 [1980] FSR 85.
17 Ibid, p 105.

be pierced to impose liability for post-incorporation activities which would have the effect of undermining limited liability as a principle. Lord Keith was in essence stating that the veil would only be pierced if the company was operating a fraud or acting as a façade, a principle established in the original *Salomon* case.

Where company is a mere façade

This exception applies when the corporate form is utilised in order to avoid an existing legal obligation or to evade limitations imposed by the law and in that respect such usage may be fraudulent. There are a number of different factual circumstances which have caused the court to hold that the corporation is being used as a façade. For example in *FG Films Ltd*[18] under-capitalisation was the basis for holding that the company was a mere façade. An American corporation, Film Group Incorporated, invested £80,000 in the making of a film. The applicant company FG Films Ltd (an English company) claimed to be the maker of the film and wished to register it as a British film. FG Films Ltd had issued capital of £100, the majority of which were owned by the president of Film Group Inc. Furthermore it had no film-making facilities and hired no staff. The court held that the English company was a façade company.

> The suggestion that this American company and that director were merely agents for the applicants is, to my mind, inconsistent with and contradicted by the evidence, and a mere travesty of the facts, as I understand and hold them to be. The applicants' intervention in the matter was purely colourable. They were brought into existence for the sole purpose of being put forward as having undertaken the very elaborate arrangements necessary for the making of this film and of enabling it thereby to qualify as a British film. The attempt has failed, and the respondent's decision not to register 'Monsoon' as a British film was, in my judgement, plainly right.[19]

Often the avoidance of an existing legal obligation will lead a court to pierce the veil of a company, often dubbed a 'sham' company. For example, in *Gilford Motor Company Ltd v Horne*[20] the defendant, Mr Horne, had covenanted with his former company not to solicit its existing customers after he had left its employ. When he left his employment with this company, he began a similar business undercutting the prices of his former employer and in direct breach of the covenant. Following legal advice he set up a company,

18 [1953] 1 WLR 483.
19 Ibid, p 485.
20 [1933] Ch 935.

JM Horne and Co Ltd (the second defendant), to take over his business and thus to do that which Mr Horne has covenanted not to do. His wife and an employee were the sole shareholders and directors. Under this guise, JM Horne and Co Ltd began to solicit customers from the plaintiff, Gilford Motor Company Ltd. On appeal, the plaintiff successfully proved that the restrictive covenant had been broken and the court granted an injunction against both defendants. Mr Gilford had attempted to use the corporate form in order to avoid the burden of a legally binding promise which pre-dated the incorporation of the defendant company. Likewise, in *Creasey v Breachwood Motors Ltd*[21] a newly formed company which was set up specifically to hold the assets of a company which was the defendant in a claim for unfair dismissal was held to be a façade. The corporate form was being used to stymie an effective payment of damages *after* that claim had arisen. However, even when the company form seems to be used for such devious purposes, the courts have moved away from making judgments based on the morality of the issues. Thus in the case of *Ord v Belhaven Pubs Ltd*,[22] the decision in *Creasy* was overruled. The actions in the latter case were unconscionable, but they were not fraudulent and therefore veil piercing was held to be unjustifiable.

Where the company is agent for the other

Although the *Salomon* case showed that a company was not automatically the agent of another company or other individual, it did not preclude the possibility of an agency relationship arising from fact. So in *Smith, Stone and Knight v Birmingham Corporation*,[23] Atkinson J attempted to categorise the circumstances that could give rise to such a relationship. In this case, a company acquired a business, registered it as a company and utilised the business as a subsidiary. The parent company held all but five shares in the subsidiary; ownership and control were effectively the same. The defendant, Birmingham Corporation, compulsorily acquired the premises owned by the subsidiary and upon which the parent company's business was carried on. The parent company claimed compensation. The Corporation claimed that the proper recipient was the subsidiary as it owned the land and the parent company was a separate entity.

In order for the parent company to claim compensation it had to show that the subsidiary was not a separate entity but was in fact an agent of the parent company. In judgment, Atkinson J devised a number of questions that could be asked in order to ascertain whether such a relationship existed in fact. These were:

21 [1992] BCC 638.
22 [1998] 2 BCLC 447.
23 [1939] 4 All ER 116.

- Were the profits of the subsidiary 'treated as the profits' of the parent company?
- Were the persons conducting the business appointed by the parent?
- Was the parent the 'head and brain' of the venture?
- Did the parent govern spending?
- Did the subsidiary make profits by its own 'skill and direction'?
- Which company was in 'effectual and constant control'?

Atkinson J concluded on the basis of these factors that the subsidiary was in fact the agent of the parent.

There are mixed authorities in respect of agency, but what does seem to be clear is that the courts will be more inclined to declare an agency relationship if to do so would redress an injustice, particularly in compensation cases like the above, where to deny compensation to the parent company would effectively thwart the purpose of the legislation. What is equally clear is that the courts will not pierce the veil in order to set aside limited liability if an agency relationship can only be shown to exist in the factual relationship between the two companies. In other words, affirmative answers to the question laid down by Atkinson J will be insufficient grounds to pierce the veil in cases where the effect is to remove limited liability. So, in *Adams Cape Industries* the court held that an agency relationship between parent and subsidiary could only be proven by evidence of an express agreement to the effect that the subsidiary was authorised by the parent to act as they did.

To determine the nationality of the company

In certain discreet circumstances, the veil may be pierced in order to ascertain the nationality of the owners and controllers of a company in order to establish their nationality as the true nationality of the company. Ordinarily a company's nationality is determined by its place of registration but in these cases the part of the veil which contains national identity is set aside, or disregarded. For example, in *Daimler Co Ltd v Continental Tyre and Rubber Co Ltd*[24] a company was incorporated in England for the purpose of selling tyres in England which were made in Germany, by the German company who held the bulk of the shares in the English company. The holders of the remaining shares were Germans resident in Germany and all the directors were Germans resident in Germany.

After the outbreak of war the company's solicitors issued a writ in the name of the plaintiff for the payment of a trade debt. The defendant alleged that the plaintiff was an alien enemy company and that the payment of the debt would therefore constitute trading with the enemy in contravention of

---

24 [1916] 2 AC 307.

The Trading With the Enemy Act 1914. The court held that 'the company was in substance a hostile partnership and therefore incapable of suing, and that any payment to it would be illegal as a trading with the enemy'.[25]

Tax evasion

Use of the corporate form in order to evade tax will always result in the court piercing the veil once the Inland Revenue maintains it has revealed a provable case of tax evasion. For example, in *Littlewoods Mail Order Stores Ltd v IRC*,[26] Littlewoods attempted to pass off a capital purchase as a running cost.

In 1947 Littlewoods began renting Jubilee House in Oxford Street from Oddfellows Friendly Society for £23,444 a year on a 99-year lease. Oddfellows had bought the building in 1947 for £605,000 but by 1958, the building was worth £2,000,000 with a rentable value of £60,000 a year. At this time 88 years remained on the lease. Oddfellows therefore had an interest in altering its arrangement with Littlewoods and Littlewoods likewise wished to possess the building on a different footing. Between these two bodies a scheme was devised so that Oddfellows could get a return on its property and Littlewoods could get the freehold and avoid a great deal of tax into the bargain. To institute this Littlewoods and Oddfellows engaged in a number of arrangements including the following. Littlewoods (the taxpayers) set up a company, Fork Manufacturing Ltd, to whom it assigned the lease. FM Ltd then sub-let to the taxpayers (Littlewoods) for a rent of £42,450 a year for 22 years. FM Ltd then acquired the freehold from Oddfellows in exchange for the assignment of the lease and therefore the rent for 22 years.

The Inland Revenue (IRC) claimed that in reality Littlewoods was acquiring the freehold for a sum of 22 × £44,450, whilst having it assessed as tax deductible because rent was tax deductible as a running expense whereas the purchase of a fixed asset was not. Littlewoods claimed that FM Ltd was a separate legal being from itself and therefore FM's ownership of the freehold was unconnected to and independent from Littlewoods' assets.

The court agreed with the IRC: Littlewoods and FM Ltd were not separate entities. And Littlewoods was the effective owner of the freehold. Lord Denning, the judge perhaps most inclined to veil piercing, put it like this:

> The courts can and often do draw aside the veil. They can, and often do, pull off the mask. They look to see what is really behind. The legislature has shown the way with group accounts and the rest. And the courts should follow suit. I think we should look at the fork company and see it for what it really is – the wholly owned subsidiary of the taxpayers. It is the creature, the puppet, of the taxpayers in point of fact; and it should

25 Ibid.
26 [1969] 1 WLR 1241.

be so regarded in point of law. The basic fact here is that the taxpayers, through their wholly owned subsidiary, have acquired a capital asset – the freehold of Jubilee House, and they have acquired it by paying an extra £19,006 a year.[27]

However, while it is very likely that a court *sans* Denning would have pierced the veil in this case, which is after all a sub-set of fraud, Denning's general point is a minority view. The doctrine of separate corporate personality specifically does not assess the integrity of the veil 'in point of fact' and then regard it so in 'in point of law'. It protects the veil in almost every circumstance, disregarding the size, nature of ownership and control and moral considerations. If it were not so, *Salomon*'s doctrine would not exist. Thus Denning's doctrines on the nature of corporate personality should be treated with extreme caution.

Alter ego for criminal or tortious liability of company that requires intention

In certain cases the intention and acts of directors and managers who are in a position to represent the mind and will of the company will be considered as the intention of the company itself. In *Lennard's Carrying Co Ltd v Asiatic Petroleum Co Ltd*[28] a shipping company lost cargoes of benzene as result of a fire caused by the unseaworthiness of the defective boilers in a ship they had chartered. The company claimed immunity from damages under s 502 of the Merchant Shipping Act, which states that no liability will arise for 'any loss or damage happening without his actual fault or privity'. The director and manager of Lennard's Carrying Co, John Lennard, did know of the defective condition of the boilers but gave no special instructions to the ship's captain. The court held that his knowledge constituted the knowledge of the company thereby rendering the company at fault. The company was liable, as John Lennard was the directing mind of company.

Similarly, in *HL Bolton (Engineering) Ltd v TJ Graham & Sons Ltd*[29] the directors claimed that the company could not have given notice on the termination of a lease because they had not met for their annual meeting. However, the court held that if the day-to-day management was left to the managers, then the will of the managers represented the will of the company. This case is popularly cited, largely because of Lord Denning's colourful description of the body corporate, of which he says:

27 Ibid, p 1254.
28 [1915] AC 705.
29 [1957] 1 QB 159.

A company may in many ways be likened to a human body. It has a brain and a nerve centre which controls what it does. It also has hands which hold the tools and act in accordance with directions from the centre. Some of the people in the company are mere servants and agents who are nothing more than the hands to do the work and cannot be said to represent the mind or will. Others are directors and managers who represent the directing mind and will of the company and control what it does. The state of mind of these managers is the state of mind of the company and is treated by law as such.[30]

In a later case, the will of the corporation was said to be held at a top management level and could not be imputed from decisions made further down the line of management.[31] Here, an assistant at the Norwich branch of Tesco wrongly priced Radiant washing powder, which at the time was on offer, and posters advertised an offer in the store. The store manager failed to notice the error. Tesco was charged with the offence of misstating the price under the Trade Descriptions Act 1968. However, s 24(1) of the Act allowed a defence where 'the commission of an offence was due to the act or default of another person' and 'the accused had taken all reasonable precautions and exercised all due diligence'. The court held that the company was only responsible for the acts and knowledge of its 'directing mind and will' as indicated by its constitution.[32] If senior management had put into place responsible and sufficient structures then they as the mind of the company had not rendered the company culpable.

Company contractual guarantees

The final exception established in common law is perhaps not an exception at all but merely the proper implementation of contracts which are not thwarted by the corporate veil. Company contractual guarantees are often offered to creditors by one company in respect of the debts of another. In enforcing this guarantee the creditor is piercing the veil to the extent that the debt is enforceable against the assets of the non-debtor company. In this way the veil is pierced to render other members (usually in the context of a group of companies) liable, if they have contracted to that effect. If the guarantee conforms to contractual standards then it is enforceable as a contract in the usual way. However, cases have arisen where a document does not have contractual force. A document that may appear to be a guarantee may fall short of this and may be termed merely a 'comfort letter' because the terms are not

---

30 Ibid, p 172.
31 *Tesco Supermarkets Ltd v Nattrass* [1972] AC 153.
32 Ibid.

sufficiently specific to be contractually binding. For example, in *Kleinwort Benson Ltd v Malaysia Mining Corporation Berhad*[33] the defendant plc in Malaysia formed a wholly owned subsidiary in England to operate as a ring dealing member of the London Metal Exchange. The plaintiffs were merchant bankers who made a loan to the subsidiary (MMC Metal Ltd) relying on a 'comfort letter' from the defendant which said: 'It is our policy to ensure that the business of the subsidiary is at all times in a position to meet its liabilities.' The loan facility was increased from £5 m to £10 m when the defendant supplied a second comfort letter in substantially the same terms.

The subsidiary went into liquidation and the defendant refused to pay sums outstanding under these arrangements contending that the letters had not been intended to impose any binding legal obligation. On appeal the court held that the defendant's statement in the letter was a statement of present fact and not a promise as to future conduct and therefore had no contractual effect.

STATUTORY EXCEPTIONS

Historically, the company form was provided to business persons and merchant traders as a privilege granted by the state. As we have seen, charters were granted for short periods and often cost the incorporators dearly. When the first public Act of 1844 extended the right to incorporate to all, it was as a response to economic needs. It was a business form delineated by government policy in legislation. The extension of limited liability to investors continued that tradition of controlled privilege and contributed to the emergence of the company as a distinct legal being whose investors lay behind and were protected by the corporate veil. Thus, when legislation is passed which undermines the veil it is passed with caution and in response to an instability or profound injustice in the system. Government intervention of this nature is also a timely reminder that the company is a creature of public statute. The problem that has provoked the most intervention into the doctrine of separate personality by the government has been the problem of creditors, and particularly unsecured creditors, who have borne huge losses created not merely through the vagaries of business success but by the reckless behaviour of company officers. Thus, the Insolvency Act 1986 provided for the personal liability of directors whose negligent or dishonest behaviour diminished the company's assets. The relevant sections include:

33 [1986] 1 WLR 379.

- s 212 of the Insolvency Act 1986;
- s 213 of the Insolvency Act 1986;
- s 214 of the Insolvency Act 1986;
- s 216 of the Insolvency Act 1986;
- s 217 of the Insolvency Act 1986.

A summary remedy against delinquent directors – s 212 of the Insolvency Act 1986

Section 212 provides a summary procedure to make persons, including company officers, liquidators, administrative receivers, company promoters but most specifically directors, liable to contribute to the company's assets for breach of fiduciary duty or any other duty owed to the company. Following an application by the official receiver, liquidator, or any creditor, a court can examine the conduct of an officer of a company to see if they have misapplied, retained or become accountable for money or property of the company, or if they have been guilty of a misfeasance or breach of duty to the company. The court can order these persons to repay all or some of the misapplied funds. The successful application of this section is illustrated in *West Mercia Safetywear Ltd (in liq) v Dodd*.[34] In this case, West Mercia Safetywear Ltd (West Mercia) was a wholly owned subsidiary of AJ Dodd & Co Ltd (Dodd). Mr Dodds was the director of both companies and both companies banked at the same bank. Dodd's overdraft was guaranteed by Mr Dodds. By May 1984 West Mercia owed Dodd Ltd about £30,000, both companies were in financial difficulties and their accountant advised Mr Dodds not to operate the company bank accounts. Contrary to this advice, Mr Dodds transferred £4,000 from Mercia's account to Dodd Ltd. In June both companies went into liquidation. The liquidator for West Mercia applied for a declaration that Mr Dodds was guilty of misfeasance and breach of trust and should repay £4,000 to West Mercia. The judge held that although Mr Dodds had acted improperly he had not breached any duty to West Mercia as the transfer was merely the repayment of a debt. On appeal, the court held that once a company was insolvent the interests of the creditors overrode the interests of the shareholders. Therefore the transfer was against the interests of the company (as the assets effectively belonged to creditors in insolvency), because it was against the interests of the creditors. Thus it could be argued that in circumstances of financial constraints, a director's duty to act in the interests of the company is a duty to act in the interest of creditors, rather than shareholders. At the very least it is a duty to protect company assets rather than to pursue profit maximisation. In this particular case, Mr Dodds was ordered to repay £4,000 to West Mercia with interest.

---

34 [1988] BCLC 250.

Fraudulent trading – s 213 of the Insolvency Act 1986

Fraudulent trading is a criminal offence under s 458 of the Companies Act 1985 regardless of whether a company is winding up. It is a civil sanction under s 213 but only when the company is in the course of winding up. This section requires that the 'business of the company has been carried on with intent to defraud creditors'.[35] The conduct must 'involve actual dishonesty, involving, according to current notions of fair trading among commercial men, real moral blame'.[36] The liquidator is the applicant and the amount of personal liability for the perpetrator is at the discretion of the court.

Some cases have suggested that fraudulent trading can include one transaction with just one creditor as in *Re L Todd (Swanscombe) Ltd*.[37] In this case, Mr Morez was a company director of a scrap metal business. It dealt with its principal customer, Mayer Newman, for many years without charging VAT. In 1985 the company went into liquidation and the following year Mr Morez was convicted of fraudulent evasion of VAT. In 1988, the Commissioners of Customs and Excise of VAT sought repayment of VAT from Morez under s 213. The court held that he was personally liable for VAT debts under this section as he had traded knowing that he was defrauding a creditor in the process.

However, a more recent case suggests that liability for fraudulent trading will only arise if the business as a whole was a vehicle for fraudulent trading. In *Morphitis v Bernasconi and Others*[38] the court held that it did not necessarily follow that whenever a fraud on a creditor was perpetrated in the course of carrying on a business that the business was being carried on with intent to defraud creditors.

Wrongful trading – s 214 of the Insolvency Act 1986

The civil sanction of wrongful trading is set out in s 214 of the Insolvency Act 1986. Under this section the liquidator of a company may apply for an order, in the course of winding up, to make a director (including a shadow director) contribute to the company's assets as the court thinks proper. A director will be liable if the company is in insolvent liquidation and it appears that trading continued (before winding up) when the *director knew or ought to have known* that there was no reasonable prospect that the company would avoid liquidation. Hitherto, a director's duty of care was not thought to be something

---

35 Section 213(1).
36 *Re Patrick and Lyon Ltd* [1933] Ch 786, p 790.
37 [1990] BCC 125.
38 [2003] 2 BCLC 53.

that should have an objective standard.[39] Under s 214(4)(a) the 'ought' standard of competency required a director to have the general knowledge, skill and experience reasonably expected from somebody carrying out the same function as a director. In addition, under s 214(4)(b) it continued to apply the subjective criteria of 'the general knowledge and skill' that the director actually possesses. Section 214(3) provides that it is a defence for a director to show he had taken every reasonable step to minimise the loss to the company. Section 214(1) provides that liability is at the court's discretion and cases which have applied this section have inclined to the view that it is designed to be compensatory rather than penal.

The case of *Re Produce Marketing Consortium Ltd (No 2)*[40] illustrates how the section is designed to work. Produce Marketing Consortium (PMC) carried on a business importing fruit as a commission agent. From 1981 PMC had traded at a loss with liabilities progressively exceeding its assets and its overdraft increasing. An overdraft of £50,000 was guaranteed by one of the directors. By 1986, the company's overdraft was over £90,000. In February 1987, the auditors concluded that business was only continuing because of its banking facility and advised the directors that they could be personally liable for fraudulent trading. PMC went into creditors' voluntary winding up and the liquidator sought an order that the two directors be liable under s 214 to the sum of £107,946. The court held that PMC was not a large company and the size of the company was important in assessing liability. There was a statutory duty to publish annual accounts and therefore the directors should have reasonably known information which would have informed them that the company should cease trading. The court therefore held the directors' contribution to the company's assets to be the amount by which the company's assets had diminished during the wrongful trading period. Or as a later case put it, the increase in 'net deficiency' between the hypothetical liquidation date and the actual date of liquidation.[41] It is perhaps unfortunate that at least on the evidence of reported cases, s 214 has had little impact on the business world, with few successful applications.

Prohibitions on the re-use of company names – sections 216 and 217 Insolvency Act 1986

Further restrictions on company names exist in order to prevent abuse of limited liability through measures that prevent the re-use of a company name (for five years) by those who were the directors or shadow directors of an

---

39 As noted in Chapters 4 and 5, American company law has an objective standard for the duty of care but this is modified in many States by the business judgment rule.

40 [1989] BCLC 520.

41 *Re Continental Assurance Company of London plc (in liquidation)* [2001] BPIR 733.

insolvent company during the 12 months prior to that company going into insolvent liquidation. These restrictions are specified in s 216 of the Insolvency Act 1986. The penalty for a contravention of s 216 is held in the following section. A director or shadow director who re-uses the name of such an insolvent company within five years of that company becoming insolvent will be personally liable for the debts of the company operating in contravention of s 216. Under this section the veil is pierced as a result of the remedy in s 217. The case of *Thorne v Silverleaf*[42] examined in the following chapter shows how the courts will utilise the provisions of ss 216 and 217.

THE HISTORICAL EMERGENCE OF THE DOCTRINE OF SEPARATE CORPORATE PERSONALITY

Historically, the judiciary recognised the separateness of the company from its members when factually the company *existed* separately from the shareholder and not before. In general, if a company was a large business whose shareholders acted as outside investors and did not hold a managerial position in the company, the judiciary tended to construe members' interests as being distinct from the interests of the company. This was true of the large charter companies in the seventeenth and eighteenth centuries and it became true of large industrial companies incorporated under the Companies Acts. Arguably, it would not be possible to construe the company as being legally separate if this did not express some material or practical reality. The doctrine after all has a practical function and practical implications, including the protection of investors from liability and the enabling of the freely transferable and saleable share.

An interesting account of the origins of the doctrine of separate corporate personality is to be found in a 1987 article, 'The conceptual foundations of modern company law'.[43] In this piece, the authors, Ireland *et al*, examine its origins from a modern Marxist socio-legal perspective. Briefly stated, in their scenario the capital-hungry economy of the nineteenth century was sustained by the sale of freely transferable marketised shares. Shareholders became holders of titles to revenue which were disconnected from the assets of the company because this facilitated an increase in the supply of capital to the company. The company by implication was construed as being disentangled and separate from shareholders *per se*.

In this section it will be argued that as evidentially compelling as this piece certainly is, it is overly economically deterministic and has overlooked the nature and importance of nineteenth-century company law in both common

---

42 [1994] 1 BCLC 637.
43 Ireland, P, Grigg-Spall, I and Kelly, D (1987) JLS 14, 1.

law and statute and the role of politics as constituent factors of this key company law doctrine. This section will examine theories on the origin of separate and corporate personality in more detail and assess the strengths and weaknesses of legal and contextual narratives.

In 'Conceptual Foundations' Ireland *et al* show how the historical reconceptualisation of shareholders' interests in the company, expressed in changes in the legal understanding of the nature of the share, resulted in a correlating reconceptualisation of the nature of the company. As the share became a definite and tradable piece of property the judiciary began to speak of the company as being a thing characterised by separateness. The company, the authors argue, ceased to be a body composed of people and instead became a thing in itself, emptied of and distinct from its members. They maintain that although traditionally, company law views the separateness of the company as arising from the legal act of incorporation (the legal effect of incorporation today), historically incorporation did not result in separation. In their words,

> An examination of eighteenth and early nineteenth century cases and texts makes it clear that incorporation did not at any time entail such a separation. Incorporation did create an entity, the incorporated company, which was legally distinguishable from the people composing it, but there was no suggestion that the entity was 'completely separate' from its members.[44]

In evidencing this proposition, Ireland *et al* cite the tendency of the judiciary to refer to companies as 'theys' rather than the modern conception of the company as an 'it'. They cite, for example, *Myers v Perigal*, where the judge stated that 'the company carried on their concerns through the agency of their directors, and were empowered to invest their capital'.[45] This use of the 'they' pronoun, they argue, is because of the different judicial interpretation of the notion and consequence of incorporation which was quite different from any post-*Salomon* understanding. Judges use the pronoun 'they' because the corporation was understood to be a group of persons, not an independent entity, an 'it'.

The second body of evidence the authors cite in support of their proposition is the legal nature of shareholding in eighteenth- and early nineteenth-century companies. The modern ordinary shareholder would generally expect a right to vote at company meetings, they would expect dividends if dividends were declared, and would enjoy any surplus assets after the company had been wound up and all creditors and preference shareholders had been

---

44 Ibid, p 150.
45 Ibid, p 151; (1851) 2 De G M & G 599.

repaid. In contrast to this model of the company share, shares in the earlier period were understood to be a property right in the assets of the company, a share within the ordinary meaning of the word. So that while the company might hold the title to company assets in the manner of a trustee, shareholders held the equitable interest. 'To possess a share in a joint stock company implied ownership of a share of the totality of the company's assets. Legally, shares in incorporated, joint stock companies, were viewed as equitable interests in the property of the company.'[46] Therefore, because shares were equitable interests in company assets, their legal nature depended on the nature of those assets. And, in determining the nature of shares, for the purpose of applying the Statute of Mortmain or Frauds, the courts routinely assessed the nature of the company's assets. Shares in a company possessed mainly of real estate were, in law, understood to be realty, and so if the assets were not real estate, the shares were construed as personalty. Explicitly demonstrating this point they cite Lord Macclesfield in a 1723 case, who said that 'the legal interest of all the stock [assets] was in the company, who are the trustees for the several members'.[47]

The shift in this judicial understanding of the share was first evidenced, they argue, in the case of *Bligh v Brent*,[48] where seemingly contrary to all previous authorities, the court held the shares in the company to be personalty rather the realty. In this case the plaintiff, the testator's heir-at-law, argued that the shares should pass to him as they were realty and in law these shares could only be passed under the testator's will to its beneficiaries and their representatives if they were personalty. According to Ireland *et al*, the court held that shares were personalty regardless of the nature of the company assets because a shareholder's interest was in the profit only. Importantly, Alderton B construed the interest of the shareholders to be in the profits alone, their interest and claim was not upon the assets but the surplus that those assets produced. Assets as distinct from profits from assets were formulated as two different forms of property, the company owning the former, the shareholder the latter. The authors argue that Alderton's view had extended to all companies by the 1850s and cite Sir John Romilly[49] in 1861 stating that shares in joint stock companies were effectively independent property, and Bacon CJ in 1871 stating that shares were no longer personal actionable rights but were instead 'freehold property'.[50] Indeed, an examination of the Statute of Mortmain cases in the nineteenth century reveals an increasing tendency by the judiciary to

---

46 Ibid, p 152.
47 *Child v Hudson Bay* (1723) P Wyms 207.
48 (1837) 2 Y & C 268.
49 *Poole v Middleton* 29 Beav 646.
50 Ireland *et al*, p 159.

construe the shares of all kinds of companies, large, small, incorporated or unincorporated to be personalty, and disconnected from the tangible assets of the company.

Thus they conclude when a share was transformed into an independent piece of property, the company was capable of being conceptualised as separate, a thing which owned its own assets and held responsibility for its own debts: 'The company was no longer a plural entity, a "they", people merged into one body; it was now a singular entity, an "it", an object emptied of people. Both the company and the share had been reified.'[51]

Ireland *et al* marry some of the theories of the more sophisticated legal writers on eighteenth-century company shares with an economic contextual approach in order to provide a method for understanding the historical emergence of this key doctrine of modern company law. However, the better legal scholars in this area, as well as providing useful source material, also provide a depth of legal and textual analysis which illustrates the importance of non-economic factors in the formation of this doctrine.

Exemplifying the former is the work of Samuel Williston, a nineteenth-century American academic and one of Harvard's brightest stars. In his 1888 article, Williston assessed many of the judgments relied upon in the article above but often made different and important distinctions.[52] Furthermore, whilst textual in his approach, Williston understands legal developments in specific areas to arise in the context of broader legal developments. In particular, in attempting to articulate the nature of a corporation, he extends his focus to the legal interests of those connected to the corporation, particularly, in this article, shareholders. And thus, like Ireland *et al*, his analysis of the particular nature of the corporation concludes that it derives from the nature and development of joint stock. However, Williston differs from Ireland *et al* in that he does not attempt a broader contextualisation of the company share as the primary financial product fuelling a rapidly developing industrial economy. Accordingly, Williston provides no explanation for these shifts in judicial thinking and as such his legal approach provides no model for understanding the dynamic of legal developments. However, his close textual readings of the cases in question and their broader legal context is informative and questions the overly neat connections made between economic development and legal thought in the previous article. Finally, as this article was written before *Salomon* was decided, the article is itself evidence of a late-nineteenth-century understanding of the separation doctrine.

Williston, in proposing that under 'old law' a share was an equitable interest in the whole concern, cites Lord Macclesfield as authority for the

---

51 Ibid, p 159.
52 Williston, S, 'History of the law of business corporations before 1800', Part II (1888) 2 Harv L Rev 4. Williston assesses mainly English cases in this article.

proposition that in pre-1800 law[53] the corporation held its assets as a trustee for the shareholders, who were 'in equity co-owners'.[54] Furthermore in evidencing the connection between shareholders' interests and the company's, he looks at cases involving the Statutes of Mortmain and Frauds, and of transfers involving real estate. He surmises that 'if the shareholders have in equity the same interest which the corporation has at law, a share will be real estate or personalty, according as the corporate property is real or personal'.[55] If the company property was real estate then the company share would be subject to the laws relating to real estate, in respect of transfers and tax. He cites a case involving the shares of the New River Water Company, where it was held that the shares were realty because the company assets were real estate.[56] Williston also assesses a group of cases involving fraudulent or mistaken transfer of shares in order to prove his proposition on the basis that if the shareholder's interest were legal, then such a transfer would not affect their rights. However, if the shareholder's interests were merely equitable, then a bone fide purchaser for value would acquire title following a transfer made without the shareholder's consent. The original shareholder would be compensated accordingly but would not be able to regain the shares. Williston shows that in eighteenth-century cases the latter view was taken. For example, he cites an 1740 case where the judge held that '. . . the company must be considered as trustees for the owner at the time he purchased this stock'.[57] Or in *Ashby v Blackwell*, where the court upheld the transfer, made without the knowledge of the original shareholders, stating that the shareholder was entitled to relief only. The company was the party who should provide that relief given that, 'a trustee, whether a private person or body corporate, must see to the reality of the authority empowering them to dispose of the trust money'.[58]

Williston provides further evidence for his proposition in the court decisions on shareholder liability for the company's debts. Criticising Blackstone's statement that 'the debts of the corporation either to it or from it are extinguished by its dissolution'[59] as 'undoubtedly, an error' he shows that the body of court opinion took the opposite view. He shows that unless there were very specific reasons not to do so, shareholders were held to be connected (in equity), to the obligations which the corporation owed to the outside world. This obligation was treated in law as part of a company's assets and they

---

53 Williston takes this date as the running point although he relies on cases which are some decades later than this.
54 Ibid, p 150.
55 Ibid.
56 Ibid.
57 Ibid, p 153.
58 Ibid, p 153, citing *Ashby v Blackwell and The Million Bank*, Ambl 503.
59 Ibid, p 161.

could be enforced through equity. Thus, in *Dr Salmon v The Hamborough Company*, the court upheld the plaintiff creditor's claim to have the company's debts paid by its members. If the company could not pay, payment would be enforced against 'every member of the said company as is to be contributory to the public charge, as shall be sufficient to satisfy the sum decreed to the plaintiff'.[60] Likewise, in a 1673 case, the judge stated that 'if losses must fall upon the creditors, such losses should be borne by those who were members of the company, who best knew their estates and credit, and not by strangers who were drawn in to trust the company upon the credit and countenance it had from such particular members'.[61] The significance of the common law rule on a member's liability for a company's debts is that it indicates the common understanding that the company and the members had a property interest in the same assets, and therefore similar liabilities if those assets became deficits. The common law rules established in English courts continued to be applied in America as late as 1826,[62] which is significant because many States had adopted company legislation which provided for limited liability for members, and by the 1830s it was generally accepted that a company member's liability would be limited.[63] *Dr Salmon* therefore indicates how persistent the notion of conjoined shareholder and company property interests really was. In England, the separation of the shareholder from the company's liability was achieved legislatively and was not the result of judicial recognition of the shareholder's separation from the company's assets and debts.[64] Indeed, even today the company constitution must state its intention in respect of its members' liability.[65]

Having proven the equitable nature of a shareholder's interest, Williston goes on to argue that the modern view on the nature of the share was established in England by the case of *Bligh v Brent* and subsequently adopted in America. Here the plaintiff's assertion that the interest of the *cestui que trust* was co-extensive with the legal interest of the trustee was, as we have seen, entirely in line with the many authorities his counsel cited. However, we now know that in this case the shares were held to be personalty. And, as the assets consisted of some real estate, Ireland *et al* surmised that this decision reflected the changing economy and function of a company share. That is, the shares in this company were declared to be personalty because shares generally had been legally reconceptualised as tradable property and were no longer understood to be equitable interests in the whole undertaking. This reconceptualisation in law was, they argued, a direct result of shares

---

60   Ibid.
61   Ibid, p 162, citing Lord Nottingham in the case of *Naylor v Brown* (1673) Finch 83.
62   Ibid, p 162.
63   As noted in Chapter 1.
64   Limited Liability Act 1855.
65   Companies Act 2006 s 9(2)(c).

becoming tradable pieces of property in fact, and *Bligh v Brent* reflected a judicial appreciation of this development. From thereon, they argued, shares were understood to be personalty, regardless of the nature of the company's assets.

The problem with these assertions is that the assets in the company in *Bligh v Brent* was mainly personalty, described in this case as five-sixths of company assets.[66] So in holding the company shares to be personalty, the court was following existing precedent. Williston notes that in 1781 the shares belonging to another water company were held to be personalty and as no reason was given for this decision he surmises that it was probably due to the low proportion of real estate in the company's assets.[67] Furthermore, although Alderson B suggests that the personalty were 'mere adjuncts to the realty', and goes on to say 'how can it signify whether some of the component parts of the undertaking consist of personal estate?',[68] the judgment seemed to rest on just that question. In both *Bligh v Brent* and the many cases examined by the court in determining the property nature of a share, the outcome was based upon a combination of the terms of the incorporating Act or charters, and a bias towards the assumption that 'in every joint stock company, the shareholder has an estate of the same nature as the company'. These two elements were given different weight in different cases. For example, in *Ex Parte The Vauxhall Bridge Company*,[69] although the incorporating Act said that shares in the company should be treated as personal estate, the court ignored this and based its decision on the nature of the company's assets. Shortly after this case, the opposite decision was reached in another case where the court held that it was the express wording of the Act which determined the nature of the shares.[70] And so although previous cases had construed the assets of a waterworks company, such as pipes and reserves, to be realty,[71] *Bligh v Brent* was decided on the wording of its charter. When the company was formed, its assets were the powers laid out in its charter, to lay piping. The real estate was purchased after its incorporation. Therefore, the court concluded, the shares were to be determined not by subsequent purchases, made in order to produce profits, but by the assets held upon incorporation. As the defence had argued, shares in this company which had previously been transferred by sale or in wills had not been treated

---

66 Op. cit., Williston, p 151.
67 Ibid, citing *Weekely v Weekely* 2 T & C 281.
68 *Bligh v Brent*, p 278. It is worth noting that cases around this period tended to distinguish between a company and a corporation. In a joint stock company the members had an interest in the property of the company whereas in a corporation this interest was vested in the corporation.
69 *Bligh v Brent*, p 278, citing 1 Glyn & Jac 101.
70 *Bligh v Brent*, citing *Lancaster Canal Company* Mont & Bligh 94.
71 *R v Chelsea Waterworks Company* 2 Nev & Man 765.

as realty. Furthermore, the court stated that 'if we look at the wording of the charter, the language is much more suitable to personal than to real estate'.[72]

This has important consequences for how we understand the legal reconceptualisation of the company and the company share, because one interpretation of *Bligh v Brent* is that it was decided according to long-standing legal thought and did not signal a huge shift in judicial understanding of the share. Another interpretation is that the law of business organisations was not based on general principles relating to types of organisation, a partnership law on the one hand and company law on the other. Instead, legal decisions were made on a case-by-case basis which did not generate universally applicable principles. Broadly this is the view taken by AB DuBois in his famous text *The English Business Company after the Bubble Act 1720–1800*[73] in which he suggests that the lack of generality is largely attributable to the affects of the Bubble Act.

DuBois notes the frequent use of the pronoun 'they' in respect of companies by legal and other authorities but interprets this differently from Williston and Ireland *et al.*[74] Rather, he argues that the eighteenth century was characterised by a paucity of legal imagination. Eighteenth-century lawyers simply failed to develop legal principles and instead dealt with issues relating to corporations in a pragmatic, case-by-case basis. Indeed, he states that:

> in those rare instances where generalisation was thought necessary, the lawyer continued piously to repeat the platitudes developed in earlier centuries and distilled in concentrated form by Lord Coke. The use of old learning was quite uncritical, and indeed the manner of repetition is so unvarying and mechanical that one is led to doubt whether any thought whatever was expended upon the philosophical conceptions underlying legal doctrine.[75]

In this dearth of general law, he argues, the legal theory relating to non-commercial organisations was frequently seized upon by 'company lawyers' with contradictory results. For example, often a corporation was at once referred to as 'like other individuals' and then referred to as 'they' or a group. DuBois notes that in *Bligh v Brent*, while Alderson B set out

---

72 *Bligh v Brent*, p 287.
73 DuBois, AB, *The English Business Company after the Bubble Act 1720–1800*, New York: The Commonwealth Fund, 1938.
74 Eg, he says: 'in a letter to the Principal Officers of His Majesty's Board of Works, on January 10, 1781, the London Assurance Corporation in claiming damages as a result of the riots in London in June, 1780, stated: "The officers will be pleased to take down the above in order that the Corporation may receive the benefit on this occasion like other individuals as they are justly entitled to the same".'
75 Ibid, p 86.

an early articulation of the separateness of a shareholder's property from the property of the company, he continued to refer to the corporation as 'they'.

This failure to develop a theory of legal personality in respect of the company, and to perpetuate a conception of a corporation as both a distinct individual and simultaneously a group, DuBois attributes to the overwhelming effect of the Bubble Act of 1720. He argues that this Act individualised every corporation, making each a business which possessed powers and characteristics that were entirely constructed by its charter. Charter corporations, therefore, were not bonded by a general law which applied to and connected them all. Instead, they were individual arrangements between the incorporators and the state; privileges granted by the state for a short period of time. DuBois maintains that 'whatever fragment of coherent theory existed relating to the business corporation was centred in that relatively frequently appearing phrase, 'the corporation is the creature of the state'.[76]

What seems clear following a close textual analysis of *Bligh v Brent* and the cases it refers to is that the judgment was specific to the facts of this case and the terms of its charter. When writers look at the judge's description of 'the' company they teleologically assume that 'the' is used in the same way as modern company law uses the term, that is to describe companies in general. So in modern company law, when a statement is made about 'the' company it is referring to or establishing a general principle which applies to all companies. Whereas cases heard at the time of *Bligh v Brent* and before were describing the nature of the company in that particular case and shareholders in that particular company. The trust analogy, utilised continuously in early cases, is instructive here. A trust has the character of its particular terms and the beneficiaries' interests are entirely derived from the character of that particular trust. Likewise, a company formed through an incorporating Act had the character of that incorporating Act and corporations formed by charter had the characteristics of that particular charter. In contrast modern companies, formed through the Companies Acts, have identifiable characteristics applicable to all companies and those involved with the company such as directors or shareholders have general rights and duties applicable to all directors and shareholders. Where a general law did connect companies it was not a law of companies but other law such that relating to property, inheritance, fraud and contract, outlined by Williston.

However, having stated that the decision in *Bligh v Brent* was an uncontroversial continuity of the judiciary's approach to understanding company shares, many of the statements made in this case were atypical. For example, Alderton B drew a picture of the company which was very modern. He

76 Ibid, p 87.

characterised a shareholder as an investor passing his funds to a corporate body in order to receive profits and a company which creates that profit through purchases upon which the shareholder has no equitable claim.

Likewise Parke B's judgment is littered with very modern descriptions of the nature of a company share and of the company itself. On the company, he states that, 'it seems to me that the company are as much distinct from the proprietors as one man is from another',[77] and later, 'the corporation is separate from the members'.[78] And of shareholders he says: 'all the subscribers have to do is to receive the net profit'.[79] These observations, though almost certainly, as I have argued, intended to describe the specific situation in *Bligh v Brent*, later found more general application.

So in the case of *Watson v Spratley*, the Court of Exchequer, in holding the shares of this unincorporated company to be personalty, made the following observations.[80] Whether dealing with a share from a large corporation or one from a small company, the share is:

> in its essential nature and quality identical. In both, the shareholder has only the right to receive dividends payable on his share: that is, a right to his just proportion of the joint stock, consisting, indeed, partly of land; but whilst he holds his share he has no interest in or separate right to the land or any part of it.[81]

Furthermore, he maintained that this essential nature was not dependent upon whether the company was incorporated or unincorporated. 'In substance and reality the interest of a shareholder in a mining unincorporated company and the incorporated joint stock company is exactly the same. In both it is in an interest in the ultimate profits.'[82]

However, this case also demonstrates how the clarity of thought in respect of the nature of a share was in process and not yet complete. Two of the judgments specifically tied their conclusion as to the nature of the shares in this case, to the specific wording in the company's constitution. So in Parke B's dissenting judgment he concluded that the nature of a shareholder's interest should be determined by the way in which the property is held. If the title is vested in the corporation, then the share is personalty; however, if it is vested with the members, then the share will be realty if the property is real estate. Thus he concluded that in this case, as the share represented an aliquot

77 *Bligh v Brent*, p 279.
78 Ibid.
79 Ibid.
80 *Watson v Spratley* (1854) Court of Exchequer 53, p 57.
81 Martin B, ibid, p 59.
82 Ibid, p 60.

portion of all the company's assets, 'both in the mine, engines machinery and all', the shares were realty.[83]

Furthermore, while Alderton B found the shares to be personalty it was on the basis that given the facts presented, the shares were not like the New Rover Company shares, where 'each individual corporator had a definite proportion of the land out of which the profit could be made'.[84] Instead, they were 'value only in the chattel interest which the parties have in the profits'.[85] Importantly, he did not base his conclusions on the 'essential nature of a company share' but upon the specific facts of this case.

However, just a few years on and the judicial interpretation of the share had gained a much more general character. In 1858, the court held that the company assets (mines) were not held on trust for individual shareholders and that their interest was in the profits gained from working those mines and nothing else.[86] Two years later a court decision held that shareholders in a joint stock company had no legal or equitable freehold interest in property – in this case the company assets were real estate. As such they could not meet the property franchise and vote.[87]

Furthermore, in the process of the consideration of *Bligh v Brent* through the courts, many of the contradictions in the judgment were shed so that a clearly identifiable shareholder and company began to emerge. In *Bligh v Brent* the company was referred to as the partnership with frequent use of plurals in reference to the company. For example, in Parke B's judgment quoted above he states 'the company *are* . . .' but in the same paragraph he refers to the corporation as an 'it'. However, by the time *Hayter v Tucker* and the *Riding* case noted above were heard, this understanding was abandoned and no such blurring of a company form with the partnership form occurred henceforth.[88] Indeed, in *Baxter v Newman*,[89] a partnership case heard just a year after *Bligh v Brent* was specifically distinguished, the partners were held to have an interest in the real estate property of the partnership corresponding to the proportion of their share of the business. Thus, by distinguishing a partnership proper from an incorporated company referred to as a partnership, the company form was emerging with an ever clearer identity.

The emergence of the doctrine of separate corporate personality was a gradual process, which embraced the interaction between legal form and

---

83 Ibid, p 58.
84 Ibid, p 62.
85 Ibid.
86 *Hayter v Tucker* (1853) 23 JP 19, 4 K & J 243.
87 *York (County) West Riding Case, Bulmer v Norris* (1860) 25 JP 8.
88 This remains the case with the exception of equitable remedies available for minority shareholders of quasi partnership type companies such as *In re Ebrahimi*.
89 (1845) 9 JP 744.

economic activity. Williston's contemporary understanding of the company form is testimony to that assertion. When Williston was writing in 1888, *Salomon* had not yet been decided, so while he described many of the elements of a company's separateness from its shareholders, he did not refer to a company being a separate legal person, emptied of people. It required the proper maturation of legal process for that, the judgment of Salomon! While the material basis for the company's separation was in place, a freely transferable share in a market for shares, the understanding of the leading international law school was that the company did not have a completely separate legal personality. The doctrine, while reflecting a material reality, did not emerge until the courts had sufficiently processed its own concepts and drawn them together into one overarching general principle. The notion of separate corporate personality for all incorporated companies was not complete until *Salomon* and so Williston could not make reference to it or indeed conceptualise the company in exactly that way.

An economic determinist perspective has a tendency to minimalise the importance of other societal facets such as law and ideology so that it often needs to overlook details which are not consistent with the economic model. On the other hand, a legal perspective sees little but the progression of a purely legal narrative and can give no explanation for these changes, nor provide a framework in which to anticipate future changes. Both approaches have their limitations, which might be transcended by an approach which embraced the relationship between law, economics and ideology. The role of limited liability legislation as formative of the doctrine of separate corporate personality is a case in point. The 1855 Limited Liability Act enabled investors to protect themselves from personal liability for their company's debts. Today, limited liability is synonymous with separate legal personality and it is difficult for students of law, taught in legal narratives alone, to conceive of the doctrine in the absence of limited liability. Yet, historically the 1855 Act and its incorporation into later consolidating Acts did not result in the immediate emergence of the doctrine of separate corporate personality, thus showing the limitations of legal narratives. However, this is not to say that economic determinism provides all the answers, because statutory limited liability did have some part in the emergence of separate corporate personality. Accordingly, limited liability can only be sensibly viewed as one of the elements which led to the reconceptualisation of the company.

Historically, the notion of limited liability was a controversial one and the Act itself was fiercely debated in and outside Parliament. Eventually, it was passed because it was believed that it would enhance investments in companies by attracting the many potential smaller investors. The Act's promoters reasoned that the wider populace would cease their reticence in regard to share purchases if they were assured that the company's debts would not fall to them personally. Clearly, as minority shareholders they would not expect to protect their investment by being actively involved in the company's business. Instead they could be outside investors, treating their shares as sources of revenue, much in the manner of a government bond.

This was the reasoning and some of it was borne out in subsequent events. For example, LM Sealy notes that following the passage of the Act, attendance at annual general meetings fell dramatically.[90] Company shareholders were observably becoming passive investors. Thus it would follow that if a significant percentage of shareholders were acting as outside investors, interested only in dividends, the judiciary would begin to conceive of shareholders in terms of their separateness from company activities and by extension the company. An enhanced popularity of a company share, which the 1855 Act undoubtedly contributed to, is an essential factor in the rise of a market in shares which Ireland *et al* rightly identify as central to the share's emergence as a tradable piece of property, disconnected from the company's tangible assets.

On the other hand, the effect of limited liability on company law history can be exaggerated. Limited liability did not unleash a public clamouring for shares any more than it greatly enhanced the numbers of entrepreneurs keen to incorporate as limited liability companies. The reasons for this seem to lie in the realm of both ideology and economics. Ideologically, the notion that limiting one's liability was an indication of dubious or sharp practice continued to dominate Victorian thinking. Limited liability, obtained under this Act both cheaply and easily, was considered by many sections of society as an indicator of immorality. And, as the parliamentary debates leading up to the Bill indicate, those in favour of limited liability as a method to enhance investment were closely pitted against those who decried it as a 'rogue's charter'. The previous fraudulent behaviour of the South Sea Company and many other smaller joint stock companies was written deeply into the public consciousness. Parliamentary committee reports indicate that the public distrusted limited liability companies, seeing little possibility of creditors and suppliers taking the risk of contracting with an organisation where none was personally responsible for the debts.[91] Within parliament MPs expressed frequent concerns that limited liability companies would undermine the good reputation of British merchants. At a very fundamental level a trader who took personal responsibility for the debts gained in the course of trading was thought to be an honest businessman. Limited liability shirked economic and moral responsibility.[92]

Furthermore, some years after the 1855 Act, the actual record of companies incorporated with limited liability tended to reinforce public distrust.

---

90 Seely, LM, *Cases and Materials in Company Law*, 2001, London: Butterworths.
91 Hannah, L, *The Rise of the Corporate Economy*, 2nd edn, 1976, London: Methuen.
92 One can observe the continuity of this ideology in present-day prohibitions on barristers operating with limited liability, a prohibition to which solicitors and even architects were subject to until very recently.

As HA Shannon's work evidences, in the period between 1856 and 1883 one-third of limited liability companies never began business, 28 per cent were declared insolvent, 32 per cent ceased operating voluntarily and 11 per cent just petered out. This left just approximately 6 per cent with a successful, ongoing trading record.[93] But the relative lack of popularity of the limited liability company may also be explained by other factors. Industrial Britain of the mid-nineteenth century had very high capital requirements, companies required capital and post-1855 investors were able to invest without personal liability. And yet, incorporations were sluggish. There is much evidence to suggest that businesses that were particularly well established, as opposed to new more speculative businesses, were generally family controlled firms. These businesses often chose to remain as unincorporated associations because the family could retain control and because they could reinvest in the firm using internally generated capital.

Work by PL Payne indicates that high profit rates in this early part of the nineteenth century, coupled with the relative ease by which unincorporated associations could be tailored to reduce personal liability, meant that there was little use for the limited liability form.[94] Furthermore, other evidence suggests that the limited liability form was attractive to investors who were themselves close to bankruptcy, which deterred wealthy investors from entangling their money with those of more dubious solvency.[95] Indeed, unlimited companies were much less prone to failure than limited companies. In the 1864 report in the register of companies, which looked at the performance of companies registered between 1856 and 1864, 24 per cent of limited companies were shown to have failed compared to only 11 per cent of unlimited companies.[96] Jeffrey's evidence shows that between 1856 and 1862, 2,488 limited liability companies were formed, although the total of paid-up share capital was only £34 m, a fifth of the £170 m invested in stock over that period.[97] The reticence to incorporate is also evidenced by comparing the numbers of incorporations in America. Between 1863 and 1890, the number of incorporated companies grew by 400 per cent, but in less industrialised America, that number was 1,400 per cent for the same period.[98]

93 Shannon, HA, 'The first five thousand limited liability companies and their duration', (1933) Economic History 4, pp 290–307.
94 Payne, PL, *British Entrepreneurship in the Nineteenth Century*, 1997, London: Macmillan.
95 Manne, HG, 'Our two corporation systems: Law and economics' (1967) Virginia Law Review 53, 259.
96 Smart, M, 'On limited liability and the developments of capital markets: An historical analysis' (1996) Working paper, University of Toronto, p 20.
97 Jeffreys, J, 'The denomination and character of shares, 1855–1885' (1948) Economic History Review.
98 Forbes, KL, 'Limited liability and the development of the business corporation' (1986) Journal of Law, Economics, and Organization 2, pp 163–77.

The English reliance on the unincorporated business form for the ideological and economic reasons noted above resulted in the relatively slow development of England's capital markets. As an adjunct to this observation, some writers have attributed Britain's failure to maintain its early international dominance with its failure to quickly develop its capital markets. For example one paper argued that:

> Britain's earlier industrial success may have led to a build-up of retained earnings among firms, allowing owners of existing, profitable ventures to delay the incorporation decision. This contributed to the problems of adverse selection in limited liability debt markets and induced a development trap for British firms.[99]

However, capital markets had been developing in England for many decades and financial arrangements between people, or *choses in action*, had been emerging as pieces of exchangeable property since the eighteenth century. *Choses in action* have been defined in various ways but the chief difference between a capital form such as a modern share and pre-eighteenth-century *choses in action* was the latter's lack of transferability. It existed as a right personal to the holder rather than a piece of intangible property which was freely transferable. An early definition of *choses in action* described them as follows:

> Things in action is when a man hath cause or may bring an action for some duty due to him, as an action of debt upon an obligation, annuity, or rent, action of covenant or ward, trespass of goods taken away, beating and such like: and because they are things whereof a man is not possessed, but for recovery of them is driven to his action, they are called things in action.[100]

Later, arrangements that were previously 'things whereof a man is not possessed' became things of which he was possessed and could dispose of although they were 'uncorporeal'. And as the meaning of a *chose in action* reformulated, so, for example, Howard Elphinstone, writing in 1893, argued that the company share was a *chose in action* with some 'diversities'. The owner of shares could enforce his rights against the company by action; however, 'he has no rights over any specific chattel belonging to the company'.[101] On the other hand the shareholder held a *prima facie* right to sell his share and thus the rights contained in it.

---

99 Op. cit., Smart, p 20.
100 Elphinstone, H (1893) 9 LQR 26, p 312, quoting Termes de la Ley, s.v. Chose in Action.
101 Ibid, p 314.

Ireland *et al*, in concurrence with Marx's work on finance capital, stated that as markets in titles to revenue developed throughout the nineteenth century, shares were no longer regarded as *choses in action* but as independent property forms. Following other titles to revenue such as government bonds, in this transformation, the company share began to become a thing in itself when, and only when, a market in shares began to develop. 'In the absence of a public share market, shares could not develop as fictitious capital with a value in themselves.'[102] A market in shares, they argued, began to develop with the popularity of the railway shares which were sold in local exchanges in small accessible denominations. And, although dividends were very depressed they continued to be very popular.

> The effects of these developments on shares, however, were qualitative as well as quantitative. Shares were not only more numerous, they were now marketable commodities, liquid assets, easily converted by their holders into money ... a gulf emerged between companies and their shareholders and between shareholders and their shares.[103]

Detailing the emergence of capital markets in Britain Michie's *The London Stock Exchange, A History*, shows that during the nineteenth century Britain's securities markets reoriented from being markets in government bonds (including foreign government bonds) to being markets in joint stock company shares. The London Stock Exchange (LSE), established in 1801, introduced the first major regulations on the sale of bonds and stocks signalling the emergence of a mature market in financial products. It imposed restrictions on membership so, for example, individuals who were involved in business were not permitted to join.[104] Furthermore, it introduced new codes of conduct.

The LSE began life dealing mainly in government bonds. However, by the mid 1820s the National Debt was producing a poor rate of return, estimated by Michie to be 3.8 per cent in 1822 and 3.3 per cent in 1824.[105] Investors switched first to foreign bonds and then second to shares. Trading in foreign bonds took place in the Foreign Funds room which was established for that purpose but, as a measure of the rising popularity of shares, by the 1830s a large proportion of the LSE's membership used this room for marketing shares. Michie estimates that by 1838 '278 brokers, out of a total membership of 675 – or 40 per cent – were involved in the buying or selling of shares, with many dealers also participating'.[106] The growing popularity of shares grew

---

102 Op. cit., Ireland *et al*, p 158.
103 Ibid, p 159.
104 Michie, R, *The London Stock Exchange, A History*, 1999, Oxford: Oxford University Press.
105 Ibid, p 53.
106 Ibid, p 59.

exponentially following the explosion of railway shares on the market. By 1845 most of the trade in the Foreign Funds room was of national railway shares, forcing the LSE to rearrange its markets and later extending into new buildings in No 9 Throgmorton Street.[107] However, much of the significance of the burgeoning market in railway shares lay in its effect on the provinces and its popularity and familiarity to the nation's people, thus normalising share owning:

> Popular as railway shares were on the LSE, threatening to overwhelm all other business, their impact on the provinces was even more dramatic. Whereas in 1825 the paid-up capital of Britain's railways was a mere £0.2 m, rising to £7.5 m in 1835, by 1840 this had increased more than sixfold to £48.1 m and then almost doubled again to £88.5 m in 1845.[108]

Furthermore,

> Membership of existing provincial stock exchanges shot up, with Liverpool reaching 220 in 1846 and Manchester 89, while a rash of new stock exchanges appeared all over the country. By the end of 1845 there were some 18 stock exchanges in existence compared with three at the beginning of the decade, and most major provincial towns possessed one.[109]

The culture of shareholding spread throughout the nation as the markets in these shares were local and accessible and such shares were issued in reasonably small denominations. In this form and within a thriving market, railway shares could freely exchange as a form of money capital. The owners of these shares were purchasing a financial investment rather than a role in a business and could not judicially or materially be described as being involved in the business. Most shareholders were distinct from the company, which was run by managers and major investors. In this context railway companies were emerging as distinct legal beings.

Industrial shares, however, lagged behind, as they lacked the two attributes of railway shares, that of being in small denominations and that of having a growing market. Later in this century the former lack was addressed by the law in the form of the 1867 Companies Act. This Act provided for the subdivision of a company's shares following a shareholder resolution. This allowed previously unwieldy shares to be transformed into saleable portions. Shares in industrial companies characterised by quasi-partnership forms of ownership which remained under the control of the original entrepreneurs or

107 Ibid, p 60.
108 Ibid, p 63.
109 Ibid.

family ownership tended to exist in very large and unwieldy denominations which were not easily marketable. The 1867 Act addressed this problem by allowing these shares to be broken down into small marketable portions.

The second issue began to change in the 1870s. Whilst trade in joint stock company shares was limited largely because there was relatively little for sale, by the 1870s businesses which had operated as partnerships began to convert into joint stock companies. In Michie's account from 1863 to 1913, 147,932 businesses were registered as joint stock companies. And while many continued to have closely held shares, by the 1880s the largest established companies began to issue shares to the general public:

> The result was a far greater awareness of, and interest in, domestic industrial and commercial securities on the London Stock Exchange. The paid-up capital of such securities quoted rose from a mere £43 m in 1883 to £690.9 m in 1903 and then to £917.6 m in 1913.[110]

The increase in shares on the market generally and the facility to have small-denomination shares substantially contributed to share marketability. But as Michie points out, an increased availability of shares did not necessarily make them attractive investment prospects so that even by 1877, it was estimated that at least 1,082 of the 1,367 issues were unmarketable. Prior to this, 'at any one time only around 10 per cent of all quoted securities could command a ready market as jobbers had to have a realistic expectation of undoing the deals they made'.[111]

The developments in the capital market, in business practice, in popular culture and in the law all contributed to the judgment in *Salomon*. The strength of Ireland *et al*'s perspective is in highlighting the importance of the burgeoning share market in changing the nature of the share and the doctrine of separate corporate personality. A market in freely transferable shares, although still dominated by railway shares, was thriving at the time of *Salomon*'s case, as was a popular understanding of the share as a claim to profits rather than the business itself. Thus their Lordships were reflecting the general nature of shareholding in late Victorian England, which did not involve shareholder liability.

However, it remains important to recognise the role of the law in this. The repeal of the Bubble Act, the more permissive regimes of the 1856 and 1862 Companies Acts, the Limited Liability Act and the 1867 Act all helped establish legal and ideological boundaries around the share allowing to it emerge and function as a separate piece of property. The share became an entitlement to dividends partly because shareholders were protected from further

110 Ibid, p 94.
111 Ibid, p 95.

business liabilities because the Limited Liability Act had made these liabilities the company's alone. Furthermore, this was a general feature of all companies so registered and not simply of those whose incorporation documents specified limited liability.

Furthermore, it is also important to recognise that the earlier judgments in cases such as *Bligh v Brent* do not advance our understanding of the doctrine of separate corporate personality as much as Ireland *et al* maintain, as these judgments were largely based on the particular facts of the case. Specifically these judgments were based upon the particular terms of the charter or act of incorporation of the company in question. So, contrary to Ireland's assertion that historically, incorporation was not the source of a company's separation, we can instead state that sometimes it was: it really depended on the bespoke terms of a company's incorporation document. No general company law existed during the first half of the nineteenth century and therefore no general principles as to the nature of the company and its shares could emerge. It is only when company law developed more principles that were applicable to all companies, in both common law and statute, that one can identify the distinct role of shareholders in a modern company. Once that is established, the boundaries of the company may be identified.

Separate corporate personality is indeed a doctrine which overwhelmingly supports and protects investors and one which recognises the two different worlds occupied by capital markets on the one hand and industrial markets on the other. But it is a doctrine which was gradually given form and articulated by the law and it is the law which is its staunchest defender.

Chapter 3

The company constitution, the company contract: ideology and the law

The company constitution refers to the body of rules which regulate the activities of those involved in the company. Under the 2006 Act the company's constitution comprises the articles of association and any resolutions relating to the company constitution.[1] It is also expected to include other important information relating to the company held in the incorporation documents. The articles of association include rules which govern the company's internal management. These rules form the terms of the statutory contract which exists between company member *qua* member and the company. Section 33 of the 2006 Act specifies that the provisions of the company's constitution 'bind the company and its members to the same extent as if there were covenants on the part of the company and of each member to observe those provisions'. Its previous incarnation in s 14 of the 1985 Act formed the basis of many cases assessing the nature of the contractual relationship between company and member.

There has been a long-standing trend in company law and company law scholarship to describe this area of law in contractual terms.[2] The company constitution and the rights of members under the constitution, in particular, have been frequently articulated within the paradigm of the contract. The siren call of this paradigm has been particularly amplified by certain aspects, or quirks, of company law. These include such things as the right of the company's incorporators to register their own articles of association, and s 33 of the 2006 Companies Act, which, as noted above, specifies a contractual relationship between shareholder and company.[3]

The purpose of this chapter is to examine critically the use of the contractual model in both company law scholarship and in the black letter law pertaining to the relationship of members to the company and to each other

---

1 Companies Act 2006, s 17.
2 And more recently to understand company law *per se* in contractual terms.
3 Previously s 14 of the 1985 Act and therefore the section cited in most relevant articles and cases to date.

identifiable in the articles and memorandum of association, and in s 33 issues. It will be argued that such contractual elements that do persist in this area of company law are small residues from companies' historical relationship with partnership law. Furthermore, it will be argued that while these residues may continue to have some significance in respect of companies that are in both management and ownership terms much more like a partnership, they have no application in larger companies. In cases involving small companies, decisions may be made which indicate a direct contractual relationship between the parties which are not mediated through the company but such decisions will only be applicable in small quasi-partnership arrangements. It will finally be demonstrated through case law and statute that the company constitution is heavily prescribed by statute and any choices that are made by the incorporators are made within a strict statutory framework. This is particularly true in respect of public companies, where wide-ranging restrictions ensure the public nature of the plc.

CONTRACTARIANISM, THE COMPANY AND THE CONSTITUTION

The contractual model for the company in this area of company law has been utilised with varying degrees of intensity by many legal thinkers. The primary concern in this chapter is with the modern variant of this, American contractarianism. It is, however, worth noting that as early as 1956 Professor Gower argued that the emergence of the English company from the (indisputably contract-based) partnership form has resulted in a continuing relationship between contract law and company law. The first English Companies Acts, he noted, were based on partnership law, indeed

> it was this familiar form of organization which the legislation of 1844 and 1855 adopted, successfully conferring on it the boons of corporate personality and limited liability. Hence the modern English business corporation has evolved from the unincorporated partnership, based on mutual agreement, rather than from the corporation, based on a grant from the state, and owes more to the partnership principles than to rules based on corporate personality.[4]

These partnership principles, he argued, made English company law ideally suited for both a small private company and a large public company precisely because 'the constitution of the English business corporation is still regarded

---

4 Gower, 'Some contrasts between British and American corporate law' (1956) Harv L Rev June Vol 69 No 8, pp 1371–2.

as essentially contractual . . . the British Companies Act relies far more on the technique of the Partnership Act, providing a standard form which applies only in the absence of contrary agreement by the parties'.[5] This standard form, which for companies limited by shares was the well-known Table A,[6] could be modified or substituted by the incorporators upon registration or altered in part by the company members at a later date.[7] Under s 7 of the Companies Act 1985, in the case of a company limited by shares, articles of association could be registered with the memorandum of association but if they were not so registered Table A[8] would be applied.[9] So, at least on first blush, it appears that the articles of association may consist of terms that the incorporators construct and agree to and in that respect it conforms to contractual norms.

However, such contractual freedoms as seem to be offered here were heavily restricted by statute. For example, s 310 of the Companies Act 1985 prohibited the inclusion of terms that purported to exempt any officer of the company from 'any liability which by virtue of any rule of law would otherwise attach to him in respect of any negligence, default, breach of duty or breach of trust of which he may be guilty in relation to the company'.[10] This statutory provision overrode any attempt to freely write the terms of the 'contract' to provide such an exemption. Furthermore, it also seemed to override Article 85 of Table A which allowed a director to retain profits made from a contract between himself and a company to which he owes a fiduciary duty, provided he has disclosed his interest to the other directors. In other words, an Article 85 disclosure which claimed to exempt a director from this breach of duty would not seem to succeed under s 310.[11]

Gower further argued that the manner in which the English share is *understood* under English law reflects the contractual character of partnership law. He asserted that the law has 'always regarded shares of stock as creatures of the company constitution and therefore as essentially contractual choses in action'.[12] As such, he notes, English company law has consistently recognised the right of the members to include in the company constitution restrictions

---

5 Ibid, p 1375.
6 Table A is a model form of regulations pertaining to the management of the company, the articles of association. It is a default model and incorporators may choose to compile their own articles of association.
7 Companies Act 1985. This has now been replaced by the Companies Act 2006, s 21.
8 Prescribed by the regulations made by the Secretary of State: Companies (Tables A to F) Regulations 1985 (1985 No 805).
9 Companies Act 1985, s 8(2).
10 Companies Act 1985, s 310(1).
11 This apparent contradiction was somewhat clumsily resolved in the case of *Movitex Ltd v Bulfield* [1988] BCLC 104.
12 Op. cit., Gower, p 1377.

on share transfers, to the extent of allowing unfettered share transfers.[13] Thus if members wished to exclude strangers from membership or preserve a company as a purely family-owned company they could do so. The effect, argued Gower, was to retain 'the essentially personal nature of the association just as effectively as in a partnership'.[14] In contrast, he saw American corporate law as tending to strike down attempts to restrict share transfer, preferring the 'property' model of the share, 'the alienation of which must not be unreasonably restrained'.[15]

The contrast with American company law principles is instructive. Modern American corporations originated from charter corporations and, as a result, that body of law contains none of the contractual norms of England's partnership-informed company law. American corporate law has delineated large companies from small companies much more successfully than in England, and has thus developed principles that are clearly intended to refer to a large company and those that are clearly intended to be for a small or 'close' company.[16] In contrast, the common law principles that are established in England apply to all companies in theory and are part of the body of company law principles, but in practice they will often apply only to a small company. So the earlier example which Gower gives on the facility for incorporators to contractually restrict share transfers applies only to private companies. A public company cannot restrict share transfers in this way.

This sole application of principles to small private companies is particularly pronounced when the principle is contractually based. So in *Ebrahimi v Westbourne Galleries*[17] (discussed in detail in Chapter 6), the courts gave a remedy to a company member who relied on understandings which were implicit in the relationship between the parties. The court effectively implied an agreement, which as its performance was thwarted meant that the court declared that the company should be wound up as it had ceased to exist for the purpose it was intended. This is a principle which could only apply to a very small company in which the relationships between the members were based on partnership's mutual trust notions.

The merging of legal principles established in the context of a small company with those established with large companies in the canon of company law goes some way to understanding why company law *per se* is associated with contractual principles. It does not, however, provide the whole answer and nor does it explain why the USA, a country without a contract-based

---

13 *Tett v Phoenix Property & Investment Co Ltd* [1984] BCLC 599.
14 Op. cit., Gower, p 1378.
15 Ibid, p 1378.
16 According to Professor Gower, American law distinguished the corporation as a public body rather than as a creature of contract earlier than English law.
17 [1973] AC 360.

corporate law, is the one to have originated and nurtured a theory of the company based on contract.[18]

Typifying this American based response is the work of Frank Easterbrook and Daniel Fischel. In their important book *The Economic Structure of Corporate Law* Easterbrook and Fischel argue that the doctrine of separate corporate personality is 'a matter of convenience rather than reality'.[19] Rather, it was usually more sensible to consider the corporation as a ' "nexus of contracts" or a set of implicit and explicit contracts'.[20] The corporation is, they remind us, a voluntary adventure in which individuals have chosen to engage, in accordance with terms they have agreed. According to the authors not only is contractarianism a better analysis of the law, but a corporate law which facilitates this voluntary character will be the most useful in promoting business success. Conversely, corporate law jurisdictions which have attempted to deviate from contractual norms invariably failed to meet business needs. In America at least: 'the history of corporations had been that firms failing to adapt their governance structures are ground under by competition. The history of corporate law has been that states attempting to force all firms into a single mold are ground under as well.'[21]

Easterbrook and Fischel argue that the corporation is constituted by the voluntary, contractual arrangements of the participants. However, they argue, these contracts may not conform to a model which contract lawyers, would recognise. Instead the terms of the agreement may be fixed by managers or investors, leaving only the price to be negotiated. In other arrangements described by the contractarians as contracts the terms may be implied by the courts or the legislatures. To the lawyer and perhaps even the layman a relationship which is defined by the courts or the legislature describes the law, in this case company law, and its provisions as found in statute and in common law, rather than in a contract. Thus far from being 'chosen' by the parties in the way of a contract, the terms upon which individuals operate business in a corporation are in fact prescribed by law; quite contrary to the way contracts work. Easterbrook and Fischel's answer to this is to argue that while these terms are provided by the law, they are 'terms that would have been negotiated had people addressed the problem explicitly'.[22] Accordingly,

---

18 Gower cited an Indiana judge in an 1860 case who said: 'A corporation is a creature existing, not by contract; but, in this country, is created or authorized by statute; and its rights, and even modes of action, may be and generally are, defined and marked out by statute; and when they are, they cannot be changed, even by the contract of the corporators.'

19 Easterbrook and Fischel, *The Economic Structure of Corporate Law*, first paperback edn, 1996, Cambridge, MA: Harvard University Press.

20 Ibid, p 12.

21 Ibid, p 13. The term 'firms' is used here, and indeed by the 'law and economics' scholars, as a catch-all term for business organisations, which include partnerships as well as corporations. The legal meaning of a firm is a partnership.

22 Ibid, p 14.

they state, 'We treat corporate law as a standard-form contract, supplying terms most venturers would have chosen but yielding to explicit terms in all but a few instances'.[23] So why don't these venturers simply negotiate as one might in the usual contractual manner? The answer is cost. The shareholder makes more money if it is not spent in costly negotiations. Thus, 'corporate law should contain the terms people would have negotiated, were the costs of negotiating at arm's length sufficiently low . . . corporate law almost always conforms to this model'.[24]

Although this seems an unusual sort of contract, they insist that it is not merely a rhetorical device, like the 'social contract' of enlightenment political theory which underpinned the American constitution. Additionally, they argue that the corporation encompasses many 'real' contracts, including those with suppliers, contractors and employees, unlike the rhetorical social contract. Furthermore, they note, the articles of incorporation are agreed by the incorporators and changes in the corporation's rules may be subsequently agreed by the majority investors. Controls over directors' decisions may be exercised by majority shareholders who may ratify a breach of duty such as self-profiting from a corporate opportunity.[25]

These observations, however, militate against the nexus of contract argument rather than support it. The real contracts made with suppliers, contractors and employees are specifically made between them and the company, a legal entity that must be capable of making such arrangements. Contracts are not made between suppliers *inter se*, between managers and employees, and they certainly are not made between suppliers, contractors, employees and shareholders. A shareholder has no legal or practical role in these arrangements and will not be responsible for debts that arise in respect of them. Furthermore, breaches of duty such as self-dealing have emerged from and are imposed by common law and not from any contractual agreement.

Yet, perhaps somewhat oddly, what really clinches the contractual argument as far as the authors are concerned is not the 'real contracts'[26] but the contracts which have terms that are in place because the market has provided information as to their efficiency through the mechanism of price. Such a term is one which shareholders would have negotiated, if it is a term that enhances share value. Indeed it is better than a negotiated term (and perhaps therefore more contractual), because market price allows the most ill-informed and least knowledgeable investor to make decisions about their investment: 'Markets transmit the value of information through price, which is more "informed" than any single participant in the market.'[27] Market price,

23 Ibid, p 15.
24 Ibid.
25 See Chapter 5.
26 Bargains which the lawyer would recognise as being a contract.
27 Ibid, p 19.

they argue, makes transparent the efficiency of non-negotiated terms more readily than any other mechanism. And, if finally these so-called contractual devices are not enough to represent the corporate participant's interest, the law can supply terms which respond to or fill in the gaps. For Easterbrook and Fischel, the American common-law system is particularly useful as it can supply terms to meet situations which the contracting parties could not have envisaged when contracting. 'Common law systems need not answer questions unless they occur. This is an economizing device.'[28]

Thus for these authors corporate law exists as different levels of contract law. It embodies so-called real contracts, it includes 'contracts' where the terms are determined by market price (a superior form of negotiated term), and includes a body of law which 'finishes' contracts between the corporate players (in a more economically efficient way than negotiation), through such mechanisms as fiduciary duties. A rather loose set of descriptions of the hitherto precise notion of a contract.

More recently Kraakman and Hansmann have developed a more sophisticated and arguably more insidious form of contractarianism, which draws in a comparative analysis of all business corporations internationally which exhibit 'five core structural characteristics'. These are legal personality, limited liability, transferable shares, centralised management under a board structure and shared ownership by contributors of capital. The authors reserve the right to include in their analysis business forms which have most of the five, as this enables them to relativise the core features and relegate the key feature of a business corporation, separate corporate personality, to just one possible characteristic a business corporation might have.

In explaining away the separate legal personality of the corporation, the trickiest area of company law for the contractarian, Kraakman and Hansmann first assert that the corporation is indeed a nexus of contracts but one in which contracting is facilitated by the 'creation of a legal person'.[29] This aids contracting because the legal person, the corporation, can act as a middle man between those that 'own or manage the firm, or are suppliers or customers of the firm'.[30] Kraakman and Hansmann depict separate corporate personality as a legal construct rationally created by individuals engaged in business as the most effective way of negotiating agreements, as if it were possible to have a large legally incorporated company without separate corporate personality. Furthermore, they argue that the main purpose of constructing this entity is to balance creditor interests and to protect both the

28 Ibid, p 35.
29 Kraakman, R and Hansmann, H, *The Anatomy of Corporate Law. A Comparative and Functional Approach*, 2005, Oxford: Oxford University Press, p 7.
30 Ibid.

assets of the business and the assets of the owners. This is achieved by constructing the business corporation as a productive, asset-owning entity. This allows separate corporate personality to facilitate two functions. First, as the corporation owns the assets it can pledge them to creditors, thus enhancing the contractual credibility of the firm. Here the authors characterise corporate creditors' interests as a priority claim on assets over and above claims of the shareholder's creditors who will be paid from corporate assets after corporate creditors. Second, it provides what they call 'liquidation protection', protecting the corporation from liquidation by disallowing shareholders from 'withdrawing their assets at will'.[31] In addition to this it protects the firm from the claims of the owner's creditors, who cannot 'foreclose on the owner's share of firm assets'.[32]

Both supposed functions are based on a distortion of the basics of company law. In the normal course of business shareholders have no claim on the company's assets and so clearly their personal creditors do not. Shareholders' creditors do not have a low priority claim against the corporate assets, they have no claim at all against them. Likewise, they cannot foreclose on the shareholders' share of the firm's assets because the shareholders do not own the corporate assets and cannot withdraw corporate assets at will. The shareholder, as a clear matter of law and economic reality, owns shares which are a claim to dividends, not corporate assets.[33] And, while it is true that upon liquidation the shareholder will receive any remaining liquidated assets after all creditors' claims and other costs have been met, from which funds they may pay their personal creditors, this does not make their creditors the corporation's creditors. It simply means that the shareholders are using their own money to pay back their own debts.

Unlike Easterbrook and Fischel, Kraakman and Hansmann do not expressly deny the separate legal personality of the company; instead they see it as a legal mechanism for making contracts effective, and they read bargains into all aspects of company law. So while legal personality[34] protects creditors' interests by prioritising them, it is as part of an exchange for something that protects shareholder's interests, that is, limited liability.

> The pattern of creditors' rights created by strong form legal personality is, in effect, the converse of that created by limited liability. It protects the assets of the form from the creditors of the firm's owners, while limited

31 Ibid.
32 Ibid.
33 See Chapter 2 for a full explanation of this assertion.
34 Which in corporations they describe as being 'strong form legal personality' as opposed to the 'weak form' legal personality of partnerships, or as we company lawyers characterise the latter, 'no legal personality'.

liability protects the assets of the firm's owners from the claims of the firm's creditors.[35]

And why does this bargain take place? Because, they state, this 'isolates the value of the firm from the personal financial affairs of the firm's owners sufficiently to permit the firm's shares to be freely traded'.[36] This is ahistorical. As corporate legal history makes clear[37] and the work of Paddy Ireland in particular details,[38] it was the increasing transferability of shares which gave rise to the real separation of the shareholder from the corporation's activity and the emergence of the doctrine of separate corporate personality, not the other way around. Again, Kraakman and Hansmann engage in distortions which attempt to construe separate corporate personality as a business choice, not a legal expression of an economic reality.

So the transferability of shares is understood as a reason for choosing separate corporate personality.[39] Transferable shares require the 'asset partitioning' provided by a firm's legal personality. They must represent only the firm's assets and not the shareholders, because otherwise the value of shares would fluctuate according to the wealth or personal debts of its shareholders. And, as shares are frequently traded, a corporation's shareholders could frequently change, thus making share valuation difficult to monitor. This assertion, while acknowledging that share values are not contingent upon the shareholders' personal wealth, still affects to connect the business assets with shareholder ownership. But in both law and in economics the company share is not a share of the company's assets; they do not own the business in the way partners own a share of the business. Yet, according to this approach shareholders remain the owners but it is a more rational and market-friendly form of ownership which allows for free transferability and a stable valuation of shares.

The issue of limited liability causes fewer theoretical problems for Kraakman and Hansmann than it does for Easterbrook and Fischel, who find it difficult to justify the privilege given to shareholders at the expense of creditors within the contractual (and therefore fair) model. For Easterbrook and Fischel this problem is only resolved by rehabilitating the company as an entity that is responsible for a creditor's debts. Kraakman and Hansmann characterise limited liability as a mechanism for achieving 'defensive assets partitioning' in that it enables shareholders to preserve their own personal assets for the benefit of their personal creditors. Conversely,

---

35 Ibid, pp 7–8.
36 Ibid, p 8.
37 See Chapter 2.
38 In Chapter 2 and below.
39 A point made earlier by Easterbrook and Fischel, who stated that limited liability was key to maintaining the fungible nature of shares.

separate personality partitions the assets of the company for creditors. So the combination of separate corporate personality and limited liability creates a rational bargain between creditor and shareholder which reduces the overall cost of capital. By viewing it this way Kraakman and Hansmann do not wander into Easterbrook and Fischel's problem of limited liability appearing as an unfair advantage to shareholders and therefore not very contractual. Instead they view limited liability as something which enhances contracting. But as this characterisation is dependent on viewing all arrangements as balancing priorities between contracting parties, limited liability is attributed with facilitating the following mutually advantageous arrangements.

> It permits creditors of the corporation to have first claim on the corporation's assets, which those creditors have a comparative advantage in evaluating and monitoring. Conversely, it permits an individual's personal creditors to have first claim on personal assets, which those creditors are in a good position to evaluate and monitor and which creditors of the corporation, conversely, are not in a good position to check.[40]

Again, this is a distortion of economic and legal reality. Corporate creditors do not have the *first* claim, they have the *only* claim unless the corporation ceases to exist by being wound up and put into liquidation. Likewise, the personal creditors of shareholders do not have a *priority* claim to the latter's assets over and above the corporation's creditors, they have the *only* claim. A corporation's creditors may only have a claim on shareholder assets if the veil is pierced and legal personality is set aside, and this is virtually impossible under English law although more common in American law.

The fourth characteristic of a business corporation, that of delegated management, is again construed as a rational and chosen arrangement between the contracting parties based on cost-efficient motives. The board is separate from shareholders because this 'economizes on the costs of decision-making by avoiding the need to inform the firm's ultimate owners and obtain their consent for all but the fundamental decisions regarding the firm'.[41] So, while long-standing empirical evidence coupled with most scholarly work on corporate governance clearly indicates that shareholders are widely dispersed, passive recipients of dividends who know little about their company, do not vote or expect to be involved in any part of the management, Kraakman and Hansmann prefer to characterise shareholder detachment from management decisions as their choice. Collective decision making is a waste of money which shareholders choose to enjoy as dividends instead of wasting in management costs. In this characterisation shareholders are involved and

---

40 Op. cit., Kraakman and Hansmann, p 9.
41 Ibid, p 12.

conscious investors in a business who realise that their interests as owners are best represented by a specialised central management, largely monitored by creditors who have a more direct relationship with asset preservation.

In examining the fifth feature of a business corporation, Kraakman and Hansmann make a final clinching bid for shareholder primacy. In corporate law, they explain, rights of ownership come only from investment in capital, unlike a partnership for example, where one may become a partner by dint of one's employment and 'typically does not presume that ownership is tied to contribution of capital'.[42] In this, it is implied that shareholders possess a greater entitlement to ownership claims than partners who merely engage in every level of the business, jointly own partnership property and are jointly and severally liable for the partnership's debts![43] In so doing they are appealing to capital as uniquely and normatively justifying ownership across any business form. Ownership, in their interpretation of the word, they explain, means the right to control the firm and the right to the net earnings of the business, both of which are entitlements arising from capital investment and are in proportion to the amount invested. Ownership, they argue, is so absolutely tied to investment that it would probably be more accurate to call a business corporation 'a special kind of producer cooperative, in which control and profits are tied to supply of a particular type of input, namely capital'.[44]

They conclude that a specialised statutory form developed because of the popularity of business corporations, the 'homogeneous interests' of shareholders and the fact that shareholder interests are the most difficult to protect contractually (the implication being that they should be protected). Thus like Easterbrook and Fischel they characterise corporate law as a way of achieving contractual ends in a cost-efficient way. But their reanimation of the shareholder as a producer in a co-operative is probably the boldest and least justifiable claim made for shareholders in large corporations to date.

The contractarian model is consistently logical only if company law is distorted and corporate history is dispensed with. This is important because history demonstrates that legal developments express social realities and are not forms constructed by the corporate players. As Ireland argues, contractarianism in the context of the company simply goes against the grain of history. For, while English company law undoubtedly originated in partnership law, thus initially taking on the latter's contractual and agency norms, it has since gone through a process of what he terms 'decontractarianism'.[45]

---

42 Ibid, p 14.
43 Partnership Act 1890.
44 Op. cit., Kraakman and Hansmann, p 13. They invite us to think of corporations as 'capital collectives'.
45 Ireland, P, 'Property and contract in contemporary corporate theory' (2003) 23 Legal Studies, p 453.

Historically, the law relating to companies shed its contractual and agency law character, a process which was completed by the end of the nineteenth century and involved such developments as the shareholder ceasing to be an equitable owner of the company assets, the share become a tradable piece of property, and the shareholder's liability being limited.[46]

Ireland notes that the introduction of limited liability in 1855 and the gradual abandonment of partly paid shares in the second half of the nineteenth century entirely severed any contractual relationship between member and third parties such as creditors and suppliers. Following the 1844 Act, he argues,

> the relationship between the shareholders of most companies and third parties ceased to be contractual at all: third party creditors now dealt not with a collection of partners liable for each other, but with companies as separate, property owning, legal (and corporate) entities. Although for a time indirect contractual links between shareholders and third parties remained, the products of unlimited liability and the residual liabilities arising out of sums unpaid on shares, these were eroded by the introduction of general limited liability in 1855 and gradually severed as shares increasingly became fully paid-up in the second half of the century.[47]

Furthermore, Ireland notes that limited liability also dissolved the practical link between shareholders as it reduced the reasons for maintaining an interest in one's fellow investors and annihilated all obligations attached to the shareholding:

> In the days of unlimited liability and partly paid up shares, for example, the residual liabilities of shareholders and the possible need of companies to make future calls provided good reasons for both companies and shareholders to be interested in who their (fellow) shareholders were and their financial wherewithal.[48]

And

> Joint stock company membership came to take the form of ownership of an unencumbered, free-standing right to revenue external to the process

---

46 Ibid.
47 Shares may be acquired without paying the full price; the remainder remains a debt to the company who may 'call up', that is require, the remainder to be paid. If they are acquired at full price then they are fully paid up.
48 Op. cit., Ireland, p 464.

of production, to which was attached no particular obligations, contractual or otherwise, either to the company itself or to outsiders.[49]

Ireland maintains that the judiciary gradually abandoned the notion of shareholders as partners, and the company and the law pertaining to it emerged as a distinct set of legal principles, far removed from any partnership origins. This shift is quintessentially articulated in the doctrine of separate corporate personality, an expression of the real separation of members from the business – a company which has disgorged its members. Thus in modern company law it is a well-established doctrine that the company is an entity which contracts in its own name, on its own account and which is responsible for its own liabilities.[50]

Ireland further argues that early contractarians Jensen and Meckling's dismissal of the corporation as 'legal fiction', a mechanism or shorthand for describing the complex network of contracts which exist between those connected with the corporation, is really a way of reconnecting shareholders with the assets and capital. The purpose of this is ideological, designed to promote the interests of shareholders and to justify their claim to the company's profits as the proper remuneration of ownership. And while the notion of the company as a 'legal fiction' is an attractive notion (the company is, after all, an *artificial* legal person), the fact that something does not exist in the natural world does not make it any more of a fiction than any other legal property. As Macpherson's work amply illustrates, property is not a thing but a political relationship, private ownership being the political right to exclude all others.[51] All things or property in the social world are delineated politically and described legally, even, or especially, intangible property that relies on legal constructs for it to emerge as an identifiable thing. The company is no more (or no less) a legal fiction than the share.

In response to Easterbrook and Fischel's contractual theories of the corporation, Ireland argues that their theory relies on constructing a business model that does not exist in reality. It certainly does not apply to large business corporations, nor to the English public company. Indeed the theory is often so flimsy that it relies on borrowing back the doctrine of separate corporate personality whenever it starts to hit too many contradictions. For example, when limited liability seems to undermine the contractual theory because it disadvantages creditors in favour of shareholders, Easterbrook and Fischel simply borrow back the corporate entity to remind us that the *company* has unlimited liability.

---

49 Ibid, p 469.
50 Given that it is a limited liability company and subject to the common law and statutory exceptions discussed in Chapter 2.
51 See Chapter 7.

The theoretical flaws in the contractarian's arguments invite the question, argues Ireland, of why they have been promulgated so fiercely over the last twenty years, or indeed, he might have asked, why they have been so widely internalised by our policy makers. The attempt to 'recontractualise' the company, Ireland argues, is an attempt to morally neutralise its activities and to render it merely a manifestation of freely negotiated agreements and market activity. It is an attempt to render the public company a private institution which is therefore above political description, in marked contrast to the post-war attempts to politicise the company by making it more of a pubic organisation.[52] It is in short, he says, 'part of a more general, ideological project aimed at providing instrumental justifications for the private appropriation by shareholders of corporate surpluses which are products of an increasingly social production process'.[53]

The contractarian argument is difficult to maintain logically, legally and historically in the context of large corporations. In respect of the black letter law which will be examined in the next part of this chapter contractarian principles are alien in all but a few discreet situations involving very small, private companies where on occasion the courts describe the relationship between the persons connected with the company in contractual terms. The law in this area shows the paucity of the contractual model. In respect of a company's formation, the incorporators must observe the strict provisions of the Companies Act and failure to do so will invariably mean that the business has not been incorporated. Furthermore, although the incorporators may design their own articles of association, Table A acting as a default model, they do so within the confines of the Companies Act and related regulations. Thus while there is a voluntary aspect to this, it is important to recognise that having choices within the regulations is not the same as having a contract. In respect of the law relating to the statutory contract between shareholder and company under s 33, one finds that the courts do not treat this as a contractual relationship wherein both parties may enforce the terms of the contract.[54] Instead, a shareholder may only enforce terms which directly relate to the rights attached to his share and not any other parts of the contract. In short, the law indicates that the contractual model has no place in the law relating to the company constitution and while the language of contract is often used, the company is understood to be a creature of statute and regulation, not of contract.

Thus, given both the content of contractarianism and the social and political context in which it emerged as a theory, and its lack of validity in company law,[55] it is difficult not to conclude, as Ireland does, that it is a highly

52 Discussed in Chapter 4.
53 Op. cit., Ireland, p 483.
54 Terms which are largely held in the articles of association.
55 This will be examined more thoroughly in Chapter 4.

ideological doctrine, encompassing and promoting the neo-liberal values which emerged in 1980s England and America.

THE COMPANY'S CONSTITUTION

The important reforms made by the Companies Act 2006 were designed to rationalise the pre-existing law. Previously, a company's memorandum of association contained, broadly, the provisions as to the name, address, purpose and capital of the company. The separate articles of association, which were subordinate to the memorandum, dealt with the internal management of the company including company meetings, procedures in declaring dividends, the scope of directors' duties and so on. Companies could divide their basic constitutional rules between the memorandum and the articles, with different rules about whether, and in what way, the rules could be changed. The new scheme remodels this arrangement, so that all that the memorandum will contain is the evidenced intention of the subscribers to form a company and to be members of that company. The articles become the primary document for all the company's constitutional issues and the memorandum of existing companies will, under s 28, be treated as the articles of association in so far as they cover those areas which are now held in the articles. Existing companies are entitled to continue using the provisions of their own constitution but may choose to adopt the new model articles under the regulations of the 2006 Act.

Among the other significant changes is that a company can now be formed by a single person (it required at least two before). A key feature of company law that remains more or less the same is the provision, previously contained in s 14 of the 1985 Act, now s 33, describing the nature of the statutory contract between member and company.

The purpose of the remainder of this chapter is to set out the law as it stands under the 2006 Companies Act in respect of a company's formation, and the law in respect of the documents which form the company's constitution and negotiate the arrangements involving the company and the company's officers, particularly the directors and the shareholders. The section also examines the way in which the courts have construed the contractual relationship of those parties involved with the company, which is usually discussed with regard to s 14 of the 1985 Companies Act, now replaced, with some small changes, by s 33 of the 2006 Act.

Company formation and the Companies Act 2006

Part 1 of the 2006 Act sets out significant reforms on company formation, replacing the relevant provisions of the 1985 Act. Section 7, which reflects the recommendations of the CLR, provides for the formation of *any* company by just one person subscribing their name to the memorandum. Previously, more than one was required in respect of all but private companies limited by shares.

Section 8 of the 2006 Act replaces s 2 of the 1985 Act (which sets out detailed requirements of the memorandum) with the requirement that the memorandum contain a statement that the subscribers want to form a company of which they will be members and will subscribe to at least one share if the company has a share capital. It must be 'authenticated'.[56] The requirements in the 1985 Act that the memorandum contain the name,[57] address[58] and objects[59] of the company together with the liability of its members,[60] whether by guarantee[61] or by shares,[62] are removed. Instead, under the new Act, this information is held either in the articles of association, other constitutional documents, or, it is not required.

One element no longer required is a specification of the objects of the company. Under the 1985 Act a company could either state particular objects in the memorandum or, alternatively, register its objects as those of a general commercial company, under s 3A. Under the new regime a company has unlimited objects *unless* the company chooses to restrict its objects by setting out its capacity in the articles of association.[63] Under s 31(1), 'unless a company's articles specifically restrict the objects of the company, its objects are unrestricted'. If a company did restrict its objects, these objects would appear in the articles of association. The general rule that amendment to the articles requires a special resolution would therefore apply.[64] In contrast, the 1985 Act had a specific section (s 4) to provide for modifications of the company's objects. A special rule persists, however, in the requirement that an amendment relating to a company's objects does not become effective until the registrar has been notified and entered the notice on the register.[65]

The changes to the content of the memorandum of association have had a knock-on effect on the documents required to register a company. The

---

56 The Registrar can specify the form of authentication required of documents submitted to him: s 1068. The concept of authentication is a broader version of signature, apt to include electronic alternatives to signing. See s 1146 for the requirements of authentication of a document or information supplied by a person to a company.
57 Companies Act 1985, s2(1)(a).
58 Ibid, s2(1)(b).
59 Ibid, s2(1)(c).
60 Ibid, s2(3).
61 Ibid, s2(4).
62 Ibid, s2(5).
63 This is very similar to the American approach first provided for in the Model Business Corporation Act 1969, s 3. The Californian Corporate Code provides that all filed articles include a prescribed 'all purposes clause' and any other additional statements may only be included to restrict the corporation's powers.
64 Section 21.
65 Companies Act 2006, s 31(2).

position now is that, in addition to delivery of the new-style memorandum, there must be:

- an application for registration, which must contain a statement of capital and initial shareholding in the case of a company that is to have share capital, or a statement of guarantee for a company limited by guarantee;
- a statement of the company's proposed officers;
- the address of the company's registered office;
- a copy of any articles of association, but only to the extent that the articles are not supplied by the default application of model articles; and
- a statement of compliance, that the requirements of the Act in relation to registration have been complied with.[66]

The application for registration itself must include the company's name; which UK jurisdiction the registered office is to be situated in (Northern Ireland, Scotland or England and Wales, although the section adds after the latter '(or Wales)'); whether liability is to be limited and if so, by share or guarantee; and whether the company will be public or private.[67]

The statement of capital and initial shareholding, which is a new document, essentially provides an account of the amount and structure of a company's share capital at the moment of registration. The old concept of the 'authorised share capital' of the company contained in the memorandum has been abolished as a result of a CLR recommendation.[68] The authorised share capital provided a limit on the amount of capital that could be issued. Now the requirement is to specify the number of shares taken by the subscribers on formation, their aggregate nominal value, the amount paid up, and, for each class of shares, prescribed particulars of the rights attached to shares, the total number of shares in the class and their aggregate nominal value. It must have information (to be prescribed) to allow the subscribers to be identified, and state, in relation to each of them, the number and kinds of shares they hold.[69]

Rather than providing information, the statement of guarantee, which must be contained in the application if the company is limited by guarantee, is an undertaking by the guarantor members that they will contribute to the assets of the company, up to a specified amount, if the company is wound up while they are members (or within a year after they cease to be a member).[70]

---

66 The registration documents are set out in s 9. Section 10 deals with the details of the statement of capital and initial shareholding; s 11 with the statement of guarantee; s 12 with the statement of proposed officers; and s 13 with the statement of compliance.
67 Section 9(2).
68 CLR Final Report, Vol 1, 2001, para 10.6.
69 Companies Act 2006 s 10.
70 Section 11.

This undertaking was previously required to be contained in the memorandum.[71] As with the previous statement, regulations will prescribe what information is required to identify members.[72]

The statement of officers requires the name and addresses of the directors, secretaries (or joint secretaries) of the company and a consent by each of these persons to act in that capacity.[73]

The articles of association

The application must contain a copy of the articles of association.[74] Under the old regime, the articles of association was the second document in the company's constitution. It was subordinate to the memorandum (despite the fact that the two documents dealt with different areas). The articles could not extend powers under the memorandum and if there were inconsistencies in the provisions of the two documents, it was the memorandum that prevailed. Under the new regime, the articles continue to set out the internal management of the company in respect of issues such as the procedures at general meeting, the appointment and removal of directors and the payment of dividends. However, under the 2006 Act it is the primary document in which all important company information is held. Section 17 (a new provision) defines the company's constitution as the articles and any additional resolutions under s 29, without any mention of the memorandum. Too much stress should not be put on this definition, however, because, first, it only applies 'unless the context otherwise requires', and second as a definition it is non-exhaustive. Nevertheless, it demonstrates the major change in the significance of the memorandum of association.

If the articles are not included then under s 20 the relevant model articles (that is those prescribed for a company of that kind being registered at that date)[75] will form the company's articles 'to the same extent as if the articles in the form of those articles had been duly registered'.[76] If articles have been included which omit or modify issues covered by the relevant model articles, then the model articles will be deemed to have been included to the extent that they have been modified or excluded.[77]

The inclination to the contractual model is highly pervasive in respect of the articles of association and the extended functions of the articles are a reflection of this. Even mainstream company law textbooks seem to accept

71 Companies Act 1985, s 2(4).
72 Companies Act 2006, s 11(2).
73 Section 12.
74 Section 9(5)(b).
75 Section 20(2).
76 Section 20(1).
77 Section 20(1)(b).

the contractual premise of the articles, regarding non-contractual aspects of this part of law as an exception to the general rule. In the seventh edition of *Gower and Davies: The Principles of Modern Company Law* the authors note that 'a remarkable feature of British company law is the extent to which it leaves regulation of the internal affairs of the company to the company itself through rules laid down in its constitution and, in particular, in its articles of association'.[78] Citing corporate governance, the division of powers between shareholders and directors, as evidence of this they footnote as a small exception to this, the Combined Code applicable to all listed companies. Thus, again, the 'general rule' is applicable only to small, unlisted, mainly private companies. Indeed, far from the articles of association evidencing contractual freedoms, they evidence the imposition of the detailed rules more appropriate to a public body than a private contract. Thus under s 7 of the 1985 Act, articles prescribing regulations for the ordering of the company may be registered, subject to certain minor administrative requirements. However, the broader picture is that the company is subject to the provisions of the Companies Act and must sensibly ensure that its regulations will not lead it to fall foul of this. Companies, therefore, largely opt to use the model regulations made by the Secretary of State. Under the 1985 Act, the relevant regulations were the Companies (Tables A to F) Regulations 1985.[79] Table A, the most significant of all of these as it was applicable to companies limited by shares, would be applied if no articles were registered or to the extent that the registered articles omit or modify Table A.[80] Such model articles have been provided by the Companies Acts since the Act of 1844.[81] As previously noted, these provisions are now held in s 20 of the 2006 Act where new model articles are applied in default.

The articles are further circumscribed by common law and statute in respect of alterations. Under the 1985 Act the articles, once registered, could be altered by a special resolution under s 9 and were required to be registered at Companies House. However, the members' power to alter the articles of association were subject to these restrictions.

The alteration could not:

- conflict with the Companies Acts;
- conflict with conditions in the memorandum;
- be illegal;
- extend or modify the memorandum;

---

78 Gower, LCB and Davies, PL, *Gower and Davies: The Principles of Modern Company Law*, 7th edn, 2003, London: Sweet & Maxwell.
79 SI 1985/805, made under Companies Act 1985, s 8.
80 Ibid.
81 Schedule A of the 1844 Companies Registration Act.

- require members to take or subscribe for more shares or increase liability to contribute without consent in writing;
- deprive members of protection under s 125 of the Companies Act 1985, which provides for the protection of a class of members if the alteration in the articles would vary their particular class rights; and
- should be 'bona fide for the benefit of the company as a whole'.

Under s 21 of the 2006 Act an amendment to the articles may be effected by a special resolution, subject to most of the same restrictions noted above. There are additional requirements in respect of provisions which are entrenched in the articles under ss 22–24, and fewer requirements in respect of the memorandum, which no longer contains anything substantive. Thus, an alteration under the 2006 Act must:

- not conflict with the Companies Acts;
- not be illegal;
- conform with s 25, which states that a member of a company is not bound by an alteration to the articles which requires him to subscribe for more shares or increases his liability to contribute to the company's share capital or any other money payable to the company;
- conform with ss 22–24;
- not deprive members of protection under s 630 of the Companies Act 2006, which provides for the protection of a class of members if the alteration in the articles would vary their particular class rights;
- be a decision taken in good faith, to promote the success of the company for the benefit of the members as a whole.

The latter three points will be developed in order.

Provisions entrenched in the articles

Under the 1985 Act, elements of the company constitution could be entrenched. Section 17 of that Act allowed the inclusion in the memorandum of provisions that could lawfully appear in the articles and as such, these provisions could be altered by a special resolution. But the section also allowed the memorandum itself to make alternative provision for the alteration of these provisions, including providing that they could not be altered.[82] Under s 17(2)(b) the memorandum could 'prohibit(s) the alteration of all or any of the conditions above referred to, and does not authorise variation or abrogation of the special rights of any class members'. Under the new regime in the 2006 Act, the memorandum has ceased to perform its old

---

82 Companies Act 1985, s 17(2)(b).

functions and so entrenchment facilities have been included in the articles of association.

Under s 22, a company may entrench specified provisions in the articles of association so that they may only be repealed or amended if particular conditions or procedures are complied with. So, clearly, a special resolution will be insufficient to make such an alteration. Such provisions may be additionally amended following a unanimous decision by all the members or by order of a court or any other authority which has the power to alter the company's articles.[83] If the company amends entrenched provisions or they are altered by a court order or that from other authorities, the company must give notice of this to the registrar[84] together with a statement of compliance.[85] The statement of compliance should certify that the amendment has been made in accordance with the company's articles or, where applicable, in accordance with the order of a court or other authority. A provision for entrenchment can only be made at the time of the company's formation or following a unanimous agreement by the members.[86] And the registrar must have notice of any such entrenchment whether by an order of a court or other authority or by the members' agreement.[87]

Alterations which vary class rights

Where a company resolution purports to alter the articles of association in such a way that the rights of a particular class are varied, statute protects the shareholders holding shares in that class by requiring them to consent to the variation.

The 1985 Act made provision for these rights in ss 125–127. It did not, however, provide a statutory definition of 'class of shares' or 'class right'. It therefore fell to the courts to attempt to define what was to be considered a class right. For example, in *Cumbrian Newspapers Group Ltd v Cumberland and Westmorland Herald Newspaper and Printing Co Ltd* the court defined two forms of right in ownership which could be described as a class right.[88] In this case, the plaintiff company Cumbrian Newspapers Group was the holder of 10.67 per cent of the issued ordinary shares in the defendant company. Shares were issued to the plaintiff in 1968 and as part of the arrangement under which the shares were issued, the defendant adopted articles of association under which the plaintiff was granted a number of rights. Of particular importance were the rights of pre-emption over the other ordinary shares in

83 Section 22(3)(a) and (b).
84 Section 23(2).
85 Section 24(2).
86 Section 22(2)(2) and (b).
87 Section 23(1).
88 [1987] Ch 1.

the defendant company, rights in respect of unissued shares and, third, the right (so long as it held not less than 10 per cent in nominal value of the issued ordinary shares of the defendant company) to appoint a director of the defendant. The purpose of these was to allow the plaintiff to prevent a take-over of the defendant.

The board of directors of the defendant made it known that they wished to convene a meeting of shareholders of the defendant to put before a general meeting a special resolution designed to cancel the articles under which the plaintiff enjoyed these special rights. The plaintiff claimed that these special rights were class rights which for the purposes of s 125 could not be varied without their consent. The court agreed, stating that the question was whether or not the rights under the relevant articles were rights attached to a class of share or merely personal rights which were unconnected to the shares. The court held that there were three different categories of rights, two of which encapsulated class rights and one which did not. The first involved 'rights or benefits which are annexed to particular shares', such as rights to participate in surplus profit on winding up. 'If the articles provide that particular shares carry particular rights not enjoyed by the holders of other shares, it is easy to conclude that the rights are 'attached to a class of shares'. The second involved rights contained in articles conferred on individuals not in their capacity as shareholders, but for an ulterior motive. Such rights did not constitute a particular class right. The third involved rights or benefits that although not attached to any particular shares, were nonetheless conferred on the beneficiary in their capacity as members or shareholders of the company. So in the earlier case of *Bushall v Faith*, the House of Lords upheld the validity of articles which provided that a director's vote should count as three (in order to prevent directors being removed from office by simple majority).[89]

In *Cumbrian Newspapers*, the plaintiff held the aforementioned rights in order to halt a take-over bid and so the defendant argued that these rights fell into the second category as being personal to the plaintiff. However, the court held that the third category applied. While the rights in question were not attached to a particular share, they were conferred on the plaintiff in its capacity as a shareholder, and if they did not hold the (ordinary) shares that they held, then they would not have been entitled to enforce them. As such they were class rights and s 125 applied.

By contrast, the new Act does set out a definition of 'classes of shares' in s 629:

> (1) For the purposes of the Companies Acts shares are of one class if the rights attached to them are in all respects uniform.

89 [1970] AC 1099.

(2) For this purpose the rights attached to shares are not regarded as different from those attached to other shares by reason only that they do not carry the same rights to dividends in the twelve months immediately following their allotment.[90]

And, on the face of it, the statutory definition is much narrower than that in *Cumbrian Newspapers*. Section 630(2)(a) states that class rights may only be varied according to the provisions of the company's articles or, if none exist, if consent of the class subject to the variation has been given.[91] This consent must either be in the form of written consent from the holders of three-quarters of the nominal value of the issued shares in this class,[92] or a special resolution passed at a separate meeting of the holders of these shares.[93] Further rights exist for the holder of at least 15 per cent of the issued shares in the class in question who did not consent to, or vote for, the variation to apply to the court to have the variation cancelled.[94] If the court after hearing the application is satisfied 'having regard to all the circumstances of the case' that the variation would 'unfairly prejudice' the class of shares the applicant represents, it will disallow the variation. The application must be made within 21 days of the consent being given[95] and the effect of making the application is that the variation has no effect until it is confirmed by the court.[96] Members of companies without share capital are similarly provided for under ss 631 and 634.

Good faith, to promote the success of the company for the benefit of the members as a whole

We deal more generally with directors' duties in Chapter 5, and in particular with the codification of general duties found in ss 170 to 187. Here, the issue is the way in which the long-standing requirement that a director should act 'bona fide and for the benefit of the company' has affected the ability of companies, or their directors, to make alterations to the articles of association.

That requirement has now been put in statutory form, in s 172 of the 2006 Act. This provides that a director must act 'in the way he considers, in good faith, would be most likely to promote the success of the company for the

---

90 This reproduces the provision in s 128(2) that shares are not to be treated as a different class from existing shares if the only difference is that dividends are not payable in the same way for the first 12 months from allotment.
91 Section 630(2)(b).
92 Section 630(4)(a).
93 Ibid.
94 Section 633(2).
95 Section 633(4)(a).
96 Section 633(4)(b).

benefit of its members'. A director, in so doing, is required to have regard to the long-term consequences of decisions; the interests of employees, the environment, and the wider community; the maintenance of a reputation for high standards of conduct, and of good relations with suppliers and customers; and the need to act fairly as between members of the company. This appears to give an expansive reading to the interests of the company. Nevertheless, existing case law on what would be considered as bona fide and for the benefit of the company in respect of an article amendment will probably still generally apply. Having said that, one area that might lead to new departures is the additional statutory requirement for a director to have regard to the need to act fairly between members of the company.

Allen v Gold Reefs of West Africa Ltd[97] has been good authority on the kinds of circumstances and principles the court will consider in respect of an alteration to the articles. The company's articles provided that it should have a lien for all debts and liabilities of any member to the company 'upon all shares (not being fully paid) held by such member'. In exchange for certain property, the company allotted Z fully paid up shares. Z also applied for shares not paid up. On his death he was indebted to the company for arrears of calls on the unpaid shares, but his assets were insufficient to pay these arrears. The company, therefore, by special resolution under the provisions contained at this time in s 50 of the Companies Act 1862, altered the above article by omitting the words 'not being fully paid up', thus creating a lien on the paid-up shares. The court held that a company may alter the terms of a contract if that contract was made in relation to an article that could by special resolution be altered. This power, which could be used against the interests of minorities, was provided for under statute but could only be exercised bona fide and for the benefit of the company. As statute was clear on these powers and their exercise benefited the company as a whole, it was made bona fide, notwithstanding that the alteration was a disadvantage to one shareholder. Such powers under statute:

> must be exercised, not only in the manner required by law, but also bona fide for the benefit of the company as a whole, and it must not be exceeded. These conditions are always implied, and are seldom, if ever, expressed. But if they are complied with I can discover no ground for judicially putting any other restrictions on the power conferred by the section than those contained in it.[98]

Following *Allen*, it was the view of the courts that the bona fides of an alteration was an issue upon which shareholders should decide, and it was to

97 [1900] 1 Ch 656.
98 Ibid, p 672.

be presumed that an alteration agreed by the members was bona fide. The court may intervene when the alteration is one which the reasonable man would not have thought of as beneficial for the company as a whole. In particular, an alteration would be suspect where it was 'so oppressive as to cast suspicion on the honesty of the persons responsible for it, or so extravagant that no reasonable man could really consider it for the benefit of the company'. However, the courts generally have not presumed that an alteration is made fraudulently or oppressively, indeed it falls to the complainant to prove that the alteration of the articles represents an improper exercise of power.

In relation to fairness between members the Australian case of *Gambotto v WCP Ltd*[99] might impact on the company's decision to alter the articles notwithstanding that the CRL specifically rejected its usefulness in English Company law.[100] In *Gambotto*, an amendment to the company's articles to enable a person holding 90 per cent of the shares to compulsorily purchase a minority shareholder's stake, was held to be invalid by the Australian High Court. The amendment would have enabled the company to save around $4 m in tax, but was not 'bona fide and for the benefit of the company', because it involved the appropriation of the 'valuable proprietary rights attaching to shares'.[101] Such an appropriation could not be justified unless the minority shareholder's continued ownership of his shares would seriously harm the company's interest. In this case the majority shareholder (through a number of wholly owned subsidiaries) held 99.7 per cent of the share in WCP Ltd. And, unlike most cases where a shareholder's expectations have been protected, this was a large public company, not a small quasi-partnership company where members might be bound by informal understandings. The decision was based on a specific elevation of the proprietary rights of shareholders *per se*, which the court stated it was bound to protect except in very extreme situations. In this respect, it is a decision in line with the current political elevation of shareholders' interests in company law reform, justified by the shareholder's 'ownership' status. Thus while the 2006 Act codifies the CLR's view that the test should be honest promotion of the company's success under s 172 above, and not *Gambotto*, the political emphasis on promoting shareholder proprietary interests may yet lead to an interpretation of s172(1)(f) along the lines of *Gambotto*.[102]

Gambotto bears a number of similarities with the much-criticised case of *Brown v British Abrasive Wheel Co Ltd*.[103] In *Brown*, an alteration of the articles to allow the 98 per cent majority shareholder to compulsorily

99 (1995) 69 ALJR 266.
100 CLR Final Report, p 169.
101 *Gambotto*, p 271.
102 *Greenhalgh v Arderne Cinemas Ltd* [1951] Ch 286.
103 [1919] 1 Ch 290; 88 LJ Ch 143.

purchase the 2 per cent minority shareholder's interest was held to be invalid. The company was in financial difficulty and the majority shareholder would only inject further capital if he was the sole owner. The court held this did not justify the alteration. The resolution was not made for bona fide reasons because it disappropriated the minority shareholder. The alteration, however, would have benefited the company as a whole but this was not enough in the absence of the requisite bona fides. Shortly after this decision, another case involving a similar alteration to the articles was held to be valid and the court reverted back to the definition of 'bona fide and for the benefit of the company' stated in *Allen v Gold Reefs*. *Brown* was criticised for holding an alteration invalid simply because the majority were found to have acted in their own interest.[104] Lord Sterndale MR and Warrington LJ stated that the judge in *Brown*, Ashbury J, was wrong to have divided the bona fides of a decision from the benefit of the company. If the majority expressed an opinion in a resolution then it was necessarily bona fide and for the benefit of the company. The was affirmed in the later case of *Shuttleworth v Cox Brothers & Co (Maidenhead) Ltd*[105] where an alteration was upheld which allowed a lifetime appointed director to be removed provided that all the other directors wrote to him requesting his resignation. The alteration was intended to effect the removal of a director who was considered to be inadequate. The court held that if in the opinion of the members the alteration was bona fide and in the interests of the company then the court would question that decision no further.

This position was modified in *Greenhalgh v Arderne Cinemas Ltd*[106] where Evershed MR held that the validity of any alteration must be judged according to two principles. First, the decision should be made honestly for the benefit of the company as a whole. And second, the phrase 'company as a whole' does not mean the company as a commercial entity but the body of shareholders. Thus the interests of a minority shareholder might be taken into account to the extent that an alteration should not discriminate against him while simultaneously giving an advantage to the majority shareholders.

The statutory duty to promote the success of the company was intended to codify the CLR's recommendation (partly based on *Greenhalgh*) that when assessing the validity of an alteration to the articles the test should be 'whether the majority honestly believe that their vote is best calculated to promote the success of the company for the benefit of its members as a whole'.[107] Thus unlike *Greenhalgh* this test does not require that the interests of all individual members be considered, or that discrimination will automatically render a

---

104 *Sidebottom v Kershaw, Leese & Co Ltd* [1920] 2 Ch 124; 89 LJ Ch 346.
105 [1927] 2 KB 9.
106 [1951] Ch 286.
107 CLR Final Report, p 169.

resolution to effect an alteration invalid, although it will be a factor to be considered. However, the statutory statement in s 172(1) reflects the *Shuttleworth/Greenhalgh* common law principles which were established when the notion of shareholder's proprietary rights were at an all time low.[108] Today, that is not the case and much of the orientation of company law reform in line with a general political outlook has supported the notion of shareholder primacy, the only real explanation for *Gambotto*. Thus decisions which affect the proprietary interests of shareholders outside those already provided for in the Companies Act may be decided according to a more pro-shareholder interpretation of 'the need to act fairly as between members of the company'.

Company names

The purpose of examining the law on company names is to show how highly regulated this area is. The incorporators have very little choice in both the character and formation of the name and the procedures in relation to adopting or changing a name. The company name also underpins the nature and importance of separate corporate personality because a company must be clearly identifiable with a name (which is its name only) because those that contract with the business are contracting with the entity, the company. The company name locates the company and enables those such as creditors to make claims against the company, in that company's name. The name also shows if the company's members have limited liability, a key piece of information for creditors.

The incorporators may choose the company's name to the extent that it conforms with the general restrictions set out in the Companies Act and may continue to use it to the extent that it does not offend any statutory or common law principle. Under the 1985 Act general restrictions were set out in s 26, which stated that a company should not be registered by a name which includes:

- 'limited', 'unlimited' or 'public limited company' other than at the end;[109]
- names including abbreviations of the above words;
- the same name as another on the registrar's index of company names;
- a name which would constitute a criminal offence in the opinion of the Secretary of State;
- a name which would be offensive in the opinion of the Secretary of State;
- in the opinion of the Secretary of State, would be likely to give the

---

108 See Chapter 4.
109 Under the Companies Act 1985, s 30, a private company limited by guarantee could exclude the word limited if (a) the objects promote commerce, art, science, religion, charity etc., and (b) the profits are not used to pay dividends.

impression that the company is connected in any way with her Majesty's Government or with any local authority.

Under the 2006 Act these restrictions are largely continued with additional restrictions such as those in respect of names which exploit another's goodwill. Other restrictions include names that are misleading to the public which are business names rather than company names. The Act also provides for ignoring trivial differences in names under certain circumstances. The wording of the relevant sections seems to give the Secretary of State much more discretion in respect of approving company names.

Section 53 states that a name is prohibited if, in the opinion of the Secretary of State,

(a) its use by the company would constitute an offence, or
(b) it is offensive.

However, names identified as sensitive words and expressions which would be likely to give the impression that the company is connected with the following are not prohibited but require approval from the Secretary of State. These include:

(a) Her Majesty's Government, any part of the Scottish administration or Her Majesty's Government in Northern Ireland,
(b) a local authority, or
(c) any public authority specified for the purposes of this section by regulations made by the Secretary of State.[110]

Other 'sensitive words or expressions' specified in regulations made by the Secretary of State require approval from the Secretary of State under s 55. Companies are still required to identify their type by having either the full title or acronym at the end of the company name. In the case of a public company, s 58 provides that it must have 'public limited company' or 'plc' at the end of the name or if a Welsh company 'cwmni cyfyngedig cyhoeddus' or 'ccc'. In the case of a private company, s 59 provides that the name must end with the word 'limited' or 'ltd'. Or, if it is a Welsh private company, 'cyfyngedig' or 'cyf'.

Section 60 replaces s 30 of the 1985 Act and provides for an exception from the requirement to use the word limited or acronym if:

(a) it is a charity,
(b) it is exempted from the requirement of that section by regulations made by the Secretary of State, or

---

110 Section 54(1).

(c)   it meets the conditions specified in –

section 61 (continuation of existing exemption: companies limited by shares), or
section 62 (continuation of existing exemption: companies limited by guarantee).

Chapter 3, ss 66 to 74, set out provisions in respect of names which are similar to other names. Section 66(1) provides that a company must not use a name that is the same as another name in the registrar's index of company names. However, s 66(2) empowers the Secretary of State to make regulations supplementing s 66 which may allow certain similarities in names to be disregarded. Or regulations may specify that names which would ordinarily be prohibited will be permitted:

(a)   in specified circumstances, or
(b)   with specified consent' (s 66(4)(a)).

Thus names which under the 1985 Act would largely be prohibited may be permitted by the Secretary of State under the 2006 Act.

Section 69 provides for the protection of an individual's goodwill, if a company name is sufficiently similar to that individual's business name as to suggest a connection. This provision puts the common law principles in this area on a statutory footing. If a proposed or registered company name is so like that of an existing business as to give the impression that it is that business or is connected to it in some capacity, such as may cause a loss to the first business, a complainant may seek relief through the common law tortious remedy of 'passing off'. The remedy for the complainant would generally be the granting of an injunction to prevent the other party from using the name. In *Ewing v Buttercup Margarine Co Ltd*[111] the plaintiff was a wholesale and retail provision merchant in Leith, Scotland. Since 1904 it had a retail chain selling dairy products under the trade name of Buttercup Dairy Company. It had 150 stores and was known as the Buttercup Company or Buttercup.

In 1916, the defendant company incorporated as a private company named The Buttercup Margarine Company. Its three directors had never heard of the plaintiff's unincorporated business and had innocently registered its business under that name after ascertaining that there was no such name on the Companies Register. The plaintiff argued that the name would lead to confusion with the general public, give the impression that the company was connected with the plaintiff's business and cause him damage.

The defendant argued that it operated in a completely different part of

111 [1917] 2 Ch 1.

Britain and that it was not possible to register and 'own' the noun buttercup. Other companies had used the name buttercup in advertising. Furthermore, the defendant company was a wholesaler and the plaintiff was a retailer. However, the court held on appeal that the prohibition under the tort of passing off on the use of existing names was not limited to using names in a manner that was 'calculated to deceive'. It was sufficient to prove that the plaintiff's goodwill would be compromised by the confusion to the public and other business associates, and the defendant company had sufficient power in its memorandum to become a retailer as well as a wholesaler.

Under s 69 the applicant may object to a company's name on the ground:

(a) that it is the same as a name associated with the applicant in which he has goodwill, or
(b) that it is sufficiently similar to such a name that its use in the United Kingdom would be likely to mislead by suggesting a connection between the company and the applicant.

Under s 69(4), if those grounds are established the objection will be upheld and the companies names adjudicator[112] will apply the remedies provided in s 73,[113] unless the respondent can show:

(a) that the name was registered before the commencement of the activities upon which the applicant relies to show goodwill; or
(b) that the company –

(i) is operating under the name, or
(ii) is proposing to do so and has incurred substantial start-up costs in preparation, or
(iii) was formerly operating under the name and is now dormant;

or
(c) that the name was registered in the ordinary course of a company formation business and the company is available for sale to the applicant on the standard terms of that business; or
(d) that the name was adopted in good faith; or
(e) that the interests of the applicant are not adversely affected to any significant extent (s 69(4)).

The Secretary of State also has powers under ss 75 and 76 to require the company to change its name if misleading information has been given for the purposes of the company's registration or the name gives a misleading indication of its activities likely to cause harm to the public. Failure of a person to

---

112 Appointed by the Secretary of State under s 70.
113 The respondents have a right to appeal against the adjudicator's judgment under s 74.

comply with either order results in liability on summary conviction to a fine and a further daily fine for each additional day of non-compliance. A company may continue to choose to change its own name following a special resolution under s 78.

Phoenix companies and prohibitions on the re-use of company names

Further restrictions on company names exist in order to prevent the abuse of limited liability through measures that prevent the re-use of the name of an insolvent company. Under s 216 of the Insolvency Act 1986, a person who was a director or shadow director of a company that has gone into insolvent liquidation any time during the last 12 months of its existence may not be connected to another company with a prohibited name for five years. Under s 216(2), a name is prohibited if it was either the exact or similar name of the insolvent company. A person is connected to a company if they are directors, or are

> in any way, whether directly or indirectly . . . concerned or take part in the promotion, formation or management of any such company, or, in any way, whether directly or indirectly . . . concerned or take part in the carrying on of a business carried on (otherwise than by a company) under a prohibited name.[114]

Such persons may not, without leave of the court, be connected to a company that uses a prohibited name for a period of five years.[115] Breach of s 216 is a criminal offence.[116]

Further to this, s 217(1)(a) states that a director or shadow director who acts in contravention to s 216 will be personally liable for all relevant debts of that company. Liability also arises for a person involved in the company's management who acts on the instructions of somebody he knows to be in contravention to s 216.[117] Relevant debts are those incurred when a person who is liable under s 216(1)(a) was involved in the management or, in the case of liability for a person acting under instructions, for the times when he was acting under instructions.

In *Thorne v Silverleaf*,[118] Mr Thorne had been the director of three companies, each of which had had the words 'Mike Spence' in its name. The first company was incorporated in 1968, and was subsequently named Mike

---

114 Insolvency Act 1986, s 216(3)(b) and (c).
115 Section 216(3).
116 Section 216(4).
117 Section 217(1)(b).
118 [1994] BCC 109.

Spence (Reading) Ltd. In 1990 it went into creditors' voluntary liquidation. The second was incorporated in 1986 and took the name of Mike Spence (Motorsport) Ltd. In 1989, it went into voluntary liquidation. The third company, Mike Spence Classic Cars Ltd, was incorporated in 1990.

Classic Cars experienced financial difficulties and a joint venture was formed between the plaintiff, Mr Silverleaf and Mr Thorne, the defendant, whereby the plaintiff would fund the purchase of stock. The company's financial position continued to deteriorate and the plaintiff complained that the terms of the joint venture had not been met and refused to supply any more funds. In 1992, accountants reported that the company owed the plaintiff £135,000 with further debts of £200,000 for unsecured creditors. The plaintiff commenced proceedings claiming the money lent to and used by the company, stating that ss 216 and 217 of the Insolvency Act 1986 were satisfied in relation to the defendant as a director of the company. The plaintiff claimed that the defendant was personally liable, jointly and severally with the company in respect of the sum owed by the company to the plaintiff.

The judgment was in favour of the plaintiff. The defendant appealed on the basis that the plaintiff aided and abetted him in committing the offence under s 216 and that on the grounds of public policy he should not be allowed to profit from his crime. However, the court held that the name of the company was so similar to that of the two previous companies as to suggest an association with them and accordingly it was a prohibited name within the meaning of s 216(2) of the 1986 Insolvency Act. The defendant satisfied the requirements of s 217 since he was involved in the management of the company in contravention of s 216. Furthermore there was no basis for denying the plaintiff a remedy under s 217 on the grounds of public policy as this was not a situation where the plaintiff was attempting to benefit from his own wrong.

As the CLR noted, proceedings under s 217 are rare, as remedies are more readily available under ss 213 and 214 of the Insolvency Act.[119] It also noted that this might be because directors had become more cautious in their re-use of names as a result of s 216. The CLR considered whether the unlimited liability in s 217 should be extended to liability for the first company's debts but ultimately concluded that this would disadvantage bona fide investors and creditors of the second company.

The CLR generally considered that phoenix companies continued to present a significant problem and were particularly concerned to tackle the problem of directors selling company assets to a second company under value, prior to putting the first company into liquidation. To deal with this problem the CLR proposed that s 320 of the 1985 Act should be extended to impose liabilities on the first company's directors if company assets were sold in the year immediately preceding winding up, if the price of the assets were not

119 CLR Final Report, Vol 1, p 326.

independently valued or if the sale was not approved by an independent majority of shareholders. In this situation the CLR recommended extending the liquidator's powers under s 322 of the 1985 Act to an amended s 320. It further recommended that leave of the court under s 216(3) should not be given if there was 'a material transfer of assets within the twelve months prior to liquidation to a new company in which the director was also interested unless the transaction complied with the amended section 320'.[120]

THE CONTRACT AND THE CONSTITUTION: THE LEGAL EFFECT OF THE COMPANY CONSTITUTION

The legal effect of the company constitution is set out in s 33 of the 2006 Act and was previously held in s 14 of the 1985 Act. Both sections identify the terms of the constitutions as being binding on both the company and the members although the 2006 Act modifies the 1985 Act in some important respects. Both sections are the most direct articulation of a contract existing between company and member, the terms of which are held in the constitution. Thus the cases which have referred to these statutory provisions test the extent to which members can enforce the terms of the constitution, the extent to which the company may enforce the terms of the constitution and who may enforce the terms against whom. In other words, these cases test the extent to which there really is a contract between member and company. Their conclusion is clear. The 'company contract' does not conform to the standards of an ordinary contract except in some limited circumstances when the court is dealing with a small private company.

It is also worth stating that in respect of the company contract the normal remedies in respect of contract do not apply. Thus the articles may not be defeated on the grounds of misrepresentation, duress, undue influence or mistake. As Steyn LJ explained in *Bratton v Oxborough*,[121] the articles of association are a form of statutory contract to which normal contractual principles cannot apply. So the vitiating factors noted above do not apply and neither may terms be implied into the contract even if (as in *Bratton*) the articles did not fully express the original intentions of the incorporators.[122] Likewise, in Read v *Astoria Garage (Streatham) Ltd*[123] a managing director who was appointed under the articles but held no service agreement was dismissed following an ordinary resolution and in accordance with the terms

---

120 Ibid, p 333. This recommendation in respect of the Insolvency Act is obviously not part of the reforms in the 2006 Act.
121 *Bratton Seymour Service Co Ltd v Oxborough* [1992] BCLC 693.
122 *Towcester Racecourse Co Ltd v Racecourse Association Ltd* [2003] 1 BCLC 260.
123 [1952] Ch 637.

of the articles. Here, no agreement as to reasonable notice would be implied because the manner of dismissal was determined by the express provisions of the articles alone.

Section 33 of the 2006 Act irons out some of the inequalities between member and company which were held in s 14 of the 1985 Act. This latter section provided that the legal effect of the memorandum and the articles[124] was that they bound company and members as if signed and sealed by each member. It was treated as signed and sealed by members but not by the company. Section 33 redresses this and instead states: 'The provisions of a company's constitution bind the company and its members to the same extent as if there were covenants on the part of the company and of each member to observe those provisions.'[125] Furthermore, the old s 14 provided that money or debts payable by members to the company was a speciality debt so that the company could pursue these debts up to 12 years after they became due. Conversely, a debt owed by company to member was merely an ordinary debt giving the member just six years to pursue moneys owing. This provision has been replaced by s 33 of the 2006 Act and revised to make the constitution equally binding on both company and member and to remove the inequality inherent in making a debt owed by member to company, 'in the nature of a speciality debt'. This section now states: 'Money payable by a member to the company under its constitution is a debt due from him to the company. In England and Wales and Northern Ireland it is of the nature of an ordinary contract debt.'[126]

Clearly the Act is attempting to construct a more expressly articulated contractual relationship between member and company which is in line with the contractarian principles the reform process has adopted. However, cases hitherto showed that s 14 did not lead the courts to construe the relationship between member and company or indeed member and member as contractual unless factually they were like contracts. So it is difficult to see how tinkering with the wording in s 33 will alter this. As Steyn LJ stated in *Bratton*, the contract between members and company is 'a statutory contract of a special nature with its own distinctive features. It derives not from a bargain struck between the parties but from the terms of the statute'.[127]

The first of these characteristics noted by Steyn LJ is that the contract is only binding in respect of the rights and obligations between the members of the company acting *qua* members. And it is consistently clear from the case

---

124 Section 14 refers to 'the memorandum and articles' as under the old Act the former was the primary constitutional document. Section 33 replaces this phrase with the words, 'a company's constitution' to reflect the new role of the memorandum, articles and other constitutional documents.
125 Section 33(1).
126 Section 33(2).
127 *Bratton Seymour Service Co Ltd v Oxborough* [1992] BCLC 693, p 698.

law that the articles bind members *qua* members only, so individuals seeking to sue under the articles may only do so in their capacity as members.[128] For example, in *Beattie v E & F Beattie Ltd*[129] the defendant director (who was also a shareholder) wished to have the dispute he was involved in with the company referred to arbitration as was provided for in the articles of association. The court held that he could not avail himself of this right as it was only available to members and not to directors. And, although he was a member, he was in dispute with the company *qua* director, rather than *qua* member.

The second of these characteristics is that if the articles contain provisions which confer rights and obligations on outsiders then these are not part of the terms that are enforceable by members against the company even if that outsider is a member as well.[130] Indeed, the only terms that are enforceable against the company by the member are those that relate to their personal rights – Steyn's third characteristic. Thus, there is clear authority for the proposition that a member may enforce the contract against the company in respect of his membership rights and the courts will intervene against a company that acts to deny those rights. So in *Pender v Lushington*[131] the court acted to ensure a shareholder's right to have his vote counted. In this case the articles limited a member's vote in a general meeting to 100 but certain shareholders had transferred their shares to nominees. The chairman ruled out the votes but the court held that the plaintiff shareholder, Mr Pender, was entitled to an injunction against the chairman's action as he had a right to have his vote recorded. Likewise in *Odessa Waterworks*,[132] the court upheld the shareholder's right to an injunction in respect of a decision of the directors to pay dividends in debenture bonds rather than cash. The court held that the director's proposal was 'inconsistent with the articles of association, and the articles alone are what the court has to consider'.[133] Furthermore, 'there was no contract with the shareholders to pay them a dividend in shares or bonds'.[134] It was their personal right to be paid in cash.

A number of cases have discussed the issue of whether the 'contract' is enforceable by one member against another. Clearly, if it was generally the case that members could directly enforce the contract against each other it would give credence to the nexus of contract theory, as the company would (at least for certain purposes) be a group of members engaging in commercial agreements. The company as a separate entity would have no function and its

---

128 Ibid.
129 [1938] Ch 708.
130 *Eley v Positive Government Security Life Assurance Co* (1875) 1 ExD 20.
131 (1877) 6 Ch D 70.
132 *Wood v Odessa Waterworks Co* (1889) Ch 636.
133 Ibid, p 639.
134 Ibid.

separateness would be a legal fiction while the members would be repersonalised in a partnership-like relationship. On the other hand, if the contract was only enforceable by a member against the company and vice versa then this would give credence to the notion that the distinct legal personality of the company was not a legal fiction.

In fact the authorities here are mixed but with one important proviso. Cases which allow a member to directly enforce the contract against another member are exclusively concerned with small companies. Here the relationships are like those in a partnership, based on trust and other informal understandings, and so the courts have often found it more appropriate to find a partnership-like solution to a problem. So, in *Rayfield v Hands* the judge stated that the memorandum and articles constituted a contract between members and was therefore directly enforceable by them without representation by the company.[135] This case involved rights relating to shares where Article 11 provided that every member who intended to transfer his shares 'shall inform the directors who will take the said shares equally between them at fair value'. The plaintiff shareholder tried to exercise this right but the directors refused to buy the shares, stating that the contract was an issue between shareholders and the company, an arrangement to which directors were not a party and that 'no relief can be obtained in the absence of the company as party to the suit'.[136] In judgment, Vaisey J examined the authority to date, finding little to support the plaintiff's claim bar Lord Herschell's dissenting judgment in *Welton v Saffery*[137] and dicta in *Hickman v Kent and Romney Marsh Sheepbreeder's Association*.[138] In the latter case Astbury J stated that 'the articles are simply a contract as between the shareholders *inter se* in respect of their rights as shareholders. They are the deed of partnership by which the shareholders agree *inter se*.'[139] And, in the former case, Lord Herschell stated that '[i]t is quite true that the articles constitute a contract between each member and the company, and that there is no contract in terms between the individual members of the company; but the articles do not any the less, in my opinion, regulate their rights *inter se*'.[140] However, Vaisey J found that authorities which indicated that the articles should be construed according to the realities of the situation were more pertinent in this case. The company here had four shareholders, three of whom were directors. Thus he stated that it was 'material to remember that this private company is one of that class of companies which bears a close analogy to a partnership'.[141] And as a partnership could 'validly and properly

135 [1960] Ch 1.
136 Ibid, p 6.
137 [1897] AC 299.
138 [1915] 1 Ch 881.
139 Op cit., Rayfield, p 7.
140 Ibid, p 5.
141 Ibid, p 9.

provide for the acquisition of the share of one partner on terms identical with those of Article 11', so could a quasi-partnership such as this company.

Thus the principle that the contract exists (in so much as it exists at all) between the legal entity, the company and the member was not questioned, but the reality of this situation meant that a partnership-type solution could be imposed and the articles were directly enforceable by the member against the directors. In the vast majority of cases the articles constitute a contract between company and member and there is no contract between the individual members of the company. Therefore the enforcement of rights against another member must be through the company, thus the solution is based in company law and not partnership law.[142]

It is finally worth noting that the statutory contract which is the articles is freely alterable by the company notwithstanding that such an alteration may cause it to breach an extrinsic contract with an outsider. Thus minority shareholders who do not want this alteration will be forced to accept it without the consent or fresh consideration required in law for a variation of an ordinary contract. So in *Punt v Symons and Co Ltd*,[143] the court held that a company could not by contract, even an extrinsic contract, exclude its power to alter the articles. This was upheld in the case of *Southern Foundries Ltd v Shirlaw*.[144] Mr Shirlaw was appointed managing director for 10 years under a 10-year service contract. When the company altered the articles to allow a principal shareholder to remove any director, the House of Lords held that the company could alter its articles to this effect, as it could not contract out the right to alter its articles. However, the company would have to pay compensation for any breach of contract that emerged from the alteration in the ordinary way.

Thus it can be seen that despite the purported contract expressed in s 14 and its previous incarnations, the courts have construed the contract in an extremely limited fashion.The fact that the courts are willing to enforce the contract in respect of enforcing personal rights but not other provisions in the articles is instructive. The contract between the member and the company does not, it seems, encompass the constitution in total, which can, as noted earlier, be altered following a special resolution whether an individual member wishes it or not. Instead the contract is limited only to the rights that accrue to ownership of a particular piece of property, the share. And, those rights are largely limited to voting rights and rights to dividend if a dividend is declared. This means that in case law, far from the members emerging as equal contracting partners with the company, they are conceived as holders of particular rights in the company, which are strictly limited and protected

142 *Welton v Saffrey* [1897] AC 299.
143 [1903] 2 Ch 506.
144 [1940] AC 701.

in both the articles and in statute. And, for the most part it is statute, not the contract, that prescribes the rights which accrue to shareholders. Shareholders are purchasers of a product and they are entitled to have certain expectations of that product. But as the case law makes clear, this does not of itself elevate them to the position of quasi-partners. Quasi-partnership solutions will be used if the company *is* a quasi-partnership and the principles established in these contexts are not utilisable in large companies. The company contract does not work at a similar level to other contracts. It usurps other contracts and may change its terms in accordance with majority requirements. The content of the articles and the other constitutional terms continue to be highly prescribed by statute, in a way which is appropriate to the protection of a kind of shareholding which does not or cannot protect its interests directly and requires the protection of statute. It is indicative of an absence of contractual control and active involvement by members rather than the contrary.

The doctrine of *ultra vires*

A company is formed for particular commercial purposes. In the case of a registered company these purposes are set out in the objects of the company which (unless under the 2006 Act) are held in the memorandum of association. Under common law a company was obliged to undertake only that business which was specified in the objects. The doctrine of *ultra vires* stated that if the company entered into a contract, the substance of which were purposes not stated in the objects, such a contract was *ultra vires* and void. Alternatively, if a company entered into a contract through an act of a director which was outside his powers to act specified in the company constitution (usually in the articles of association or a company resolution), the contract was *ultra vires* the director and voidable at the instance of the company. It was also a breach of fiduciary duty. Any member or creditor or persons officially representing creditors were empowered under common law to have such transactions declared *ultra vires*. In this way some managerial power was retained by the individuals involved in the company. They had lent money or goods to the company or had purchased shares and so were entitled to ensure that their investment would go towards the kinds of business activities specified in the company's constitution. They were also entitled to ensure that directors complied with the restrictions upon their powers under the constitution.

It was something of a last resort doctrine but it was an effective mechanism by which investors could protect their investment. However, since the first application of the *ultra vires* doctrine to registered companies this protection has been whittled away. Company stakeholders have become increasingly passive and correspondingly so have their powers of intervention. This has occurred over three main phases.

First, the doctrine itself was applied with increasing latitude by the judiciary who moved from a strict application in 1875 to an increasingly flexible application in the succeeding decades. Second, the 1989 Act made contracts which were outside the company's objects or outside the directors' authority enforceable, but made directors liable for any losses suffered by the company. It also left any residual powers to halt *ultra vires* acts in the hands of members only, leaving out creditors. Third, the 2006 Act no longer requires companies to specify their objects and removed the small powers of intervention left to members in the 1989 Act.

In phase one, the doctrine of *ultra vires* in early cases was first applied very strictly but was later applied very loosely. In early cases, a company did not have the power to do acts which were not precisely specified in its constitution and the judiciary showed little flexibility in respect of this requirement. So, in *Ashbury Railway Carriage & Iron Co v Riche*,[145] a company incorporated under the Companies Act 1862 stated as its objects 'to make, sell, lend or hire, railway carriages, wagons, plant, machinery etc'.[146] The House of Lords declared a contract to finance the construction of a railway in Belgium to be *ultra vires* and void because such a contract was not specified in the objects. Furthermore, although clause 4 of the objects provided that 'an extension of the company business beyond or for other than the objects or purposes expressed or implied in the memorandum of association shall take place only in pursuance of a special resolution', the House of Lords stated that ratification (even by all the shareholders) would have been ineffective.

> Where a company is formed on the principle of having the liability of its members limited to the amount unpaid on their shares . . . the memorandum of association shall contain . . . the objects for which the proposed company is to be established . . . the company . . . is to be an existence and to be a coming into existence for those objects and for those objects alone.[147]

This case was the start of a long journey towards judicial leniency in respect of *ultra vires* contracts. The first step was taken in *A-G v Great Eastern Railway Co*[148] where a company incorporated by statute to acquire two existing railway companies and to construct another railway wanted to hire locomotives and stock from another company. The court decided that this contract would not be *ultra vires* as it was reasonably incidental to the main objects.

---

145 1875 LR 7 HL 653.
146 Clause 3 of the memorandum.
147 Op cit., judgment p 665.
148 (1880) 5 App Cas 4731.

Later in this phase, the judiciary began to take an ever more lenient attitude to the construction of the objects clause. In an earlier case[149] the court declared that a company had failed to achieve the business for which it was incorporated by reason that it had not attained one of the clauses (upon which all the other objects were said to be ancillary), and so the company was wound up for just and equitable reasons. But by 1918 the courts accepted a clause making each separate object in each sub-clause an equal and independent object.[150] In this case, Essequibo, a rubber company, had a long objects clause that ended with a clause that the objects should not be restrictively construed and that each paragraph should be regarded as conferring a separate and independent object. Each clause was held to be substantive and not subsidiary to the main or leading object. Essequibo entered into an agreement to underwrite an issue of shares from another company. Later, when both companies were in liquidation the liquidator sought an application to render that transaction *ultra vires* and void. The court said that the validity of the clause could be upheld, underwriting the issue of shares was not *ultra vires* and the memorandum had been correctly compiled with. This case facilitated the practice of creating long lists of object clauses.

By the 1960s the courts went as far as to accept the validity of a subjective objects clause. In *Bell Houses Ltd v City Wall Properties Ltd*,[151] the court upheld the validity of a clause that empowered the plaintiff company to

> carry on any other trade or business whatsoever which can, in the opinion of the board of directors, be advantageously carried on by the company in connection with or as ancillary to any of the above businesses of the general business of the company.[152]

Furthermore, despite judicial antipathy to companies making non-commercial payments, famously encompassed in the statement that 'there shall be no cakes and ale except such as are required for the benefit of the company', it gradually developed an increasingly tolerant attitude to gratuitous payments.[153] In the early period, even if a company held an express clause in its objects stating that it could make a gratuitous payment of some kind, the judiciary continued to test the validity of acts made in pursuance of those clauses according to whether the act was bona fide and for the benefit of the company.[154] Later, however, the courts upheld some payments if they were bona fide and for the benefit of the company and reasonably incidental to the

---

149 *Re German Date Coffee Company* (1882) Ch 20, 169.
150 *Cotman v Brougham* (1918) AC 514.
151 (1966) 1 QB 207.
152 Ibid.
153 *Hutton v West Cork Ry Co* (1883) 23 Ch D 654.
154 *Re Lee, Behrens & Co Ltd* [1932] 2 Ch 46.

business. In *Evans v Brunner Mond & Co*[155] the plaintiff, a shareholder, challenged the decision of the company to distribute to universities and scientific institutions the sum of £100,000 in furtherance of scientific education. Although a resolution authorising this distribution had been passed by an overwhelming majority of shareholders, he argued that the motion instituted an activity that was not incidental to the company's business and was not for the benefit of the company. He argued that the rightful beneficiaries of the money would only benefit to a very small degree while the cost of the gift to the company was very great. The court, however, upheld the gift saying that as the company was

> in constant need of a reserve of scientifically trained men for the purposes of its business – and the business cannot be maintained if the supply of such men is deficient – that a deficiency is almost inevitable unless substantial inducements are forthcoming to attract men to scientific study and research – that the best agencies for directing these studies are well equipped universities.[156]

Later still, where there was an express clause allowing the company to make gifts the courts upheld acts made in pursuance of such a clause without applying the bona fide and for the benefit of the company test. So in 1970, in the case of *Charterbridge Corp Ltd v Lloyds Bank Ltd*,[157] the court held that an agreement to guarantee another company's debts although made without payment in return was *intra vires* as there was an express object in the memorandum allowing such guarantees. Later, the courts showed even greater latitude by allowing a payment that was not necessarily incidental to the company's business or for the benefit of the company, on the basis that non-commercial clauses would be upheld.[158] However, if no such clause existed the courts would continue to assess whether such gratuitous payments were bona fide and for the benefit of the company.[159]

In the second phase, the provisions on *ultra vires* contracts in the 1989 Act radically reformulated the *ultra vires* doctrine. Under these new sections, which were subsequently incorporated into the Companies Act 1985, a contract entered into by the company which was beyond its capacity would no longer be void; however, a director would be liable to the company for any loss. Section 35(1) of the 1985 Act stated that a company's capacity was not limited by its memorandum but retained directors' liability in s 35(3) which stated that 'it remains the duty of the directors to observe any limitations on

---

155 (1921) 1 Ch 359.
156 Ibid, p 369.
157 [1970] Ch 62.
158 *Re Horsley & Weight Ltd* (1982) 3 All ER 1045.
159 *Simmonds v Heffer* [1983] BCLC 298.

their powers flowing from the company's constitution'. A director would only avoid liability for this act if the company agreed to allow it by a special resolution. A shareholder could continue to exercise some autonomous intervention if the transaction in question had not yet become a legal obligation. Under s 35(2) a member could bring proceedings to restrain the doing of an act which was outside the company's capacity if it was at a pre-contract stage or if it referred to a donation, neither of which arrangements were legally enforceable.[160]

Under s 35A a transaction which involved a director acting outside his powers under the constitution was no longer voidable by the company if the person dealing with the company was acting in 'good faith' in his dealings. Good faith in this context was presumed under s 35A(2)(c) and bad faith would not be assumed 'by reason only of his knowing that an act is beyond the powers of the directors under the company's constitution' under s 35(2)(b). Section 35A(4) reproduced the same shareholder intervention as held in s 35(2) and s 35A(5) made directors liable for any loss to the company caused by their exceeding their authority. In contrast to s 35(3), an ordinary resolution would be sufficient to effect ratification of a director's breach of duty. A person would not be considered to be acting in good faith if he was connected with the company in the ways specified in s 322A of the 1985 Act.

By the by, the provisions on directors' authority were somewhat untidy. Section 35A stated that 'the power of the board of directors to bind the company, or authorise others to do so, shall be deemed to be free of any limitation under the company's constitution'. This seemed to imply that only transactions agreed by the board of directors would fall under s 35A but that it would not apply to transactions entered into by single directors. The latter transactions would continue to be covered by the old common law protections. These protections began with *Turquand's* rule[161] in 1856, which stated that when a company denies that an individual (usually a director) has the authority to bind the company and therefore the company was not bound to certain transactions, the court may uphold a claim by a third party who believed that the individual did have the authority to do so. That belief needed to be reasonable and to be reasonable there must have been no constructive notice of the individual's lack of authority. Therefore if the limitation on the individual's authority was held in the company constitution, the third party was deemed to have constructive notice of it and the company would not be bound to the transaction. Constructive notice was abolished by s 35B of the 1985 Act which stated that 'a party to a transaction is not bound to enquire as to whether it is permitted by the company's memorandum or as

---

160 *Re Halt Garage Ltd* [1982] 3 All ER 1016.
161 *Royal British Bank v Turquand* (1856) 6 E & B 327. This rule was really an application of agency principles.

to any limitation on the powers of the board of directors to bind the company or authorise others to do so'. Thus *Turquand*'s rule was modified to only include those cases where the company 'holds out' an individual as acting with the company's authority.[162] Latterly it has been suggested that s 35A may apply to transactions undertaken by one single director.[163]

In the third phase and in accordance with the recommendations of the CLR's Final Report, companies formed under the 2006 Act will have unrestricted capacity unless they specifically choose to limit their objects. Section 31(1) of the 2006 Act states that 'unless the company's articles specifically restrict the objects of the company, its objects are unrestricted'. Furthermore, if a company wishes to make any amendments to its objects it must give notice to the registrar, who will register them and it will take effect from the date of the notice on the register.[164] Any such amendment will not affect any rights or obligations of the company 'or render defective any legal proceedings by or against it'.[165]

In respect of companies which continue to restrict their capacity in their articles s 39 of the 2006 Act replaces s 35 of the 1985 Act with the following revisions. Section 35(2) and (3) have been removed as superfluous given that a company may have unlimited objects and a director's liability in respect of failure to observe the company constitution is now held in s 171 of the 2006 Act.[166] Section 39(1) and (2) of the new Act replace s 35(1) and (4) of the old Act.

Section 40 restates ss 35A and 35B of the 1985 Act except that first, the part of s 35B which referred to enquiries into limitations in the company's memorandum has been removed, and second, 'the power of the board of directors' (held in s 35A(1) of the 1985 Act) is replaced by the phrase 'the power of the directors'. This suggests that s 40 is applicable to the acts of all directors and not just the acts of a fully quorate board.

Section 41 restates s 322A of the 1985 Act and states that whether a person is dealing in good faith with the company in accordance with s 40 depends on whether he or she is an insider or an outsider.[167] An insider includes a director of the company or of its holding company or a person connected with any such director, and their involvement will render the transaction voidable at the instance of the company.[168] In any event, such a party will be liable to account to the company for any gain he made from the transaction and to indemnify the company for any loss or damages resulting from the

162 *Freeman & Lockyer v Buckhurst Park Properties Ltd* [1964] 2 QB 630.
163 *Smith v Henniker-Major & Co* [2002] BCC 544.
164 Section 31(2).
165 Section 31(3).
166 See Chapter 5.
167 Section 41(1).
168 Section 41(2)(b).

transaction.[169] Section 41(4) lists a number of circumstances when the transaction becomes no longer voidable in line with the old s 322A.

Thus it can be seen that the residual managerial powers or powers of intervention that existed for those with a stake in the company have been whittled to nothing. Again, the provisions in respect of the company constitution show company members are not treated as bargaining individuals empowered to halt unconstitutional acts, no matter how small their stake. Instead they are treated as they are, passive recipients of dividends who are expected to leave the management of the company to directors and majority owners.

169 Section 41(3).

Chapter 4

Corporate governance I: the theories in context

Corporate governance broadly refers to the political, economic, cultural, social and legal mechanisms which govern the activities of corporations. It covers a vast array of scholarship, government policy and law which lay various claims to the proper emphasis of corporate governance, the nature of the company and problems of internal control. American scholarship has continued to set the agenda in this area and as there are such similarities between American corporate law, English company law and corporate ownership patterns, it will be substantially drawn upon in this chapter.

Corporate governance concerns in England and similarly in America are centred on the basic agreed premise that share ownership is widely dispersed between many shareholders, none of whom hold a controlling interest. For example, one study indicated that in England's top 20 companies, no one shareholder owns more than 20 per cent of the stock.[1] Corporate governance discussions, therefore, are largely focused on the issue of management and how to control it. In the absence of a controlling shareholder who can guide management in a shareholder-centred direction, management may pursue non-shareholder-orientated goals. This theory, the premise of most corporate governance, is widely attributed to Berle and Means's 1933 study outlined below. However, the interpretation of and response to this theory have been varying. Much of the orientation of corporate governance concerns in England have been about how to control directors and how to ensure that they pursue the interests of shareholders and not themselves. In the next chapter we will see the varied mechanisms used by the judiciary to affect just that end, but broadly speaking under common law, a director is a fiduciary who owes a duty of utmost honesty to the company. Here the company is generally construed as the interests of shareholders as a whole. Accordingly, a director will be in breach of his fiduciary duty if he acts in his own self-interest under the self-dealing rules. The control of directors' activity is also

---

1 La Porta, R, Lopez-de-Silanes, F and Scheifer, A, 'Corporate ownership around the world' (1999) 54 J Fin 471.

the concern of a number of government reports published from the 1990s onwards and now incorporated in the Combined Code.

On the other hand, it is clear from much of the post-war literature on corporate governance and the separation of ownership from control thesis (discussed later in this chapter) that the notion of a company whose directors were no longer bound by the shareholder-orientated goal of profit maximisation was for a time greeted as an entirely positive development in British capitalism. Corporations in this period began to be conceived as public organisations, capable of balancing the interests of all those involved from shareholders to consumers and employees. The corporation was viewed as a vehicle for social progress as well as dividend creation. However, from the 1980s onwards the emphasis of corporate governance discussions has been around achieving profit maximisation and shareholder primacy. The most dominant theory here is contractarianism, which recommends the promotion of shareholders' interests through such mechanisms as minimising agency costs and facilitating market control. Agency costs, an issue which often features in American literature on corporate governance post–1980, refers to the cost to the company of monitoring directors to ensure their compliance with profit maximisation goals. In English and American corporations, agency costs are said to be reduced by market- and law-based mechanisms, such as hostile takeovers, information from capital markets and minimal legislative interference.

Other areas of scholarship discussed includes the 'law matters' thesis. Here, Anglo-American corporate law is said to exhibit 'good law' tendencies because these systems enable capital markets to develop by encouraging wide share dispersal. In contrast continental Europe, and civil law systems in general, are said to exhibit 'bad law' tendencies, which inhibit share dispersal and instead encourage the continuance of controlling shareholder patterns within companies or the continuance of family-owned firms. In these jurisdictions capital markets are relatively underdeveloped, a situation which is considered to hinder economic development. Good law systems are said to be characterised by mechanisms which enhance share dispersal. These include a strong legal tradition of protecting minority rights which encourage small investors and a national political context which is conducive to the development of 'good law'.

Alternatively, other writers indicate that shareholding in Anglo-American companies is less widely dispersed than the figures would suggest or at least the significance or effect of the higher dispersal is exaggerated. Furthermore, higher levels of dispersal might indicate a greater level of concentration of wealth rather than greater levels of wealth distribution because in high-dispersal economies a smaller proportion of a company's stock is required to maintain control. From this perspective, the Anglo-American company acts as a much more efficient vehicle for enhancing the wealth of the wealthiest of society than its European counterparts.

The vast ocean of literature on this subject means that only a small but representative pool of scholarship may be drawn upon. This chapter will be organised under the following headings:

- the emergence of the 'separation of ownership from control' thesis;
- the nature of ownership and control in a Berle–Means corporation and the era of the social corporation;
- anti-organisationalism, neo-liberalism and the free market: corporate governance and shareholders;
- neo-liberalism translated into corporate governance: the problem of management in the Berle–Means corporation;
- politics, law and ideology;
- economic ownership and the refutation of the separation thesis;
- the third way, company reform and 'enlightened shareholder value'.

THE EMERGENCE OF THE 'SEPARATION OF OWNERSHIP FROM CONTROL' THESIS

The 'separation of ownership from control' thesis emerged from an empirical study of America's largest corporations undertaken by Adolf Berle and Gardiner Means in the wake of the Wall Street crash of 1929. Their thesis formed a significant part of the intellectual landscape which replaced the laissez-faire ideology which had previously dominated American economic policy. Together with Louis D Brandeis, Adolf Berle and Gardiner Means became the primary architects of Roosevelt's 'New Deal' package in respect of corporate activity and provided the theoretical and practical basis for new controls over America's security market. Legislatively, this included the 1933 Securities Act (designed to ensure an informed market of investments) and the Securities Exchange Act of 1934 (aimed at correcting trading abuses).[2]

Louis Brandeis's main theoretical contribution was to insist upon greater disclosure in order to flush out the interconnection between finance, industry and infrastructure which was harmful to competition and industrial development. Furthermore, he argued that a lack of disclosure gave false information to investors as to the real value of securities. In *Other People's Money* he had argued that interlocking directorates meant conflicts of interests were unavoidable and enabled the few to profit at the expense of the many, smaller investors.

Brandeis's analysis of the problem of big business led him to conclude that capitalism needed to be more open. He therefore recommended that federal

---

2 The Glass–Steagal Act forbade commercial banks to play on the stock market in order to draw a distinction between investment and commercial banking.

law should emphasise disclosure on securities which he summed up in his famous adage, 'sunlight is said to be the best of disinfectants; electric light is the most efficient policeman'.[3] In Brandeis's view, the availability of information for investors would scupper the financier's ability to charge misleading prices and create financial bubbles. Information would protect the investor and safeguard the integrity of the market.

Likewise, Berle and Means agreed on the necessity for federal legislation to protect investors. Their research had made it clear that shareholders were too powerless and passive to protect themselves because the growth of the capital market and large corporations had resulted in a separation of ownership from control. In this ground-breaking thesis on corporate governance they argued that power within large corporations had shifted from investors to managers, which they demonstrated by the empirical studies published in *The Modern Corporation and Private Property*.[4] Written in the wake of the crash, this book contained detailed empirical data about stock ownership patterns in large corporations which showed that even the largest stockholders held only a tiny percentage of the whole. Their evidence indicated that business had undergone an 'evolution of control', from 'control through complete ownership' to 'majority control', to 'control through legal device', to 'minority control', through to the full and final evolution, 'managerial control'. It was an evolution of control which resulted in a shift of power from those that owned the corporation, stockholders, to those that controlled it, the managers.[5]

Briefly stated, they argued that complete ownership existed when a single individual or a small group owned all or almost all of the stock. As the owner retained legal powers of ownership and could use it to elect and dominate management, ownership and control were *ad idem*.[6] In a majority-controlled business, most of the powers of sole ownership were retained by the majority stockholder although a minority owner could block special resolutions such as charter amendments, thus undermining the absolute nature of the majority's control. However, if there were a number of minority shareholders, their ability to act with one voice against the majority would be severely hindered. In both scenarios control was still exercised by stockholders, those who owned.[7]

In control by legal device, strategic minority ownership could ensure control of the corporation without the need for a majority holding. Berle and Means used the example of 'pyramiding', where a stockholder owning the majority of the stock in the corporation at the top of the pyramid could

---

3 Today, disclosure laws in America are referred to as sunshine laws.
4 Berle, A and Means, G, *The Modern Corporation and Private Property*, 1932, London, Macmillan.
5 Ibid, p 67.
6 Ibid.
7 Ibid.

control all the other corporations further down the pyramid. They observed, for example, that the Van Sweringen brothers controlled eight railroads worth $2 bn with $20 m in stock through use of the pyramid system.[8]

In a minority-controlled corporation, a minority stockholder could control the activities of the corporation because the other stockholders were many and scattered. Furthermore, minority control could be bolstered by the issue of non-voting stock. For example, their evidence showed that Rockefeller tended to own around only 14.9 per cent of Standard Oil stock, but few would suggest that Rockefeller did not exercise absolute control over 'his' company.[9]

The final stage in the evolution of control, management control, is the distinctive portion of their analysis. Management control, they maintained, prevailed in large corporations where stockholders had no economic power or personal desire to exercise control. In a management-controlled corporation, the wide distribution of stockholding resulted in no one stockholder having sufficient voting power to control the activities of its management. And, as management itself would have little or no stock, their self-interest would be better served by making pro-management decisions than it would by making decisions beneficial to shareholders. The latter approach might benefit them in their capacity as shareholders, but would be minimal compared with the more direct benefits of pro-management decisions such as self-rewarding bonus schemes. In this scenario, control over the corporation was in the hands of, and serving the interests of, those whose self-interest might not be the same as the owner's. So, unlike the previous models, control in these large corporations, later referred to as Berle–Means corporations, became disconnected from ownership.[10]

Berle and Means's separation of ownership from control thesis has dominated all subsequent debates on corporate governance and is the premise on which all discussions on corporate governance rest. However, its meaning and significance change in accordance with the political context in which it is expressly or impliedly being interpreted.[11] Broadly speaking, during periods when the political environment is characterised by a broad-based socialism, the ideological, legal and policy response to corporate governance tends to emphasise Berle and Means' analysis of the weakened nature of ownership in

8 Ibid, p 69.
9 Ibid, p 77.
10 Berle and Means defined management-controlled corporations with examples like the Pennsylvania Railroad Co, whose top 20 stockholders owned just 310,518 shares or 2.7 per cent of the total stocks and its 19 directors held just 0.7 per cent of the total stock. Likewise, the United States Steel Corporation's 13 directors held just 1.4 per cent of total stock. Figures from 1928.
11 Impliedly, because the separation is so embedded in corporate governance that many writers have ceased even referring to it.

the widely held corporation and thereby the potential for social change that this happenstance presents. Discussion orientates around the possibilities of constructing socially responsive and responsible corporations that can deliver socialist or social democratic policy objectives. However, when neo-liberal, pro-market thought is in the hegemony, the academy, business and government emphasise the management accountability portion of Berle and Means' thesis. That is, the political values of liberalism such as individualism, personal and economic freedom, require that business operates for market goals rather than social goals. And, as the primary market goal of business is profit maximisation, and, as that goal serves the interests of shareholders, shareholder primacy becomes the desired goal of corporate governance for neo-liberals. Strategies to ensure that shareholder primacy is pursued involve various mechanisms to ensure that directors are fully focused to that end and are not pursuing the interests of other interested groups such as employees. The purest neo-liberal thought insists that the market generates enough controls to achieve management compliance and thus the aim of government should be non-intervention in companies and non-interference in the 'free' market. Others suggest that the government needs to intervene in market activities and corporate law in order to create the conditions for a free market. Both views essentially agree that the market is the source of corporate governance and the role of policy and corporate law is to support market activity.

The contemporary politics of the present administration have done little in substance to deviate from the neo-liberal position. New Labour's third way politics have maintained a pro-market, pro-shareholder position while continuing a little of the social democratic rhetoric Labour previously represented. As we shall see in the final section, this approach is reflected in the reform process.

The following sections assess the prevailing political hegemony during the periods which proceeded Berle and Means' thesis. They assess the effect of these politics on the way in which corporate governance has been conceived and the way that different parts of the separation thesis have been emphasised.

THE NATURE OF OWNERSHIP AND CONTROL IN A BERLE–MEANS CORPORATION AND THE ERA OF THE SOCIAL CORPORATION

In *The Modern Corporation and Private Property* Berle and Means mapped out the evolution of control *and ownership* in large corporations. Ownership, they argued, had become something that was 'passive' and devoid of 'spiritual values'. The shareholders of large corporations could not directly employ their wealth, the value of which was dependent on outside forces which were entirely out of their control.[12] However, for Berle and Means such a development did not mean that economic catastrophe was inevitable. Nor did it necessarily mean that directors needed to be more carefully monitored. The evolution in ownership really meant that control needed to be exercised differently. Ownership of stocks in a large management-controlled corporation meant ownership of a liquid asset whose value was dependent on outside forces. The entitlement of an owner was, therefore, to have the liquidity of his asset maintained and its unrestricted transferability protected. The owner was also entitled to unencumbered, accurate information on the value of his property. It was therefore incumbent upon the 'controllers' of companies and on the law to ensure and protect these rights.

However, according to Berle and Means, the stockowner should not expect rights over and above those stated. In particular, he could not demand the same rights of ownership as could the owners of more tangible properties such as land because unlike the latter owners, stock owners bore little responsibility for their property. The stockowner did not and could not exercise control over his property aside from selling it. Ownership of stocks was a passive arrangement that did not involve or require the creative energy of the owner or indeed involve any of the personal responsibilities generally associated with ownership.[13] For Berle and Means, stockholding was originally a property right but when the large corporation separated ownership from control, 'ownership' became a smaller bundle of legal rights that had an *historical* relationship with property rights but were not property rights *themselves*.[14] The corporation was no longer subject to the demands of private ownership. The new passivity of stockowners in large corporations meant that they had forfeited the extensive rights and obligations of property ownership, and in the absence of an involved ownership the corporation was reconstructed as something more like a public institution. Accordingly, they argued, the fiduciary duty of a director in a widely held corporation should be akin to a trustee of a public organisation. Here the director's duty to shareholders' concerns would be of a limited nature, deferring to the director's obligation to consider the well-being of the organisation as a whole.

The significance of the revised nature of stock owning in the modern corporation was famously debated by AA Berle and Merrick Dodd in the Harvard Law Review. Berle and Means' position articulated above divided into two polarised positions, with Dodds postulating the pluralist perspective and Berle arguing for greater managerial accountability. Both of these positions held sway in the succeeding decades.

Unwittingly commencing the debate, Berle, assuming that there was no

---

12 Op. cit., Berle and Means, p 79.
13 Particularly in a limited liability company.
14 Ibid, p 297.

existing mechanism to control corporate managers, concluded that only a strong reassertion of the director's fiduciary duties to act in the interest of stockholders could prevent managerial abuse. In 'Corporate powers as powers in trust'[15] he set out five areas of corporate power in order to demonstrate that any such powers were, in law, subject to equitable limitations which assured that managerial actions were exercised solely in the interest of stockholders.

In response, Dodds argued that the traditional view, that directors owed a duty to maximise profits for stockholders, was based on assumptions that were no longer true and no longer acceptable to the public and business world alike.[16] The first assumption was that the corporation is private property, which Dodds argued has rarely prevailed in business law and ethics and which in the context of large corporations with absent owners and professional managers was entirely inaccurate.[17]

> Business – which is the economic organisation of society – is private property only in a qualified sense, and society may properly demand that it be carried on in such a way as to safeguard the interests of those who deal with it either as employees or consumers even if the proprietary rights of its owners are thereby curtailed.[18]

The second assumption, that stockholders were the beneficiaries to whom managers as trustees were bound to represent, was likewise inaccurate. He argued that whether one considered the distinct legal personality of a company to emerge because of the legal act of incorporation,[19] thus rendering it a legal construct, or whether one considered it to have emerged because of 'the very nature of things', in the legal realism tradition, the conclusion was the same. Directors owed a fiduciary duty to act in the interests of the entity, not in the interests of individual stockholders. And what the law construed as the entity was something of a movable feast. The America of the 1930s, he argued, was much more inclined to construe the interest of the entity to be expressed as the interests of employees and consumers as well as stockholders. For example he quotes part of Swope's[20] plan for industry in which

---

15 Berle, A, 'Corporate powers as powers in trust' (1930–31) 44 Harv L Rev 1049. These included the power to issue stock, the power to withhold dividends, the power to acquire stock in another corporation, the power to amend the corporate charter and the power to merge.
16 Dodds, M, 'For whom are managers trustees?' (1931–32) 45 Harv L Rev 1162.
17 Dodds reviews a number of legislative controls that have prevailed over business organisation and the substantial degree of social planning in respect of public utilities.
18 Op. cit., Dodds, p 1162.
19 A view Dodds calls the traditional view.
20 President of the General Electric Company.

he states that, 'organised industry should take the lead, recognising its responsibility to its employees, to the public, and to its stockholders.'[21] He also refers to a leading business executive statement on a manager's duty as being first to investors, ensuring that their capital is 'safe, honestly and wisely used', second to employees, third to customers and last to the general public. Furthermore, he notes an increased judicial willingness to allow directors to take socially responsible decisions including an acceptance of charitable donations from corporations. Dodds concluded that the prevailing judicial and business view was that 'those who manage our business corporations should concern themselves with the interests of employees, consumers, and the general public, as well as stockholders'.[22]

In answer to this, Berle set out the social purpose of pursuing and protecting the legal arguments he articulated in his previous article. He argued that in the absence of a strong administrative body capable of responsibly negotiating the differing claims against a corporation, the primacy of shareholders' claims should be fiercely protected. If neither a strong government nor fiduciary duties were in place the result was that 'management and control become absolute'.[23] A system which was based on private ownership, he argued, should protect the interests of private ownership. To do otherwise would be to jeopardise the welfare of ordinary people whose wealth was now that of the passive bond or stockholders, who were entirely dependent on the actions of a handful of managers. To replace a director's fiduciary duty to stockholders with one which gave directors more discretion (suggested by Dodds as a means to enhance social responsibility), he argued, was to 'simply hand[ed] over weakly to the present administrators with a pious wish that something nice will come of it all'.[24] It would, he argued, create, 'economic civil war'.

Mr Swope and Mr Young were, he argued, noble exceptions to the rule of self-interested management. Thus he concluded:

> With due appreciation of the fact that the appraisal is bitterly unjust to many men in the corporate system [such as those mentioned above] it must be conceded at present, that relatively unbridled scope of management has, to date, brought forward in the main seizure of power without recognition of responsibility – ambition without courage.[25]

Ultimately, Berle did not believe that it was possible to make capitalism less

---

21 Op. cit., Dodds, p 1155.
22 Op. cit., Dodds, p 1156.
23 Berle, AA, 'For whom corporate managers are trustees' (1931–32) 45 Harv L Rev 1367.
24 Ibid, p 1368.
25 Ibid, p 1370.

capitalistic. In a capitalist private property economy, the ordinary person's interests could only be protected by protecting both his property and his liberty. Accordingly he maintained that a more fundamental change in society was required before the corporation could act in a more self-consciously ethical manner. Socialism, not capitalism could support a social corporation as capitalism without managerial accountability would merely lead to managerial abuse.

Given Berle's premise of socialism for a social corporation, it seemed entirely feasible that the strong organisational-based system that existed in post-war Britain overcame the problems of accountability in large dispersed organisations noted by Berle. In this political context the social corporation promoted by Dodds could become a reality and part of the programme of socialist reform pursued by the Labour Party.

Post-war Britain from the universities to the workplace was highly radicalised.[26] A Labour government was voted in with an overwhelming majority, charged with improving the lives of ordinary people. Historians such as Eric Hobsbawn and EP Thompson wrote people's histories in the Marxist tradition. Left-wing and Marxist economists such as Paul Sweezy and Harry Magdoff held the moral high ground. From the revolutionaries to the reformists all were agreed that organisations were the key to engineering a society which could attend to social need, heralding a new egalitarian society, free from poverty and oppression. 'Organisationalism', as it will henceforth be referred to, was the virtually uncontested strategy for societal progress. FA Hayek and later Milton Friedman were the most notable of organisationalism's critics but at the time their ideas appeared to be rather eccentric. They would be rehabilitated in the 1980s after organisationalism's demise, but in the interim, the main political disagreements in and around the Labour Party were over strategies to achieve socialism rather than whether socialism was a desirable achievement. That argument for the moment had been convincingly won.

The separation of ownership from control debate found its place in the social democratic left. Within the Labour Party this was exemplified by CAR Crosland MP's own brand of social democracy, which reflected much of the optimism surrounding the emergence of corporations. In his classic manifesto *The Future of Socialism* Crosland argued that business was no longer dominated by the demands of ownership and the business class had lost its superior position to the state.[27] He argued that in contrast to the supremacy enjoyed by business in the 1930s and before (when the government took an active role in supporting business and high unemployment meant that

---

26 This was echoed in post-war Europe and America; however, this study is limited to a discussion of English corporate governance and the influences that prevailed.

27 Crosland, C, *The Future of Socialism*, London: Jonathan Cape.

the labour force had little power to resist),[28] the post-war economy had empowered both the state and the working person. This shift in power he attributed to three developments in British society. The first development was that 'decisive sources and levers of economic power have been transferred from private business to other hands'.[29] Public authorities, including national-ised industries, had taken control over much of the economy. Within nation-alised industries 'economic decisions in the basic sector have passed out of the hands of the capitalist class into the hands of a new and largely autonomous class of public industrial managers'.[30] As well as being the country's largest employer, Crosland argued that public authorities wielded a 'substantially greater power over business decisions even when these remain in private hands'.[31] This was because politically, the government had commit-ted itself to orientating fiscal policy to affect such social measures as full employment. Furthermore, it taxed directly and indirectly to encourage particular production patterns.

The second development was the enhanced political power of the work-force. Economic prosperity and government policy had meant that it was a seller's market for employees. Trade unions had strengthened and their demands were generally met. The labour force's security was business's insecurity. Part of the reason for business's subordination to its workforce resulted from the third development Crosland identified, that of the 'psycho-logical revolution within industry and the altered role of profit'.[32] Crosland argued that a number of factors had shifted power over business away from the capitalist or share-owning class to specialised non-share-owning man-agers. The 'diversity and technical intricacy' of industry meant a much greater reliance on experts, rather than the merely wealthy, so that 'scientists and specialised technicians [were] appointed to boards of directors'.[33] As well as the emergence of the Berle–Means corporation, Crosland argued that there were additional factors within British society that had undermined the actual and psychological strength of shareholders. Economic growth had increased company size, tax policies made private companies less feasible than large public companies and managers, paid by wages not dividends, had only small incentives to heed the interests of shareholders. Indeed, argued Crosland, they had little need to heed the capitalist class as a whole as their ability to plough back profits into industry (rather than return high dividends to shareholders) meant that companies were much more independent from

28 Crosland cites the plight of the Jarrow workers as a potent symbol of capital dominance and governmental compliance.
29 Ibid, p 7.
30 Ibid, p 11.
31 Ibid, p 7.
32 Ibid, p 14.
33 Ibid, p 15.

financial institutions than they had been before the war. Furthermore, managers' personal prestige was not dependent on profitability. Indeed in the post-war socialist climate, it could equally be enhanced 'by gaining a reputation as a progressive employer, who introduces co-partnership or profit sharing schemes'.[34] Buzzwords such as 'co-operation', 'participation', 'communication', 'democratic leadership' and 'permissive management' littered boardroom discussion.[35] Crosland even went as far as to say that the manager 'longs for the approval of the sociologist'![36] It was a trend in business that continued late into the 1970s, demonstrable in many examples including a CBI Committee which said that a company must be a 'good citizen in business',[37] or the Institute of Directors stating that directors owed a duty to 'employees, customers and creditors as well as . . . in some degree to the state'.[38] Indeed, it is probably worth mentioning anecdotally, and in order to give a flavour of the time, that the state was the preferred environment in which to pursue professional aspirations, with brighter students pursuing careers in the public sector leaving the less able to take jobs in the second choice private sector.

For Crosland, these shifts in both corporate governance and the economy as a whole meant that British capitalism had undergone a fundamental change which rendered the Marxist arguments in favour of fundamental economic shifts 'obsolete'. Such theories, he argued, were premised on nineteenth-century capitalism to which the post-war economy bore no resemblance. Economic power had shifted from both industrial and finance capitalists into the hands of specialised management, employees, trade unions and government. 'Is this still capitalism?' he asked. His answer was 'No'.[39]

> In the basic industries, nationalisation has wholly deprived the capitalist class of its power of decision. But it has been similarly deprived in much of the private sector. The growth of the managerial joint stock corporation has transferred the function of decision making to a largely non-owning class of salaried executives, who suffer singularly little interference from the nominal owners. Even this new business class finds its freedom of action limited to an extent which its capitalist predecessors never did – partly from the growth in the role of government but mainly by the growth in the power of labour, stemming generally from the rise in

34 Ibid, p 17.
35 Ibid, p 19.
36 Ibid.
37 Quoted in Ireland, P, 'Toward a less degenerate capitalism? Corporate governance, stakeholding and the company' (1996) 23 JLS.
38 Ibid, quoting CBI Committee, 'The social responsibilities of the British public company' (1973) 23 Institute of Directors, *Guidelines for Directors*, 13.
39 Op. cit., Crosland, p 42.

trade union strength and specifically from the altered conditions of the labour market.[40]

Ireland argues that the height of the British establishment's acknowledgement of the 'end of capitalism', in the Labour administration of 1974–79, came in the form of the Bullock report.[41] Premised on the assumption that shareholders had no practical or moral claim on the activities or loyalties of directors, its main proposal was the equal number of worker and shareholder representatives on the boards of large companies.[42] If shareholder-orientated goals need no longer be pursued, then the character of British capitalism could be moulded by the composition and policies of the company board as Crosland had described. The company board could therefore act as a mediator of government policy, imbued with the social goals of a socialist administration. The swift and negative response by industry to the possibility of worker participation on the board heralded the radical societal shift away from Labour's social democratic policies and to its polar opposite, the neo-liberalism of the 1979 Conservative administration under the leadership of Margaret Thatcher. With this new administration came the abandonment of the corporate governance goals of social corporations and the re-adoption of shareholder primacy goals.

ANTI-ORGANISATIONALISM, NEO-LIBERALISM AND THE FREE MARKET: CORPORATE GOVERNANCE AND SHAREHOLDERS

In England in the 1980s, the economic and political effects of the previous decade laid the foundation for the emergence of a strong, reconstituted Conservative Party, whose ideology has been subsequently dubbed the New Right or Neo-Liberalism. British society prior to their electoral victory was characterised by internal conflicts and contradictions which can, to a great degree, explain the emergence of this new Conservative Party.[43] As Stuart Hall describes, the two primary contradictions in British society were the demands of the market economy and the policy responses of the Labour Government. The British economy, engulfed in recession, placed demands upon the social democratic Labour Party which lost them their political and moral credibility. They could no longer claim to represent working people whilst requiring that same class to conform to the constraints of a capitalist crisis.

---

40 Ibid, p 30.
41 Op cit. Ireland on the Report of the Committee of Inquiry on Industrial Democracy, 1977, Cmnd 6706.
42 In 1976 the same strategy was adopted in large firms in Germany.
43 Hall, S, 'The politics of Thatcherism', 1983, London, Lawrence and Wishart, pp 19–30.

Throughout the 1970s, Callaghan's Labour Government introduced the harsh monetarist policies advised by the IMF and slashed spending on the welfare state. Later, when these policies were re-adopted by the new Thatcher Government, they were heralded as responsible, innovative and liberating. This suggests that ideology was the dominant feature of successful policy decisions. The Conservatives could adopt the previously unpopular policies of the Labour Government because they expressed them in a different way and they did not carry the political baggage of Labourism. Such policies, in the hands of the Labour Government, were seen as treacherous and authoritarian. Labour had represented itself as the party of the working class, and so in order to impose less socialist economic policies it needed to persuade its voters of the unlikely proposition that these policies were ultimately in working people's interest. A short-term deprivation that would pave the way for long-term prosperity. However, the ideological initiatives to liken the interests of workers to the success of capitalism, characterised by Hall as 'corporatist . . . incorporating sections of the working class and unions into the bargain between state, capital and labour', floundered.[44] The problem with this political approach to economic crisis was, argued Hall, Labour's inability to appear to represent the people it governed. And although Labour had always encompassed different political thought from the socialism of Tony Benn to the social democracy of Crosland, its economic policies in this period looked hypocritical.[45] The Labour Party appeared to betray the class it represented and they responded by participating in the huge industrial unrest which dominated England in the 1970s.

In this context the New Right and subsequently 'Thatcherism' was able to convey the clarity of vision that Labour's policies could not, argued Hall. They were able to capitalise upon Labour's political dilemmas by treating popular perceptions of Labour as an authoritarian government as a reality. Ideologically, Thatcherism linked social welfare policies with intrusive anti-individual state activities, neatly disassociating itself from both. According to Hall, the Conservative Party enhanced its popularity by side-stepping the issue of being a party representing a particular class interest and, instead, advanced what he called a 'people to party' approach. It represented the nation, while the Labour Party represented class interests. And, in order to represent one class Labour had needed to create an interventionist and controlling state.

The New Right's populist approach was encapsulated in anti-state rhetoric such as the abolition of the 'nanny state' which was said to both encourage scroungers and stifled entrepreneurialism. In the context of interventionist

44 Ibid, p 24.
45 Ibid, p 26. Hall states that ' "Labourism" is not a homogenous political entity but a complex political formation. It is not the expression of the working class "in government", but the principal means of the political representation of the class.'

Labour policies, argues Hall, this rhetoric was a covert and highly successful attack on Labour and social democratic politics generally. Importantly, it followed Milton Friedman's line of connecting personal freedom with a free market. Since the 1950s Friedman had been putting the case for business governed only by the market and not by social policies and had co-founded the Chicago School of Economics based on a neo-liberal economic theory. Friedman received the Nobel Prize in economics in 1976 and created an economic theory, monetarism. However, it took the failure of the left and the project of organisationalism to make his theories part of mainstream thought. The 1980s made him the man of the moment. In 1962 he had argued that only the market produced both economic prosperity and promoted a free society.[46] Accordingly, the unencumbered company was a moral imperative and engineering a company's activities in the interests of employees simply wrong, the actions of a freedom-hating minority. At the time of publication his ideas were mildly eccentric. By the 1980s they were common sense.

Coupled with Friedman's monetarist economics, the New Right's rhetoric drew from the classic articulations of liberalism. Intellectuals such as Adam Smith, John Stuart Mill and, in particular, Hayek were drawn upon as masters of common sense for their reasoned antipathy to state intervention and their association of laissez-faire policies with individual liberty and economic progress. Hayek was especially acute on this point, writing, as he was, in the aftermath of fascism. A lone voice in the post-war 'organisationalism', Hayek directly associated a thriving dynamic economy with a minimalist state that was underpinned by the rule of law. In contrast, an interventionist government, one which controlled the economy rather than allowing a market of contracting individuals to operate freely was necessarily, he argued, arbitrary and discriminatory. Such a government could not function under a legal system whose rules were, 'fixed and announced beforehand', it required flexibility to respond to circumstances as they arose, in a manner that was unencumbered by a priori legislation.[47]

Hayek argued that legislation passed by an interventionist government was merely the expression of party politics and involved rules with a substantive content, designed to achieve a particular end. Under an interventionist government, individuals could not rely on a known status quo and could not predict the actions of their state. In order to achieve self-expression and economic growth, individuals required a system of pre-set, formal rules to which all, including government, were subject. With such a system individuals could 'predict actions of the state which may affect these plans'[48] and

---

46 Friedman, M, *Capitalism and Freedom*, 1962, Chicago: University of Chicago Press.
47 Hayek, F, *The Road to Serfdom*, 1976, London: Routledge, Kegan and Paul. First published 1944.
48 Ibid.

only under these conditions could a free market operate. For Hayek, it was only the rule of law that could prevent government undermining individual property rights and suppressing individual effort, two key elements of the allegedly entrepreneurial spirit much vaunted in the 1980s.

A society of individuals pursuing their own economic objectives within 'formal and generalised' rules gave rise to what Hayek called a 'spontaneous order', or what Adam Smith similarly called 'the invisible hand of the market'. In *Law, Legislation and Liberty*,[49] Hayek expanded his theory on the dynamic character of spontaneous order, justifying it on the basis that as individuals possessed better local information than the state and possessed a self-interest in making use of it, an economy based on individual self-interest, a free market, would be bound to thrive. Individuals possessed the most accurate knowledge of their own circumstances, local resources and potential for growth and profit making. And, unlike the state, it was the individual who had access to the most precise and up-to-date 'decentralised' and 'fragmented' knowledge, and it was the individual who had the greatest self-interest in making use of this knowledge toward the furtherance of his own enrichment and ultimately the enrichment of society as a whole.

Centralised planning, argued Hayek, stymied the intrinsic power of the individual, disabling him from taking full advantage of his unique position. 'Hence the familiar fact that the more the state plans, the more difficult planning becomes for the individual.'[50] According to Hayek, a planned economy, such as that pursued to a degree under organisationalism, although dressed up as creating the greater human good, in fact encouraged discrimination, and suppressed creativity and freedom, a perspective to which the New Right readily subscribed. Thatcher's Government drew from this language of liberty and identified its attainment with the restriction and reduction of the machinations of the state.

From this perspective and within the context of this neo-liberal hegemony, the company would no longer be conceived as a public institution in which managers responded to the policy objectives of central government. In Hayek's view, even the most benign policy objectives were inherently anti-liberal and open to abuse. In a free society, government made no substantial intervention into economic activity. The company as a vehicle for the economy was therefore the concern of private citizens, whose pursuit of wealth would enhance the overall wealth and well-being of society. Shareholders were economic actors, in possession of private property, the share. They were entitled to have the company run in the interests of their private property and no such entitlement should be extended to those without such private property interests, such as employees. Individual private property was central to

---

49 Hayek, FA, *Law, Legislation and Liberty*, 1979, Chicago: University of Chicago Press.
50 Op. cit., Hayek, *The Road to Serfdom*, p 57.

the New Right's attack on post-war welfarism. In an ingenious conjunction of its anti-state welfare ideology and that of individual private property, council houses were sold to their occupants, taken from council control and transformed into the private property of former council house tenants.

Philosophically, the orientation of the rule of law around the protection of private property, maintained by liberal thinkers from Locke to Hayek, is justified on the basis that these individual rights act as a buffer against the intervention of the state. Freedom, formal equality and private property are, for liberals, intrinsically connected by '. . . recalling the link . . . between having a property in one's person and being a free man'.[51] It is the freedom of the individual to sell their personal skills and strengths in the market for a price determined by market forces that is the starting point for the ascendance of private property. Thus,

> having this most basic right in my own person seems to entail having the most basic of liberal freedoms – contractual liberty, liberty of occupation, association and movement and so on – and it is compromised whenever these freedoms are abridged. The connection between property and the basic liberties is in these cases constitutive and not just instrumental.[52]

For modern liberal thinkers it is the subservience of private property rights in person and things to the dictates of collectivism and the state that create a situation where 'we move away from private property to communal or collective institutions, [and] the practical knowledge available to society is diluted or attenuated'.[53] Under collectivism, the individual is constrained by the values of others. The result according to Grey is that 'Communal systems of ownership embody a bias against risk and novelty – a fact which may go far to explain the technological stagnation of the world's socialist economies'.[54]

The New Right, therefore, were adverse to the notion that private industry should be constrained by public or non-economic criteria. Interference with the spontaneous order of the market was akin to socialism and all its accompanying evils. Thus, when the *Committee to Review the Functioning of Financial Institutions*, appointed under the premiership of James Callaghan but published in 1980 under the government of Margaret Thatcher, noted that 'criticism [of company policy] by small-scale shareholders or by financial journalists constrained as it is by the laws of libel, can frequently be ignored',[55]

---

51 Gray, J, *Liberalism*, 1995, Buckingham: Open University Press, p 58.
52 Ibid, p 63.
53 Ibid.
54 Ibid, p 65.
55 Committee to Review the Functioning of Financial Institutions, 1980, p 249.

the New Right's response was to do nothing. Instead of introducing policies that would redress this balance of power, its response was to allow the market, in this case majority shareholders, to retain its hegemony. Likewise, the Bullock Report's recommendation of shareholder and employee representation on the board of directors was legislatively expressed in the toothless s 309 of the Companies Act 1985, which states that 'directors of a company are to have regard in the performance of their functions . . . the interests of the company's employees in general, as well as the interests of its members'.

Labour's vision of the company as an inclusive and socially responsible institution driven by concerns other than profit was not shared by the New Right.[56] The Conservative Party wished to portray itself as a non-interventionist government presiding over a free market which emphasised individualism and the regressive nature of welfarism, and in so doing it reasserted nineteenth-century liberal philosophy. It chimed with Milton Friedman's avocation of profit maximisation and shareholder primacy.[57] According to Friedman, corporate social responsibility was the wrongful distribution of shareholders' property. Managers were agents for shareholders' interests, custodians of private capital. They were not, as post-war labourism maintained, a form of public servant.

NEO-LIBERALISM TRANSLATED INTO CORPORATE GOVERNANCE: THE PROBLEM OF MANAGEMENT IN THE BERLE–MEANS CORPORATION

From the 1980s onwards the predominant theories and policies on corporate governance continued to be based upon the Berle and Means control and ownership division. However, neo-liberal approaches to corporate governance in contrast to the previous era sought to reassert profit maximisation as the primary goal of the corporation and therefore the primary duty of a director. The new elevation of profit maximisation as the goal of the corporation was importantly politics driven. It was the reassertion of the rights of the owning classes over the employed classes.

This new political emphasis drove a fundamental change in corporate

---

56 This perspective affected other business organisations. Historically, the mutual building society was an institution that had been, in many ways, socially engineered in order to reify the rewards of thrift and hard work to working people. In the, albeit partisan, words of Sir Herbert Ashworth, former chairman of the Nationwide Building Society, 'they are admirable institutions which have made a significant contribution to the welfare of the people of this country by fostering saving and promoting home ownership'.[56] No mention of profitability here. Ashworth, H, *The Building Society Story*, 1980, London: Franey, Preface.

57 Friedman, 'The social responsibility of business is to increase its profits', *New York Times*, 13 September 1970.

governance perspectives and goals. While the corporate governance vehicle for ensuring equality and socialist political goals was pluralism and shared control, so the corporate governance vehicle for ensuring profit maximisation was the elevation of the shareholder. Indeed, there is little moral or even legal justification for the elevation of the shareholder otherwise.[58]

The connection of free market economics and the law where the latter was viewed as a mechanism to promote the former is the basis of the 'law and economics' movement which originated in the Chicago School of Economics.[59] Its neo-liberal perspective determined that the only forum for ensuring the proper operation of business is the 'free market'. Thus the free-market, neo-liberal theories of the Chicago School, in the context of corporate law, emphasises the importance of a corporate law which promotes the free market. From a 'law and economics' perspective developed in the Chicago School, pro-market corporate laws may be ones which do little to inhibit the intentions or decisions of the 'players', those involved with the corporation, or conversely they may intervene in commercial arrangements in order to ensure free-market transactions.

The first theory which articulated neo-liberal theory in the context of the business corporation is generally thought to be held in Ronald Coase's article 'The nature of the firm' written in 1937.[60] In this article he characterised the corporation as a set of transactions between those involved in the business. The basics of this theory were developed by scholars within the law and economics movement referred to as contractarians.[61] The application of Coase's model of the corporation by the contractarians as just a set of arrangements between individuals and its corresponding denial of the corporation as an entity may be summarised in the notion that the corporation is merely a 'nexus of contracts'. This term was first coined by Jensen and Meckling in their famous article of 1976.[62] In their nexus of contracts model, individuals within a business engage in private market contracts, bargains which are overseen and guided by managers. As the company is only a legal fiction,[63] the manager does not act as an agent for the company but for the shareholder.

Shareholders, particularly those in large corporations, are forced to rely on the honesty and competence of their managers, a situation which presents a constant or structural risk that managers will act in their own self-interest or

---

58 See Ireland and Greenwood, below.
59 Known simply as the Chicago School.
60 Coase, R, 'The nature of the firm' (1937) 4 Economica 386.
61 Given the hegemonous nature of the perspective it has featured in Chapters 1, 3, 5 and 6 of this book.
62 Jenson, M and Meckling, W, 'Theory of the firm: managerial behavior, agency costs and ownership structure', 3 J Fin Econ 305, 1976.
63 The 'personhood' of a corporation is a matter of convenience rather than reality. Easterbrook and Fischel, 'The corporate contract' (1989) Columbia L Rev, Vol 89, p 1426.

for interests other than those of their principal. The costs associated with reducing or annihilating this risk are called 'agency costs'. These are borne by shareholders who have no fixed claim against the company, unlike creditors, but who are instead paid according to the available profit. If agency costs are high, then dividends will be reduced and stock will fall in price.

In this model corporate law's *raison d'être* is the reduction of agency costs and accordingly, any law which fails to do this should be removed. For the most part, however, it is not the law which reduces agency costs but the market, which includes the financial markets, labour markets, and markets in managerial expertise. A manager that fails to reduce agency costs will quickly be exposed by corporate information such as share prices, which will jeopardise his relationship with his existing and future employers. Thus the market provides managers with a huge incentive to succeed. Furthermore, according to contractarianism the market also constructs corporate law itself, so that only rules which support the market will, and indeed should, survive. This is particularly true in America where the competition for incorporations noted in Chapter 1 means that states adopt the laws which are most desirable to incorporators, thus changes in corporate law are very quick and responsive to market needs. However, it is also demonstrable in Britain where both the judiciary and the legislator have attempted to create a market- and shareholder-friendly body of rules. Indeed, the stated aims of the reform process were to create a company law for a competitive economy.

From the contractarian perspective, as corporate governance (reconstrued as reducing agency costs) is largely achieved by the market, corporate law is often given a different role. For example, a director's fiduciary duties would, from a classical legal perspective, be understood as a mechanism for ensuring that directors act in the interests of the company, usually understood to be shareholders' interest as a whole. Such duties would therefore help ensure that the company was governed in the interest of shareholders. However, the contractarian approach to fiduciary duties reduces the function of fiduciary duties to that of perfecting the contract between agent (the manager/director) and principal (shareholders). According to Easterbrook and Fischel a contract between shareholders ('holders of residual claims') and managers exists, but the terms are impressionistic with no specific duties expressly stated. So, 'to make such arrangements palatable to investors, managers must pledge their careful and honest services'.[64] Thus shareholders receive the benefit of fiduciary duties in exchange for enduring no 'explicit promises', that is, no guarantee of dividend.

However, this is not to suppose that fiduciary duties will be carefully monitored at all times. To retain monitors of directors would involve creating

64 Easterbrook and Fischel, *The Economic Structure of Corporate Law*, Cambridge, MA: Harvard University Press, p 90.

another layer of management which might itself fail to meet its remit but more importantly would create higher agency costs. The absence of monitoring, they argue, reflects the law's protection of directors in their routine decision making while in other less routine circumstances, such as for self-dealing, heavily penalising them. A director might make wrong or negligent decisions, but the cost of bringing this to court would outweigh the benefits to the corporation and may result in the loss of an otherwise useful agent. Thus the business judgment rule, which protects directors from liability for negligent or costly decisions if they were made honestly, does so for the good of the business. On the other hand, self-dealing is likely to be a one-off act by a previous or outgoing director involving a large financial loss to the business. In that case it is cost-efficient to pursue a director for beach of a fiduciary duty and the law responds accordingly.

Likewise, Kraakman and Hansmann argue that in America, the law is a relatively weak mechanism for protecting shareholder interests. Even in Delaware, shareholders have little power compared to their international counterparts. They have 'less power to shape corporate policy', 'US boards have far more latitude to defend against hostile takeovers' and 'US securities law burdens consultation and proxy solicitation among large shareholders more heavily than the law of any other jurisdiction'.[65] Other mechanisms, such things as high compensation packages for directors, are much better at achieving shareholder primacy. The UK, they argue, differs from the US in that the law is much more shareholder-friendly. Probably as a result of the power of institutional shareholders, they surmise, shareholders have greater control over corporate governance structures and greater facility to put forward important motions at general meeting such as those relating to mergers. Furthermore, the City Code places many important restrictions on manager decisions. Overall, though, they conclude that legal corporate governance mechanisms are much weaker on corporate governance than 'ownership structures, managerial culture, and the political power of mangers and employees'.[66]

The notion that the free market provides corporate governance is encapsulated in the notion of the 'market for corporate control'. For example the information produced by the market forces managers to constantly improve their performance. Indeed, 'few markets are as efficient as capital markets':[67]

Accurate price signals in capital markets contribute to the efficiency of labor markets. Share price information provides a relatively low-cost

---

65 Kraakman, R and Hansmann, H, *The Anatomy of Corporate Law: A Comparative and Functional Approach*, 2005, Oxford: Oxford University Press, p 67.
66 Ibid, p 70.
67 Op. cit., Easterbrook, p 96.

method of evaluating the performance of corporate managers. Such information can be used (imperfectly) to set managers' compensation within the firm as well as to measure their opportunity wage in external labor markets.[68]

Moreover, information on poor managerial performance will lead even the most inexperienced investor to pay less for shares in that company. Somewhat oddly, Easterbrook and Fischel argue that this is because 'the more investors believe that their dollars will be used by those in control of firms in ways inconsistent with maximising the value of the firm, the less they will pay for shares'. This statement not only assumes that the purchase price of shares goes to the company (it does not, only the purchase price of IPOs goes to the company and the vast majority of shares are sold on the secondary share market), it recreates an entity, 'the firm', which has a value! Along similar lines, there is a great deal of literature which argues that poor managerial performance leads to low share prices, which lead to hostile takeover bids, which generally lead to the removal of the incumbent directors.

Hostile takeovers are those undertaken against the directors' wishes and where the bidder directly approaches the 'target' company's shareholders. The role of hostile takeovers in corporate governance was first mooted by Manne in his 1965 article.[69] Manne argued that the radical deregulation of hostile takeovers would enable a market for corporate control which would benefit shareholders. Woven into a more contractarian model, this market for corporate control is justifiable because managers are agents of shareholders and are therefore obliged to welcome bids which produce the greatest value for shareholders. And although the nexus of contract model assumes that there are more players than just managers and shareholders and therefore more claims than those of shareholders, their interest is elevated above others because they are, as stated earlier, 'residual risk bearers'. So, while successful hostile takeover bids might be against the interests of employees and directors who might lose their jobs, or the local community who may lose a useful industry and suffer from the increased unemployment of its citizens, corporate law should protect, or at least not hinder, the ability of shareholders to make premiums from such bids.

This approach reflects Friedman's assertion that the social responsibility of corporations is to make money. And as Easterbrook and Fischel make clear, takeover bids make money: 'Stock prices rise, by 30 per cent and more. Investors in targets realised $346 billion in the decade 1977–1986 and investors in purchasers realised additional gains in the billions.'[70] Furthermore,

68 Ibid.
69 Manne, 'Mergers and the market for corporate control', (1965) 73 J Pol Econ 110, 1965.
70 Op. cit., Easterbrook, p 198.

they argue that hostile takeover bids, while representing a small proportion of similar corporate activity (numbering, they estimate, around 40 to 50 per year) act as an important disciplining mechanism. This is because they tend to happen to firms that are producing lower than average profits, within industries that are as a whole 'lagging behind the national average'.[71]

However, from a contractarian perspective, corporate law has failed to fully reflect and facilitate the market mechanism of hostile takeovers. In the case of *Unocal v Mesa Petroleum Co*, the Delaware Supreme Court, centre for the common law on corporations, held that it was a director's duty to consider the negative effects of a hostile bid on the enterprise as a whole.[72] The court specifically emphasised that this would include the effects on non-shareholders as well as shareholders. Furthermore, in response to some of the negative social effects wrought by hostile bids, many states have adopted anti-takeover measures. Additionally, many firms have adopted anti-takeover measures, most known as poison pills, and most states have signalled their approval of pills. The cost to Delaware firms, according to Easterbrook and Fischel, is about 2.6 per cent of equity value.[73]

Corporate governance under the contractarian model neatly sidesteps the issue of power within the corporation which characterises all other discussions on this issue. Ownership is not separated from control as there are no real owners and nothing real that may be owned. Instead, this model replaces owners with 'residual risk takers' who exchange money and relative financial vulnerability for managers' loyalty. A non-negotiated standard form contract exists between shareholder and manager which is constructed by company law but most efficiently monitored by market mechanisms. By construing governance in this way, contractarianism attempts to neutralise the power relations within and outside a corporation. If all relations are contractual and contract is based on choice, freedom and the implicit equality of the players, then there can be no question of unfair distribution of wealth and exploitation. However, it is important to remember that no intellectual movement emerges from a vacuum. This is a theory which is entirely opposed to the interventionist, socially responsible society promoted by the left and dominant in the post-war years and has created a rationale for the promotion of its polar opposite, the free market. It is the intellectual basis for Gordon Gekko's claim that 'greed is good', and the most influential body of scholarship on company law today.

---

71 Ibid.
72 493 A 2d 946, 955–56 (Del 1985).
73 Op. cit., Easterbrook, p 197.

POLITICS, LAW AND IDEOLOGY

In contrast to the contractarian approach of the law and economics thinkers a number of scholars have demonstrated that corporate governance is formed not through the logic of the free market but through other mechanisms – politics, law and ideology. In assessing each of these three factors in turn this section will discuss some of the work of Mark Roe, Paddy Ireland and Daniel Greenwood respectively. Mark Roe's work shows how company law and the market are subject to the political policies of a national government, which he demonstrates through a comparative analysis of corporate governance in Europe, England and America. Paddy Ireland's work shows how the law misconstrued shareholders in large companies as owners because of the way it developed historically and became constrained by its own internal logic. This he demonstrates by analysing the relationship between usury laws, partnership law and company law. Finally, Daniel Greenwood's piece argues that shareholder claims to primacy and in particular to the profits of business is neither justified by law nor economics but instead represents an ideological victory for investors and managers over the competing interests of employees, consumers and the community at large.

Mark Roe

Roe maintains that the success of mechanisms for achieving corporate governance in England and America are dependent upon a particular form of government. Thus while market control mechanisms such as hostile takeovers might be effective here, they are not easily translatable into the corporate activities of corporations in continental Europe. For example until 1999, when Vodafone took over Mannesmann, there had never been a successful hostile takeover in Germany. Roe argues that to different degrees the politics of social democracy stymied such market-based attempts at managerial discipline.

> Hostile takeovers were notoriously harder in continental Europe than in the United States and Britain . . . they regularly foundered due to the political pressure one would expect in a social democracy, as workers campaigned to block the takeovers and politicians sided with employees and against capital owners.[74]

In France, hostile takeovers were more frequent than in Germany but such takeovers were always subject to some form of Ministry scrutiny. Roe notes that, 'the Ministry rarely approved a takeover without a social plan in place,

---

74 Roe, MJ, 'Political preconditions to separating ownership from control' (2000–01), 53 Stanford L Rev 539, p 558.

one that had the offeror renouncing laying off any employee at the target for two to five years.'[75] Furthermore, the Minister of Finance in France stated his immediate aversion to very high priced takeovers because the buyer would be looking for a swift and immediate profit which could be detrimental to employees' interests! In contrast, Anglo-American thinking specifically values high prices and immediate high profits and would not consider employee interests a factor, much less a deciding factor.

Roe maintains that it is the political context of corporate governance that determines whether managers will pursue shareholder interests in preference to other connected persons including themselves. European social democracies, he maintains, pressure managers to pursue goals which are not shareholder-orientated but are socially orientated. In particular, social democracies seek stability for employees, an aim, among others, which Roe maintains would be the natural, preferred option for managers. Problematically, the effect of social democracies on corporate governance is to ensure the continuation of family firms, suppression of stock dispersal and to hamper capital development.

Germany is a prime example of social democracy's promotion of employees' interests. Here employees' interests are pursued directly through employee representation on the company's supervisory board and less directly through government policy. The former arrangement arose from the post-war agreement that Germany's coal and steel industry would be co-determined equally by employees and shareholders. Later, the principle was extended to a one-third employee representation on the boards and then one-half of larger firms in 1976.[76]

The effect of co-determination, Roe shows, has a direct effect on share value. For example when the 1976 Act raised the minimum employee representation on boards in larger firms to one-half, one study cited by Roe estimated that the loss to productivity was between 13 per cent and 14 per cent while others estimated that co-determination reduced market-to-book ratio by 27 per cent.[77] Even in the absence of co-determination, Roe maintains that Germany's social democratic politics favour policies which protect employees' interests to the detriment of shareholders'. For example, Roe cites an instance when Gerhard Schröder nationalised a steel mill rather than risk employees' jobs in a possible restructuring by a foreign firm.[78]

---

75 Ibid, p 559.
76 Ibid, p 547, referring to an article by Katharina Pister, 'Codetermination: A sociopolitical model with governance externalities', in Blair, MM and Roe, MJ (eds) (1999) Employees and Corporate Governance 163, 167–69.
77 Ibid, p 550, citing Roe. FitzRoy, FR and Kraft, K, 'Economic effects of codetermination' (1993) 95 Scandinavian J Econ 365, 374, and Gorton, G and Schmidd, F, 'Class struggle inside the firm? A study of German codetermination', NBER Working Paper No W7945, 2000.
78 Ibid, p 552.

Roe maintains that social democracy reduced shareholder value first because its pro- employee policies marry with a manager's self-interest and second because the mechanisms which reduce agency costs in English and American companies are stymied in a social democracy. As managerialists Jenson and Meckling indicated, managerial goals, unhampered by shareholders' interests, include empire building, protecting their professional position and personal popularity.[79] The unencumbered manager will tend to use their discretion over the use of company profits to expand the company's real and human capital, enhancing both their comfort and power. They will be risk-averse even though taking risks may increase profits, as risks may endanger their position. They will take more leisure time and larger financial rewards than shareholders might wish. They will avoid restructuring a business which would mean invariably shedding employees in times of economic crisis because it is both painful and unpopular. And while all of the above are contrary to the interests of shareholders, many of these dispositions, as Roe points out, 'fit well with employees' goals'.[80] Like managers, 'Employees also are averse to risks to the firm, as their human capital is tied up in the firm and they are not fully diversified. Employees also prefer that the firm expand, not downsize, because expanding often yields them promotion opportunities, whilst downsizing risks leaving them unemployed.'[81]

Thus, Roe concludes, a social democracy in pursuing the interests of employees reinforces rather than counters natural managerial goals. As shareholders' interests are sidelined, so is the desirability of shares and shareholding as a form of outsider investment. Investment in shares only makes financial sense if one has a large controlling interest, and this is particularly so when social democracy is coupled with co-determination.

According to Roe, this explains why the majority of stock in German firms remains within a family group, and stock ownership does not become dispersed. He explains the scenario thus. In order to ensure that dividends remain an organisational goal of the business, family owners act directly as the firm's managers and do not hire professional managers (who are likely to pursue managerial or social democratic goals). The profitability of the firm and by extension the value of their stock relies upon their direction and upon their commitment to monitoring business performance. If they wished to sell their stock they would not be able to receive its present value because that value is ensured by their active involvement in the running of the business. Their absence would reduce the profitability of the firm and the value of the stock. Alternatively, if they sought to compensate for their absence by creating a strengthened board, which undertook such measures as regular

79 Op. cit., Jenson and Meckling.
80 Ibid, p 551.
81 Ibid.

meeting, rewarding profit maximisation and engaging independent advisors[82] the firm's profitability would probably remain unchanged or even improve. However, given the social democratic pressure upon managers, there would be no guarantee that this profit would not return directly to employees. Indeed, says Roe, an identifiable percentage of 10–20 per cent would be likely to return to employees in some form of benefit.[83] The choice for the family owner who wants to sell is to launch an IPO of their shares at a discount, or to sell the stock as a block to another individual or group that will take over the managing function. The former strategy would aid share dispersal in Germany but would mean sustaining a loss, which the latter choice would not. Not surprisingly, block sales are common in Germany. Roe concludes that 'German social democracy, institutionalised in corporate governance via codetermination, induces this firm to stay private, so as to avoid the costs to shareholders of an enhanced labor voice inside the firm. Social democracy in the form of a supervisory board codetermination mixes badly with the public firm.'[84] And, argues Roe, even without such co-determination as is found in German companies, social democracies successfully thwart 'shareholder value' and thereby sustain the continuance of large family holdings.

In contrast, he argues, America and to a lesser extent England have developed mechanisms for reducing the agency costs outlined above which have enabled a dispersed share market. Continental Europe, however, is unable to use these mechanisms because the very politics of social democracy undermines them.

Roe's work here is interesting and informative. It amply illustrates how politics is at least *nearly* as significant as economics in informing company law. Thus, a separation of ownership from control may be enhanced by the economic requirement of capital which fuelled, for example, railway construction in England and railroads in America. But the conditions for this share dispersal must be a pro-shareholder political environment. Without this, the wealthiest in society cannot be sure that their interests will be pursued as a matter of course and will be obliged to maintain their majority stake.

Thus, extending from the themes developed in Roe's paper, it is clear that share dispersal will not, in itself, result in a society dominated by managerial goals. Contrary to the views of Crosland and others it cannot result in a fully 'socialised' corporation, where managers will pursue the interests of employees, or follow the social policies of their government. This is because

---

82 Measures that are part of the usual mechanism for ensuring shareholder value in Anglo-American companies.
83 Roe cites statistics which show that following the 1976 codetermination law this amount, on average, was lost to shareholder value.
84 Ibid, p 550.

large shareholders would not allow their stock to be dispersed if this would be the outcome. The only conditions where large shareholders would divest themselves of stock is when they can be sure that such an action would not harm their investments. According to Roe, the conditions for this are political. What does the government believe to be the right orientation for company managers? What does the judiciary believe to be the right focus of a director's attention? In other words, share ownership is more dispersed in England (as well as America) because the political conditions were and are so conducive to shareholders' interest. And the judiciary, through doctrines such as *ultra vires* and through its slant on a director's fiduciary duties, displays a much greater commitment to shareholders' interests than to other people connected to the company such as employees, consumers and even creditors.

Paddy Ireland

In 'The myth of shareholder ownership' Ireland maintains that the root cause or justification for distinguishing a shareholder who makes a money contribution from a creditor who does the same is that the shareholder is said to have risked his capital whereas the creditor has not.[85] A shareholder has invested his capital in the corporation whereas the creditor has merely lent his money for a limited period of time. The importance of risk in distinguishing the two has long historic origins, which Ireland traces back to the moral abhorrence and legal prohibitions against money lending, or usury. Usury was distinguishable from other forms of money investment because the usurer parted with ownership of his property for a period of time and did not risk that property during the period it was lent. Ireland notes that the moral aversion to usury is clearly articulated in the classics where Aristotle railed against the unnatural arts of the usurer. According to Aristotle, money facilitated human happiness because it helped cohere society by creating a symbolic value which made exchange a simpler process than bartering commodities. Usury subverted the fairness of exchange because it gave something that was a symbol of value, a value in itself. So for example, while one coin might represent the value of a chicken, if a usurer lent that coin for one year, it might be worth the value of two chickens. While a chicken might reproduce itself in a year, it was unnatural that a symbol of value, money, might do the same. Money was barren, the chicken was not, therefore the activities of the usurer subverted the nature of money and in so doing subverted the harmony of society.

Ireland argues that usury was condemned in Ancient Greece and, filtering through Christian doctrines, condemned in Britain for many centuries. For the most part usury was defined as charging more than 5 per cent interest on

85 Ireland, P, 'The myth of shareholder ownership' (2001) MLR.

loans and the penalties were harsh. Although during the Elizabethan period this was increased to 10 per cent, which indicated the basic problem of usury laws for British capitalism. However, anti-usury laws were firmly entrenched in British society both through the Christian church and its accompanying anti-Semitism – they were part of the moral fabric of British society. On the other hand capitalism required capital and that meant extensive borrowing, but the limits on interest set by the usury laws made lending unattractive. According to Ireland, the judiciary responded to this conundrum in an interesting and innovative way. Throughout the eighteenth and part of the nineteenth centuries, British capitalism was rapidly developing. The usury laws retained a general application but certain financial institutions were explicitly exempted from its provisions.[86] Individuals, however, were not exempted and could not on the face of it invest in business for a good rate of return. The partnership was the dominant vehicle for business during this period and investment was crucial for business development. Thus, following the decision in *Grace v Smith*[87] the judiciary adopted a practice of construing investors in partnerships as partners, even though they were not declared as such and played no part in the business. By construing them thus investors could enjoy high rates of return without incurring the penalties of the usury laws. Investing capital was sufficient to qualify as 'business in common with a view of profit', the later statutory definition of a partnership, which retained enjoying the profit as *prima facie* evidence of partnership.[88] Partners, who merely invested in the partnership, were morally exempted from the usury law because unlike the usurer they were risking their capital. Partners owned and controlled the business, they were all equally entitled to the firm's profits, and personally responsible for the firm's debts.

Inevitably, the judiciary's approach to lending in a partnership resulted in cases when an investor/partner faced such a huge personal liability for the firm's debts that he sought to be reconstrued as a creditor, one to whom debts were owed.[89] This situation and the Hobson's choice it presented were witnessed in a 1787 letter where a partner in the Cornish Metal Company was advised thus: 'I told him the point of law was clear and that he was a partner in a trading company and liable to pay all deficiencies, and that if he was not a partner he was liable under the statute of usury to forfeit three times his capital.'[90]

---

86 Building societies, for example, were specifically exempted under the Benefit Building Societies Act 1836.
87 (1775).
88 Partnership Act 1890. Section 2(3)(d) provides that a loan paid in line with profit and accompanies with a loan agreement will not give rise to the assumption of partnership, but this was passed after the Usury law was repealed.
89 *Re Megavand* (1887).
90 DuBois, AB, *The English Business Company after the Bubble Act*, 1938, New York: The Commonwealth Fund, p 257.

Ireland maintains that when early companies evolved from the roots of partnership law, the same values which construed an investor in a partnership as a partner, likewise served to construe an investor in a company as an owner. In early companies formed under the Companies Act 1844, this was more understandable as the few hundred companies formed under this Act did not provide for members' limited liability and members retained some proprietary connection to the company assets. In other words they were not dissimilar to partnerships. However, as company law responded to the changing nature of the company and its shareholders, it developed as a distinct area of law with distinct principles. This, perhaps, should have been a time when the notion of shareholder as owner/partner was abandoned, but it was not. It was this failure to fully shake off the values of partnership law (which had allowed pure investors to be considered as partners to avoid the usury laws), which Ireland asserts is the reason why shareholders today retain their status as owners. Thus, notwithstanding the polar differences between a general partner and a modern shareholder, the latter continue to be regarded as the *raison d'être* of corporate governance procedures. Ireland's interesting theory provides a fascinating account of the role of law, but it doesn't entirely explain why the fiction of shareholder ownership has not been revised to reflect the economic reality of most shareholders. Why has it been so resilient? Or indeed, does it matter that it results from a historical misconception if the result of maintaining the fiction of shareholder ownership is in contractarian terms, economically efficient. The following piece provides some answers to this by drawing out the importance of ideology in retaining the shareholder as owner.

Daniel Greenwood

Greenwood opens his 2006 article on American corporate law by asserting that shareholders are not owners and are not deserving of the fruits of corporate ownership, namely corporate profits: 'Everybody knows that shareholders receive dividends because they are entitled to the residual returns of a public corporation. Everyone is wrong.'[91] He argues that no theory that justifies shareholders' claims stands up to scrutiny at either the level of law or of economics. Instead, Greenwood argues that shareholder primacy is largely the result of CEOs' successful pursuit of their self-interest, which is much better served through association with shareholders than by association with employees. An ideology which supports shareholder primacy, he maintains, is one that supports managerial goals. Thus he is diametrically opposed to both the agency costs analysis and Berle and Means' thesis. Furthermore, the victory of top managers and wealthy shareholders has been the elevation of shareholder interests at the level of scholarship, law and government policy.

91 Greenwood, DJ, 'The dividend problem', ExpressO Preprint Series, 2006, Paper 1185, p 1.

He argues that across the spectrum of corporate governance theories and corporate law scholarship there is a startling accordance with the notion that shareholders are entitled to the corporation's profit which at different levels of coherence is justified as the entitlement of ownership. Those who say explicitly that shareholders are the owners justify shareholders' entitlement to profits as a logical attribute of ownership while the nexus of contract theorists who theoretically consider the notion of ownership as irrelevant argue that the entitlement to profit arises from the bargain made by shareholders. For the latter, shareholders cannot really be owners because the corporation only exists as a fiction. However, they conversely maintain that the corporation (despite being a fiction) should be run in shareholders' interests – a conclusion which, Greenwood maintains, cannot be justified by the notion of market bargains.

Greenwood argues that whether one considers economic analysis or whether one considers black letter doctrine, there is no justification for shareholders' claims to 'the residual returns of a public corporation'.[92] Under the former analysis, he argues, shareholders who are 'purely fungible providers of a purely fungible commodity' have no intrinsic claim to profit in a capitalist system.[93] In a market, each player is rewarded according to the market value of his contribution. A purely financial contribution in a capital-saturated market should not provide such high returns as those enjoyed by shareholders. 'Accordingly, market-based analyses of the firm should conclude that shareholder returns result from a market distortion.'[94]

Furthermore, he argues, black letter legal doctrine makes clear that shareholders are not 'owners' or 'principals' and have no legal claim on corporate assets, even as 'trust beneficiaries'.[95] And, although the ownership and control debate is predicated on the corporation as property which is owned by shareholders, 'the legal reality is that shareholders have political voting rights in an organisation, not rights of ownership'.[96] He concludes that the claims of shareholders as owners result from ideology promulgated by CEOs to justify shifting profit away 'from employees to the CEO/shareholder alliance'. An alliance, he argues, which is much more pertinent to the self-interest of both groups than the purported alliance between managers and employees previously noted in corporate governance debates: 'those conflicts are dwarfed by the common interests of the two groups'.[97]

Greenwood argues that the origins of the problem lie in the historical reconceptualisation of the corporation which has erroneously allowed private

92 Ibid,
93 Ibid, p 2.
94 Ibid.
95 Ibid.
96 Ibid.
97 Ibid.

interests to determine social production. Early corporations were under-stood to deserve privileges and protection from the state because they were engaging in public works which the state would otherwise have undertaken. However, later, when corporations were engaged in private industry they were reconceptualised as private individuals, citizens that were understood to need protection *from* state interference. So, in 1886 the Supreme Court said that corporations could enjoy the same rights as natural people in respect of the right to due process under the equal protection clause of the Fourteenth Amendment.[98] Private owners, not the state, would prevail upon the governance of corporations.

The corporation was reconceptualised as something which promoted pri-vate interests and those private interests were articulated in law to be those of shareholders. And, in the famous pronouncement on whose interest the cor-poration should be run the court stated that 'a business corporation is organ-ised and carried on primarily for the profit of the shareholders. The powers of the directors are to be employed to that end. The discretion of directors . . . does not extend to a change in the end itself.'[99]

Greenwood maintains that the CEO and shareholder alliance is evidenced by the managerial decisions actually made, which, he argues, are far more pro-shareholder than the law requires. Greenwood asserts that notwithstand-ing the pronouncements in *Dodge*, both corporate law generally and the doc-trine of separate corporate personality specifically give the directors huge discretion in the performance of their duties. Dividend law, for example, does not give shareholders a right to the company's profits. In law, all surplus is owned by the corporation unless it declares a dividend.[100]

Furthermore, he argues the business judgment rule even after *Smith v Gorkom*[101] prevails and the courts only really interfere in clear incidences of self-dealing or insider dealing. Indeed, he argues, the courts have been traditionally lax in respect of directors' activities so that even in the highly unionised post-war period the courts didn't interfere if the corporation was run in the interests of 'unionised employees and middle-level management'.[102] Directors are largely left to their own devices and even when deciding their own level of remuneration, 'no American court has yet set any limit to the amount a public corporation's fully informed board may publicly pay its CEO. Even if the board had no evidence that services were valuable or priced correctly.'[103]

98 Ibid, *Santa Clara v Southern Pacific RR*, 118 US 394.
99 Ibid, *Utah Dodge v Ford Motor Co* (1919) 170 NW 669 Mich.
100 In most American states the RMBCA 6.40(7) – where declared dividends are treated as an unsecured debt in line with other unsecured debt – applies. In England ss 263 and 264 of the 1985 Act applied.
101 Discussed in Chapter 1.
102 Ibid, p 8.
103 Ibid, p 9, citing *Brehm v Eisner* (2000) 746 A2d 244 (Del).

Shareholder primacy is particularly emphasised by law and economics scholars. But as Greenwood points out, it is particularly difficult to justify shareholder returns in the nexus of contract theories. A shareholder's claim must be based on the negotiated agreement (albeit not as an ordinary contract) but shareholders possess neither a contractual claim on profits nor a claim based on market value. Shareholders, he concludes, are merely a 'factor of production' who have a product (capital) which firms buy with stock (or rent with debentures). In a negotiated agreement they would get the market price for this product but not a claim to corporate profits. Thus 'it is virtually inconceivable that shareholders would be able to win a share of the rents in a competitive market. Shareholder returns, therefore, must be the result of a non-competitive process that cannot be legitimated by market claims.'[104] Thus by taking on the contractarian claims that the corporate players receive that which they have bargained for, he demonstrates that such a bargain is so grossly favourable to shareholders that no market could sustain it and their claims could only be the result of other machinations.

ECONOMIC OWNERSHIP AND THE REFUTATION OF THE SEPARATION THESIS

There is a growing amount of scholarship which indicates that there has been no separation of control from ownership, and at least for major shareholders, control of the corporation has remained firmly held. Economic ownership within this perspective refers to the kind of ownership possessed by the wealthiest investors who continue to exercise control over the corporation and may be distinguished from other shareholders who are the separate, passive recipients of dividends of Berle and Means' thesis.

An article by Michel De Vroey in 1976 showed that the dispersed ownership patterns in England and America did not result in a loss of shareholder control over the corporation. Indeed, conversely, his study concluded that share dispersal among the many has tended to *enhance* rather than undermine their power resulting in the increasing tendency for economic power in the corporation to be held by an increasingly smaller elite.[105] According to De Vroey, the joint stock company generated a number of phenomena. These include the distinction and functional separation of ownership from the managing role, the dispersal of share ownership among the public and, lastly (the part that Berle and Means minimise), the concentration of power in the hands of large shareholders.

Utilising C Bettleheim's models of ownership, De Vroey demonstrates that

104 Ibid, p 9.
105 De Vroey, M, 'The separation of ownership and control in large corporations' (1975) Review of Radical Political Economics Vol 7, No 2, p 1.

within a corporation there are three forms of ownership: possession, economic ownership and legal ownership.[106] The first concept refers to the ability to put the company to work and therefore describes the 'ownership' of the manager. The second concept describes ownership that possesses the power to assign or dispose of the assets in question and the third concept describes the ownership rights of the title-holder of a share. The latter two concepts are connected because they both involve the right to vote, a right that is part of legal ownership and an entitlement to dividend. They differ, however, because in order to have effective voting power it is necessary for the shareholder to have a sufficient number of shares to pass the desired resolutions. Therefore, an economic owner will possess legal ownership but a legal owner may not be an economic owner.

The economic owner will hold the amount of stock required to control the outcome of major resolutions, including those that may dispose of directors. Thus although the manager has 'possession' of the corporation, managing the day-to-day running of the business, he does so with an eye on the interests of the economic owners. In De Vroey's view, the emergence of the non-owning manager merely represents a stage of capitalist development when the rich no longer justify their claim to profits by dint of their entrepreneurial or managerial input into production. Their claim is justified by ownership of shares alone while the managerial tasks are undertaken by skilled employees. The 'why have a dog and bark yourself?' approach.

Furthermore, and indeed crucially, as legal ownership spreads a large minority of shareholders require a smaller percentage of the total stock in order to exercise economic ownership because other stockholders are too dispersed to organise effectively.[107] So rather than share dispersal inhibiting the control of large investors it enhances control as they may now invest in and control many more companies. First because managers/employees perform the routine tasks of managing the business and second because the large investor may retain economic control with a smaller stake in any given business, liberating capital to be invested elsewhere. In De Vroey's words, 'the corporate system allows an increase of the power sphere of big capitalists who now control larger economic units with a reduced proportion of legal ownership'.[108] Or, in the somewhat archaic language of R Hilferding cited by De Vroey:

> With the extension of the shares system, capitalist ownership is increasingly transformed into a restricted ownership, giving nominal rights to the capitalist without allowing possibility to exert any real influence of

---

106 Bettleheim, C, *Economic Calculation and Forms of Property*, 1976, Routledge & Kegan Paul.
107 Op. cit., De Vroey.
108 Ibid, p 3.

the production process. The ownership of a great number of capitalists is constantly being restricted and their unlimited disposition of the productive process is suppressed. But, on the other hand, the circle of masters of production becomes more restricted. Capitalists form a society in the governing of which most of them have no voice. The effective disposition of the means of production is in the hands of the people who have only partially contributed to it.[109]

In this way De Vroey radically departs from the managerialist school of thought originating with Berle and Means by essentially denying their final stage of evolution, managerial control. Indeed, De Vroey's analysis (and Hilferding's, although he predated the managerialists) is posited on the continuation of minority control in large corporations. Hilferding's assertion that production is controlled by 'people who have only partially contributed to it' describes the ownership of Rockefeller and the Van Swering brothers noted by Berle and Means. Accordingly, his perspective provides a mechanism for re-interpreting statistics which, on the face of it, chime with the separation thesis. In a set of statistics derived from managerialists Smith and Franklin, and cited by De Vroey, there appears at first blush to be clear evidence of share dispersal and a corresponding diminishing of the wealthiest investors' ownership in and thus control over corporations. Here we can see that while in 1953, the wealthiest 0.5 per cent of society held 77 per cent of all stock, by 1969 this had dropped to 44 per cent of all stock. Likewise, in 1953 the wealthiest 1 per cent owned 86.3 per cent of all stock but by 1969 this had dropped to 50.8 per cent.[110] These decreases were steady in the intervening years. However, when one considers these statistics in the context of a massive increase in the number of shares and shareholders the statistics paint a different picture. In De Vroey's words, 'If the overall dispersion increases, which seems to be the case (the New York Stock Exchange figures show an increase of nearly 500 per cent in the number of shareholders between 1952 and 1970) the limit of economic ownership in terms of percentage of total stock has consequently lowered.'[111] Furthermore he notes that it is in the interests of large investors to keep 'participation in ownership close to this limit so as to function using other people's funds and to be able to take part more freely in new ventures'.[112]

This perspective may aid a new interpretation of comparative statistics on share dispersal. For example, a study which analysed the 20 largest

109 Hilferding, R, *Le Capital Financier*, 1970, Paris: Editions de Minuit, p 33, quoted by De Vroey, p 3.
110 Op. cit., De Vroey, p 5.
111 Ibid.
112 Ibid.

companies in each country concluded that English and American companies have a high incidence of dispersed ownership while in contrast continental Europe has more closely held firms.[113] Here, the authors set the point at which a firm could be described as *diffusely owned* as when there is no one owner who owns more than 20 per cent of the stock. Accordingly all such companies in England could be described as diffusely owned as were 80 per cent of companies in America. In contrast, in Belgium and Austria the figure was 5 per cent, in Italy 20 per cent, in Norway and Sweden 25 per cent, in the Netherlands 30 per cent, in Germany 50 per cent and in France 60 per cent.[114]

However, this high level of dispersal in English and American companies does not necessarily denote a low level of shareholder control. As De Vroey maintains, shareholder control may be exercised through economic owner-ship, made possible by the high level of dispersal of all shares not held by an economic owner. In this way, under 20 per cent of the shares may be more than enough to exercise economic control where shares are widely dispersed. This chimes with Roe's argument that in Europe large, often family, share-holdings maintain a majority stake in the business because this is the only mechanism by which they may maintain control. It would be curious to imagine that the wealthy in England and America are not likewise con-cerned to maintain control, preferring instead to leave their wealth to chance. More likely is that large investors in Anglo-American corporations have proportionally smaller stakes in the business than their European counter-parts because share dispersal allows them to maintain control through a smaller stake. This allows them to diversify and to extend their influence in a way that is not available to European investors. This possibly is borne out by other work on control patterns in Anglo-American corporations. For example, DL McConaughty states that while there has been a tendency for share dispersal in over 20 per cent of America's largest corporations, the founding family, not simply an outside economic owner, 'retains significant influence'.[115] Furthermore, research from Anderson, Mansi and Reeb showed that 20 per cent of large American publicly traded firms have families with shareholdings of 20 per cent or more.[116] In 1998, 34 per cent of Standard and Poor's 500 Corporations had founder family equity of

113 Op. cit., La Porta.
114 Ibid, figures. These figures may be misleading in their underestimation of closely held busi-nesses in Europe. For example, these figures suggest a large percentage of widely held companies in France whereas that figure would drop to 30 per cent were the cut-off point to be set at 10 per cent. Furthermore, Italy has many small family-owned firms and few public companies and these statistics only look at public companies.
115 McConaughty, DL, *et al*, 'Founding family controlled firms: efficiency and value' (1998) 7 Rev of Financial Economics 1, p 8.
116 'Founding family ownership and the agency cost of debts' (2003) J Fin Econ, p 269.

18 per cent.[117] Even in the absence of a family holding shareholders seem to operate as a group when their interests are threatened. In 1993, the shareholders of IBM, Westinghouse and Kodak emerged from their supposed passivity to dismiss their poorly performing directors. And in England, 'performance pay became the rallying call for British investors'.[118]

There is also a significant body of literature which charts the rise of institutional shareholders and which indicates that dispersed share ownership has become reunited under the umbrella of such institutions which can effectively represent shareholders' interests. In America by 1994, institutions owned 40 per cent of all shares, although as *The Economist* noted, as they came late to the market they were obliged to buy shares in small and medium-sized companies and adopted a 'hands off' strategy.[119] In contrast institutional shareholding in Britain has a much longer tradition so that some institutions have a very significant shareholding in the business of around 5 per cent.[120] Additionally, as a group, institutional shareholders make up the vast majority of shareholders in Britain. Statistics cited by Ronald Gilson show that in 2004, 81 per cent of shares were held by institutional investors while only 8 per cent were owned by families.[121] Other statistics are lower, showing a steady rise from 29 per cent in 1963 to a high in 1998 of 70 per cent, dropping to 48 per cent by 2004.[122] Notwithstanding this difference, institutional shareholders, as a whole, retain a significant proportion of company shares.

However, the rise of the institutional shareholder is only really significant as a vehicle to promote shareholders' interests if they act in unity, and the evidence on this is mixed. Lee Roach argues that despite the factors which would make institutional investors well suited for interventionist activities (including the fact most are based in the city, they operate in a lenient legal environment, and it is relatively cheap to communicate through their various trade associations), institutional investors have taken a relatively passive approach to shareholding. This he attributes to a number of factors, or barriers to acting as a coalition. First the costs of acting as a coalition are high, although communication is cheap, including legal expenses and the cost of information. The 'free rider' problem, where other shareholders benefit from the activity and expenditure of the involved shareholder, is cited as a reason for institutional investors' passivity. Furthermore, when undertaking action against the company's management, institutional investors need to know the position of their portfolio companies. Loach argues that the monitoring of

117 Ibid.
118 *The Economist*, Survey, 'Watching the boss', 29 January 1994.
119 Ibid, p 6.
120 Ibid.
121 Op. cit., Gilson.
122 Roach, L, 'CEOs, chairmen and fat cats: the institutions are watching you' (2006) Company Lawyer 27, p 299.

these companies is woefully poor: 'even the largest investment companies tend to have small monitoring staffs'.[123] And such staff as there are are poorly trained and ill prepared to take on the required task of active monitoring despite their huge and international portfolios. Conflicts of interests both legal and in terms of reputation are another barrier to coalitions. Loach posits the example of a fund manager who will have connections with banking firms who in turn will have connections to many companies who may be affiliated to the company which the fund manager wishes to confront. He may therefore decline to do so as 'fund managers who develop an anti-manager reputation will lose business and find it harder to attract new clients'.[124]

Loach identifies the third barrier to activism as being the desire of institutional investors for 'soft information', that is information which the managers supply to them rather than to the general public, and presumably doesn't constitute insider dealing. Loach maintains that 'if an institution is in possession of truly material non-public information, then it can make abnormal returns even in an efficient market.'[125] The fourth barrier Loach terms 'behind the scenes activism', and refers to the exchange which takes place between managers and institutional investors. If the latter made public their concerns it may trigger a rush to sell shares and a corresponding loss to share value, so to avoid this, managers will attend to the grievances of their institutional investors behind the scenes. This latter barrier does, of course, denote institutional investor activism and perhaps does demonstrate a reconnection of ownership to control; however, the other three barriers do not and instead indicate clear advantages to institutional investors in remaining passive. Indeed, Loach notes that the more recent attempts at institutional investor activity which have centred on high executive remuneration have resulted in unexpected and negative outcomes. For example, when the institutional investors of GlaxoSmithKline discovered that its CEO Jean-Paul Garnier was about to be awarded an £11 m remuneration package, they successfully campaigned to persuade shareholders to reject the proposal. However, Loach maintains that the non-institutional investors were spurred on by their success with Garnier to set their sights on the executives of Aviva, Standard Life and Prudential, the institutional investors themselves!

Thus it can be seen that while institutional investors hold a large proportion of British shares, they are traditionally inactive or at least publicly inactive. The reasons for this are partly staffing policies which are not geared up for high-level monitoring. However, the overwhelming evidence suggests that their self-interest is better served by operating privately, making their views known to the executive and benefiting from non-public information. A

123 Roach, L, 'CEOs, chairmen and fat cats: the institutions are watching you' (2006) Company Lawyer 27, p 299.
124 Ibid, p 300.
125 Ibid.

flexible understanding between institutional investors and managers is much more mutually advantageous than a long-drawn-out and public battle over pay, the amounts of which are tiny when compared with company profits. In these ways institutional investors do not differ from economic owners and further evidence the argument that no separation between ownership and control exists outside that experienced by the small investor.

THE THIRD WAY, COMPANY REFORM AND 'ENLIGHTENED SHAREHOLDER VALUE'

In this section it will be argued that the politics of New Labour have greatly affected the orientation of contemporary corporate governance perspectives. It will be argued that while the politics of New Labour is primarily committed to a market economy, it shies from the rhetoric of the free market, preferring instead the rhetoric of *inclusion*. The political perspective of New Labour is best demonstrated by outlining the thoughts of the authors of the three influential books on the subject. These are, in descending importance, Anthony Gidden's *The Third Way*,[126] Will Hutton's *The State We're In*[127] and Charles Leadbetter's *Living On Thin Air*.[128]

The 'third way' politics of New Labour may be understood as the outcome of a reaction against old-style socialism (a broad umbrella containing the 'far left' and the Labour Party of the 1970s) and the neo-liberal politics of Thatcherism. The generally acknowledged architect of the political notion of 'the third way' is Anthony Giddens in his influential book of the same name. Here he described third way politics as an attempt to connect the social welfare principles of socialism with a strong national market operating in a global context. Giddens constructed this model through a critique of socialism and neo-liberalism and concluded that while both schools of thought were flawed, modern society and the consciousness of the populace generally remained entrenched in certain elements of both. For example, he argued, the individualism of the 1980s had left a residual aversion to many of the activities of the welfare state. During this decade, in particular, the welfare state had been criticised by the right for being undemocratic and for suppressing personal liberty, criticisms that had a powerful appeal because they were, in part, true. Giddens himself described the welfare state as being 'bureaucratic, alienating and inefficient'.[129]

However, he notes, these tenacious notions of individualism have not led to a corresponding aversion to the making of welfare claims. Neither has it

126 1998, Polity Press.
127 1996, London: Jonathan Cape.
128 1999, Viking Press.
129 Op. cit., Giddens, p 113.

affected the population's moral affinity to the 'socialist' principle of providing for the vulnerable. At first blush, he argued it might appear that these two perspectives, individualism and socialism, were incompatible. However, third way politics could encapsulate both perspectives and these two seemingly irreconcilable positions could cohabit in a world where increased individual liberty was coupled with increased individual responsibility. 'Having abandoned collectivism, third way politics looks for a new relationship between the individual and the community, a redefinition of rights and obligations.'[130]

Expanding individualism would mean expanding individual obligations. Thus, he argued, a consciousness must be nurtured which allowed for a responsible, mature individualism. So, in respect of the welfare state, 'third way politics sees these problems not as a signal to dismantle the welfare state, but as part of the reason to reconstruct it'.[131]

Third way politics identified the role of the state, not in the minimalist style of the neo-liberal's Hayekian vision, nor in the intervention vision of the socialists. Instead, the role of the state was to promote the market while maintaining a more generalised prosperity through some limited government intervention in its activities:

> Classical social democracy thought of wealth creation as almost incidental to its basic concerns with economic security and redistribution. The neoliberals placed competition and the generating of wealth much more to the forefront. Third way politics also gives very strong emphasis to these qualities, which have an urgent importance given the nature of the global market place. They will not be developed, however, if individuals are abandoned to sink or swim in an economic whirlpool. Government has an essential role to play in investing in the human resources and infrastructure needed to develop an entrepreneurial culture.[132]

Third way politics deployed a 'social investment state', which aimed to create a 'new mixed economy' that would comprise a 'synergy between public and private sectors, utilising the dynamism of markets but with the public interest in mind'.[133]

In third way politics, the balanced combination of public and private sectors was important for a number of reasons. An overly dominant market tended to perpetuate inequality, as evidenced by the great differentials in meritocratic societies such as the USA, the UK and New Zealand. However, an overly public, welfare economy tended to create a 'dependency culture'. In third way politics, the key to moving toward greater equality in a modern

130 Ibid, p 64.
131 Ibid, p 113.
132 Ibid, p 99.
133 Ibid, p 100.

society was the elimination of *social exclusion*. Third way politics viewed 'equality as inclusion and inequality as exclusion'.[134]

> Inclusion refers in its broadest sense to citizenship, to the civil and politi-
> cal rights and obligations that all members of a society should have, not
> just formally, but as a reality of their lives. It also refers to opportunities
> and to involvement in public space. In a society where work remains
> central to self-esteem and standard of living, access to work is one main
> context of opportunity. Education is another, and would be so even if it
> weren't so important for the employment possibilities to which it is
> relevant.[135]

In order to counteract the many forms of social exclusion which perpetuated inequality, third way politics would construct an 'inclusive society', utilising the ingredients of 'equality as inclusion, limited meritocracy, renewal of pub-lic space (civic liberalism) beyond the work society, positive welfare and a social investment state'.[136] The trend towards a socially excluding society could be reversed through a 'civic liberalism' which encouraged a political and economic commitment from the richer elements of society to the poorer. Furthermore, a private solution could be found to public welfare programmes if the middle classes possessed a self-interest in maintaining the welfare state. This self-interest could be satisfied by improving the services offered by the welfare state, elevating welfare from a 'safety net' for the poor into a series of high-quality services, which all classes could enjoy. Indeed, he argued, 'where "welfare" assumes only a negative connotation and it is targeted largely at the poor, as has tended to happen in the US, the results are divisive'.[137]

Thus, third way politics seeks to encourage the market economy, while ensuring that its tendency towards social division is tempered by some limited state intervention to encourage socially responsible and community-sensitive commerce. In this way, third way politics accommodates aspirations for indi-vidual freedom by making that freedom dependent on a commitment to certain social obligations. In the context of the welfare state, the freedom of individuals to enjoy its benefits should be tempered by their obligation to pay for its continual improvement, and to limit personal claims to state benefits, education and healthcare by taking a more responsible attitude to work, childcare and healthy living. In the context of artificial legal individuals, such as the company, the individual freedom to operate in the market must be tempered with social obligations to communities and the environment.

134 Ibid, p 102.
135 Ibid, p 103.
136 Ibid, p 105.
137 Ibid, p 108.

The notion of the 'socially responsible business' was also discussed at length by another writer with the ear of New Labour, Will Hutton, former editor of *The Observer* newspaper. His version of third way politics was discussed under the concept of 'stakeholder capitalism' in his briefly important book, *The State We're In*.[138] In this treatise he argued for the encouragement of the socially responsible corporation in which the interests of all 'stakeholders' were negotiated. These 'stakeholders' would include consumers, employees, creditors and local communities, as well as the well-established interests of shareholders. This approach would encourage a commitment from all those concerned with the corporation and would give them a reason to pursue the prosperity of the business, an outcome clearly popular with business owners. Hutton's more radical message, however, was that business should not be run purely for the purpose of creating profit. The interest of shareholders' dividends was only one of the interests that business should pursue. Shareholders were just one among many types of stakeholder and should take their place among a number of other priorities.

Hutton's socially responsive business held clear socialist undertones, yet in spite of this, 'stakeholder capitalism' remained a buzz phrase of New Labour for many years, although the policies were not pursued. In contrast, third way notions have retained their popularity with the policies of New Labour coupled with the occasional ideological garnish such as that presented by Charles Leadbeater in his book, *Living on Thin Air: The New Economy*.[139]

Like Giddens, Leadbetter argued that the old class system had disappeared and, with it, traditional methods of retaining social order. However, unlike Giddens, Leadbetter attempts to understand this in terms of the material basis of social order. The economy, he argued, has shifted from industrial production to a 'knowledge-based economy', but has done so while attempting to retain the institutions of social order that maintained and described the older economy. So, despite moving into a knowledge-based economy with all its potential democratic and safe connotations, individuals were experiencing their life as fraught with increasing anxiety. However, he argued, this sense of anxiety and powerlessness was not a personal failing but an institutional failing. While the economy has undergone huge changes, the institutions that contained and sustained the economy had not. Indeed, the institutions that exist today were, in all their major characteristics, institutions designed to meet the needs of industrial Victorian England.

The nineteenth century was revolutionary because the Victorians matched their scientific and technological innovations with radical institutional innovations: the extension of democracy, the creation of local govern-

138 Op. cit., Hutton.
139 Op. cit., Leadbeater.

ment, the birth of modern savings and insurance schemes, the development of a professional civil service, the rise of trade unions and the emergence of the research based university. We live with the institutions the nineteenth century handed down to us. Our highly uneven capacity for innovation is the fundamental source of our unease. We are scientific and technological revolutionaries, but political and institutional conservatives.[140]

The 'new economy', which to a greater extent is viewed as developing naturally and organically, required new institutions to be artificially created through government policy. Thus, the market itself demands third way politics in order that it may continue to prosper. New Labour's attempt to reorganise welfare, work and social order is not so much autonomous political policy as a sensitive response to the requirements of the new 'knowledge-based economy'. Little wonder then that Tony Blair is cited on the back cover as saying: 'Charles Leadbetter is an extraordinarily interesting thinker. His book raises critical questions for Britain's future. I know it will be widely read and debated.'[141]

The stated challenge of the New Labour Government was to reconstruct a social order appropriate to the demands of a new economy. The question was, would it reflect Gidden's third way or Hutton's stakeholding? These two possible directions for company law reform were assessed in some detail in the CLR's consultation document in 1999.[142] The third way approach was reflected under the heading of 'enlightened shareholder value' while the stakeholder approach was reflected under the heading 'pluralist approaches'.

Enlightened shareholder value

The enlightened shareholder value approach advocates the continuation of a company law which promotes the interests of shareholders by acknowledging that this may be best achieved by taking account of the interests of others connected with the company.

Exclusive focus on the short-term financial bottom line, in the erroneous belief that this equates to shareholder value, will often be incompatible with the cultivation of co-operative relationships, which are likely to involve short-term costs but to bring greater benefits in the longer term.

140 Ibid, preface.
141 Ibid, cover page.
142 'Modern company law for a competitive economy: the strategic framework', consultation document, February 1999.

> Thus the law as currently expressed and understood fails to deliver the necessary inclusive approach.[143]

The CLR noted that the practical advantage of adopting the enlightened shareholder value approach is that it would not involve a fundamental change in the orientation of company law which is concerned to maximise shareholder wealth. It would, however, involve a little modification. The CLR maintained that the law as it was expressed tended to 'lead to an undue focus on the short term and the narrow interest of members at the expense of what is in the broader and longer term sense of the enterprise'.[144] This, the CLR suggested, could be addressed by reformulating directors' duties to give effect to the enlightened shareholder value approach. The current law, with its emphasis on a director acting in the interests of members as a whole including future members and its restraints on a director improperly using his power, enabled directors to take account of broader enlightened shareholder value concerns. Instead, however, directors tended to pursue short-term narrow ends and the law tended to support this. The CLR stated that 'it is in our view clear, as a matter of policy, that in many circumstances directors should adopt the broader and longer term (inclusive) view of their role.'[145] The reason they did, they proposed, was because of a lack of knowledge and understanding of the law. The aim of law reform, from this perspective, would be to clarify the position in law, creating clear signposts for directors which would enable them to steer the company in the interests of wider concerns. Importantly, this approach would not entail a radical reform of the law. Instead it would express the law in such a way as to allow directors to take an enlightened shareholder value approach.

However enlightened shareholder value is a third way policy and as such it attempts to construe the market's usual pursuit of profit as something that is first desirable and second something which is best achieved by considering the interests of all. A seemingly inclusive approach rather than an exclusive approach, it locates the achievement of this inclusive approach in the polishing up of the status quo and relies more upon wishful thinking than rigorous analysis. Its assumption that the failures arise because people need more advice, more education, more codes of practice in order to do the right thing is typical of contemporary policy making. For as the CLR notes, the law already exists to enable an enlightened shareholder value approach and yet directors don't take his route. Is it because of ignorance? Yes, say enlightened shareholder value advocates. Or is it that the market measures success by profitability which is achieved by specifically ignoring the interests of other

143 Ibid, p 37.
144 Ibid, p 39.
145 Ibid, p 40.

players such as employees and suppliers? A company achieves profitability if the capital it spends on production is less than it gains on the sale of its products. Thus, arguably, greater profit is achieved by reducing its wage and supply costs.

The pluralist approach

The pluralist approach as characterised by the CLR would shift the orientation of directors' duties away from shareholders only, to include shareholders and all other persons concerned with the company including employees, suppliers, creditors, consumers and the wider public (other stakeholders). It promotes this radical approach because:

> the present law in making shareholders' interests ultimately overriding, may create, or reinforce, an environment in which relationships are difficult to sustain. This increases the level of inefficient risk between those managing companies and employees, suppliers and others, on whom the company depends for factors of production and who depend in turn on the company for a secure environment within which to make the commitments necessary to provide them.[146]

In order to create this conducive environment all the many parts of the Companies Act that give shareholders control would have to be replaced with provisions which balanced these powers between all stakeholders. This radical reformulation of company law and the way in which it would affect business culture, argued the CLR, would be unpopular. Furthermore, directors would be unclear as to whom they were accountable and this would, according to the CLR, 'dangerously distract management into a political balancing style at the expense of economic growth and international competitiveness'.[147]

As the pluralist's stakeholding premise assumes a convergence of self-interest between all stakeholders which should be reflected in governance structures such as board representation, the CLR presented a number of objections to the assertion that this approach would be better for profitability. These are well founded. As the empirical evidence presented by Roe illustrates, systems which enhance employee/stakeholder interests are not as profitable as those that promote shareholder interests. Stakeholding, as presented by the CLR, although in contrast to Hutton's approach, presents a new model of the socialised corporation which is different from the post-war model discussed earlier in that it is promoted as something that will increase

146 Ibid, p 42.
147 Ibid, p 44.

profitability. It promotes a social institution as something which is in fact a superior market institution. This is not only wrong, it misses the point of the social corporation. It was never supposed that a social approach to corporate governance would enhance shareholder value, quite the opposite. It was supposed that it would create a fairer and more socialised society which provided safe and well-paid positions for employees, good inexpensive products for consumers and would address environmental and community issues. The price for these social goods was profitability and it was a price worth paying. This is more in line with Hutton's stakeholding notion and one which would have seriously radicalised both the law and society as a whole.

However, in contemporary society the notion that a company should operate non-profit goals is seen as eccentric at best. And while a bald neo-liberal approach is considered too stark, too individualistic, too greedy, the aims of neo-liberalism, the enhancement of private ownership are unquestioned. It is a matter of style. Profit-maximise, but call it inclusion. This 'have your cake and eat it' approach of both the enlightened shareholder value and pluralist approach is more palatable in the former hue because it does not require the structural changes and loss of profit-making potential which the pluralist threatens. And so the CLR later abandoned stakeholding's pluralism and its possible connotations of the social corporations in favour of enlightened shareholder value. The subsequent legalisation closely reflects this.

The Companies Act 2006 in respect of governance issues is best comprehended as an ideological creature of its time. It is a point in the process of corporate governance discussions. In its preferment of the free market with the rhetoric of socialism, it concurs with the abandonment of non-profit-orientated goals but reconstructs the social corporation. Unlike Dodd's social corporation it does so in words only, requiring directors to only consider the interests of other stakeholders and only when in honest pursuit of the promotion of the success of the company for the benefit of its members. The dominant ideology in legal scholarship contractarianism gave enlightened shareholder value some intellectual credibility. Furthermore, it enabled the reform process to reformulate the power relations within the company as bargains between company players, borrowing the assumptions of equality and fairness of contractual agreements. But companies are the structures within which the wealth of society is organised and enlightened shareholder value organises this wealth for the benefit of shareholders – and that isn't equal or fair.

Chapter 5

Corporate governance II: directors' fiduciary duties

Prior to the Joint Stock Companies Act 1844,[1] the penalties of the Bubble Act would be visited upon businesses which traded freely transferable shares without the permission of a royal charter. Otherwise, business either engaged in the arduous task of gaining incorporation through a private Act of Parliament or operated as an unincorporated association such as a partnership or as a Deed of Settlement company. In statutory companies, a director's duties were those set out in the incorporating Act. In partnerships, all partners were entitled to manage and owed a duty of utmost trust to the other partners who were all agents for each other and responsible for all the partnership's activities and debts. In Deed of Settlement companies those who managed the business were trustees who held the title to the company for the beneficiaries, the shareholders. As trustees, they owed a fiduciary duty to the beneficiaries to act with absolute honesty entirely eschewing self-interest in their actions and intentions. Correspondingly, shareholders as beneficial owners had both an interest in the company's assets and (unless there was an agreement in the deed to the contrary) undertook unlimited liability for the company's debts.

The emergence of the company as a self-owning entity distinct from the shareholders had a corresponding effect on the nature of directors' fiduciary duties. Duties shifted from being owed to the shareholders to being owed to a company now emptied of people. Correspondingly, legislation such as the Limited Liability Act 1855 divorced shareholders from financial responsibility for the company's financial arrangements. Shareholders' ownership in the company became ownership of the newly reconceptualised share, and in ownership of this property, shareholders were protected through statutory limited liability and through voting rights in the company. The doctrine of separate corporate personality meant that the shareholder did not own the assets of the company: 'neither a shareholder nor a simple creditor of a company has any insurable interest in any particular asset of the

1 7 & 8 Vict c 110 & 111.

company'.[2] What they did own was title to revenue and other residual rights of ownership such as voting rights. Thus a shareholder remained the owner, by dint of owning a *function* of the company – the fruit of its activity, that of making profits.

With shareholders' interests and ownership more clearly delineated, describing the boundaries of the company should have been, in principle, much simpler. The company was everything that the shareholder did not own. It was assets, human and tangible, contracts, business associations and goodwill. In short it was the productive assets of the company divorced, in law, from human ownership. Taken as a whole, companies now represented the productive assets of society as a whole.

In respect of directors' fiduciary duties, company law has wrestled with the challenges presented by the doctrine of separate corporate personality because, as a direct result of this doctrine, the question arose – what is the company? In order for a director to fulfil his duty to the company, the law must have an answer to this question. The answers have varied. In some cases the company is construed as its assets, but in others it is construed as the *function* of the assets, that of making profits. When the company first emerged as a separate legal being the tendency of the judiciary was to view the company as a function of its assets. In this period directors' duties reflected both the continuity of trustee principles and a newer pro-investor approach. By construing the company as being its function, shareholders' interests were more directly and immediately promoted. For example, the old law on dividends emphasised the company as being a dividend-creating organisation whose interests were protected when its directors pursued dividend-creating policies. As we shall see, this approach often subordinated to the protection of company assets and thus the interests of a company creditor. Furthermore, it soon became clear that when this orientation was pursued too rigorously, the company's assets and ultimately its potential to make profits were put at risk.

Later, this early emphasis on the company as function was superseded by a judicial understanding of the company as being its productive assets. In this period the emphasis was on a director's duty to act in the manner of a trustee of the company's assets, although the nature of a company's assets could be construed quite widely including goodwill and business opportunities as well as the more obvious tangible assets. This new emphasis on the company's

---

2 The view taken of shareholders' ownership rights in *Macaura v Northern Assurance Co Ltd* [1925] AC 619. The process of separating company property from shareholder property was a process that began with large companies. By the end of the century this conception was regarded as correct regardless of the size of the company.

assets also brought creditors into the equation. Finally, from around the 1980s, the ideological emphasis has been upon the company as a competitive contractual being in the same way as a director may be. This contrasts with the law's previous strict approach to a director profiting from his fiduciary position. In this climate a director's duty to his company will only be breached when he benefits from something which the company could have enjoyed, even if the benefit is something he himself would not have enjoyed had he not been a director.

In this, English law is reflecting the long-established position of American corporate law where a director may obtain a benefit in the course of his employment as long as the company wasn't a real competitor. This period is interesting because while the larger most significant companies have a dispersed and passive membership whose separateness is evident both materially and legally, the reigning ideology is neo-liberal contractarianism which constructs and relies upon an active capital investor. The interplay between these three factors results in the company being construed as a nexus of contracts in which the competing interests of the contractees are pursued and encapsulated. The company as competitor becomes, ideologically, the company as a nexus of competition within a competitive market, and the facility for a director to pursue corporate opportunities is understood in terms of agency costs.

These three periods will be discussed under the following headings:

- the company as defined by its function;
- the company as defined by its assets; and
- the company defined as competitor or a nexus of competition.

Within these periods, a director's fiduciary duty to act in good faith and the duty not to profit personally from a fiduciary position will be considered. In discussing the contemporary position under the 2006 Act, the duty not to abuse given powers, the duty of confidentiality and the duty of care will also be discussed. The 2006 Act attempts to encapsulate a director's duty within the contractarian framework and to remove linguistic references to the trustee principles established over many decades of case law. Whether the courts will eschew such a large body of law is unlikely, although in interpreting the statutory provisions some modifications are likely.

In setting out these three periods, it must be appreciated that not every case precisely conforms to the normative values of its time. The interplay of the three formative factors of company law: law; ideology and economy will often produce judgments which seem slightly out of place. Furthermore, no period abruptly stops, but instead seeps into the next, gradually losing influence and relevance.

DIRECTORS' DUTIES TO THE COMPANY AS FUNCTION (1850–1910)

The functional is the dominant perspective of the period of early modern company law up to the first decade of the twentieth century. During this time there was a great deal of law which suggested that a director's fiduciary duty was owed solely to the function or purpose of a company: that of making profits. Invariably, the short-term interest of the shareholders, in the form of dividends, was seen to be of greater importance than the protection of company assets, which provided comfort to creditors. And although the general principle that the company is represented by the interests of shareholders persists (and indeed has become enhanced by the recent company law reform), this period differs in that its interpretation of that interest is both exclusive and pertains specifically to the short-term interest in dividends.[3]

During this period a director would not be in breach of his duty to the company if he diminished company assets in order to pay dividends. That is not to say that there was a total absence of restrictions in respect of the payment of dividends. Clause 73 of Table A stated that 'no dividend shall be payable except out of profits arising from the business of the company'.[4] However, in court this restriction was modified by the judiciary's liberal interpretation of profit. In an 1880 case, Lord Jessel concluded that when assessing the legality of dividends, the court need not consider capital losses from previous years.[5] In this case a tramway company had failed to maintain company assets, or to set aside a maintenance fund, notwithstanding that the articles stated that the directors should 'before recommending a dividend, set aside out of the profits of the company . . . such sums as they think proper as a reserve fund for maintenance, repairs, depreciation, and renewals'.[6] As a result of their failure to do so, an injunction was granted against the company's declaration of a dividend and in response, an action to dissolve the injunction was successfully brought to court by a preference shareholder. The court held that the issue was not whether the value of the assets had diminished, or indeed whether the failure to observe the articles should be rectified, but whether or not there were sufficient profits made *that year* to pay dividends. If there were sufficient, then a dividend could be paid without consideration of the assets.

The courts did make some attempts to protect the assets of the company.

---

3 The 'obligation to act bona fide in the interests of the company has been defined as an obligation to act in the interests of the shareholders.' *Farrar's Company Law*, 4th edn, p 381.

4 Companies Acts 1862 Table A. Article 74 also stated that directors may consider making appropriate repairs to company assets before declaring a dividend but were under no obligation to do so.

5 *Dent v London Tramways Company* (1880) 16 Ch D 344.

6 Ibid, p 348.

In *Trevor v Whitworth*,[7] the court established the capital maintenance rule that a company could not buy back its own shares. However, in stark contrast to this approach a case immediately preceding *Trevor* had the Court of Appeal stating that 'it is entirely with the shareholders to decide whether the excess shall be divided among them or set apart as a reserve fund for replacing assets, and the court has no power to intervene with their decision however foolish or imprudent it may be'.[8]

Even in the context of the *Trevor* case, Lord Watson commented that 'paid up capital may be diminished or lost in the course of trading, that is a result which no legislation can prevent'.[9] There was no requirement to replace assets lost in trading before a dividend was declared. The Companies Act had made only one restriction in respect of the declaration of dividends, that no dividend could be paid except out of profits. In *Flitcroft's* case,[10] dividends which were paid on false accounts put forward by the directors which made debts look like assets were held to be personally repayable by the directors responsible notwithstanding that they had not personally benefited from the dividends. They were held to be trustees of the money of the company and if they, in breach of their duty, caused those moneys to be taken from the company, they were required like trustees to replace those moneys.

However, the protection of assets that might diminish in value as a result of pursuing profits for dividends was not an objective of the Companies Acts. So, in *Lee v Neuchatel Asphalte Co*[11] it was held that 'there was nothing in the Companies Acts . . . to impose on the company any obligation to set apart a sinking fund to meet the depreciation in the value of a wasting product'. Furthermore, *Lee* emphasised that the power to restore wasting assets lay not with the creditors, who relied on the assets as security, but with the shareholders, whose sole economic interest lay in dividends. The problems for creditors were further exacerbated by the court's failure to find an adequate definition of profit, making the funds designated available for the payment of dividends ultimately a movable feast.[12]

Thus in this context a director's fiduciary duty was not breached by diminishing company assets nor by undermining creditors' interests. The duty to the company was not to protect tangible property but to protect the short-term interests of shareholdings. It was a narrower duty even than making the company profitable, which potentially benefits all persons connected to the

---

7 (1887) 12 App Cas 409.
8 *Lee v Neuchatel Asphalte Co* (1889) 41 Ch D 1, p 10.
9 *Trevor v Whitworth* (1887) 12 App Cas 409.
10 (1882) 21 Ch D 519.
11 *Lee v Neuchatel Asphalte*, p 1.
12 Weiner, J, 'The theory of Anglo-American dividend law: the English cases' (1918) Columbia L Rev.

company. It was a duty which was fulfilled by the declaration of profits at any long-term cost.

Self-dealing

Throughout, a key area for the law relating to directors' duties is how they should be regulated when there is an actual or potential conflict between the interests of the company the director is supposed to serve and his own personal interests. The strict rules on 'self-dealing', as this situation is called, reflects the continuation of the trustee principles into the modern company. The strict principles of trusteeship were transported into a director's duties there to remain, subject to certain modifications (discussed below), until the 2006 Act. The strict application of these principles was famously articulated by Lord Cranworth *in Aberdeen Railway Company v Blaikie Brothers*.[13] The House of Lords struck down a contract under which the company had agreed to buy an order of chairs from a firm in which one of the directors of the company was a partner. By being represented on both sides of the bargain, the director had put himself in a position entirely inimitable to his duty to the company.

> A corporate body can only act through agents, and it is of course the duty of those agents so to act as best to promote the interests of the corporation whose affairs they are conducting. Such agents have duties to discharge of a fiduciary nature toward their principal. And it is a rule of universal application, that no-one, having such duties to discharge, shall be allowed to enter into engagements in which he has, or can have, a personal interest conflicting, or which may possibly conflict, with the interests of those whom he is bound to protect. So strictly is this principle adhered to, that no question is allowed to be raised as to the fairness or unfairness of a contract so entered into.

Directors were fiduciaries who owed a duty of complete loyalty to the company, the principal. That duty would only be fulfilled if the director avoided all situations where he had a personal interest that might possibly conflict with that of the company. Failure to do so would be a breach of duty which would allow the company to avoid the contract or make the director accountable to the company for any personal gains. Furthermore, the fairness or otherwise of the contract entered into was an irrelevant consideration and might not be raised. As we shall see, subsequent provisions in Table A and in legislation have permitted a director to enter into a transaction which entails such a conflict, so long as he makes an appropriate declaration of interest

---

13 (1854) 1 Macq 461.

(although *Aberdeen* remained the default position). Furthermore, following the 2006 Act, the fairness of the transaction is one of the criteria which the court will consider when assessing whether a director has breached his statutory duty. But at this earlier point, the law's position on conflict of interests was immutable and unflinching. Directors were performing a public function, not a negotiable contract, and the company was a public body, intrinsically connected to society.

DIRECTORS' DUTIES TO THE COMPANY AS ASSETS (1910–1980)

While shareholders became increasingly detached from any personal involvement in the company, the company's directors remained both conceptually and practically bound to the management of its working assets. In this model of the company, the relationship between director and shareholder is entirely severed and no longer mirrors the relationship that subsists between partners in a firm. Instead, a director's fiduciary duty is owed to an entity distinct from shareholders and no longer represents a fiduciary relationship owed to the shareholders.

This is the view taken in *Percival v Wright*, the leading case on the question of 'to whom does the director owe a fiduciary duty'. In this case Swinfen Eady J held that the directors owed a duty to act in 'the best interests of the company as a whole', and that directors were not 'trustees for individual shareholders'.[14] In this case, which was an action to set aside the sale of shares in a limited company, the company secretary had been approached by a number of shareholders who wished to sell their shares and requested his help and advice in their disposal. This company was a private one, and the shares could not be valued in and sold on the stock market. Furthermore, the company's memorandum provided that the shares could not be sold without the approval of the board of directors. The plaintiff shareholders stated the price they would accept and the company chairman wrote to their solicitor offering to purchase the shares. A sale was agreed with the chairman disclosing that the shares would be divided into three lots, two of which would be held by two other directors. After the transaction was completed, the shareholders discovered that the board had been approached by a third party, a Mr Holden, who had offered a considerable sum for the entire undertaking with the intention of selling the company onto a new company. Although no firm offer had ever been made by Mr Holden and although negotiations fell through, the court was not convinced that the board ever seriously entertained his offer.

14 [1902] 2 Ch 421.

The plaintiffs argued that the directors were in a fiduciary position to them and should have disclosed the negotiations with Holden. Counsel for the plaintiffs argued that the company should be understood as 'merely the sum of the shares',[15] which at law belonged to the company but in equity belonged to the shareholders. Accordingly, they were the beneficiaries of the company and the directors were 'trustees of the sale of the undertaking'.[16] Counsel contended that the directors were under a duty to disclose all related negotiations to the beneficiaries. Furthermore, they argued, 'in this respect the shareholders inter se are in the same position as partners . . . If managing partners employ an agent to sell their business, he cannot purchase the share of a sleeping partner without disclosing the fact of his employment. Incorporation cannot affect this broad equitable principle.'[17] What we can see in this argument is a clear articulation of old company law, when the company was not distinct and separate from the shareholders and where incorporation meant that the company held the legal title to the whole undertaking and members held the equity. It is a reference to companies that were not 'its' but 'theys', whose shareholders were like partners in their relationship to the assets and in their personal liability for the businesses' debts. Thus, the most compelling argument against this argument was a firm articulation of the doctrine of separate corporate personality and its ramification:

> The company is a legal entity quite distinct from the shareholders: Salomon v Salomon & Co; so that a sale by a mortgagee to a company in which he is a shareholder is neither in form or substance a sale to himself.[18]

In judgment, Swinfen Eady J sought to show that separate corporate personality severed the directors' duty to the company from the interests of individual shareholders. Swinfen Eady J set out established authorities on the definition of a director's duties in the context of the modern, separate company. The first two citations involve earlier cases, where the issue was a director's personal liability for the company's financial undertakings, and hence the court had been keen to stress a director's representative function:

> Directors are the mere trustees or agents of the company – trustees of the company's money and property – agents in the transactions which they enter into on behalf of the company.[19]

---

15 Ibid, p 423.
16 Ibid.
17 Ibid.
18 Defence counsel in *Percival*, ibid, p 424.
19 *Great Eastern Ry Co v Turner* (1872–3) LR 8 Ch App 149, quoted *Percival*, p 425.

And,

> Directors are called trustees. They are no doubt trustees of assets which have come into their hands, or which are under their control, but they are not trustees of a debt due to the company. The company is the creditor, and, as I said before, they are only the managing partners.[20]

And later,

> Although directors are not properly speaking trustees, yet they have always been considered and treated as trustees of money which comes to their hands or which is actually under their control; and ever since joint stock companies were invented directors have been held liable to make good moneys which they have misapplied upon the same footing as if they were trustees, and it has always been held that they are not entitled to the benefit of the old Statute of Limitations because they have committed breaches of trust, and are in respect of such moneys to be treated as trustees.[21]

The judge goes on to explain that because the fiduciary duty is owed to the *assets* of the company there are necessarily strict rules on self-dealing under English law, summed up in the overarching imperative for a director to act bona fide and in the best interests of the company. This is a shift of emphasis from the previous pro- dividend approach. He concludes that the nature of incorporation alters the position of shareholders so that they are not like partners and cannot conjoin themselves with the business so as to make a director's fiduciary duty, which is owed to the company, one that is owed to them also:

> It was strenuously urged that, though incorporation affected the relations of the shareholders to the external world, the company thereby becoming a distinct entity, the position of the shareholders inter se was not affected, and was the same as that of partners or shareholders in an unincorporated company. I am unable to adopt that view.[22]

The decision in *Percival v Wright* meant that a director's fiduciary duty was owed to the company and that the company was not the individual shareholders, but a bundle of moneys and other non-financial assets (whose value

20 *In Re Forest of Dean Coal Mining Co* (1878–79) LR 10 Ch D 450, per Jessel MR, quoted *Percival*, p 426.
21 *Re Lands Allotment Co* [1894] 1 Ch 616, p 631, quoted *Percival*, p 428.
22 Ibid.

they must attempt to enhance). And it was only when the company was owned by a small number of shareholders who might reasonably expect to be acquainted with the running of the business, such as to make this company like a partnership or a 'quasi- partnership', that this position might be modified. The director was legally conceived as owing a duty to the company entity, but not to the shareholders, when materially the company was a distinct being.

It should also be noted that in certain discreet circumstances the court has taken the view, at least by implication, that a director's duty is owed to its creditors. So in *Winkworth v Edward Baron Development Co Ltd*[23] a husband and wife who were directors used as their home a freehold property purchased by the company. Prior to this they had purchased shares in the company costing £115,000, using money from the company bank account.

Some months later, and without the wife's consent, the husband mortgaged the house to the appellant, Winkworth. The company subsequently become insolvent and when it defaulted on the payment of the mortgage, Winkworth brought an action for possession. On appeal, the House of Lords held the withdrawal of £115,000 from the company's account to purchase the company's own shares was a breach of their fiduciary duties to the company and its creditors, as was the wife's failure to discover the mortgaging of the property. Accordingly, equity would not operate on behalf of these parties. Likewise in *West Mercia Safetywear Ltd (in liq) v Dodd*,[24] the director was held to be breach of his duty to the company for transferring some assets from one company to another in respect of an outstanding debt. The court held that once a company was insolvent the interests of the creditors overrode the interests of the shareholders. Therefore the transfer was against the company's best interest because it was against the interests of the creditors.[25]

The emphasis on a director's trustee relationship to the company as assets was most vividly reflected in the 'no-profit' rules, which stated that a director could not personally benefit from his fiduciary position. And, during most of the second period under discussion, the no-profit rules were uncompromisingly strict, requiring a director to account for all and any benefits he had gained as a result of his fiduciary position. In respect of conflict of interest situations, whether there was a breach which would allow the company to either avoid the contract or to require the directors to return to any profits made from the transaction would depend on whether consent has been received or an appropriate disclosure made. Both acts would imply that a

---

23 [1987] 1 All ER 114.
24 (1988) BCLC 250.
25 *Brady v Brady* (1988) BCLC 20, *Re DKG Contractors Ltd* (1990) BCC 903, *Re Purpoint Ltd* (1991) BCC 121, *Knight v Frost* (1999) 1 BCLC 364.

director had acted bona fide and was not therefore in breach. However, a director remains a trustee for company assets, including non-tangible assets such as business opportunities. Thus, in respect of corporate opportunities, in the early part of this period a director would be liable regardless of whether his actions were taken in good faith and for the benefit of the company. However, later cases indicate a greater willingness to assess the bona fides of a director's actions and to impose liability only if the director has not acted in good faith.

Self-profiting

Conflicts of interest

As we saw in *Aberdeen*, self-profiting from a conflict of interest situation can involve the director contracting *with* the company. This section will deal with a number of modifications made in respect of this sort of conflict of interest. In the following section, we will consider another species of self-profiting, in which a director benefits from personal use of company property, such as business associates or corporate opportunities. Both involve conflicts of interest but the former breach has been subject to a number of modifications which will be considered first. The subsequent section will assess the judicial reasoning on self-profiting, illustrated by a number of important corporate opportunity cases.

The first of these modifications to note was introduced into the standard form articles of association provided for in the Companies Acts by the beginning of the twentieth century. The most recent version is Article 85, in Table A, the standard form made under the 1985 Act. The broad approach has been to prevent a director being penalised for having an interest in a transaction in which his company was involved provided he had disclosed that interest. In full, Article 85 provides:

> Subject to the provisions of the Act, and provided that he has disclosed to the directors the nature and extent of any material interest of his, a director
>
> (a) may be party to, or otherwise interested in, any transaction or arrangement with the company or in which the company is otherwise interested;
>
> (b) may be a director or other officer of, or employed by, or a party to any transaction or arrangement with, or otherwise interested in, any body corporate promoted by the company or in which the company is otherwise interested; and
>
> (c) shall not, by reason of his office, be accountable to the company for any benefit which he derives from any such office or employment or

> from any such transaction or arrangement or from any interest in
> any such body corporate and no such transaction or arrangement
> shall be liable to be avoided on the ground of any such interest or
> benefit.

Thus a director would only be accountable to the company for any personal profiting if he had failed to make an appropriately full disclosure, given,
of course, that his company's articles included Article 85 or a similar
provision.

As a separate operation of law, s 317 of the 1985 Act requires a director to
disclose such an interest promptly. Statutory provisions requiring a director
to disclose any interest in company contracts were first introduced in s 81 of
the Companies Act 1928.[26] Failure to make such a disclosure would result in a
fine,[27] but this penalty would not cancel out the operation of the common-law
rule in *Aberdeen*.[28] So in *Guinness plc v Saunders*,[29] a director was required
to return the £5.2 m he had received from Guinness for services and advice
on a take-over because (*inter alia*) he had not disclosed the agreement to the
board. Lord Templeman stated that it was contrary to the position of a
trustee to profit from his position outside of that allowed under the trust
document. Section 317 created a criminal offence of failing to disclose an
interest. In contrast, principles under *Aberdeen* were equitable principles,
where the remedy was to recreate fairness.

This no-conflict rule arose in the trustee principles of the nineteenth century so that disclosure will not relieve a director from liability if the equitable
principle of good faith has not been met. Thus in *Neptune (Vehicle Washing
Equipment) Ltd v Fitzgerald (No 2)*,[30] a company brought an action against
its former sole director who, at a board meeting of the company attended by
the defendant and the company secretary, had resolved as sole director that
his own service contract should be terminated and had resolved that the sum
of £100,892 should be paid to him by way of recompense for the termination of his contract of employment. The defendant argued that he had
made sufficient declaration in line with the company's articles but the court
held that:

> The company's articles excluded the strict equitable rule against self-
> dealing but that did not entail that the director was relieved from his

---

26 Section 317(1) and (2). Section 317 has now been replaced by s 184 of the 2006 Act.
27 Section 317(7).
28 Section 317(9).
29 [1988] 2 All ER 940.
30 [1996] Ch 274.

other obligations to the company, including his duty to act bona fide in the company's interests.[31]

Even if he had disclosed his interest, which would have been to himself, in the court's words, a statutory pause for thought, it would not have relieved him of his duty to act with bona fides. The monetary award to himself was a breach of that duty.

Indeed, the duty to act in good faith had been found to underpin all a director's actions, so the court concluded in *Movitex v Bulfield*,[32] in which an apparent conflict arose between Article 85 and s 320 of the 1985 Act. This section provided that the company's articles could not exclude a director's liability 'which by virtue of any rule of law would otherwise attach to him in respect of any negligence, default, breach of duty or breach of trust of which he may be guilty in relation to the company'.[33] On the face of it, Article 85 appeared to do that which s 320 prohibited by excluding liability for a breach of the duty to avoid conflicts of interests albeit following disclosure. The court concluded, however, that there would only be a conflict if the articles provided for modification of the duty to act bona fide and for the benefit of the company. Conflicts of interests could be modified, although not excluded, in the articles.

Corporate opportunities

Self-profiting from a corporate opportunity involves a director personally benefiting from company property such as business contacts and business information obtained from the company while under a fiduciary obligation to that company.

The early case of *Cook v Deeks*[34] is instructive, placing as it does great emphasis on a director's trustee-like relationship to company assets. In this case three of the four directors in the Toronto Construction Company Limited used their majority votes to pass a resolution to the effect that the company had no interest in a contract with the Canadian Pacific Railway Company. They then secured the contract for a new company which they had formed for this purpose. The plaintiff director, Mr Cook, claimed that they had diverted a business opportunity away from the company and therefore they should be made to account for the profits made from the contract to the company. The court agreed, finding that 'the contract in question was entered into under such circumstances that the directors could not retain the benefit

31 Ibid.
32 *Movitex v Bulfield* [1988] BCLC 104.
33 Companies Act 1985, s 320(1).
34 *Cook v Deeks and others* [1916] 1 AC 554.

for themselves, then it belonged in equity to the company and ought to have been dealt with as an asset of the company'.[35]

A reasonable enough conclusion. Yet the context of these transactions lends a different complexion to the decision and informs us of the distinctly fiduciary nature of a director's duty. It was, in fact, the defendants, GS Deeks and GM Deeks, together with a third, Mr Hird, who had a long-lasting and successful history of working with the railway company. Indeed, they had formed the Toronto Construction Company to undertake a particular contract for the railway. By the time the contract in question was put out to tender, however, the relationship between these defendants and Mr Cook, the plaintiff, had become extremely difficult and the latter clearly desired to sever relations permanently. In 1907, disagreements had already resulted in the dissolution of a number of partnerships they were involved in and the defendants could have separated from the plaintiff by using their majority votes to affect a voluntary liquidation of the company. Instead they chose to tender for the contract under the auspices of the company, hide negotiations from Mr Cook and use their majority to pass the questioned resolution. As individuals, it was the Deeks and Hird who actually undertook the business with the railway, not Mr Cook. Their lordships agreed with the trial judge's statement that Mr Cook was 'a business associate who they deemed and I think rightly deemed, unsatisfactory from a business point of view'.[36] So from a personal and business standpoint the defendant's severance from Mr Cook was entirely understandable, yet it was their failure to openly sever their relationship with the company that gave rise to the onerous penalty visited upon them. Once the company was formed, and the defendants became directors, their relationship with the entity became that of fiduciaries, requiring utmost honesty, and a commitment to put the interests of the company above their own self-interests. This applied notwithstanding that they were majority shareholders because shareholders, majority or otherwise, are not the company and the law on directors' duties resists all attempts to conflate shareholders with the company:

> Men who assume the complete control of a company's business must remember that they are not at liberty to sacrifice the interests which they are bound to protect, and while ostensibly acting for the company, divert in their own favour business which should properly belong to the company.[37]

So while it was clearly the case that the defendants were continuing a business relationship (within which they had worked for many years, without

35 Ibid, p 565.
36 Ibid, p 4.
37 *Cook v Deeks*, p 563.

any useful assistance from the plaintiff), they could not personally benefit from it. They had committed themselves to subordinating their self-interest to the interest of the company and while the company continued to exist, their actions amounted to self-dealing and a breach of their fiduciary duty.

Until quite recently the cases made it clear that the motives of the directors in breach were not a relevant consideration for the court. The *act* of self-dealing constituted a breach and the director's *motives* never mended the breach. This point was made clear in *Regal (Hastings) Ltd v Gulliver*.[38] In this case, the appellant company owned a cinema and its directors wanted to acquire the lease of two other cinemas in order to sell the whole undertaking as a small chain. They formed a subsidiary company in order to acquire and hold these leases but the landlord would not let to the subsidiary unless it either had more paid-up capital or alternatively the directors gave a personal guarantee for the rents. Regal was unable to purchase more than 2,000 £1 shares and so the directors (who did not want to give personal guarantees), the chairman and the solicitor purchased additional shares thereby capitalising the subsidiary to the landlord's satisfaction. In this, the judges agreed that the directors had acted with bona fides, intending to act in the interests of Regal. The four directors took 500 shares each, the chairman (Gulliver) found outside subscribers for 500 and the solicitor (Garton) took the final 500. Three weeks after these transactions the directors decided not to purchase the cinemas but instead sold all the shares in the two companies. The purchasers then issued a writ requiring the directors, the chairman and the solicitor to account to the company for the profit they had made from the sale, some £2 16s 1d per share.

The House of Lords made clear that a director's accountability for self-dealing did not rest upon the bona fides of his actions. They concurred with Lord Russell in the Court of Appeal that the liability which arises from a fiduciary position did not depend on fraud or an absence of bona fides. However, they reversed the decision of the court of first instance and the Court of Appeal, which found the directors not accountable to the company for profits made. Lord Porter stated that the correct legal proposition in respect of a director profiting from his fiduciary position is that 'one occupying a position of trust must not make a profit which he can acquire only by use of his fiduciary position, or, if he does, he must account for the profit so made.'[39] Lord Porter went further, ruling that liability of this kind 'does not depend upon breach of duty but upon the proposition that a director must not make a profit out of property acquired by reason of his relationship to the company of which he is director'.[40] The act in itself is sufficient. No fraud,

38 [1942] 1 All ER 378.
39 Ibid, p 395.
40 Ibid.

lapse of duty or even negligence is required. Finally Lord Porter added that the fact that the company could not have enjoyed the opportunity which enriched the fiduciary, for other reasons, does not alter a director's account-ability in this context. The profit belongs to the company, 'even though the property by means of which he made it was not and could not have been acquired on its behalf'.[41]

This latter proposition is followed in many later cases. In *Industrial Development Consultants Ltd v Cooley*,[42] a director was held to account to the company for the profit he gained from a contract with a business relationship he formed while a director of a company, IDC, even though IDC probably would not have gained that contract. As managing director of IDC, Mr Cooley, an architect, was involved in negotiations with the Eastern Gas Board for the construction of four depots. These negotiations collapsed as the Board did not want to contract with IDC, and really required the skills of an architect. The following year Mr Cooley entered into correspondence with the Board over a period of months. In June the new deputy of the Board strongly intimated to Mr Cooley that they wished him to take on the project independently from his company. A few days later, Mr Cooley sought to sever his employment with IDC by feigning serious ill health and was released from his position on 1 August. On 6 August he contracted with the Gas Board. There are similarities with *Regal (Hastings)*, in that in both cases the com-pany was, for different reasons, unable to benefit from the transaction in question. In IDC much emphasis was placed upon Lord Cranbrook's famous speech in *Aberdeen* in which he said:

> And it is a rule of universal application, that no one, having such duties to discharge, shall be allowed to enter into engagements in which he has, or can have, a personal interest conflicting, or which possibly may conflict, with the interests of those whom he is bound to protect.[43]

IDC may have had a later opportunity to gain the contract, so Mr Cooley's usurpation of the contract may have conflicted with IDC's interests. The *possibility* of an actual conflict gives rise to the breach of duty and the court would not find that there was absolutely no possibility that IDC would have gained the contract. *Regal (Hastings)* also differs from this case in that at the point when the contract in dispute was made, Mr Cooley was no longer managing director of IDC, whereas Regal's directors purchased the shares while still employed as such. Under English law, a fiduciary will cease to owe a duty to the principal once the contractual relationship is severed. However,

41 Ibid.
42 [1972] 2 All ER 162.
43 *Aberdeen Ry v Blaikie Bros* (1854) 1 Macq 461, p 471.

Mr Cooley's resignation was deemed to be irrelevant because it was his actions in negotiating with the Gas Board *before* his resignation which constituted the breach. The breach was that 'he embarked on a deliberate policy and course of conduct which put his personal interest as a potential contracting party with the Eastern Gas Board in direct conflict with his pre-existing and continuing duty as managing director of the plaintiffs'.[44] The fact that he had severed his contractual relationship by 'foul' means was noted as an indicator of dishonesty but was not the principal reason for holding him accountable. Thus, in this case, like *Regal (Hastings)*, it was not the bona fides of the directors' action that was definitive in holding them accountable, although it was more of a factual feature in *IDC*.

The importance of the bona fides of a director's act of resignation in determining whether the fiduciary duty ceased with the resignation was found to be of greater importance in a similar appeal case in Canada, heard after *IDC*.[45] In this case two senior executives resigned from their position in the company, Canadian Aero Service Ltd. They then acquired for their new company a business opportunity which they had been maturing on behalf of Canadian Aero Service. The court held them accountable to Canadian Aero Service because as fiduciaries they could not pursue a business opportunity which their principal was actively maturing. This applied even after they had resigned if that resignation 'may be fairly said to have been prompted or influenced by a wish to acquire for himself the opportunity sought by the company'.[46] Resignation would have allowed them to pursue a contract in competition with their old fiduciary if their reasons for resigning were bona fide.

The importance of the bona fides of a director's reasons for resignation when he subsequently and successfully competed with his old principal was fully endorsed in the later case of *Island Export Finance Ltd v Umunna*.[47] The company director was held not to be in breach of his fiduciary duty when he personally benefited from a contract with a party with whom the plaintiff, IEF, had previously contracted, and with whom he originally had contact by dint of his employment with IEF. At the time that the director, Mr Umunna, profited from this contract (undertaken with the Cameroon Postal Authority), he had already resigned from his position with IEF. However, previous authorities such as *IDC v Cooley* and *Canadian Aero Service v O'Malley* held that resignation would not sever the fiduciary relationship between director and company if the resignation was prompted by the desire to exploit a corporate opportunity which emerged while he was working for the company.

44 Ibid, p 472.
45 *Canadian Aero Service v O'Malley* (1971) 23 DLR (3d) 632.
46 Ibid.
47 *IEF v Umunna* [1986] BCLC 460.

Mr Umunna had worked for IEF Ltd as a managing director for a number of years but the court felt that this was in name only as the major decisions were made by the controlling shareholder, Mr Lewis. The business of IEF was based in the Cameroons, where Mr Lewis had a number of business interests. Mr Lewis seems to have been instrumental in achieving a business association between IEF and the Cameroon Postal Authority.

Throughout Mr Umunna's time with IEF he had expressed dissatisfaction with a number of business decisions made by Mr Lewis and in particular with the way he, Mr Umunna, had been treated. Mr Umunna eventually resigned his position and later approached the postal authority with a proposal for the supply of new post boxes which they accepted. IEF claimed that Mr Umunna should account to the company for any profits he made from this latter transaction, arguing that he had intended to develop and exploit an independent business relationship with the postal authority while he was a fiduciary of IEF. The courts agreed that Mr Umunna probably did consider future contracts; in their words, 'if he had been asked at that date whether he contemplated that he might obtain orders for postal caller boxes from the Cameroons, I have no doubt that he would have replied that he did'.[48] However, merely contemplating this did not constitute a breach because in the court's view the resignation itself was prompted by his dissatisfaction with his treatment. The judge stated that he rejected 'the suggestion that the exploitation of the opportunity was his primary or indeed an important motive in his resignation', although he did think that Mr Umunna desired to 'branch out on his own by seeking through Benosi, to open up West African business for himself'.[49]

Another key factor in this decision was that IEF were not actively pursuing any repeat orders with the Cameroons, nor were they important players in this particular market, although in a general sense they did consider approaching the Cameroons in respect of future propositions. In summary, there was no breach of duty because first Mr Umunna's resignation was not prompted by a desire to exploit this business opportunity and second because IEF was not 'maturing a business opportunity' with the Cameroons.

This ruling is quite a departure from that of *Regal (Hastings)*. In *Regal (Hastings)* not only was the company not maturing a business opportunity but it had no financial ability to make the disputed transactions, unlike IEF, who did contemplate future transactions but not ones that were sufficiently well formed at the relevant periods. Furthermore, the directors in *Regal (Hastings)* appeared to act entirely in the interests of the company, whereas Mr Umunna's actions were more self-interested albeit prompted by the difficult position in which Mr Lewis had placed him. In *IEF*, the judge moved

48 [1986] BCLC 477.
49 Ibid, p 476.

from the strict liability approach of *Regal (Hastings)* to a more complicated consideration of the factual situation which essentially hinged on one central factor, that of the bona fides of the director's actions. Mr Umunna's intentions were not to act against the interests of the company, or to deprive the company of a corporate opportunity which properly belonged to it. Though his actions might have deprived the company in the long term, there was not a competition for a specific contract. Although knowledge of such opportunities in the Cameroons came to Mr Umunna as a result of his position with IEF, this did not make such knowledge the property of the company. Indeed to restrain Mr Umunna from using such knowledge when no longer a fiduciary would amount to an unlawful restraint of trade. 'Directors, no less than employees, acquire a general fund of knowledge and expertise in the course of their work, and it is plainly in the public interest that they should be free to exploit it in a new position.'[50]

THE COMPANY AS COMPETITOR: A NEXUS OF COMPETITIONS (1980 ONWARDS)

IEF v Umunna continued to reflect the judicial understanding of the company as a bundle of tangible and intangible properties to which the director owes a fiduciary duty. Furthermore, it reflected the growing importance of the director's bona fides, a consideration central to *Canadian Aero Service*, and significant in *IDC v Cooley*. In those respects *IEF* falls into the previous section. However, it also illustrates the third period because it goes much further towards reconceptualising the company as a competitor. Mr Umunna was not required to account to IEF Ltd because his resignation was prompted by bona fide reasons and it was not maturing a business opportunity with the Cameroons. To impose liability when these two conditions had been satisfied would amount to an unlawful restraint of trade. Mr Umunna was entitled to personally profit from business contacts and knowledge acquired as a fiduciary as long as his resignation was not prompted by a desire to usurp a specific maturing business interest. He was further entitled to compete with IEF when he had legitimately ceased to be a fiduciary. This is quite distinct reasoning from that in *Canadian Aero Service*, where the judge stated that a director would be called to account if, after resignation, a business opportunity arose as a result of contacts made while a fiduciary: 'where it was his position with the company rather than a fresh initiative that led him to the opportunity which he later acquired'. Thus, if the bona fides of a director's action are in place, he is entitled to compete with his former principal so long

50 Ibid, p 482.

as the particular transaction in question was not one which the principal was maturing at the time of the director's employment. Following *IEF*, as long he does not exploit the maturing opportunity, the ex-director may compete, and do so using business contacts which his old principal was interested in maintaining in a general way, and may deprive his old principal of future, even (generally) anticipated business.

So, in the recent case of *CMS Dolphin Limited v Paul Maurice Simonet, Blue (GB) Limited*,[51] the managing director, Mr Simonet's actions were tested according to their bona fides. He and Mr Ball had established an advertising agency. Mr Ball provided the finance while Mr Simonet did the work and brought in the clients. The two fell out, and Mr Simonet resigned, taking many of the staff and clients with him to his newly formed competitor agency, Blue (GB) Ltd.

The judgment makes clear that Mr Simonet was entitled, as a general principle, to benefit from associations and contacts made while a fiduciary. Accordingly, if he had resigned for reasons unconnected to gaining CMSD's customers then he would not be in breach. English law allows a fiduciary to resign even if to do so would undermine the prospects of the company. Furthermore, after he has resigned, a fiduciary may, following *IEF*, use his 'general fund of skill knowledge, or his personal connections, to compete'.[52] The question of liability therefore lay in his intention in resigning, not in the act of resigning itself and the subsequent use of business connections. Considering the evidence of the behaviour of the parties, the court chose to disbelieve Mr Simonet's 'disingenuous' account, according to which he had been frustrated and marginalised by Mr Ball. Rather, the court concluded that he put and intended to put his personal interests first and did not act in the best interests of the company.

In *Plus Group Ltd v Pyke*,[53] a director was found not to be accountable for diverting a corporate opportunity because at the time of the alleged breach he was effectively, although not formally, resigned from his position. In assessing whether there had been a breach, the court laid great emphasis on the factual details of the transactions and relationships, moving away from the strict liability approach of *Regal (Hastings)* which, if applied, would surely have told against the defendant director. The plaintiff had been owned and controlled equally by the defendant, Mr Pyke and Mr Plank, but at the time of the alleged breach, Mr Pyke had been effectively excluded from the management for a significant period of time.

In approaching the company as a competitor, in a competitive market, these cases reflected the decision in the earlier Canadian case of *Peso Silver*

51 [2001] 2 BCLC.
52 [2001] WL 535670 (Ch D) para 95.
53 [2002] 2 BCLC 201.

Mines.[54] In this case, a director was held not to be liable to account for profits made from a transaction of which he had become acquainted in his capacity as a fiduciary. The director, Mr Cropper, and the rest of the board had been presented with an offer to purchase speculative mining properties which were situated close to the plaintiff's property. The plaintiff held 20 square miles of mineral claims in Yukon (acquisitions which were said to have strained its finances), and had been advised by its engineers that it should focus its finances on these properties. The board decided to reject the offer, a decision which the court stated was 'an honest and considered decision of the appellant's board of directors as a whole and done in the best of faith and solely in the interest of the appellant'.[55] Offers of these kinds were routinely presented to the board, at a rate of two or three a week. Later, the same mining rights were presented to Mr Cropper, with the suggestion that he join a group of investors, in order to hold these rights as a shareholder in a company which would be formed for that purpose. Mr Cropper agreed, and the company, called 'Cross Bow', was incorporated.

Mr Cropper remained director of Peso Silver Mines throughout these transactions but the following year, Peso had a new shareholder, Charter Oil Company Ltd, who required a new board, with five additional directors. Mr Cropper became Vice President under a new President, Mr Walker. These two men quickly disagreed, and it was in this spirit of bad feeling that a memorandum was sent to Mr Cropper from the Chairman requiring that 'all officers of Peso Silver Mines make full disclosure of their connection with any other mining companies'.[56] Mr Cropper declared his interest in Cross Bow and this later resulted in a motion to dismiss him from his position in Peso because of his earlier refusal to hand over his interests in Cross Bow. Peso later took action against Mr Cropper to make him liable to account for profits made from Cross Bow.

The Canadian Appeal Court found in favour of Mr Cropper, rather surprisingly given that its decision was based almost entirely by concurring with the decision in *Regal (Hastings)*. The court agreed with the appellant's argument that liability neither depends on the bona fides of a fiduciary's actions nor the fact that the principle could not have benefited from the disputed transactions. Liability, the appellants argued, arose solely because profit was made 'by reason and in course of that fiduciary relationship'.[57] However, the court took a very narrow reading of a statement in Lord Porter's speech that liability arose not from breach of duty but '*by reason of*

---

54 [1966] 58 DLR (2nd) 1.
55 Ibid.
56 *Peso*, para 17.
57 Ibid, para 23.

his relationship to the company of which he is a director',[58] to find that liability could only arise if the *reason* for acquiring the corporate opportunity was *because* of the directorship. It then stated that it was 'impossible to say that the respondent obtained the interests he holds in Cross Bow and Mayo by reason of the fact that he was director of the appellant and in the course of the execution of that office'. Mr Cropper could not be liable notwithstanding that like the *Regal (Hastings)* directors, this was knowledge he gained while a fiduciary, of which the company did not avail itself because of decisions made by the directors in good faith.

It is difficult to see how a case which purported to apply *Regal (Hastings)* would not find Mr Cropper liable. The result is rendered even more opaque when the justification for distinguishing the two cases is based on a 'hypothetical model' discussed by Lord Greene in his minority speech. Lord Greene had said that if directors made a bona fide decision not to invest their company's money in some proposed business and then later decide to invest their own money, they should not be held to account for the profits they make. Lord Russell's curt response (following a long and considered speech) to this was 'I can only say that to my mind the facts of this hypothetical situation bear but little resemblance to the story with which we have had to deal'.[59] Twenty years on, the judgment in *Peso* held that the fact that Lord Russell addressed Lord Greene's hypothetical situation at all implied that he concurred with the legal principle it articulated. Furthermore, the court held that as Lord Greene's model so closely described the facts of *Peso, Regal (Hastings)* was authority for asserting that Mr Cropper was not liable to account.

Arguably, basing a judgment on the possible implications of a short comment in a long speech is stretching the point somewhat. It is equally plausible that Lord Russell addressed the hypothetical because he was giving a very thorough speech, in which all points were addressed, and mentioned this one merely to say it was irrelevant and so no further discussion of its legal implications were required. The decision in *Peso* is perhaps best explained by political and ideological shifts, rather than the seamless continuity with the judgment in *Regal (Hastings)* which the judges claimed. In particular the ideological perspective of legal reasoning in American cases is heavily reflected in *Peso* as it was in recent thinking on conflict situations in England.

American law in respect of a director's duties is dominated by two questions, that of the bona fides of the director's actions and whether the director acted in actual competition with his principal. For example a New England case in 1918 held a director to be in breach of his duty to avoid a conflict of

---

58 *Regal (Hastings) v Gulliver* [1942] 1 All ER 378.
59 Ibid, p 154.

interest and loyalty because he had caused the plaintiff to enter into a contract on unfavourable terms with another company for whom he was a director.[60] The plaintiff power company had contracted to provide power to the Woollen company at a fixed price for five years. However, the court made clear that it was not merely that the defendant had presided on the boards of both companies but that he had exerted an influence on the plaintiff to ensure it entered into a bad bargain. He had known that the Woollen Company's electricity requirements were set to rapidly increase but had not informed the board of the plaintiff. Judge Cardozo stated that a fiduciary should not take advantage of his position on both sides of the transaction and held the contract voidable at the instance of the plaintiff company.

In *Broz v Cellular Information Systems Inc* (1996), Broz was the sole president and sole shareholder in RFBC Inc.[61] Broz was also an outside director of the respondent company, Cellular Information Systems Inc (CIS). CIS had recently experienced severe financial difficulties resulting in bankruptcy proceedings and the shedding of 15 licence agreements. At the time of the disputed transactions, CIS was negotiating a loan and was not in a position to make any new acquisitions. In his capacity as a director of RFBC, Broz was approached to purchase a licence relating to an area in Michigan which was adjacent to an area for which CIS were licensees. Broz decided that RFBC would purchase it but he did not present the opportunity to CIS, nor had he formally presented his plans to its board. RFBC began a bidding battle with Pricecellular Inc, a company that was proposing a merger with CIS. Nine days before the merger took place Broz acquired the licence. He was subsequently dismissed from his position with CIS, together with the other directors. Pricecellular's replacement nominees brought an action claiming that Broz had diverted a corporate opportunity and held the licence on a constructive trust. Reversing Delaware's Court of Chancery decision, the Supreme Court held that Broz was under no formal duty to present the Michigan licence to the CIS board. Furthermore, the opportunity had come to Broz in his private capacity and finally that CIS lacked both the interest and financial capacity to acquire the licence.

In reaching this decision, the Supreme Court explained that the principles relating to corporate opportunities were as laid down in an earlier Delaware case.[62] This case stated that a corporate officer or director may not take a business opportunity for his own if the following conditions were satisfied. First, if the corporation was financially able to exploit the opportunity. Second, if the opportunity was within the corporation's line of business and if the corporation had an interest or expectancy in the opportunity. And

---

60 *Globe Woollen Co v Utica Gas and Electric Co* (1918) 121 NE 378.
61 *Broz v Cellular Information Systems Inc* 673 A 2d 148 (Del 1996).
62 *Guft v Loft Inc*, 5 A 2d 503 (Del 1961).

third, if by taking the opportunity for his own, the corporate fiduciary would thereby be placed in a position inimitable to his duties to the corporation. Referred to as the 'line of business' test, it narrowed the 'interest or expectancy' test first articulated in 1899.[63] This test established that a director would have usurped a corporate opportunity where the corporation had an existing interest in the opportunity or an expectation based on an existing right. The court was clear that when a director acquired for himself an opportunity which his corporation had been pursuing but had subsequently abandoned, he would not have usurped a corporate opportunity and would not be liable to account.

COMPANY LAW REFORM

In addressing reform in the area of a director's duties the judiciary's more recent leniency toward the no-profit rule has dovetailed with the law and economics, contractarian approach of the reform process.

In the Law Commission Consultation Paper of 1998, the first significant statement on directors' duties in the reform process, the Commission set out its commitment to approaching this area of law from a law and economics perspective.[64] By way of general introduction the Commission emphasised two points as its guiding principles for reform. First, the economic importance of directors operating within clear guidelines: 'unclear law creates unnecessary costs and inhibits decision-making and therefore competitiveness'.[65] And, second, that company law is 'a functional area of law: it must facilitate commercial activity and enable, or at least not prevent, the delivery of benefits to all the company's stakeholders'.[66]

In Part 3 of the Consultation Paper (CP), the Commission further developed the law and economics perspective it would adopt. This perspective was useful, it argued, first because it could be used to 'evaluate particular legal provisions in terms of how they enhance efficiency'.[67] It would enable an assessment of how far the existing rules promote the proper allocation of resources, or 'allocative efficiency', closely connected to the notion of

---

63 *Lagard v Anniston Lime & Stone Company* 28 So 199 (Ala 1899).
64 The DTI undertook several reports on the issue of directors prior to this study but they either proposed to defer to the impending Commission's report or were not directly concerned with directors' duties. They included the DTI's consultative document on the Companies Act 1985, Schedule 6 (October 1991), DTI Working Party 1993–95 on directors' duties and a consultative document named Disclosure of Directors' Shareholdings. The Law Commission also undertook a feasibility study on private companies in November 1994.
65 Law Commission Consultation Paper No 153, 'Company directors: regulating conflicts of interest and formulating a statement of duties', p 6.
66 Ibid.
67 Ibid, p 33.

'dynamic efficiency', which allows for innovation in achieving efficiency. The second benefit of economic analysis, contended the Commission, was that it allowed the effects of changes in the law to be predicted.

Drawing straight from the heart of law and economics contractarianism, the Commission declared agency costs to be key to law reform. Agency costs, it declared, citing Lord Hoffman, are the 'cost associated with having your property managed by someone else', an inevitable result of the separation of ownership from control in larger companies noted by Berle and Means. The purpose of law reform from this perspective would be to provide mechanisms which reduced agency costs. This it can do by 'making bargaining more effective, thereby contributing to both technical and allocative efficiency'.[68] Problematically, as argued in Chapter 4, this definition of agency costs is tied to the fallacious notion that shareholders are active owners who are dealing or bargaining with their agents and require a legal framework for monitoring and bargaining costs. In reality, the large corporations where a separation of ownership from control occurs, have shareholders that are passive and detached from the activity of the corporation, who do not make bargains and do not own the business but own only an entitlement to dividends. This particular take on agency costs is a deviation from the classic account of agency costs where they are conceived as costs (to shareholders) consequent on managers pursuing ends other than shareholder value which they can do because there is a control gap between shareholders and managers.

Indeed, the Commission recognised that the agent/principal model does not operate in law in the way that the economic concept requires. In English law, it acknowledges, directors are the agents and the company is the principal. Shareholders do not enter into this equation except in their association with the 'interest of the company', as noted in the earlier cases. However, the Commission seemed undeterred by this fundamental characteristic of company law, stating that 'the economic concept of "agency" is concerned with the costs which arise from delegation, rather than the precise juridical relationship to which the delegation gives rise'.[69] Thus presumably, the precise juridical relationship can be disposed of as a 'legal fiction' à la Jensen and Meckling, in order to accommodate the more desirable economic definitions. A curious position for law reformers to take, perhaps, and yet they continue further with the contractual model in which shareholders have assumed the role of principal.

> Efficiency will be increased if an incentive structure can be put in place which will align the interests of the parties as far as possible. This set of incentives may be thought of, in a loose sense, as a contract or

68 Ibid, p 35.
69 Ibid, p 35, footnote 7.

governance structure which is the result, in part, of bargaining between the parties, even though not all aspects of the arrangement would be regarded as contractual in the juridical sense of constituting a legally binding agreement.[70]

Thus, in this construction of the bargaining which exists in some real or vague sense between the parties, the Commission, not content with side-stepping the fundamental principles of company law, now contend that we should dispense with our legal understanding of contract law. The problem with this approach is not that it fails to reflect long-standing legal principles. It is problematic because legal doctrines such as separate corporate personality reflect real economic realities; to reformulate them is to reconstruct concepts to reflect an ideological aspiration. In this context it is recasting the role of principal in order to justify the promotion of shareholders' interests. And the constant use of the word bargain, albeit as a form of contract, not a contract 'in all aspects', is an ideological attempt to recast shareholders as actively negotiating principals. Like Easterbrook and Fischel before it,[71] the Commission holds the company contract to be more contractual precisely because it does not conform to the norms of contract law. So, in the bargain between shareholder and manager:

there will come a point when the costs of anticipating and dealing with future contingencies outweigh the benefits of explicit contracting. Hence, any express agreement is bound to be incomplete to some degree, and to that extent less than 'perfectly' efficient.[72]

And, like Easterbrook and Fischel, they conceptualise company law as merely a mechanism for perfecting the corporate contract:

Here, company law plays an important role in supplying a set of background rules which fulfil a number of functions, including filling in the gaps in express contractual arrangements and facilitating bargaining between the parties.[73]

Having embraced the contractarian premise, the Commission examines the fiduciary relationship in order to discern whether this relationship as presently construed, which they argue is essentially the contractual relationship between directors and shareholders, is economically efficient. They conclude

70 Ibid, p 35.
71 See Chapter 3.
72 Ibid, p 36.
73 Ibid, p 36.

that the fiduciary principle does have an economic rationale, but economic arguments for imposing a fiduciary relationship on directors are mixed. For example, Cooter and Friedmann argue that the duty of loyalty is an incentive structure which ensures that directors act in the best interests of the company,[74] and where 'the open ended standard is said to be justified by the high costs of express contracting over the terms of the fiduciaries' performance',[75] given the many opportunities the fiduciary might have for self-dealing. Alternatively, the Commission cites Daniels' argument that too strict an application of fiduciary duties might give rise to 'second-order effects', such as 'premature resignations', or may result in directors demanding further remuneration to compensate them for their commercial self-restraint.[76] Finally, the Commission notes the considerable literature on the market for corporate control where mechanisms such as hostile take-overs are said to ensure the loyal attention of directors.

Thus the Commission surmised that to properly reflect economic considerations a balance between the competing concerns would be required. In ensuring economic efficiency and competitiveness, a director's duty should not include absolute prohibitions but mutually beneficial negotiated agreements that might, for example, include a director taking advantage of a corporate opportunity. These 'contractual' arrangements would largely not be expressly agreed, like for example a contract, but would instead rely upon 'penalty default rules'. These rules are liabilities that may be avoided but only 'at a cost of time and resources'. For example, under Article 85 of Table A, a director may be involved in a transaction which entails a conflict of interest so long as he discloses his interest to the other directors. The purpose of law reform from this perspective would be to provide clear guidelines as to the nature and extent of fiduciary duties and clarity as to the nature and applicability of new 'penalty default rules'.

The DTI's subsequent reports on directors' duties concurred with both the ideological approach of the Law Commission and its recommendations to have clearly stated directors' duties and a penalty default regime, together with a thorough reorganisation of Chapter X of the Companies Act 1985.[77] The resulting legislation, the 2006 Act, creates a regime which, while largely similar to that under the 1985 Act, provides more facility for a director to pursue other commercial interests outside the interests of his company and attempts to codify the many varied judicial interpretations put upon the directors' fiduciary duties. It explicitly inhibits the judiciary from creating new

---

74 Ibid, p 37, citing Cooter, R and Friedmann, B, 'The fiduciary relationship: its economic character and legal consequences' (1991) 66 NYU L Rev 1045.

75 Ibid, p 37.

76 Ibid, p 39.

77 CLR, 'Completing the structure: final report', Chapter 3.

duties and implicitly limits the interpretation of existing duties. It creates a clearer regulatory regime in which directors may operate and largely removes the criminal penalties attaching to directors' activities.

How important were the contractarian theories which informed the reformers to the formation of the final Act? There is, of course, no simple answer. The removal of many of the prohibitions and their replacement with default rules such as disclosure and consent does align with the Commission's contractarian-informed notion of company law as default rules, or a standard form contract; a regime which describes the private contracting of players involved in a joint commercial endeavour. Equally, however, the provisions of the new Act in respect of directors' duties sets out a detailed regulatory regime, covering all the principal aspects of a director's activities prescribing both how a director should act and the penalties if he does not: a regime which describes the regulation of the public activities of a pubic institution to which and in which all players have clearly designated roles, rights and responsibilities. In the end perhaps the importance of contractarianism lies not in its effect on actual legislation (which must in the end encapsulate the economic reality of the separate company with inactive shareholders), but in its ideology of the company as private, not public, concern.

THE COMPANIES ACT 2006 AND DIRECTORS' DUTIES

Summary of the Government white paper 2005

In 2005, the Government published a white paper recording its conclusions following the consultation process on the earlier green paper. The principal conclusions of the white paper are summarised below.

The Companies Reform Bill will contain a statutory statement of directors' duties drafted in such a way as reflects 'modern behaviour'. In accordance with proposals from the CLR the goal of directors should be 'the success of the company for the benefit of its members as a whole', which would be reached by embracing 'an enlightened shareholder value' approach. This approach would consider managerial decisions in the context of the concerns of consumers, employees, suppliers and the general community.[78]

Corporate opportunities which presently require the company's consent would be exploitable by a director following permission from the board acting independently of the interested and therefore conflicted director. In respect of directors' conflicts of interest and the reform of Part 10 of the Companies Act 1985, the white paper stated that the Bill would set out a new simplified structure with transactions requiring shareholder approval such as

---

78 The statutory form of this intention, s 172, is much less inclusive that that described in the white paper.

loans, payments for loss of office, and property transactions brought together. It would allow loans to directors following shareholder consent. It would require disclosure of connected persons' interests and service contracts to shareholders and would require disclosure of interests in contracts to other directors as soon as was reasonably possible.

The Companies Act 2006

Sections 170–188 of the Companies Act 2006 set out the general duties of directors. These duties are a codification of the existing equitable and common law principles stated in such a way as to take account of the variations that exist within existing case law and to allow the law on directors' duties to continue to develop. Section 170 states that the statutory duties set out in ss 171–177 are based on common law rules and equitable principles but are to have effect in place of those rules.[79] However, when interpreting the statutory duty, regard can be had to previous case law as an aid to interpretation.[80]

Codifying a body of rules which are case-based and therefore have slightly varying principles are not easily distilled into a set of clearly identifiable principles. The government, in codifying these principles, therefore has taken account of the aims and recommendation of the CLR's Final Report which incorporated the recommendations of the Law Commission's report on company directors. These recommendations were summarised in Chapter 3 of the Final Report. In putting directors' duties in a statutory form the CLR wanted to 'provide greater clarity on what is expected of directors and make the law more accessible', thus enabling better company governance.[81] In particular this would clarify who the company was run for (which in their view was primarily shareholders), and how the interests of other stakeholders would be met in the context of modern business practices. The CLR sought to make 'development in the law more predictable', while allowing the courts to continue to develop this area.[82] Finally it wanted to put the rules in respect of conflicts of interest in line with 'the accepted norms of business practice'.[83]

In respect of the reforms on conflicts of interest which include transactions with the company and corporate opportunities the regime is greatly liberalised. In the former conflict situation only a declaration of interest is required under ss 177 and 182 and in respect of the corporate opportunities, authorisation from the board is required under s 175. In order to be effective, this authorisation must be made without the participation of the interested director.

---

79 Section 170(3).
80 Section 170(4).
81 Final Report, Vol 1, p 40.
82 Ibid, p 41.
83 Ibid.

Under this chapter the duties are owed by every person that is a director including de facto directors and in certain circumstances former directors. The duties also apply to shadow directors (defined in s 251) to the extent that the equitable and common law rules codified in this chapter applied. Each duty is cumulative and directors must abide by each individual duty and each breach is enforceable in the same way as any breach of a fiduciary duty. The consequences of a breach can include the payment of damages to the company, restoration of company property, rescission of a contract in which the director is interested or making the director accountable for any profits made from the breach.

The duties

Section 171 states that a director must 'act in accordance with the company's constitution',[84] reflecting the CLR's view that the constitution should prevail over the possible self-interests of controlling shareholders.[85] Section 171 also requires directors to exercise their powers solely for the 'purposes for which they were conferred'.[86]

Section 172 is the key section which determines the orientation of all the subsequent duties. It replaces the trustee-based notion that a director should act bona fide and for the benefit of the company with a statutory duty to promote the success of the company for the benefit of its *members* as a whole, in good faith.[87] This should be understood with regard to the CLR's proposal that good faith would be measured by the successful promotion of the company for the members.[88]

In promoting the interests of the members of a whole, s 172(1)(a)–f) requires the directors to have regard to the following matters:

(a) the likely consequences of any decision in the long term,
(b) the interests of the company's employees,
(c) the need to foster the company's business relationships with suppliers, customers and others,
(d) the impact of the company's operations on the community and the environment,
(e) the desirability of the company maintaining a reputation for high standards of business conduct, and
(f) the need to act fairly as between members of the company.

---

84 Section 171(1). See Chapter 3 on *ultra vires*.
85 Op. cit., 'Completing the structure', Chapter 3, para 3.17, p 39.
86 Section 171(2).
87 Section 172(1).
88 Op. cit., 'Completing the structure', Chapter 3, para 3.19.

As we have seen, the case law which will be used to aid interpretation of these sections has, in various forms, construed the best interests of the company as being the interests of the shareholders. And, as the case law of gratuitous payments or gifts indicates, the judiciary have been particularly averse to construing the interests of the company as the interests of the employees. Indeed, it is counterintuitive that the interests of shareholders could be best pursued by considering the interests of employees, unless those employees are highly skilled and difficult to replace. Otherwise, such decisions which benefit employees, such as wage rises and better conditions, are likely to run directly contrary to the profit-maximising, dividend-declaring interests of shareholders. Having regard to such issues as high standards, the community and the environment, on the other hand, are easier to reconcile with profitability particularly given the present concern with corporate social responsibility.

This 'take all into account after shareholders' section encapsulates the 'enlightened shareholder value' approach preferred by the CLR and the government. As argued in the previous chapter, 'enlightened shareholder value' is a compromise approach between a number of conflicting ideologies. The orthodox neo-liberalism approach which promotes shareholder interest and profit maximisation as the sole concern of corporate governance came under pressure from the ideology of a broader stakeholder approach as the former's 'greed is good' approach seemed to precipitate a number of corporate scandals. Partly in response to this but also continuing an ideological crusade against the notion of the company as a social institution, contractarianism provided the law academy with an ideological cover for the re-assertion of neo-liberal, pro-shareholder approaches which infects the policy community through agencies like the Law Commission and the CLR. The compromise (or third-way triangulation) solution is 'enlightened shareholder value', a fallacious assertion that *as a matter of fact* there is no conflict between shareholder value and wider socially responsible corporate activity.

The result is a *legislative* cop-out, because in the nature of things, you can't legislate social facts into existence like this. Section 172(1) doesn't make it *true* that acting for the good of the company will amount to acting for long-term rather than short-term gain, be in the interests of the employees or for good relations with suppliers and consumers or for the good of the environment. All it requires is that the director should *think about* whether it will or not.

For practical reasons, the enlightened shareholder value approach is modified in respect of charitable concerns, and in order to comply with the Insolvency Act. Subsection 2 states that if the company's purposes include purposes other than the benefit of the members, then that will be treated as promoting the prosperity of the company. Subsection 3 states that this section is subject to other rules which may require the directors to act in the interests of creditors, such as when the company is in financial difficulties.[89]

Under s 173 a director has a duty to exercise independent judgment which, under subsection (2), is not infringed by acting in accordance with an agreement entered into by the company which restricts that judgment or by acting in accordance with the company's constitution.[90] In understanding the first part of this section reference may be made to cases such as *Dawson International plc v Coats Paton plc*.[91] In this case Dawson International plc (Dawson) alleged that there had been a number of meetings between its directors and the directors of Coats Paton plc to discuss the terms of a take-over of Coats. Both made a joint press announcement of the terms of the bid. Dawson claimed that Coats had also agreed not to co-operate with a rival bidder if one emerged. Coats entered into negotiations with Vantina Viyella plc and an agreed take-over of Coats by Viyella was announced.

Dawson raised an action against Coats in which it claimed that they had breached the agreement not to enter into other negotiations. Coats argued that such a contract would have been contrary to the fiduciary duty that the directors owed to individual shareholders to advise them on the merits of any take-over bid and not to limit their independent judgment. The court held that such a duty was not directly owed to shareholders but if directors took it upon themselves to give advice to current shareholders then they had a duty not to advise fraudulently or negligently but in good faith under ordinary principles of law. However, if the directors decided in good faith that it was in the interests of the company to enter into an agreement such as that with Dawson, which afforded the company a substantial payment, they could enter into such a contract without being in breach of their fiduciary duties.[92]

The long-anticipated duty to exercise reasonable care, skill and diligence in accordance with both objective and subjective standards is now held in s 174. Previously, the judiciary were prepared to tolerate high levels of incompetence in the company directors. For the most part the courts held that the duty required from a director was not the common law duty of care of the reasonable man but was better described as an equitable duty, analogous to a trustee. *In Re City Equitable Fire Assurance Co Ltd*,[93] a director's duty was encompassed by three basic propositions. First, a director was expected to exercise no greater care or skill than that expected from a person of his knowledge and experience, a subjective test. Second, there was no requirement that a director should give his full time and attention to affairs of the

---

89 Op. cit., *West Mercia Safetywear Ltd (in liq) v Dodd* and the Insolvency Act 1986, ss 212–214.
90 Section 174(2)(a) and (b).
91 [1989] BCLC 233.
92 *Fulham Football Club Ltd v Cabra Estates plc* (1994) BCLC 363. Substantial payments were made for a similarly restrictive agreement.
93 [1925] Ch 407.

company. And, third, where management was properly delegated, a director was justified, in the absence of grounds for suspicion, in trusting an official to perform his duties honestly. Again, in Farrar it is noted that 'the courts regarded directors as pleasant, if sometimes incompetent, amateurs who did not possess any particular executive skills and upon whom it would have been unreasonable to impose onerous standards of care and skill'.[94] More recently the courts have adopted a more objective test when assessing a director's competency. In *Dorchester Finance Co Ltd v Stebbing*,[95] the court rejected the argument that the directors could rely upon the competence and diligence of auditors and renounce all supervisory functions. Here the directors who were non-executives were chartered accountants who were employed for their skills and therefore had to display such skill as could reasonably be expected of persons with their knowledge and experience. They had at all times to take such care as a prudent man would take on his own behalf. Likewise in *Re Barings*,[96] a director was held to be in breach for failing to properly monitor the activities of somebody in a lower management position such as his level of remuneration would have reasonably required of him.

The statutory duty of care and skill reflects the recommendation of the Law Commission that it be a dual test, a 'twofold objective/subjective test'[97] with regard to 'the function of a particular director and the circumstances of the company'.[98] The wording of s 214 of the 1986 Insolvency Act was looked upon favourably by both the Commission and the Review and the 2006 Act reflects this. The level of care and skill required is:

the care, skill and diligence that would be exercised by a reasonable diligent person with–

(a) the general knowledge, skill and experience that may be reasonably be expected of a person carrying out the functions carried out by the director in relations to the company, and

(b) the general knowledge, skill and experience that the director has (s 174(2)(a) and (b))

The duty to avoid conflicts of interest is held in s 175. This section particularly includes conflicts involving corporate opportunities such as the 'exploitation of any property, information or opportunity'.[99] Furthermore and in line with the principles in *Regal (Hastings) et al*, 'it is immaterial

---

94 Op. cit., *Farrar*, p 392.
95 (1977) (1989) BCLC 498.
96 *Secretary of State for Trade and Industry v Baker (No 1)* [1998] BCC 583.
97 Law Commission No 261, para 5.20, p 52.
98 Ibid.
99 Section 175(2).

whether the company could take advantage of the property, information or opportunity'.[100] Subsection 1 requires a director to avoid conflicts which conflict or might possibly conflict with the interests of the company. This differs from the common law principle that a director should avoid situations in which his self-interest may possibly conflict with his duty to the company in that the new wording requires a possible external conflict with the company, not an internal conflict with the multiple roles a fiduciary might assume. It plays much more closely to the 'company as a market competitor' notion and anticipates the forthcoming acceptance of director's actions which may constitute an internal conflict but do not jeopardise the interests of the company, either objectively or in the view of the directors. Accordingly, subsection 4 states that this duty is not infringed, '(a) if the situation cannot reasonably be regarded as likely to give rise to a conflict of interest'. Thus this provision gives a statutory expression to the reasoning in the conflict cases discussed in the 'company as competitor' section, and allows the court to decide objectively whether the director's actions were in conflict with the interests of the company.[101] Alternatively, subsection 4 allows a director to avoid liability if 'the matter has been authorised by the directors'.[102]

Authorisation may only be given if the company is a private company with nothing in its constitution which invalidates a proposal to authorise.[103] Or, if the company is a public company authorisation may only be given if there is a provision in its articles allowing such a proposal.[104] In both cases this authorisation is only effective if the vote of any interested director was not counted and any quorum requirements are met.[105]

Under s 176 a director may not accept any benefits from a third party (other than payment for services rendered) given because he is a director, if such an acceptance would reasonably be regarded as conflicting or possibly conflicting with the interests of the company. Thus a director may personally benefit from his position if it causes no reasonably identifiable disadvantage to the company, another departure from trustee principles.

Section 177 provides that a director must declare the nature and extent of any proposed transaction or arrangement with the company in which he has a direct or indirect interest. This declaration may be made at a meeting of directors, by notice in writing under s 184 or by general notice under s 185.[106] A fresh declaration must be made if the original declaration becomes

---

100 Ibid.
101 Eg, op. cit. *IEF v Umunna, Peso Silver Mines, Broz v Cellular*.
102 Section 175(4)(b).
103 Section 175(5)(a).
104 Section 175(5)(b).
105 Section 175(6).
106 Section 177(2).

inaccurate or incomplete[107] and it must be made before the company enters into the transaction or arrangement.[108] Failure to do the above will constitute a breach of duty. However, this section does not apply if the director is not aware of the transaction and it is reasonable that he is not.[109] Furthermore, a director need not declare an interest if it 'cannot reasonably be regarded as likely to give rise to a conflict of interest',[110] or to the extent that the directors already know about it.[111] Lastly he will not need to make a declaration if it concerns the terms of his service contract which are in the process of being considered by the other directors.[112]

Similar provisions are made in respect of a declaration of interests in existing contracts or arrangements under s 182. Under s 182(1) a director must make a declaration to the other directors which under subsection 2 may be made at a meeting, or by notice in writing or by general notice. A fresh declaration must be made should the original become inaccurate or incomplete and any such declaration must be made 'as soon as is reasonably practicable'.[113] Subsections 5 and 6 are identical to the corresponding subsections in s 177. Under s 183 a director who fails to comply with s 182 commits an offence and is liable to a fine.[114]

If any provisions in respect of declarations or consents are complied with then the director will not be in breach of his duty to the company.[115] Absent this, any breach of ss 171–177 will result in the consequences that were applicable under the old common law and equitable principles.[116] Furthermore, in respect of duties under ss 175 and 176, a director will still be subject to these after he has ceased to be a director. In the case of conflicts of interest under s 175, the duty will continue 'as regards the exploitation of any property, information or opportunity of which he became aware at a time when he was a director'.[117] Or, in respect of the duty not to accept benefits from third parties, 'as regards things done or omitted by him before he ceased to be a director'.[118]

In the case of a declaration of interest under s 182 by a shadow director, such a declaration may only be made by notice in writing in accordance with

107 Section 177(3).
108 Section 177(4).
109 Section 177(5).
110 Section 177(6)(a).
111 Section 177(6)(b).
112 Section 177(6)(c).
113 Section 182(3) and (4) respectively.
114 Replacing s 317 of the 1985 Act.
115 Section 180.
116 Section 178.
117 Section 170(2)(a) following *IDC v Cooley*.
118 Section 170(2)(b).

s 184.[119] A shadow director, encapsulating the ruling in *Re Hydrodam*,[120] is 'a person in accordance with whose directions or instructions the directors of the company are accustomed to act but does not include a professional advisor.

Other chapters in Part 10 include the following important provisions which are given in overview form only.

Chapter 1: The appointment and removal of directors. Sections 154–169

Section 154 requires a private company to have at least one director and a public company to have at least two. Section 155 requires that at least one of these directors must be a natural person, to deal with the problem of the accountability of holding companies who under the previous Act might be the only directors. Under s 157 a director must be at least 16 years of age and any who are not at the time this section comes into force will cease to be directors. Sections 162–167 specify the requirements of a register of directors including the requirement that the company must keep a register of its directors' residential addresses. Under s 168 a director may be removed by an ordinary resolution of the company's members but has certain rights to protest under s 169.

Chapter 4: Transactions with directors requiring approval of members

In this chapter, all transactions which require the approval of members are drawn together. All criminal penalties in respect of these transactions are removed and the civil remedies in respect of failure to get members' approval for substantial property transactions, loans, quasi-loans and credit transactions are aligned. Chapter 4 covers long-term service contracts, substantial property transactions, loans, quasi-loans, credit transactions and payments for loss of office.

1. Long-term service contracts
Sections 188 and 189 replace s 319 of the 1985 Act. Member approval is required for all service contracts over two years and failure to get this approval will allow the company to terminate the contract at any time following reasonable notice.

2. Substantial property transactions
Sections 190–196 replace ss 320–322 of the 1985 Act and require members'

---

119 Section 187.
120 Section 251.

approval when the company buys or sells a non-cash asset to a director of the company or a director of its holding company, a person connected with a director of the company or to a director of its holding company worth more than £5,000. Approval is required if the transaction is worth more than £100,000 or 10 per cent of the company's net assets.

3. Loans, quasi-loans and credit transactions

Section 197 requires members' approval for loans, quasi-loans and credit transactions made to directors in private companies which are not associated with a public company. Sections 197, 198, 200 and 201 require members' approval for loans, quasi-loans and credit transactions made to directors in public companies or private companies associated with public companies. Members' approval is not required for loans, quasi-loans and credit transactions which do not exceed £50,000 if this money is to fund expenditure on company business,[121] or for money lent to finance a director's defence costs for breaches of duty or any related regulatory action,[122] or for loans and quasi-loans not exceeding £10,000 and credit transactions under £15,000.[123]

4. Payments for loss of office

Sections 215 to 222 require members' approval for such payments.

Chapter 5: Directors' service contracts

This chapter requires that a director's service contract be available for inspection up to a year after they have left.[124] Failure to comply will result in a fine of £1,000 for every officer in default and £100/day for all subsequent non-compliance. Section 229 allows members to inspect the contracts free of charge and s 230 applies these rules to shadow directors as well as directors. Sections 228–230 replace section 318 of the 1985 Act.

Chapter 6: Contracts with sole members who are directors

Under s 231, such contracts must be recorded in writing unless they are those entered into in the normal course of the company's business. Failure to comply results in the responsible company officers' liability for a fine not exceeding £5,000. This section replaces s 322B of the 1985 Act.

---

121 Section 204.
122 Sections 205 and 206 respectively.
123 Section 207.
124 Sections 228 and 227. Section 227 is new.

Chapter 7: Directors' liabilities

Under s 232 a company is prohibited from exempting a director from negligence, breach of duty or breach of trust and any provision in the company's articles which attempts to do so is void. This replaces s 310 of the 1985 Act. Sections 233–238 set out various provisions in respect of a company's provision of insurance or indemnification for its directors. Section 239 provides that any decision by a company to ratify an action which constitutes negligence, default, breach of duty or breach of trust must be taken without the votes of the director in question or any person connected to the director.[125] Otherwise all existing rules on ratification remain.

Chapter 8: Directors' residential addresses: protection from disclosure

The purpose of this chapter is to put into statutory form the recommendations of the CLR that a director may choose to either put his residential address on public record, as under the 1985 Act, or to provide a service address which would be on public record. Their residential address would be held on a separate secure register to which access would be restricted. Section 240 prohibits a company providing its directors' home addresses without their consent. Section 243 allows the registrar to use or disclose a director's address for certain limited ends such as when he needs to communicate with the director. Under s 244 anyone with sufficient interest may apply to the court for an order to disclose the protected address. This may be because the service address is ineffective[126] or to enforce a court order.[127]

Chapter 9: Supplementary provisions

Under this chapter a number of terms are closely defined. Under ss 252–256 persons that are connected with the company are defined, including members of the director's family under s 253, a body corporate under s 254 and an associate body corporate under s 256.[128] It also includes a company in which the director has a controlling interest, defined as more than 50 per cent of the shares.[129] Section 248 sets out certain requirements in respect of records of directors' meetings, including the requirement to keep the records for 10 years. Section 250 defines a director and s 251 defines a shadow director;

---

125 Defined in s 252.
126 Section 244(1).
127 Section 244(2).
128 A connected body corporate is one in which the director owns at least 20 per cent of the shares. Section 256 is new.
129 Section 255.

both reproduce the definitions under the 1985 Act. Finally, s 247 replaces s 719 of the 1985 Act and provides that directors may make provisions for employees including ex-employees but may not rely on this section to make payments for themselves or for former directors or to shadow directors. Subsection 6 provides that such payments may only be made following a resolution of the members unless the articles allow such authorisations to be made by the board. All such payments must be made out of profits and before the company commences winding up.

CONCLUSION

The reform process and the resulting legislation on directors' duties have promoted the ideology of shareholder primacy. The provisions in s 172 mean that all the duties which a director owes to the company, be it a duty to be reasonably competent, honest or to act with discretion, are to be exercised in such a way that primarily pursues shareholder interest. The ideology of contractarianism has facilitated a modern and sophisticated justification for focusing 'the best interests of the company' in this way. But it is wrong, both methodologically and morally. The company is made of arrangements between people as the contractarians rightly assert, but this makes it a social as well as an economic actor, which must be reflected in giving it a broad public nature. Accordingly, directors' duties should take proper account of the interests of all engaged persons and not simply privilege shareholders.

Chapter 6

Corporate governance III: minority shareholder protection

Minority shareholder protection is vital to corporate governance. In the words of La Porta *et al*, 'corporate governance is, to a large extent, a set of mechanisms through which outside investors protect themselves against expropriation by the insiders'.[1] The reform process in respect of the law on minority protection has attended to two key perspectives, the 'law matters' perspective and contractarianism. The first position posits the notion that minority shareholding will only be attractive and thus encourage the wide share dispersal which characterises Anglo-American corporations if there are sufficient legal protections for shareholders without a majority holding. The second perspective asserts that unfettered minority rights are not economic-ally efficient as ultimately the costs to the business from a minority action are costs that are borne by shareholders with the largest stake in the business. This position advocates strong controls over minority rights. The law matters thesis and contractarianism will be briefly examined in the first part of this chapter in so far as they relate to minority shareholder protection. The chapter will then examine the law on minority protection as it has developed, the aims and ideological influences of the reform process in respect of minority protection and its legislative expression in the 2006 Act.

THEORY AND MINORITY PROTECTION

Law matters

As we saw in Chapter 4, Mark Roe argued that the most important factors in creating an environment which encourages wide share dispersal is politics. A political environment that facilitates state control over business will dis-courage the sale of large, usually family stakes in businesses, where such

---

1 La Porta *et al*, 'Investor protection and corporate governance' (2000) 58 Journal of Financial Economics, 3, p 4.

shareholders require a majority stake in order to ensure the pursuit of their self-interest. Other work has emphasised the importance of law in creating an environment which encourages wide share dispersal. In particular, a body of work from La Porta *et al* indicates the crucial nature of laws and enforcement procedures which protect minority shareholders:

> Company, bankruptcy, and securities laws specifically describe some of the rights of corporate insiders and outside investors. These laws, and the quality of their enforcement by the regulators and the courts, are essential elements of corporate governance and finance. When investor rights such as the voting rights of the shareholders and the reorganization and liquidation rights of the creditors are extensive and well enforced by regulators or courts, investors are willing to finance firms. In contrast, when the legal system does not protect outside investors, corporate governance and external finance do not work well.[2]

Indeed, La Porta *et al* claim that legal systems in their entirety will allow or disallow minority shareholder protection. Their research indicates that the historical development of common law systems, originating in post civil war England, was responding to parliamentary attempts to protect private property against the crown. They argue that this emphasis on individual private property has enabled common-law systems to value the protection of the private property interests of minority shareholders. Thus, they maintain, 'civil law is associated with greater government intervention in economic activity and weaker protection of private property than common law', leading to 'inferior protection of the rights of outside investors in civil law countries'.[3]

In regard to financial markets La Porta *et al* maintain that systems which protect minorities have more valuable stock markets because when investors are protected from expropriation they will pay more for stock. In their 1997 study they provide evidence that 'countries that protect shareholders have more valuable stock markets, larger numbers of listed securities per capita, and a higher rate of IPO (initial public offering) activity than do the unprotected countries'.[4] This may also be demonstrated, they argue, by a comparison of two major Eastern European economies in transition. In Poland, they argue, the adoption of strong securities legislation has resulted in the emergence of a thriving capital market. In contrast, the Czech Republic 'chose neither to introduce tough securities laws nor to create a powerful market regulator at the time of privatization'.[5] Now, 'Czech markets have

2 Ibid, p 4.
3 Ibid, p 12.
4 Ibid, p 15.
5 Ibid, p 22.

been plagued by massive expropriation of minority shareholders',[6] so that 'in contrast to the Polish market, the Czech market stagnated, with hundreds of companies getting delisted and virtually no public equity financing by firms'.[7]

According to La Porta *et al*, one of the attributes of 'good law' is rules which can be easily enforced. This often means rules which can be imposed within an existing enforcement structure rather than the construction of perfect rules which cannot be enforced without the further construction of an enforcement agency. A connected issue here is the clarity of the rules in question and the procedures for enforcing those rules. In this respect, the 2006 Act has done much to clarify both the law and the procedures concerning minority protection.

Contractarianism

Contractarianism in the context of company law maintains that the law should operate to produce the bargain that parties would have come to if they were actually bargaining. By constructing the bargain, therefore, company law reduces the cost of actually bargaining, thus fulfilling the purpose of good company law, which should be to produce the most cost-efficient results – cost-efficient results being those that produce the greatest return for investors. Accordingly, contractarianism has a tendency to consider minority shareholder protection as not cost-efficient and therefore something which company law could happily abandon.

Exemplifying this position are Easterbrook and Fischel, who maintain that minority shareholder provisions have a tendency to misallocate funds they give power to shareholders who may have a very tiny stake in the business. In respect of the derivative action they state that 'holders of small stakes have little incentive to consult the effect of the action on other shareholders, the supposed beneficiaries, who ultimately bear the costs'.[8] Indeed, the 'determining characteristic of the derivative action is the lack of any link between stake and reward – not only on the judge's part but also on the plaintiff's'.[9] Furthermore, they argue, a derivative suit will be to the advantage of other outsiders such as attorneys who will be keen to pursue a case despite its lack of merits and without regard to the interests of the company because it pays them to do so. In contrast, 'the value of the managers' time cannot be recouped, no matter how frivolous the action'.[10]

Accordingly, they argue, the most cost-efficient way to judge the decisions

---

6 Ibid.
7 Ibid, pp 22–23.
8 Easterbrook and Fischel, *The Economic Structure of Corporate Law*, first paperback edn, 1996, Cambridge, MA: Harvard University Press, p 101.
9 Ibid.
10 Ibid.

of managers is not through the views of minority shareholders or judges, who are poorly equipped to do so, but through the views of managers themselves. A decision that might look 'hasty' to the outsider might be the most economically efficient decision for the experienced manager. Corporate law, they maintain, recognises the economic efficiency of limiting minority shareholder actions by such mechanisms as the business judgment rule, which takes most corporate decisions outside of the realm of scrutiny.[11] Furthermore, they argue that even the supposedly wrongdoing director is in a more economically efficient position to judge the rightness of his actions than the minority shareholder. They conclude by commending the existing restrictions on derivative actions and tacitly recommending further restrictions. 'Our discussion of the poor incentives of small shareholders and their attorneys to maximize the value of the firm implies that legal rules should place restrictions on the ability to bring derivative suits.'[12]

Indeed, it is the many restrictions which exist in respect of minority shareholder protection in England and America which leads Brian Cheffins to critique the 'law matters' thesis.[13] How, he asks, can a rule such as that of *Foss v Harbottle* (discussed below) create confidence for minority shareholders thus encouraging wide share dispersal? Concurring with the contractarian approach he argues that regulation which ensures an open and free market is a much better mechanism for achieving good governance of corporations. Both America and Britain had poor legal protection for its minority shareholders, 'instead in both countries other institutions provided investors with sufficient confidence to purchase tiny percentages of equity in publicly quoted companies, thus allowing the widely dispersed share ownership that characterizes the Berle–Means corporation to emerge'.[14]

While case law developed fiduciary duties for directors in principle, the problem for minority shareholders was one of enforceability. The best protection for minorities was market controls, in short a manager's record for producing dividends. 'In fact, if not in law, at the moment we are thrown back on the obvious conclusion that a stockholder's right lies in the expectation of fair dealing rather than in the ability to enforce legal claims.'[15] Small investors were induced to invest by the clarity of information produced by the market and its institutions. For example, he noted, the New York Stock Exchange (NYSE) would reject applications to list companies that lacked an adequate

---

11 In that it allows a director to avoid claims resulting form his poor or even negligent decisions on the basis that the decision taken was a business judgment which is assumed in law to have been made honestly.
12 Ibid, p 105.
13 Cheffins, BR, 'Law as bedrock: The foundations of an economy dominated by widely held public companies.' (2003) 23 OJLS 1, pp 1–23.
14 Ibid p 7.
15 Ibid, p 10.

earnings record or who operated in high-risk businesses such as petroleum and mining. The NYSE 'saw itself as a guardian of the financial quality of the issuers listed on it'.[16] Furthermore, in 1909 it sought to enhance corporate disclosure by imposing 'a requirement that listed companies distribute annual financial reports to their shareholders and from that point onwards carried out a strong campaign to improve the quantity and quality of disclosure'.[17]

Likewise, Cheffins argues, in the UK, shares only became truly dispersed once the market had taken on measures to protect and inform investors, many aping the controls already adopted in America. Following the Second World War, he states, the London Stock Exchange engaged in much greater quality control, addressing 'various matters of potential concern to outside investors by strengthening its listing rules. Topics dealt with included disclosure, insider trading and other forms of self dealing by directors and controlling shareholders.'[18] Similarly, the Take-over Panel, whose code, originating in the 1950s and largely determines take-over practices, took as its guiding principle the fair and equal treatment of all investors. Cheffins concludes that 'market dynamics, together with privately-orientated regulatory initiatives, did much more than the legal system to enhance the confidence of British investors as the Berle–Means corporation became dominant'.[19] And 'market orientated mechanisms did more to induce investors to own equity in companies characterized by a separation of ownership and control'.[20]

The reform of the law on minority protection creates a clear statutory regime in which minority shareholders may pursue derivative actions. These reforms reflect the law matters thesis. However, in this reform are contained a number of procedures and checks which halt the pursuit of an action if this action is not in the interests of the company or cost-efficient. These reforms reflect the contractarian thesis.

It is usual for textbooks to discuss other minority shareholder protections, which include statutory protections under s 122(1)(g) of the 1986 Insolvency Act and s 459 Companies Act 1985, in the same chapter or section, and to that extent this chapter conforms to this approach. However, in governance terms these other protections perform quite a different role to that of the derivative action. Derivative actions refer to the legal mechanisms which allow a minority shareholder to change the balance of power within the corporation (at least temporarily) on the company's behalf. On the other hand, statutory protections such as petitions for unfairly prejudicial conduct only apply in quasi-partnership companies and not large companies characterised

16 Ibid, p 11.
17 Ibid.
18 Ibid, p 14.
19 Ibid.
20 Ibid, p 22.

by dispersed share ownership. These are remedies which allow informal understandings between members of a company (composed of a very small number of people who act as if in a partnership) to be enforced because their relationships are sufficiently close for non-contractual relations to be the *modus operandi*. These businesses do not fall under the reform project of encouraging 'enlightened shareholder value' which applies to the large companies which constitute most of the economy and accordingly, there is little change in this statutory regime.

THE LAW ON MINORITY SHAREHOLDER PROTECTION

Common-law derivative actions

In the area of minority shareholder protection the law has been dominated by a rule that was established in case of *Foss v Harbottle*.[21] This case concerned a corporation, not a modern registered company. Furthermore, the decision and reasoning were almost certainly intended to apply to the specifics of this case alone and not to have a general application to registered companies, which at the time did not exist. *Foss v Harbottle*, like the early corporation cases discussed in the previous chapters, was so decided because of the particular terms of this company's Act of incorporation and *despite* any general principles in law.

In *Foss v Harbottle*, two minority shareholders who complained that the company directors had sold their own land to the company at an inflated price were denied redress by the courts. The reason given by the Vice-Chancellor for this was that although the corporation was the *cestui que* trust,

> the majority of the proprietors at a special general meeting assembled, independently of any general rules of law upon the subject, by the very terms of the incorporation in the present case, has power to bind the whole body, and every individual corporator must be taken to have come into the corporation upon the terms of being so bound.[22]

The reason the minority had no redress was because the particular terms of the company's incorporation enabled the company's decisions to be made by a majority of shareholders at a special general meeting. The company was described as 'little more than a partnership', and the judge expressed regret that the shareholders were being deprived of their 'civil rights'. Thus, one

21 (1843) 2 Hare 461, 67 ER 189.
22 Ibid, p 195.

might reasonably expect this judgment to have very limited application. Instead, however, this judgment becomes authority for the proposition that no individual member can sue in respect of any wrong which is ratifiable by ordinary resolution of the members.[23] Initially this was constrained by the particular terms of the company's constitution so that in *Mozley v Alston*[24] the court articulated the 'rule in *Foss v Harbottle*' to be that an individual shareholder could not bring an action to the courts to complain about an irregularity in the way in which the company's affairs were being conducted if there was a constitutional facility to ratify the wrong. If there wasn't, then presumably *Foss v Harbottle* would not apply.

But, once modern company law had fully articulated what was ratifiable by a simple majority in general law, the notion that ratification automatically put a stop to any legal action by a disgruntled shareholder became the general rule. And, once the company had developed into a distinct economic being and was conceptualised in law as a separate legal being the 'proper plaintiff' rule was grafted onto the rule in *Foss v Harbottle*.[25] The 'proper plaintiff' rule states that in respect of a wrong done to a company the proper plaintiff is the company and not the shareholder. So the rule in *Foss v Harbottle* is now understood to be that:

- in respect of a wrong done to a company the proper plaintiff is the company; and
- no individual member can sue in respect of any wrong which is ratifiable by ordinary resolution of the members; and
- actions by individual members can only be done under an exception to the general rule.

Under common-law rules developed in the latter half of the nineteenth century, a member could bring an action against those doing wrong to the company, in their own name, but ultimately on the company's behalf. In other words, exceptions to the rule in *Foss v Harbottle* developed. They could take this derivative action if the company was not in a position to protect its own interests because the wrongdoers were in effective control.[26] The wrong in question would need to be a substantial breach of duty and/or a fraud against the company. Thus to bring a derivative action the minority shareholder was obliged to establish both a wrong against the company and that the wrong-doers were in such control of the company as to prevent any legal action by the company.

---

23 Now modified by the Companies Act 2006, examined later in this chapter.
24 (1847) 1 Ph 90; 16 LJ Ch 217.
25 Neither *Foss v Harbottle* nor *Mozley v Alston* articulated the proper plaintiff rule.
26 *Atwool v Merryweather* [1867] LR 5 Eq 464n; 37 LJ Ch 35.

Negligence alone has been consistently considered to be an insufficient wrong on which to base a derivative action. In *Pavlides v Jenson*,[27] minority shareholders alleged that the directors were grossly negligent in selling a company asset. The court held that there was no cause of action as there was no fraud alleged, nor had the directors personally benefited from the transaction. However, in *Daniels v Daniels*,[28] a similar gross undervaluation of company assets did constitute an actionable wrong, because in this case the directors had bought the land themselves.[29] The court held that under the exceptions to *Foss v Harbottle* there was no requirement to fulfil the strict criteria of fraud. Such an action could be brought for negligence if such a breach had personally benefited the wrongdoers. As Vinelott J later wryly noted, 'to put up with foolish directors is one thing; to put up with directors who are so foolish that they make a profit of £115,000 odd at the expense of the company is quite another'.[30]

Alternatively, majority action which was clearly not in the interests of the company has been sufficient grounds upon which to pursue a derivative action. In *Estmanco (Kilner House) v GLC*,[31] the Greater London Council (GLC) formed a company to continue its work of selling long leases on a block of 60 refurbished flats. The company had £3,000 of share capital which was divided into 60 shares valued at £50 which carried one vote. Under its articles of association the company was to allot one share to each new tenant but the votes were to remain vested in the GLC until all the shares were sold. Until that had occurred the GLC remained the sole voter at company meetings. In 1981 the GLC entered into an agreement under seal that included an undertaking that they would use all their efforts to sell the flats on a long lease. Following a change in housing policy the council's housing committee passed a resolution to the effect that the remaining 48 unsold flats should be let to 'high priority applicants on its housing list'.[32] The three directors of the company, who were also employees of the GLC but who were fully empowered to act independently in the best interest of the company, sought to enforce the company's contract with the council. At an extraordinary general meeting a resolution was passed on the votes of the sole shareholder, the GLC, in which the directors were instructed to withdraw all action in respect of the contract. The application to take a derivative action was bought by one of Estmanco's tenants and the court held that the

---

27 [1956] Ch 565.
28 [1978] Ch 406.
29 In this case the two directors caused the company to sell the land to one of them and then four years later caused the company to rebuy the land at 28 times the amount the director paid for it.
30 *Prudential Assurance Co Ltd v Newman Industries Ltd* (No 2) [1981] Ch 257, p 315.
31 *Estmanco (Kilner House) Ltd v Greater London Council* [1982] 1 WLR 2.
32 Ibid, p 3.

discontinuation of the action in respect of the contract gave the applicant sufficient interest to pursue an action. The wrong was in ignoring the company's best interests, depriving minority members of the chance to vote and 'stultifying the purpose for which the company was formed'.[33] The court considered the exceptions of 'fraud on a minority' to be sufficiently wide to cover enforcement of covenants, citing Templeman J's judgment in *Daniels* that 'a minority shareholder who has no other remedy may sue where directors use their powers, intentionally or unintentionally, fraudulently or negligently, in a manner which benefits themselves at the expense of the company.[34]

Megarry VC stated that the principle stood without the self-dealing aspect in *Daniels*. The core wrong was misuse of power.

> Apart from the benefit to themselves at the company's expense, the essence of the matter seems to be an abuse or misuse of power. 'Fraud' in the phrase 'fraud on a minority' seems to be being used as comprising not only fraud at common law but also fraud in the wider equitable sense of that term, as in the equitable concept of a fraud on a power.[35]

The second arm of the exception to *Foss v Harbottle*, that of wrongdoers in control, is perhaps more controversial. In *Pavlides v Jenson*, the action failed both for the absence of fraud, as previously examined, but also because the directors did not technically control the company which was wronged. The directors, however, did make up the majority of the board of the company's holding company, but, strictly speaking, 'the shareholders of the shareholding company could in general meeting decide differently and disagree with the directors of that company'.[36] In *Pavlides*, Danckwerts J required that control be *de jure* control rather than what it was, *de facto* control.

In contrast, Vinelott J's judgment in *Prudential Assurance v Newman*[37] considered control to be a procedural issue and one that was flexible once fraud had been established. If justice would be thwarted by allowing *de jure* control to be the only basis upon which to pursue a derivative action then the courts, he stated, should have the flexibility to consider *de facto* control. In *Prudential* the wrongdoers in question were two directors on the board of Newman Industries Ltd. First they presented a series of false or confusing documents to the board and then having misled the 'independent valuer' presented a misleading circular to Newman's shareholders. As a result they

33 Ibid, p 4.
34 *Daniels v Daniels* [1978] Ch 406, p 414.
35 *Estmanco (Kilner House) Ltd v Greater London Council* [1982] 1 WLR 2, p 12.
36 *Pavlides v Jenson* [1956] Ch 565, p 577.
37 *Prudential Assurance v Newman Industries Ltd* [1980] 2 WLR 339.

succeeded in persuading a small majority at an extraordinary meeting to pass a resolution approving fraudulent transactions worth £425,000. The directors owned a holding company which owned TBG Ltd, a major shareholder in Newman Ltd, and the recipient of many of Newman's assets. However, TBG did not vote on the resolution and the directors were not in *de jure* control of either the board or the shares of Newman. Could a derivative action be maintained notwithstanding that the wrongdoers were not in *de jure* control?

Citing some early authorities Vinelott J argued that the notions of interests of justice have consistently insisted that issues of control should be flexibly approached to include those in a position to influence as well as those with actual control.

He later referred to Lord Davey in *Burland v Earle*,[38] who stated that the proper plaintiff rule is a *prima facie* rule only. To further support this approach, he cited Jenkins LJ in *Edwards v Halliwell*,[39] who stated that 'the rule is not an inflexible rule and [that it] will be relaxed where necessary in the interests of justice'. On Jessel MR's pronouncements on the exceptions to *Foss v Harbottle*,[40] Vinelott J surmised that Jessel MR clearly considered that an action could be brought when the company's interests would be defeated if the minority could not act in circumstances when the wrongdoers were not majority shareholders but were in control. Thus he concluded that the court should be able to assess all the circumstances of a case in order to determine whether the majority is disinterestedly pursuing the best interests of the company.

The 'justice of the case' principle upon which Vinelott based his *de facto* control notion was rejected by the Court of Appeal, which considered the principle too wide and too difficult to apply except when a judge was determining the preliminary issue of whether a shareholder had a right to bring a derivative action at all. Indeed, the court held that the question of whether the rule in *Foss v Harbottle* applied to any particular set of circumstances should, where possible, be decided as a preliminary issue and not left for determination at the trial. However, the 'control' issue is by no means settled in law, and, in the context of large public companies where most shareholders will be governed by a more powerful group, be it directors or a large, visible minority shareholder, it is of arguable wisdom to disregard Vinelott's '*de facto* control' test.

Statutory protections

Statute has for many years provided a small number of remedies for minority shareholders whose company's affairs are conducted in such a manner that

---

38 [1902] AC 83.
39 [1950] 2 All ER 1064, p 1067.
40 In the case of *Russell v Wakefield Waterworks Co* LR 20 Eq 474.

they are being treated unfairly and contrary to any informal understanding they had with those in control of the company, who may be directors or may be the majority shareholder(s). An informal understanding is one that is not held in a contract but is instead an understanding of how the company will be run which has not been put in a legal form because the mutual trust between the parties made such formalities unnecessary.

Section 122(1)(g) of the 1986 Insolvency Act

A minority shareholder may apply to the court to have the company wound up on 'just and equitable' grounds under s 122(1)(g) of the 1986 Insolvency Act.[41] The factors which the court will consider in reaching this conclusion were amply stated in the well-known case of *Ebrahimi v Westbourne Galleries Ltd*,[42] particularly in the judgments of Lord Wilberforce and Lord Cross of Chelsea. These judgments have a wide-reaching importance providing a basis for interpreting the more widely used remedy under s 459, discussed below and informing the CLR's thinking on minority protection more generally.

The fact that the inequity of the conduct complained of is a breach of some significant but informal understanding implies that this remedy and indeed a petition under s 459 is usually only applicable in small private companies where the members have had close communications capable of being significant understandings. The members of such companies are likely to have previously undertaken their business under the partnership form, incorporating the business as a company some time into their business relationship. Under such circumstances, it would be expected that the manner in which the business was undertaken as a partnership would continue notwithstanding that the business was now a company to which new formalities and rules applied. Thus much of what the members expected would not be reflected in the company constitution or within the Company Acts but would be contained in mutual understandings of the continuance of partnership-like relations. In *Ebrahimi*, Westbourne Galleries Ltd was typical of this type of company, characterised by Lord Wilberforce as a quasi-partnership.

In this case, Mr Ebrahimi and Mr Nizar were partners for a period of 14 years before transferring the business to a private company. They held both shares and managerial positions in such a manner that reflected their previous relationship, that is in equal amounts of shares and equal directorships. Soon after the company's incorporation, Mr Nizar's son joined the business as a director and both Mr Ebrahimi and his father gave him 20 per cent of their shares. This meant that Mr Ebrahimi now held a

---

41 Section 122(1)(g) states that the company may be wound up if 'the court is of the opinion that it is just and equitable that the company should be wound up'.

42 *Ebrahimi v Westbourne Galleries Ltd* [1973] AC 360.

20 per cent shareholding and Mr Nizar and his son together held 60 per cent. As majority shareholders they voted on an ordinary resolution to have Mr Ebrahimi removed from his directorship. And, as all the company's profits were paid as directors' remuneration rather than dividends Mr Ebrahimi was effectively removed from both the management of the business and its profits. The court held that the company should be dissolved on 'just and equitable' grounds because the character of the company was one that was based on mutual trust and this had been lost, leaving Mr Ebrahimi with no right to the profits and no power to dispose of his shares. Lord Wilberforce stated that the 'just and equitable' provision enables 'the court to subject the exercise of legal rights to equitable consideration; considerations, that is, of a personal character arising between one individual and another, which may make it unjust, or inequitable, to insist on legal rights, or to exercise them in a particular way'.[43] And although the circumstances in which those considerations will apply are not clear cut, he stated, it would probably include more than one of the following elements. First, 'an association formed on the basis of a personal relationship, involving mutual confidence'.[44] Second, that all or some of the members will participate in the company's management and third, where the member's stake in the business is restricted, 'so that if confidence is lost, or one member is removed from management, he cannot take out his stake and go elsewhere'.[45]

Section 459 Companies Act 1985

A member of a company may petition to the court under s 459 on the grounds that the company's affairs are being conducted in a manner which is 'unfairly prejudicial' to some or all of the members. Under s 461 if the court was satisfied that a petition is well founded it has discretion to make 'such order as it thinks fit'. This specifically included making an order to regulate the company's future activities, making an order to stop doing the act complained of or to act if the complaint was a failure to act, making an order authorising civil action in the company's name on its behalf and finally making an order requiring the company or any members of the company to purchase the petitioner's shares. The value of shares could either be made pro rata, a percentage of the total value of the company, or discounted for being a minority holding. In *Bird v Precision*,[46] the court held that in general, shares were to be valued on a pro rata basis, particularly if the shares were purchased at the time of incorporation. Shares that had been purchased later and

---

43 Ibid, p 279.
44 Ibid.
45 Ibid.
46 *Re Bird Precision Bellows Ltd* [1986] Ch 658.

where the petitioner had either been excluded from management for bona fide reasons might be valued on a discounted basis.[47]

The precise terms of s 459 were introduced in 1980[48] following a recommendation from the Jenkins Committee in 1962, and it is by far the most popular and significant mechanism for minority shareholder redress, as the empirical work undertaken by the Law Commission and discussed later testifies.

As Lord Hoffman stated in *Re Saul D Harrison and Sons plc*,[49] (examined below), the term 'unfairly prejudicial' was selected by Parliament specifically because it was 'deliberately imprecise',[50] thus allowing the courts wider powers of interpretation than that provided by the earlier s 210 of the 1948 Companies Act. Furthermore, he stated, s 210, which was intended to provide a similar remedy for minority shareholders, had been 'too restrictively construed'. Having included the term 'oppressive' which the House of Lords had interpreted as 'burdensome, harsh and wrongful' it 'gave rise to some uncertainly as to whether "wrongful" required actual illegality or invasion of legal rights'.[51]

In *Re Saul* the Court of Appeal held that a s 459 petition could only be brought if the petitioner had failed to have his 'legitimate expectation met'. These expectations could be found in the company's constitution, other external agreements and a shared understanding of a fundamental nature; a fundamental understanding between the shareholders which formed the basis of their association but was not in contractual form. In this case, there was no evidence that the latter two existed and thus only the articles of association expressed legitimate expectations. As the defendants had acted within their powers under the articles and had not breached their fiduciary duties, the petition was dismissed. Neill LJ set a number of guidelines to the 'correct approach' to the concept of 'unfairly prejudicial'. First, Lord Wilberforce in *Ebrahimi* stressed that 'unfairly prejudicial' were general words which should be used flexibly but that this should be tempered with Lord Hoffman's appeal to control the scope of the definition.[52] Second, the conduct should relate to the company of which the petitioner is a member and third, the conduct must be both unfair and prejudicial. Fourth, 'unfairly' covered legitimate expectations which encompassed legal rights held in the memorandum and articles and equitable considerations.

In *O'Neill v Phillips*,[53] Lord Hoffman radically reduced the scope of

---

47 The empirical evidence gathered by the Law Commission (next section) suggests that the latter method of valuation is rarely ordered by the courts.
48 Section 75. This became s 459 in the Companies Act 1985.
49 [1995] 1 BCLC 14.
50 *Saul* [1995] 1 BCLC 14, p 17.
51 Ibid.
52 *In Re a Company (No 007623 of 1984)* [1986] BCLC 362.
53 *O'Neill and another v Phillips and others, Re a company (No 00709 of 1992)* [1992] 2 BCLC 1.

unfairly prejudicial conduct. Indeed, he accepted culpability in its extension following his characterisation of unfairly prejudicial acts in *Re Saul* to be ones which offended the petitioner's 'legitimate expectation'. His use of an essentially public law term allowed the concept to 'lead a life of its own', making it 'capable of giving rise to equitable restraints in circumstances to which the traditional equitable principles have no application'.[54] The purpose of his judgment in this case was to clarify the scope of equitable restraints.

In *O'Neill*, the petitioner had worked as an employee of Pectal Ltd and having impressed its majority shareholder (Mr Philips), had been given 25 per cent of the shares and promoted to a directorship. Mr Phillips gradually withdrew from the business, leaving O'Neill as *de facto* managing director and relinquishing two-thirds of his dividends in order that O'Neill would receive 50 per cent of the profits through dividends and wages. There had been some negotiations between the two shareholders in respect of Mr O'Neill obtaining a 50 per cent shareholding, but these were never concluded. After a period of time, the business began to fail and Mr Phillips regained management control, having reduced his opinion of Mr O'Neill's abilities. He determined that Mr O'Neill would no longer be paid 50 per cent of the dividends and would instead receive dividends accruing to his 25 per cent shareholding plus a director's salary. O'Neill issued a petition under s 459, which was dismissed at first instance because the judge found that Mr Phillips had not promised to give Mr O'Neill half of the profits or half of the shares. The Court of Appeal allowed Mr O'Neill's appeal ordering Mr Philips to buy the petitioner's shares: 'O had a legitimate expectation that he would receive an equal share of the profits and additional shares and that P's denial of those expectations was unfairly prejudicial to O's interest as a member and had forced him out of the company.'[55]

The House of Lords upheld the respondent's appeal on the basis that a s 459 petition could only be granted if the conduct complained of fell within the normal ambit of equitable consideration. Thus a promise to do something may not be enforceable in law but may be binding under equity. However, in this case the judge had found that no promise had been made and therefore 'there was no basis, consistent with principles of equity, for a court to hold that P had behaved unfairly'.[56] An expectation that something would happen, albeit reasonably, did not give rise to the operation of equity. Lord Hoffman explained this in the context of the purpose and history of company law and of English law *per se*. A company was a commercial arrangement the terms of which were to be found for the most part in the

54 Ibid, p 11.
55 Ibid, p 1.
56 Ibid, p 2.

company constitution. All members both know and have agreed to these terms. However, company law's 'seamless[ly]' emergence from partnership law meant that it carried much of the baggage of partnership's good faith principles. Therefore, although in general the company and its members will be governed by the express terms of the constitution there will be some circumstances when 'equitable considerations make it unfair for those conducting the affairs of the company to rely upon their strict legal powers. Thus unfairness may consist in a breach of the rules or in using the rules in a manner which equity would regard as contrary to good faith'.[57] However, that which equity considers contrary to good faith is strictly limited to established equitable concerns. Indeed, stated Hoffman, it is only a quirk of the English legal system that a dichotomy is drawn between the legal (that which is strictly by the letter) and the equitable (that which is justice-based). Courts of Law and Courts of Equity once amalgamated continued the practice of distinguishing the two approaches. Other legal systems approach issues without such distinction, the stick of the law followed by the salve of equity. Hoffman notes that continental systems introduce a general requirement of good faith into contractual arrangements, which, Hoffman implies,[58] is the more sensible approach that achieves the desired outcome of s 459 with less complication. The question to ask in a s 459 situation is what is the plain meaning of the terms such as to give rise to honest expectation.

Furthermore, he stated that there needed to be inequitable behaviour for s 459 to apply. The notion that the breakdown in relations between, in this case, Mr Phillips and Mr O'Neill, would justify a petition was without authority. Drawing upon the reform process, Hoffman argued that the Law Commission's case for no fault exit at will rights for quasi-partnership type companies indicated that it clearly did not consider s 459 to already contain this remedy.[59] This was a proposition to which he subscribed.

O'Neill was to have a profound impact on the reform process as its restrictive approach was said by the CLR to render obsolete a number of the Law Commission's recommendations, discussed below. However, the strict application of equitable considerations required under *O'Neill* would probably not inhibit the continued application of many earlier cases to present cases if they involved equitable considerations.

A significant misuse of powers would continue to fall under the *O'Neill* restrictions. For example *Scottish Co-operative Society Ltd v Meyer*,[60] whence

---

57 Ibid, p 8.
58 Although he says a new approach would cause uncertainty, he also states that 'it (traditional English theory) is derived from arrangements for the administration of justice which were abandoned over a century ago.' Ibid, p 8.
59 This proposed that private companies adopt a clause in the articles which allowed shareholders to have their interest purchased on a no-fault basis.
60 [1959] AC 342 (HL).

the strict interpretation of the term 'oppressive' (noted by Lord Hoffman in *Re Saul*) originated, involved a misuse of powers by the majority shareholders in the company. The minority shareholders were two directors who were brought into the company for their expertise and ability to secure the licence to produce the product rayon, which the company required. The majority shareholders later caused the company to transfer its business to another subsidiary and cut off the company's supply of raw materials. The company was left without business and without profits, to the great detriment of the minority shareholders who had no interest in the subsidiary company. The court held that the company's affairs had been conducted in a way that was burdensome, harsh and wrongful and ordered the company to purchase the petitioners' share at a fair value.

Exclusion of a member from the management of a quasi-partnership company, such as that in *Ebrahimi*, would continue to constitute unfairly prejudicial conduct. Diverting corporate assets and business opportunities[61] would continue to provide good grounds for a petition, as would excessive remuneration to directors enabled by having voting control over the company.[62]

REFORM AND MINORITY PROTECTION

Reform and s 459

In 1997 the Law Commission published its report on shareholder remedies in which it made detailed recommendations in respect of ss 459–461 of the Companies Act 1985, the common-law rule of *Foss v Harbottle* and its exceptions.[63]

The Commission's empirical research indicated that the more common remedy sought by minority shareholders was for unfairly prejudicial conduct under ss 459–461. Furthermore, research indicted that this remedy was almost exclusively sought by shareholders in very small companies. Of the court files relating to s 459 petitions presented to the Companies Court between January 1994 and December 1996, 233 out of 254 were inspected.[64] Of these, 70.4 per cent of the petitioners were minority shareholders and 96.6 per cent involved private companies. 33.9 per cent of petitions involved companies with only two shareholders and 48.1 per cent of

---

61 *Re London School of Electronics Ltd* [1986] Ch 211.
62 *Re Cumana Ltd* [1986] BCLC 430. The Appeal Court concurred with Vinelott J's findings at first instance that the two-thirds majority shareholder and director had procured for himself remuneration far in excess of what he had earned.
63 The Law Commission (Law Com No 246) Shareholder Remedies. 1997 Report on a Reference under s 3 (1)(e) of the Law Commission Act 1965.
64 Ibid, p 177 Appendix J, Statistics relating to the filing of s 459 petitions.

petitions involved companies with fewer than five shareholders.[65] Only 4.3 per cent of petitions involved companies with more than 10 shareholders.[66] In 35.6 per cent of the petitions, *Ebrahimi* considerations of mutual trust and confidence were pleaded and in 64.4 per cent exclusion from management was alleged. The main relief sought under s 461 was the purchase of the petitioner's shares, totalling 69.5 per cent of all petitions inspected.[67] The Law Commission, therefore, proposed reform which would reflect need and give better access to the overwhelmingly commonest form of shareholder complaint and remedy – a s 459 petition submitted by a minority shareholder in a company with fewer than 10 shareholders, who complained of exclusion from management in a company previously characterised by mutual trust and who sought the remedy of share purchase.

The Commission's recommendations were partly informed by the costs in s 459 proceedings which could often far exceed the value of the shareholding in question. The Commission cites the case of *Re Elgindata Ltd*,[68] in which the parties incurred costs of £320,000 after 43 days in court, in an action relating to shareholdings that were eventually valued at £24,600. However, for the most part the Commission concluded that the excessive costs could be dealt with by active judicial case management, being developed at the time in the then Draft Civil Proceedings Rules.

In the earlier Consultation Paper, the Commission had proposed a new additional unfair prejudice remedy for smaller companies if two *Ebrahimi* conditions had been satisfied. The first condition was whether the 'association formed or continued on the basis of a personal relationship, involving mutual confidence'. The second condition was the question of whether there was 'an agreement, or understanding, that all, or some (for there may be "sleeping members"), of the shareholders shall participate in the conduct of the business'.[69]

However, following concerns from respondents to the Paper the Commission put forward an alternative recommendation that might achieve the same result for those shareholders in an *Ebrahimi* type situation. This involved the inclusion of two presumptions in proceedings under s 459. The first presumption was that if the shareholder had been excluded from management, such conduct would be presumed to be unfairly prejudicial if the company in question was a private company limited by shares. This presumption would apply 'where the petitioner has been removed as a director or has been prevented from carrying out all or substantially all of his functions as a

---

65 Ibid, p 178.
66 With 3 per cent stated as not known.
67 Ibid, p 179.
68 [1991] BCLC 959 cited at p 3 note 14.
69 Ibid, p 25.

director'.[70] Furthermore, it would only apply if the company was owner-managed and the petitioner held no less than 10 per cent of the voting rights 'capable of being exercised at general meetings of the company on all, or substantially all, matters ... in his own name'.[71] This presumption also required that all or mostly all of the shareholders were also directors so that it would be reasonable to assume that the petitioner expected to be involved in the company's management.

The second presumption proposed was that if the first presumption was satisfied then the petitioner's shares should be valued on a pro rata basis rather than discounted on the basis that it was a less valuable minority holding. This should apply unless the court otherwise directed.

The Commission further recommended that there should be a time limit for bringing claims under s 459 and that winding up should be added to the list of remedies available under s 461 but that a petitioner should obtain leave of the court if he seeks winding up on just and equitable grounds under s 122, in addition to his s 459 proceedings. The Commission further recommended the incorporation of an 'exit clause' in Table A which was dismissed by the CLR in 'Developing the framework' as it 'would not be used in practice because on commercial grounds it would not be incorporated in company constitutions by well informed founders ... For ill-informed founders it would be a trap'.[72]

The CLR considered the Commission's proposals in 'Developing the framework' and rejected both the two presumptions and the inclusion of a winding up remedy in s 461. On the presumptions the CLR stated that 'on balance we are inclined to doubt whether a case for the presumptions has been made'.[73] And, on the winding up remedy it stated that such an inclusion would endanger 'the viability of companies'.[74] These views were largely reached because of the decision in O'Neill which had not been heard when the Commission published its recommendations. This case, as previously noted, had held the scope of s 459 to be more restrictive than previously considered. As such, the CLR argued, the practical concerns voiced by the Commission which it had felt would be met by the presumptions, would instead be met by greater clarity in case law. Section 459 would be likely to apply to a much narrower range of cases following Lord Hoffman's reasoning in O'Neill.

In 'Completing the Structure' the CLR concluded that the O'Neill decision was sound and provided a clear and fair limit to the kinds of issue that

---

70 Ibid, p 34.
71 Ibid, p 35.
72 'Modern company law for a competitive economy: developing the framework', para 4.103, p 120. Lord Hoffman had in O'Neill previously dismissed these two presumptions as merely reflecting existing practice and therefore surplus to requirements.
73 Op. cit., 'Developing the framework', p 121.
74 Ibid.

would be actionable under s 459.[75] The CLR concurred with the House of Lords that a s 459 petition must be based upon a 'departure from an agreement, broadly defined, between those concerned, to be identified from their words or conduct'.[76] As this amply dealt with the problems of 'lengthy and undisciplined' proceedings, the Law Commission's proposal on presumptions was impliedly rejected. Subsequent reports considered the issue on presumptions to be dropped.[77]

Reform and derivative actions

The Commission considered that the right for a shareholder to bring a derivative action in respect of a wrong done to the company was both sound and one that could be appropriately brought under statutory control. The Commission noted that New Zealand, South Africa and Japan had introduced a statutory derivative action and therefore in the context of global corporations it was 'highly desirable' for England to follow suit. The Commission proposed that a new statutory derivative action should be introduced in respect of 'claims arising out of a breach of directors' duties'. And while it considered that in some cases there may not be a breach of duty[78] or that claims may not *arise* from a breach of duty but from the activities of a majority shareholder,[79] it considered such cases to have a remedy under s 459. The new action should, the Commission argued, be limited to directors' breach of duty only and should not be extended to employees or officers other than directors.[80]

The Commission further recommended that the new statutory derivative action should include negligence as an actionable wrongdoing. As previously noted, a derivative action could only be bought on the basis of negligence if that negligence profited those in breach.[81] And, as the Commission recommended explicitly allowing a breach to cover negligence as well as a statutory fault by a director, it proposed that the new derivative action should include a phrase similar to that already held in ss 310 and 727 of the Companies Act 1985: that of 'negligence, default, breach of duty or breach of trust'. It also recommended that legislation make explicit that this new action would cover conflict of interest situations.

---

75 'Although the majority of views expressed in responses to 'Developing the framework' were in favour of reversing *O'Neill* and thereby extending the scope of the remedy, after careful consideration we came down against this'. Modern Company Law: Final Report, p 163.
76 Op. cit., 'Completing the structure', para 5.79, p 97.
77 Modern Company Law: Final Report, p 163 stated that as no support had been extended for the presumptions and winding up, the Review focused on the scope of *O'Neill*.
78 *Movitex Ltd v Bulfield* [1988] BCLC 1040.
79 *Estmanco (Kilner House) Ltd v Greater London Council* [1982] 1 WLR 2.
80 Law Com No 246, p 84.
81 *Daniels v Daniels* [1978] Ch 406.

As a solution to some of the issues which emerged from their empirical work, the Commission recommended that the procedure to pursue a derivative action should be simplified and set out in the rules of court. The claimant should give 28 days' notice to the company of his intention to pursue a derivative action and then be required to obtain leave of he court to pursue the claim. In respect of the issue of leave, the court should consider the 'applicant's good faith, the interests of the company; that the wrong has been, or may be, approved in general meeting; the views of an independent organ and the availability of alternative remedies'.[82] Thus while an effective ratification would continue to bar a derivative action, the fact that the wrong is ratifiable is only one of the factors which the court should consider when assessing leave. The court would retain the power to adjourn proceedings to allow a meeting of shareholders. It further recommended that any action started by the company which has not been diligently pursued could be continued as a derivative action by a member of the company.

In response to these recommendations the CLR expressed their broad support subject to a number of additional queries and clarifications. The first concerned the effect of a company deciding not to sue and the second ratification or possible ratification of a wrongful act upon a derivative action. The third concerned the extension of actionable breaches of duty to negligent acts by a director in the absence of self-profiting.

The decision not to sue is usually a management one, thus if some or all of the management are associated with the wrong then a decision not to redress this wrong should be distinguished from other management decisions. Therefore, the CLR concluded that 'in all ordinary circumstances the derivative procedure should be confined to cases where one or more members of the board of directors are implicated in the wrong or by some special association with the wrongdoer and the board fails to institute proceedings'.[83] The CLR concurred with the Commission that employees' wrongs and those of other officers should be dealt with by the board and not under a derivative action.

In respect of ratification the CLR supported the Commission's view that effective ratification should remain a complete bar to a derivative action but sought to clarify the nature of 'effective'. What constituted 'effective' and 'lawful' ratification? The CLR acknowledged that there were clear identifiable circumstances when ratification would not be lawful already established in law. These included ratification of an *ultra vires* act, ratification of a wrong in respect of a member's personal rights, ratification of a wrong which constituted a breach of the articles,[84] and ratification where the wrongdoers were

82 Ibid, p 91.
83 'Developing the framework' para 4.118, p 129.
84 *Edwards v Halliwell* [1950] 2 All ER 1064.

the majority shareholders, or at least in effective control of the votes.[85] All the above exceptions (except the fourth circumstance) involved wrongs that were inherently unratifiable. The question remained, therefore, if a transaction was inherently ratifiable could a director *qua* shareholder vote? The CLR maintained that 'to be effective, ratification should be carried out by a sufficient majority of disinterested shareholders'.[86]

The CLR concurred with the Commission's recommendation that a wrong should be extended to negligent acts by a director and that the basis of a derivative action should be set out in statute. It further agreed with the Commission's recommended three- stage procedure.[87] Furthermore, the CLR proposed a simplified approach to ratification that they argued was necessary when negligence was included among actionable wrongs. Fraudulent wrongs are justifiably unratifiable because it is unacceptable in wider society. Outside of this, the question of whether to ratify or not or whether to sue should depend upon the court's assessment of who is in the best position to assess what is in the best interest of the company. That is, is it the minority shareholder or some other body?

In 'Completing the structure', the CLR confirmed their adoption for a simplified ratification process so that

the question of the validity of a decision:

- By the members of the company to ratify a wrong on the company by the directors (whether or not a fraud); or
- By the members of the board or of the company not to pursue such a wrong;

should depend on whether the necessary majority had been reached without the need to rely upon the votes of the wrongdoers, or of those who were substantially under their influence, or who had a personal interest in the condoning of the wrong.[88]

---

85 Op. cit., *Prudential*.
86 Op. cit., 'Developing the framework', p 129.
87 In addition the CLR suggested that further consideration should be given to situations when a shareholder suffered a separate loss from that which the company suffered and whether there should be an express provision to state that where the loss to the shareholder is contingent upon a direct loss to the company, the shareholder may only sue if the company improperly refuses to redress its own losses. Otherwise, such indirect loss is only recoverable by a shareholder by suit of the company.

This position was confirmed in the CLR's subsequent paper although they reserved their position as the issue was coming up in the House of Lords in the near future thus provoking a shift in perspective. In the event, by the time that the CLR's Final Report was published, the House of Lords had confirmed their provisional view and thus the Final Report made no other modifications.
88 Completing para 5.85, p 99.

The adoption of this approach was also guided by the desire to put ratification of wrongs on the same statutory footing as ratification of a breach of a director's statutory duties and to set it out in primary legislation. The CLR noted that there had been many negative responses to their suggestion that for wrongs which had not been ratified the court should decide whether to allow an action to proceed on the basis of what was in the best interests of the company.[89] They therefore counter-proposed that the court should have discretion to consider the merits of giving leave for derivative action based on all relevant circumstances especially the best interests of the company and the principles on directors' duties.[90] The Final Report confirmed the proposals of the previous report in respect of a statutory derivative action, ratification and the role of the courts.

The recommendations of the CLR in respect of derivative actions were approved in the 2005 white paper as 'an important mechanism by which shareholders can hold directors to account for the proper exercise of their duties in pursuit of their company's short and long term interest'.[91] Creating a statutory derivative action was conceived as a method for increasing shareholder control over the activities of directors and, in the paper's words, 'enhancing shareholder engagement'.[92] Ideologically it promotes the interests and engagement of all shareholders including minority shareholders, but it does not substantially increase minority powers. The reforms therefore do not substantially deviate from the contractarian views on minority shareholder protection.

MINORITY PROTECTION AND THE COMPANIES ACT 2006

A statutory derivative action

The 2006 Act provides for a new statutory derivative action under ss 260–264 in Part II Chapter 1, Derivative Claims in England and Wales or Northern Ireland. Here, a derivative action is available for breach of the duty to exercise reasonable care, skill and diligence without having to prove that the wrongdoers personally benefited from this breach. Furthermore, the applicant will not have to prove that the wrongdoing directors controlled the majority of shares. These sections also provide for a two-stage procedure for permission to continue a derivative action. At the first stage the applicant must make a

---

89   Ibid, para 5.86.
90   Para 3.40, 'Developing the framework'.
91   Company Law Reform, Cm 6456, p 24.
92   Section 3 of the paper, entitled 'Enhancing shareholder engagement and a long-term investment culture'.

prima facie case for the claim providing evidence for this. No evidence is required from the defendant. If no *prima facie* case is proven at this point then the courts must dismiss the application. At the second stage the court considers evidence from the company. The court is bound to consider a number of factors in deciding whether to give permission to continue and it must refuse permission according to other factors set out in these sections.

Section 260 sets out the nature of a derivative claim. Under sub-section (1) a member of a company may apply for proceedings '(a) in respect of a cause of action vested in the company, and (b) seeking relief on behalf of the company.' Under sub-section (2) a derivative claim may be made in pursuance of unfairly prejudicial proceeding under s 994 as well as under this chapter. Under sub-section (3) (as recommended by the Commission) a claim can be bought in respect of negligence in respect of 'an actual or proposed act or omission involving negligence, default, breach of duty or breach of trust by a director of the company'.[93] This section also provides that claims may be brought against third parties. Under sub-section (4) a member may bring a claim in respect of wrongdoings which occurred before his membership. And under sub-section (5) (reference to a director) this includes shadow and a former directors.[94]

The procedure for bringing a derivative action is as follows. Under s 261, a member must first apply to the court for permission to bring the action.[95] The court may then take the following course of action. It may consider that the evidence provided does not 'disclose a *prima facie* case for giving permission'[96] and therefore 'must dismiss the application'.[97] In addition the court 'may make any consequential order it thinks fit', for example a costs order.[98]

If the application is not dismissed at that point the court may require that certain evidence be provided by the company and may adjourn to give sufficient time for that evidence to be gathered.[99] On hearing the application the court may simply give permission for the applicant 'to continue the claim on such terms as it thinks fit'.[100] Or 'refuse permission and dismiss the claim'[101] or 'adjourn the proceedings on the application and give such directions as it thinks fit'.[102]

---

93 Section 260(3), reflecting the language in ss 310 and 727 of the 1985 Act.
94 *Re Hydrodam*, a director for the purposes of the Insolvency Act 1986 s 214 included *de facto* directors.
95 Section 261(1).
96 Section 261 (2).
97 Section 261(2)(a).
98 Section 262(2)(b).
99 Section 261(3) (a) and (b).
100 Section 261 (4)(a).
101 Section 261(4)(b).
102 Section 261(4)(c).

An alternative route to obtaining permission to pursue a derivative claim is when the company has begun a claim and the cause of action is one which falls within the criteria in Part II Chapter 1 of the 2006 Act.[103] A member may apply to the court for permission to continue a claim as a derivative action because 'the manner in which the company commenced or continued the claim amounts to an abuse of the process of the court'.[104] Or (in partial accordance with the Commission's recommendations), 'the company has failed to prosecute the claim diligently, and it is appropriate for the member to continue the claim as a derivative claim'.[105] This application will be treated exactly as a s 260 application, that is, the court may immediately dismiss it,[106] it may require additional evidence[107] and might hear the evidence and give permission to proceed,[108] refuse permission[109] or adjourn proceedings and give such directions as it thinks appropriate.[110] Under s 264, a member may apply to continue a derivative action brought by another member, if that claim was initiated by the first member,[111] or was one taken over from an action brought by the company,[112] or 'has continued a derivative claim under this section'.[113]

Section 263 sets out the circumstances in which the court must refuse permission under both ss 261 and 262. The court must do so if it is satisfied that a person who was acting to promote the success of the company would not continue the claim,[114] or it is a proposed act which the company has authorised,[115] or the act has occurred but it was either authorised by the company or subsequently ratified.[116] And ratification must not depend on the votes of the wrongdoing director.

In accordance with the Commission's recommendations as to what the court should consider when deciding on giving permission, s 263(3) states that the court must take into account:

(a) whether the member is acting in good faith in seeking to continue the claim;

103 Section 262(1)(a) and (b).
104 Section 262(2)(a).
105 Section 262(2)(b) and (c).
106 Section 262(3).
107 Section 262(4)(a).
108 Section 262(5)(a).
109 Section 262(5)(b).
110 Section 262(5)(c).
111 Section 264 (1)(a).
112 Section 264(1)(b).
113 Section 264(1)(c).
114 Section 263(2)(a).
115 Section 263(2)(b).
116 Section 263(2)(c).

(b) the importance that a person acting in accordance with section 172 (duty to promote the success of the company) would attach to continuing it;

(c) where the cause of action results from an act or omission that is yet to occur, whether the act or omission could be, and in circumstances would be likely to be –

    (i) authorised by the company before it occurs, or

    (ii) ratified by the company after it occurs;

(d) where the cause of action arises from the omission that has already occurred, whether the act or omission could be, and in the circumstances would be likely to be ratified by the company;

(e) whether the company has decided not to pursue the claim;

(f) whether the act or omission in respect of which the claim is brought gives rise to a cause of action that the member could pursue in his own right rather than on behalf of the company.[117]

Under sub-section (4) the court must pay special attention to the views of disinterested, independent shareholders. Sub-section (5) bequeaths the Secretary of State with the power to make regulations on the criteria the courts must consider when deciding to give leave to continue a derivative action. In so doing he must consult all appropriate persons and all the regulations will be subject to affirmative resolution procedure.[118]

Petition for 'unfairly prejudicial' conduct

The remedies available when a company's affairs have been conducted in a manner which is 'unfairly prejudicial' to the interests of the company's members, which were held in ss 459–461 of the 1985 Act, are now reproduced in the Companies Act 2006. The effects of the Financial Services and Markets Act 2000 had already been incorporated into s 460. Here, an order on application of the Secretary of State applied to a company in respect of which he had received a report under s 437[119] or had exercised his powers under s 447[120] or s 448,[121] additionally included companies in respect of which,

(c) the Secretary of State or the Financial Services Authority has exercised his or its powers under Part XI of the Financial Services and Markets Act 2000; or

---

117 Companies Act 2006, s 263(3).
118 Section 263(6) and (7).
119 An inspector's report.
120 Secretary of State's power to require production of documents.
121 Warrant to enter and search premises.

(d) the Secretary of State has received a report from an investigator
    appointed by him or the Financial Services Authority under that
    Part.[122]

Section 459 of the 1985 Act is reproduced in s 994 of the Companies Act
2006, with sub-section (1) now divided into (a) and (b). Section 460 is reproduced in s 995 of the 2006 Act with a little reorganisation so sub-section (1)
of the 1985 Act is now sub-section (2) of the 2006 Act and sub-section
(1A) of the 1985 Act is now sub-section (1) of the 2006 Act. The provision
stating that the Secretary of State may bring a petition in addition to or
instead of presenting a petition to wind up the company, which was held
in brackets in s 460(1)(b) of the 1985 Act, is now held in its own subsection, s 995(3). Section 460(2) of the 1985 Act is now s 995(4) of the 2006
Act.

The powers of the court held in s 461 of the 1985 Act are held in s 996 of
the 2006 Act. Under s 996, the court's order may:

(a) regulate the conduct of the company's affairs in the future;
(b) require the company–

    (i) to refrain from doing or continuing an act complained of, or
    (ii) to do an act that the petitioner has complained it had omitted to
         do;

(c) authorise civil proceedings to be brought in the name and on behalf
    of the company by such person or persons and on such terms as the
    court may direct;
(d) require the company not to make any, or any specified, alterations in
    its articles without the leave of the court;[123]
(e) provide for the purchase of the shares of any members of the com-
    pany by other members or by the company itself and, in the case of
    a purchase by the company itself, the reduction of the company's
    capital accordingly' (Companies Act 2006 s 996(2)).

The 2006 Act sets out the procedures in respect of an alteration to the
company's constitution following an order of the court following a petition
under this part. If the court's order either alters the constitution or gives the
company leave to make alterations to its constitution, the company must
deliver a copy of the order to the registrar under s 998(1) and must do so
within 14 days under sub-section (2) unless the court has otherwise allowed.

---

122 Companies Act 1985, s 460 (1A).
123 This was not identified as a separate remedy under s 461 but was clearly intended as a
    remedy as the provision stating that leave of the court was required. This was held in
    s 461(3).

Under sub-section (3) of this section, the company and every officer of the company commits an offence if they fail to comply with this section and under sub-section (4) will be liable to a fine and a daily default for continued contravention.

CONCLUSION

Derivative actions under the common law were articulated as exceptions to the rule in *Foss v Harbottle* although the rule itself became modified when the doctrine of separate corporate personality became part of the body of company law. The exception was strictly construed and generally required a fraud against the company when the company was not in a position to protect its own interests because the wrongdoers were in control. Negligence was an insufficient wrong to fulfil the exception unless it was an extreme negligence which profited the wrongdoer. The wrongdoers in control were generally the managers but not infrequently, as in *Estmanco*, they were the majority shareholders. Moreover, *de facto* control was deemed too wide to constitute control under this exception notwithstanding Vinelott J's attempt to do so in *Prudential*. It was therefore difficult for minority shareholders to pursue a derivative action and this has bolstered majority shareholder and manager control over the company.

The new statutory derivative action in extending wrongdoing to cover negligent acts which do not profit the wrongdoer and in allowing an action without proof that the wrongdoers control the majority of shares has dispensed with a number of obstacles to a derivative action. By including negligence it is reflecting the new expectations of competency required of directors and focuses a derivative on directors and away from shareholders which would exclude *Estmanco* type situations. A director's negligence is now actionable which will surely focus director attention. Furthermore, by no longer requiring actual control and allowing *de jure* control these sections place a non-shareholding manager within the scope of a derivative action. This is a partial reflection of Vinelott's judgment in *Prudential* except that it excludes majority shareholders unless they can be construed as shadow directors defined in s 251. It extends the responsibilities of professional managers while limiting the application of a derivative action to large investors.

From a law matters perspective the reforms are welcome in that they clarify the law on derivative action by putting it on a statutory footing and on the face of it provide greater facility for minority shareholders to address wrongs against the company. It also provides clear guidelines on the matters which the court must consider in respect of derivative actions. From a contractarian point of view also this is, potentially, a cost-efficient reform in that it places greater controls on the agent's activities but allows minority shareholders to engage in the monitoring. These reforms, however, would only be effective if the minority shareholder was stopped from pursuing costly and frivolous actions. This latter element is catered for by the two-stage procedure described above where the courts may dispense with the action fairly early on in the proceedings. The reforms provide a clear but narrowly focused basis for derivative actions which will add value to shareholdings while arresting undesirable complaints before they affect the company and its officers. It is a neatly constructed conjunction of law matters and contractarian influences.

Chapter 7

From mutuality to plc –
building societies: a case study

> We are sending this pristine maiden, the building societies, out into the financial jungle where dangers abound and rapists throng. Why, in any sense, loosen the lock on the chastity belt?
>
> Austin Mitchell MP[1]

Over the previous chapters we have seen how companies came to company law through the roots of the law on unincorporated associations, charter and statutory companies and within an ideological and economic context. In this chapter we will present a historical and critical account of how building societies came to company law. The distinguishing characteristic of building societies that are not companies is that they are mutual societies. The legal mechanism by which they cease to be mutual societies is known as demutualisation or conversion. However, as we shall see, mutuality is an attribute that originated as a response to a particular set of social and economic imperatives and was subsequently moulded by ideology and economics. Thus the shedding of mutual status is part of a historical process which was completed for the most part by the end of the twentieth century and is best understood in a contextual analysis.

Early building societies were small collectives of local people who made monthly contributions, at a set amount. The purpose of this was to save enough to facilitate all the members' purchase of property, with property allocated to one member at a time when the collective fund was sufficient. The member to whom this property was allocated was usually chosen through a lottery system. Members would continue to save until all the membership had purchased a property after which the society would come to end. Early building societies were known as 'terminating societies' because of this. The first known building society was called Ketley's Society and was formed in

---

1 HC Hansard 1985, Debate on the Building Societies Bill, p 945.

Birmingham in 1767. Like most of the early societies it was formed in the local hostelry from which it took its name.

Building societies operated for over 60 years without any legislation specifically designed for their usage, their internal organisation prescribed by the members rather than by legislation. Despite this, most building societies organised themselves in a fairly similar manner. Although there were many differences in the cost of subscriptions, methods of allocating property and penalties for defaulting members, societies operated under a system whereby members received equal benefits for equal contributions and once all members had been allocated housing, the society was terminated. However, the absence of legislation placed a question mark over their legality. Some building societies registered themselves as friendly societies under the 1793 Act. It is uncertain, however, if this did anything to improve their legitimacy as this legislation was designed for societies to raise funds to relieve poverty caused by unemployment, death or illness. The ambivalent legality of building societies was further exacerbated by the Bubble Act of 1720, because building societies operated by allocating shares to their members through subscriptions, (shares that could be transferred in many cases) and they did so without obtaining a charter or an Act of Parliament. This question was raised in court and in 1812 the question of whether the Bubble Act applied to the activities of building societies was answered in the negative.[2] However, it was not until some years later that building societies had legislation that specifically legitimated their activities. In 1836 the Benefit Building Society Act was passed, with its stated aim to 'afford Encouragement and Protection to such Societies and the Property obtained therewith'.[3] But while this bill acknowledged the existence of building societies among 'the industrious classes', parliamentary records prior to 1836 indicate that there was little concern or knowledge of building societies within contemporary governing bodies. The Bill was passed with no recorded debate and, perhaps for this reason, became subsequently renowned for the ambiguity of its drafting.

Contained in nine short sections it made lawful the establishment of building societies and enabled them to take action against defaulting and fraudulent members by 'such reasonable Fines, Penalties, and Forfeitures upon the several Members of any such society who shall offend any such rules'.[4] Societies were exempted from the payment of stamp duty on the transfer of shares.[5] In return for this legal protection societies were made subject to the

---

2 *Pratt v Hutchinson* (1812) 15 East KB 511. The court found that membership-based restrictions on the transferability of shares meant that the Bubble Act did not apply to building societies.

3 The Benefit Building Societies Act 1936, Preamble.

4 Ibid, s 1.

5 Ibid, s 8.

laws pertaining to usury[6] and were prohibited from investing in 'any savings bank, or with the commissioners for the reduction of national debt'.[7] Building societies could now register as a specific form of friendly society with the Registrar for Friendly Societies.

However, by the time this Act was passed, terminating societies had already been shaped by their social and ideological origins.

THE ORIGINS OF MUTUALITY

The mutuality of building societies originated in the context of the social and material needs of the newly emerging working class, who were landless, but possessed some financial means. Furthermore, mutuality arose in a period of heightened political change and shifting allegiances.

The gradual transformation of the economy from agricultural production to commodity production was accelerated by the passage of hundreds of enclosure Acts at the end of the eighteenth century which extinguished the long-held rights in land held by members of the community. From 1761 to 1780 over a thousand such Acts were passed with a further 900 passed from 1781 to 1800.[8] Furthermore, between 1793 and 1813, 2,260,000 acres of land were put into cultivation following the passage of a further 1,883 Acts.[9] This had the obvious effect of creating a landless labour force on the one hand, and on the other, the concept that land was a commodity, the title to which could be owned privately. In a dramatic surge of change, the labourer was transformed from an individual whose occupation was partly governed by the social hierarchy of a close geography into one who privately 'owned' his ability to work.

The semi-feudal social hierarchy that largely determined status, work and reward was, with the emergence of the market system of production, replaced by the notion that work was a commodity that could be exchanged like any other commodity by the individual who 'owned' it. In the absence of slavery (for slavery continued to operate in the British colonies among white as well as black people),[10] this particular commodity was owned by the individual that actually performed the activity. Thus, the worker could exchange his property for a reward that was, at least in theory, negotiated by himself and the individual who wished to purchase it. With that transaction completed, the worker could then exchange the negotiated value of his work for other commodities that he required or desired. And, with the emergence of land as a

---

6 Ibid, s 2.
7 Ibid, s 6.
8 Halevy, E, *A History of English People in 1815*, 1924, T Fisher Unwin Ltd, p 261.
9 Ibid.
10 Zinn, H, *A People's History of the United States*, 1999, Longman.

commodity that could be purchased, that desired commodity could be a home. So, it was these factors, representing material changes in the English economy, that presented the initial and crucial context for the emergence of mutuality.

Related to these factors were the diverse ideologies that legitimated this method of economic organisation and those that modified it. The ideology of the old system, semi-feudalism, and the ideology of the new market system were factors in constructing mutuality. The philosophy of the old system was connected to conservative ideology while the philosophy of the new was connected to the ideas of liberalism.

The ideas of conservatism, unlike liberalism, did not have a set of formal philosophers to articulate them,[11] but it is possible to understand conservatism as a set of ideas through the writing and speeches of conservative politicians. Foremost in this group was Whig politician Edmund Burke, whose treatise against the French revolution insisted upon the need for social hierarchy and strong government.[12] It reflected the classical works of Aristotle and Plato, who believed that society existed as a predetermined fact based on the natural hierarchy of individuals. For Aristotle, hierarchy was articulated mainly in terms of the humours, an ideology of which legitimated women's inferiority to men.[13]

For Plato, hierarchy was understood in terms of the 'metal' of the individual's soul, the purest 'metal' being possessed by the philosophers who strove to understand the truth and therefore understand the divine; the meanest metal being possessed by artists, who sought merely to reproduce, in a useless form, that which already existed in a useful form.[14] Thus, for the philosophy of Plato, Aristotle, and the conservative thinking that it informed, society was an organic whole, composed of inferior and superior beings. Social order, a state where humanity could be productive and creative, resulted from

---

11 Thomas Hobbes has been claimed as a conservative philosopher for his emphasis on the need for a strong 'Leviathan' state. He has also been claimed as a liberal thinker for his emphasis on individual 'natural' attributes.

12 Burke, E, *Reflections of the Revolution in France*, London: Owen.

13 According to the notions of thinkers like Aristotle, men were supposedly possessed of dry hot (superior) humours whereas women possessed cool, damp (inferior) humours. These notions explained the external nature of male genitalia and the internal nature of female genitalia, the latter being merely inverse male organs that had insufficient 'heat' to externalise (Aristotle, *The Works of Aristotle*, 1990, Chicago Press).

According to Talbot, these ideological quasi-biological notions continued in English thinking until the rise of science and rationalism. For example, a pregnancy resulting from an alleged rape would disbar any action by the alleged victim. This was because a woman, understood to be an inverse man, produced her 'seed' upon pleasurable ejaculation, like a man. Pregnancy required the female seed and thus orgasm, therefore the copulation must have been pleasurable and could not have been forced, a view of conception that continued until science better understood human ovulation (Talbot, unpublished).

14 Plato, *The Republic*, 2nd edn (revised) 1984, Penguin Books.

an acceptance and enforcement of the natural hierarchy; be that between men and women, Philosopher King and artist or rich and poor. For the conservative thinker, failure to observe this natural order would result in a brutal and destructive society.

This way of understanding social reality served admirably to legitimise the fixed social hierarchy of feudalism that had underpinned England's agricultural economy until around the seventeenth century. Broadly speaking, individuals were born into a particular social stratum in which they remained until death, generation after generation *ad infinitum*. Social stratification determined rights in the land, duties to superiors, responsibilities to inferiors and familial reward. Social mobility was virtually non-existent. Questions such as 'what will I be', and 'who am I' were irrelevant for the ordinary person. The church and state interpreted the Bible to emphasise hierarchy rather than equality. Already nostalgic when it was written, this approach is as exemplified in the hymn 'All things bright and beautiful', whose Christian message outlined a hierarchically organised world. Everything had a place in creation. God himself had rubber stamped inequality, extending from the lowliest animal to hierarchy in the human social world:

> The rich man in his castle, the poor man at his gate,
> He made them high and lowly and each to his estate.[15]

However, this understanding of social reality could not describe or legitimise the new burgeoning market economy. As one writer put it,

> Exchange, or the circulation of commodities, is predicated on the mutual recognition of one another as owners by those engaged in exchange. This acknowledgment, appearing in the form of an inner conviction or of the categorical imperative, is the maximum conceivable height to which commodity-producing society can rise. But in addition to this maximum to be realised, it is sufficient for commodity owners to act as if they acknowledged one another mutually as proprietors. Moral conduct here is contrasted with legal conduct, which is characterised as such irrespective of the motive which generated it.[16]

So, in contrast to conservatism, liberal ontology placed the individual before society. For the liberal, society was merely the decision of an amalgamation of separate autonomous individuals to come together in order to pursue individual self-interest. The form that society took was not a given fact, and certainly not divinely ordained, but depended upon a series of decisions that

15 William Monk, 'All things bright and beautiful', 1848.
16 Pashukanis, EB, *Law and Marxism*, 1989, Pluto Press, p 162.

private but pragmatic individuals had taken. A dynamic society was one that properly reflected the will of individuals and that could not occur unless those individuals were free to make choices. Thus, liberal thought tended to stand for social equality and freedom of expression coupled with personal responsibility for those decisions, and society was understood as a market for the exchange of freely made material choices.

Legally, the responsibilities of individualism and the absence of morality outside the values individuals choose to adopt were, and are, most readily reflected in modern contract law. In a world of autonomous individuals engaging in exchange relationships of their own choosing, contract personified the new role of the state in liberal, market capitalism. The state's role in the liberal view is essentially that of enforcer of agreements made between 'free' individuals vigorously pursuing their own interests and desires, rather than one of enforcing hierarchy and social order.

In his classic book, PS Atiyah traces the connection between liberalism, the free market and contract.[17] He argues that it was liberal notions of autonomy and personal responsibility that provided the philosophical rationale for the courts' re-conceptualisation of contract in nineteenth-century England. According to Atiyah, during the period between 1770 and 1870, liberal values and ideas shaped the law's attitude to the making of contracts. Judgments assumed that all consequences of a contract were the product of the will of the parties, so the courts would not intervene if the parties had made a bad bargain and would not consider the possibility or consequences of inequality of bargaining power between the parties. In contrast, the courts' attitude to the making of agreements in the eighteenth century emphasised and actively imposed a standard of fairness based upon custom. The law and the courts (usually in the form of lay justices) would actively intervene and void or amend contracts on a wide variety of grounds. Atiyah concludes that in keeping with rule of law ideology, nineteenth-century courts adopted a formal non-interventionist stance to the making of contracts, a stance radically divorced from the moral notions of eighteenth-century England.

Freedom of contract and freedom to contract was essential for the development of the new market economy and liberalism defended this freedom by providing it with a philosophical rationale and ideological justification. But the market, with its requirement for freely contracting individuals, conflicted with many of the norms of the semi-feudal hierarchy from which it arose. Market ideology conflicted with feudal ideology and it was in the context of this conflict that building societies emerged. In a time of acute conflict between the old and the new society, building societies become the products of, and to a certain extent architects of, the conflicts and resolutions that ensued. Conservative thinkers under Pitt sought, and for the most part

17 Atiyah, PS, *Rise and Fall of the Freedom of Contract*, 1979, Oxford: Clarendon Press.

obtained, strict anti-collectives legislation. Politicians such as Edmund Burke eloquently described the social chaos that would ensue if individual desire triumphed over a fixed hierarchical social order. Accordingly, organised collectives seeking social change were something to be feared and repressed. The social equality explained as a universal right by Thomas Paine (writing in response to Burke's own *Reflections on the French Revolution*), was the first step to anarchy. In this context, Paine's practical entreaties to seize the potential of that point in history, to address the question of

> whether man shall inherit his rights, and universal civilisation take place? Whether the fruits of his labour shall be enjoyed by himself, or consumed by the profligacy of governments? Whether robbery shall be banished from courts and wretchedness from countries?[18]

were dismissed as pandering to a mob mentality. Likewise, conservative criticisms of equality and freedom were prosaically expressed in the philosophical writings of Donatien-Alphonse-François de Sade, who offered a stark insight into contemporary critics of early liberal individualism. Writing in eighteenth-century France, the Marquis echoed the sentiments of English philosopher Thomas Hobbes, published over a century before. In de Sade's brutal, erotic world, his fictitious characters show that the unfettered individual will commit any manner of atrocity in order to satisfy desire and that the absence of state interference in the life of the individual induces a reversion to animalism. Accordingly, as it is only social conventions such as morality which make murder or rape into crimes, a world without such conventions would degenerate into brutality. In the words of de Sade's 'libertine' hero Dolmance in instruction to his fifteen-year-old 'pupil':

> It was the early Christians who, daily persecuted for their ridiculous beliefs, used to cry: 'Don't burn us! Don't flay us! Nature says that man must not do unto others what he would not have others do unto him!' Fools! How could Nature, who always urges us to delight in ourselves, who never suggests any other instincts, other notions, other inspiration, assure us in the next moment that we must not, on the other hand, choose to love ourselves should it cause others pain? Ah, believe me, Eugenie, Mother Nature never speaks to us save of ourselves; there is nought so egotistic as her message, and what we most clearly divine

---

18 Paine, T, *Rights of Man, being an Answer to Mr Burke's Attack on the French Revolution*, 1792, Fleet Street, p 215. An offer by the publisher for the copyright for £1,000 was made although this was said in a later publication to be inspired by a desire to suppress publication and appease the English Government. 'This offer was promptly declined by Mr Paine, who wrote for the benefit of mankind and not for pecuniary reward.' New York: Liberty Books, Freethought Press, vi.

therefrom is the immutable and sacred counsel: prefer thyself, love thyself, no matter at whose expense.[19]

In parliament, and in contrast to these conservative fears about the social degenerative effects of liberty, stood the more progressive pro-market elements of the Whig Party. Politicians such as William Sheridan, a rhetorician equal to Burke, argued against the Pitt Government and in favour of the freedom of individuals to organise and to enjoy freedom from the increased state restrictions that followed the French Revolution and which he described as 'hysterical'.[20]

In this political climate, many working people found themselves in an unhappy and unique situation. Suffering from the demise of a semi-feudal social support system and often disappropriated from their homes, working persons needed to create their own system of support and their own access to accommodation. Low wages and insecure working conditions meant that individualised private solutions to these social needs was not an option, collective solutions would have to be found. The dominant views of the state, however, still grounded in semi-feudal politics (now denuded of its socially responsible elements), mitigated against collective activity. In contrast, the liberal's support of individual expression and independence did give some ideological space to expand.

The eighteenth century witnessed the emergence of collectives of working people who organised (under the legal form of a friendly society) to provide a 'safety net' for the insecurities of working life. However, because of the political climate, these societies overtly underlined their uncontroversial nature through the strict policing of their membership. Members of such societies could be disbarred for drunkenness, swearing oaths against the King, political discussion, adultery, and even for contracting venereal disease.

Originating as far back as the late seventeenth century, the early friendly societies predated building societies. However, building societies tended to operate as friendly societies and so closely did they mirror each other's organisational forms that many early building societies followed the friendly societies' practice of operating through trustees. Furthermore, following the Friendly Societies Act of 1793, many building societies registered themselves as friendly societies. According to Cleary 'this made their legal position clear and extended to them the exemption from stamp duties' granted by the Act.[21]

Created and maintained as 'self-help' groups for working people and operating independently from recognised state authorities, friendly society aims were largely to circumvent the grosser failures of the market to deal with

---

19 de Sade, DAF, *The Philosophy of the Boudoir*, 1995, London: Creation Books, p 56.
20 Hansard (1793) 33 George III 'Debate on Mr Sheridan's Motion'.
21 Cleary, J, *The Building Society Movement*, 1965, Elek Books, p 14.

problems of social welfare, such as unemployment or injury and death in the workplace. Generally, members paid a monthly subscription into a central fund and in return were insured to a small degree against the vicissitudes of working life.

For employers, seeking the maximum output from labour in return for minimum responsibility towards the workforce, the objectives of friendly societies had something to be desired. As Alan Fox notes, while the relationship between employee and employer maintained its feudal origins in respect to the 'servant's' obligation to the 'master', 'the commitment of the whole person as against the segmental attachment of the alienated',[22] the 'master' required the limitation of responsibilities to his servants to that which could be encapsulated in pure contract. Furthermore, in purely economic terms, the relief provided by friendly societies 'reduced the number of paupers thrown upon the parish and in this way prevented the poor rates from becoming too heavy a burden on the taxpayer'.[23]

However, inherent in the practice of collective organisations lay the possibility of a political threat to the existing balance of power. As one historian noted 'what was a friendly society but a popular club likely during a time of political agitation, to become a centre of Jacobin propaganda?'.[24] And, as Gosden makes clear in his historical account of friendly societies, the early nineteenth century was marked by fears about their politically destabilising effect. Home Office papers from this period evidence this.[25] For example, in 1813, six employers in engineering firms sent a memorial complaining about the activities of their journeymen. In it they stated that 'laws are artfully and efficaciously evaded and defeated by and under the mask of Benefit Societies, institutions that have created, cherished and given effect to the most dangerous combinations among the several journeymen of our district'.[26] And in 1801, FM Eden, an individual generally sympathetic to the needs of the working community, stated that 'association is the prevalent malady of our times. In all cases its real object should be ascertained, and its progress vigilantly watched by those who are entrusted with the governance of this country'.[27]

Membership of diverse friendly societies represented a significant proportion of the working population. At the turn of the nineteenth century the population of England stood at an estimated 10 million.[28] In 1802 there

---

22 Fox, A, *Beyond Contract*, Oxford, 1977.
23 Op. cit., Halevy, p 287.
24 Ibid, p 288.
25 Gosden, PHJH, *The Friendly Societies in England 1815–1875*, 1961.
26 Ibid, quoting HO 42/172 Manchester UP, 1961.
27 Quoted by Gosden, p 158, taken from Eden, FM, Observation on friendly societies, 1801, p 24.
28 Cornish, WR, *Law and Society in England 1750–1950*, 1989, London: Sweet & Maxwell.

existed 9,672 societies and by 1815 the number of members' friendly societies was estimated to be 925,429.[29] The numerical popularity of friendly societies within the context of such political flux was enough to alarm the most objective observers. For example, in P Colquhoun's *A Treatise on Indigence* he states that with 164,424 different meetings taking place in 9,672 inns, individuals, 'ill-informed', 'open to seduction and heated by political frenzy, artfully worked up . . . may alarm and afflict the peaceful subject'.[30]

Collective organisation on the basis of shared interests was made possible by the breakdown of feudalism and the enhanced mobility of labour. This, argue many commentators, led to a new consciousness in working people – distinct and potentially more destabilising than the random activities of 'the mob'. Asa Briggs argued that the rapid disintegration of 'ascribed status' as a mode of social organisation prior to the eighteenth century resulted in the evolution of groups organised around the broad principle of 'justice' and a notion of class as 'a group far from homogenous but with realisable ambitions as a group and not a mere collection of individuals'.[31] It was this new consciousness which gave rise to highly politicised collectives among which friendly societies were counted.

> In the new towns there were large numbers of working men's friendly clubs and trade societies and employees' associations and combinations, the former looking to 'unions' for strength, the latter binding themselves together to protect their interests both against the farmer and the artisan.[32]

It is true that friendly societies did have the potential to be incorporated into politically radical movements and occasionally realised that potential, famously encapsulated in the plight of the Tolpuddle Martyrs. However, it is perhaps too tempting for social historians to overemphasise the radicalism of early workers' collectives in their efforts to promote the notion of the working person as an actor rather than a victim of historical events. Some friendly societies did, no doubt, provide some relief to those engaged in trade disputes. However, what is more apparent from the objects of friendly societies is their conscious attempt to appeal to the more 'respectable' elements of the working class and of their promotion of the values of abstention, hard work and saving, coupled with collectivism. Their radicalism lay not in their involvement with political issues, such as universal suffrage, but in maintaining economic independence from both government and employers by an insistence upon meticulous organisation within societies and standards of

29 Statistics from appendix No 1 of the Fourth Report of the 1874 Royal Commission Report into Friendly and Benefit Building Societies.
30 Op. cit., Gosden, p 158.
31 Briggs, A, *The Age of Improvement 1783–1867*, 1959, Longman, p 65.
32 Ibid.

behaviour from its members. For example, as early as 1688 the articles and regulations for governing the Town Porters' Friendly Society, instituted on 12 March of that year, required members to be

> of sound constitution, free of maim, bruise, hereditary or constitutional disease, capable to gain an honest livelihood by their employment, of good moral character, and his wife, if he has one, in good health.[33]

The rules and regulations of the Trades Society at Annan stated in article 1 that 'every person who should be admitted a member of this society be of good repute, and of sober life'.[34] Similarly the rules for the United Philanthropists Society, instituted in 1833, stated that a member must be 'a man of credit and reputation, his earning not less than twenty-four shillings per week, and not afflicted with diseases of any kind whatsoever'.[35]

Drunkenness was particularly frowned upon. The Castle Eden Friendly Society fined members one shilling for each offence of 'drunkenness, fighting, betting and cursing' while at a meeting.[36] The Trades Society controlled drinking at meetings by only authorising elected officers to order drinks for the assembly and members attempting to order their own drinks were fined sixpence.[37] Claims for benefit in relation to harms that were considered to be self-inflicted were almost universally precluded by Societies:

> No person shall receive any benefit from the stock of this society that had any distemper prior to his entrance, or whose sickness, lameness or blindness, shall be caused by his own defence, or by being in any riot or drunkenness, or the venereal disease.[38]
>
> If his distemper is found to be forged or the result of excessive drinking, fighting or quarrelling, he shall be dispelled from the society.[39]
>
> No benefit will be forthcoming if sickness is caused by drunkenness, fighting, unlawful or needless exercise, or from immoral conduct of any kind.[40]

Furthermore, expulsions for engagements in illegal activity were commonplace regardless of whether such actions were connected to, or affected, the

---

33 Article 3 of the articles and regulations of the Town Porters' Friendly Society printed at the St. Michael Press by C M'Lachan, 1801.
34 Article 1 of the Trades Society at Annan, ibid.
35 Article 3 of the rules of the Philanthropists' Society.
36 Article 27 of the Castle Eden Friendly Society.
37 Article 18 of the rules of the Trades Society.
38 Article 5, The Society of Taylors, Stanhope Street, Clare Market, London, 1787.
39 Article 34, The Town Porters' Friendly Society.
40 Article 11, The Angel Inn Friendly Society, Bedford, 1826.

member's role in the society. For example, the Town Porters' Societies' articles stated that:

> When a member shall be judicially convicted of theft, or any other crime inferring infamy and moral depravity he shall therefore be deprived of all further connection with the Society and shall forfeit all he has contributed to the funds and be expelled from the Society as an unworthy member.[41]

Similarly, article 14 of the Angel Society's rules stated that 'if any member be convicted of felony, perjury, fraud, or notable crime that may bring disgrace on the society, he shall be excluded'.[42]

To be sure, such strict policing of members indicated a clear moral agenda (it was the whole moral and economic person that was required by Societies), but it was a morality that was internally generated. As historian David Neave argued in his archival study of friendly societies in rural East Riding, this was a morality of a distinctive working class character, not a set of moral codes imposed by middle class concerns. Although organised to help individuals, it was an organisation based on collectivity, 'the labels of "individualism" and "self help" should be replaced by "collectivism" and "mutual aid" and there is little sign of "social exclusiveness" '.[43] In addition, this form of moral policing spoke of a desire to maintain some independence from the state by proving their collective ability to self-regulate. Political radicalism by members would have invited state intrusion and was generally unwanted in these stoically independent organisations. Clearly underlining this point, the Beneficit Society of Tinwold (1793) stated in their articles that 'none shall be admitted into this Society who are suspected of being friendly to the new fangled doctrines of Liberty and Equality and the Rights of Man as set forth by Thomas Paine and his adherents'.[44] By presenting a moral and non-provocative image it 'was earnestly hoped that benevolent institutions of this nature may not be cramped by rules'.[45]

In the context of rising 'laissez-faire' policies this hope was, to a great extent, realised in the latter part of the nineteenth century, as the government acknowledged the virtue of ensuring friendly societies' relative independence from the state. In response to arguments for the establishment of a highly regulated 'National Friendly Society managed and therefore virtually

---

41 Article 44 of the Town Porters' Society.
42 Article 14 of the Angel Society's rules.
43 David Neave, *Mutual Aid in The Victorian Countryside: Friendly Societies in the Rural East Riding 1830–1914*, 1991, p 98.
44 Quoted in Gower's *Principles of Company Law*, 1992, London: Sweet & Maxwell, p 31.
45 Preface to the rules and articles of the Castle Eden Friendly Society.

guaranteed by the Government',[46] the Friendly Societies Commission concluded that 'the great object of fostering a spirit of independence among the people is attained by a system which leaves them to make their own provision against sickness and their own ability to work and to bear the consequences if they make an inadequate or improper one'.[47] State interference, it argued, should be limited to the provision of information upon which societies may base financial decisions and the correlation of friendly societies' accounts 'with care to publish that guarantee is not to be implied ... sound tables may be framed, and it is intended that the condition of every society should come under periodic review'.[48] As Gosden argued, 'the principal enemy of independence was thought to be state aid or interference in the field of friendly society activity'.[49] Thus the 1875 Act, though far lengthier than previous legislation, broadly speaking limited state interference in friendly societies to the issue of registration.

Following friendly societies' lead, the early collectives that put money into a common fund in order to purchase property (or building societies as they became known) were small and conservative, with the limited aim of saving collectively in order to fund the purchase of land or housing for the members. Their aim, the purchase of property, was an opportunity presented by the rise of the market but one that was proscribed by the political environment.

The limited aims of early building societies meant that every member joined for the same limited purpose and, expecting the same outcomes from membership, they contributed broadly to the same degree. Each member saved and each member obtained property as a result of this continued commitment. When the objective of providing property for each member was achieved, the society terminated. Originally, therefore, mutuality was not constructed by legislation or governmental policy but was something that described a method of organisation that arose organically from a particular historical context.

However, as the particular purpose of building societies was to advance such funds as were sufficient for its members to purchase property, societies found themselves involved the acquisition of an element of social life that was, and is, charged with political character. In the eighteenth century, the legal conceptualisation of property encompassed the evolution of socio-economic relations in Britain as both a material reality and a potent symbol of an emerging new order. It was the arena within which much of the ideological dispute between Whig and Tory took place and it was the arena within which much of the arguments for constitutional reform were fought. The

46 Fourth Report, Friendly Societies Commission, cxcii.
47 Ibid.
48 Fourth Report, Friendly Societies Commission, ccxviii.
49 Op. cit., Gosden, p 163.

reconceptualisation of property directly affected large swathes of the population by rendering them homeless and without their traditional means of survival, but facilitated the unique historical development of the market economy enabling Britain to become the first industrialised economy in the world. With the weight of history bearing down upon the issue of property, it would not be surprising that, as building societies maintained as their object the acquisition of property, the politics of property would have a profound impact on the development of the building society movement. The emergence of early building societies encapsulated a basic conflict, for while the members of building societies were 'buying into' the norms of a market economy through the acquisition of private housing or land, they were maintaining a more desirable position of independence and self-determination.

As noted earlier, the creation of private property in the land was almost entirely completed by the passage of hundreds of Enclosure Acts in the latter half of the eighteenth century. Over a thousand Enclosure Acts were passed from 1761 to 1780, with 900 being passed from 1781 to 1800.[50] In the period spanning 1793 to 1813, 1,883 such Acts were passed, putting 2,260,000 acres of land into cultivation.[51] By this process, 'common land lying continually fallow on which everyone had the right to pasture his cow, to cut a little wood, and dry some leaf, became by virtue of the Enclosure Act, the private property of an individual owner'.[52] Or as EP Thompson puts it, prior to enclosure and engrossment laws, land was held subject to a 'hierarchy of co-incident use-rights', a hierarchy that correlated to an individual's social status.[53]

Property rights in land prior to the domination of the market economy did not merely denote an individual's wealth. More significantly, it demonstrated an individual's political, social and legal status. Formally, there was little in the way of a universally socially stratified justice, although there were many exceptions to the principles of common law. For example, Scottish miners remained as 'bound labour' until 1774, slavery remained legal until 1772, while the Master and Servant Acts (the first passed in 1823), which made breach of contract by an employee a criminal offence, was not repealed until 1875. Under the common law, servants continued to be treated as the chattels of the master. Cornish cites a number of cases in the nineteenth century where servants were punished for very minor acts. Indeed, he states, an underage servant could be physically punished without repercussions for the master unless beaten to death. In that event case the master could face imprisonment or be required to pay damages.[54] However, property dominated the legal system by the fact that appointment to legal office carried a property

---

50 Op. cit., Atiyah, pp 26–27.
51 Op. cit., Halevy, p 201.
52 Ibid.
53 Thompson, EP, *Whigs and Hunters: The Origins of the Black Act*, 1977, Pelican Books.
54 Op. cit., Cornish, p 287.

qualification. Cornish, while maintaining that there was a long-standing tradition of common law in England, indicates that social position remained the cornerstone of legal appointment. Judges in the higher courts, or Royal courts, were men of 'considerable social position'.[55] Indeed, he argues, 'it would have been remarkable had it been otherwise. Those who acquired the highest office were expected to purchase an estate commensurate with their station; and they had to show the social accomplishment befitting their place in the order of precedence.'[56] Lower down the judicial hierarchy, justices of the peace were drawn from lesser property owners and jurors too were selected by a 'householder property qualification'.[57] Indeed, those who administered justice were those who had the most to gain from existing property arrangements. In the towns, 'mill- and mine-owners were drawn onto benches, to continue there the hostilities over discipline and conditions that infected many work-places.'[58]

Atiyah, in *The Rise and Fall of the Freedom of Contract*, notes that until the complete emergence of the market economy, it was property law that dominated the English legal system, usurped in the latter part of the eighteenth century by contract law. He argued that 'this transition from property to a law of contract relating to property merely reflects the now familiar process by which the significance of property rights changed from their use value to their exchange value'.[59] Transformed under the market economy, property emerged as just another commodity, valued by the market. Previously, property denoted stability, continuity and heritage, providing for material needs and ensuring the continuity of relationships of deference and domination. However, Atiyah's assertion that the increased ability to alienate and exchange property (through the contract form) had depoliticised property is not in accord with other important work on the nature of property. Macpherson, for example, argues that property itself is not neutral, but representative of a particular set of social and political relationships.[60] He argues that when (and only when) property is for the most part held as private property it appears to be the case that 'property is a thing'. This is because the right to both enjoy and dispose of property is held by one legal entity. The true essence of property is that it exists as a 'political right between persons'. And, in the case of private property, it is the political right to exclude all persons from use of the thing. Alternatively, common property represents a shared mutual right of all individuals to the thing. Property rights are, by their very nature, only

---

55 Ibid, p 21.
56 Ibid, p 22.
57 Ibid, p 20.
58 Ibid.
59 Op. cit., Atiyah, p 103.
60 Quoted by Macpherson, CB in *The Political Theory of Possessive Individualism: Hobbes to Locke*, 1962, Oxford: Clarendon Press, p 123.

meaningful when accompanied by a political and coercive organisation that is capable of enforcing recognition of these rights. Private property, therefore, is only a meaningful right because of the political phenomenon of the state, an organised, specialised system of enforcement that ensures private property owners' absolute right to exclude others – the nature of a right being entirely derived from its enforceability as a claim and the enforceability of that claim depending upon a particular set of political relations.

In pre-capitalist agricultural England, an individual's legal rights to the land gave a highly visible testimony to their social status. Thus, at the level of politics, real property ownership entirely determined an individual's right to enfranchisement. Ownership of property was central to the right to vote and remained relevant even after the Reform Act of 1868.[61] Macpherson argues that the association of property rights with political (voting) rights had posited itself in the English consciousness for many centuries and this association was so deeply and universally entrenched that it was part of the ideology of the ruling class and radical working class groups alike. In the protracted debates on enfranchisement in the seventeenth century, that most radical of organisations, the Levellers, consistently excluded the possibility of giving the right to vote to wage labourers, beggars and to those receiving alms. The Levellers argued that these men could not experience the independence of mind and freedom that ownership of their own means of subsistence would have given them. Freedom was associated with private property ownership, and free will could only be expressed by the free-born Englishman, free because he was not dependent on the property of another. In debate with Oliver Cromwell, the Leveller Petty stated:

> I conceive the reason why we would exclude apprentices or servants, or those who take alms, is because they depend on the will of other men and should be afraid to displease (them). For servants and apprentices, they are included in their masters, and so for those that receive alms from door to door.[62]

While the Levellers argued on the basis of pragmatism or merely an acknowledgement of material reality, political philosophers, in the emerging liberal tradition, presented private property as a universal, natural and even moral right. John Locke and those following in the Lockean tradition argued that private ownership was an intrinsic quality of a physical object, and that private property ownership was intrinsic to human nature. The 'natural state' of mankind was to be engaged in private property ownership, even if that property was limited to 'property in self'. Adam Smith emphasised the importance of legislation that underpinned the absolute nature of private

---

61 Reform Act 1868.
62 Quoted by Macpherson, op. cit., p 123.

property rights as essential toward facilitating the exchange of goods and services. As a corollary to this, government should be restrained in its power to intervene with individual property rights; private property rights should be maintained as an immutable principle to which all other interests, including that of the governments, should be subordinate. The political theory of private property was co-opted (notwithstanding its libertarian potential) into the politics of Whig landowners who were undoubtedly keen to uphold the immutable right to private property as against the interference of sovereign or state.

Thus, property underpinned the ideology and aspirations of diverse groups in England and the economic, social and political relations therein. For the working class, private property ownership, if only in one's labour, determined freedom, in the sense of freedom from a fixed occupation. Thus material freedom was seen as a crucial mainstay of political freedoms. For the landed Whig classes, the maintenance of private property sustained a privileged lifestyle, as a moral imperative. Politically and philosophically, Whigs associated with the ascending liberal principles. The political correlation between the aims of building societies and liberalism created powerful if not pragmatic advocates for the movement. The universal right of individuals to make choices as to how they utilised and acquired property in self and other commodities served both these groups' interests.

The correlation of these interests crystallised in a surprising and ingenious manner in the middle of the nineteenth century with the emergence of a particular strand of building societies, the freehold land societies. This movement incorporated the political aspiration of working men to achieve enfranchisement and private property in land with the political aspiration of liberal politicians.

Following the passage of the Reform Bill in 1832, the vote was extended to those who owned property worth £10 in the boroughs and in the counties to £10 copyholders, £10 long-leasers and £50 medium leaseholders as well as the existing 40-shilling freeholders. This meant that building societies could play a direct role in the extension of the franchise through the provision of property of sufficient value to allow the owner to meet the voting qualifications.

In 1847, the first society to operate for the joint purpose of obtaining both property and the vote was established by a James Taylor and was called the Birmingham Freehold Land Society. This organisation and the others that followed represented a hybrid of both constitutional reform groups and building societies. Initially registering as friendly societies, when the legitimacy of advancing funds for the purchase of property was fully appreciated following the 1836 Act, subsequent societies tended to register under the Building Societies Act.

Strictly within legal limits and aimed precisely at Conservative strongholds in the counties, Taylor organised collectives of 40-shilling freeholders.

Working people were invited to become members of the society and to form a common fund based on small weekly subscriptions with which freehold land was purchased and distributed among its members in small plots. As long as the plots maintained a market value of 40 shillings, members obtained a county vote. At the end of the first year, subscriptions amounted to £500 per month and allotments had been made to over 200 members. The movement spread rapidly throughout the country and after only three years consisted of 80 similar societies with 30,000 members subscribing for 40,000 shares with paid up subscriptions of £170,000. As building societies, they operated under trustees who guaranteed mortgages and on occasion put up the initial funds for purchasing property. Up until the 1852 election, trustees were drawn from the ranks of liberal politicians. Particularly prominent in the freehold land movement were anti-corn law leaguers and free marketeers Richard Cobden and John Bright, whose success through the freehold land vehicle was often perceived as highly disreputable. As an article, *More Faggot Votes – New Purchase by the League*, in the Morning Herald of 1852 stated:

> An estate containing between 400 and 500 acres of land, situated at Horfield, two miles from Bristol, has just been bought by Cobden, Sir Joshua Walmsley and another Anti-Corn Law Leaguer; for the purpose of creating 1000 40s freeholds in West Gloustershire. The property is bought at 40L. per acre, and belonged to the Rev. Mr Richards, whose solicitor took it to a country farmer looking man, who, when he had paid the deposit, gave the names of Cobden *et al* as the purchasers. Mr Richards has since ascertained that the estate is positively bought for these parties, and the purpose named.[63]

The mood of the freehold land movement in contrast was focused and inspired:

> Economy is the beginning of independence. A man who is always hanging on the verge of debt, is in a state not far removed from that of slavery. He is in bondage to others, and must accept the terms they dictate to him. He is not his own master, he cannot help looking servile.[64]

However, by accumulating some property and engaging in a thrifty existence,

> his self respect is maintained and he can still walk tall without the fear of parish overseers. He is no burden to society – neither himself nor his little

---

63 Quoted in the Freeholder's Circular No 6, 2 August 1852.
64 Ibid, 'Independence for working men', p 75.

ones. His character is unimpaired, his virtue untainted; he looks forward with hope; he can neither be bought or sold.[65]

The potential of this movement was soon realised in the cities and in 1849 the *National Freehold Land Society* was started with the purpose of extending the franchise and land ownership in more industrialised areas. It opened with 750 members subscribing for 1,500 shares and quickly became the largest of all such societies. By 1852, *The National* boasted 9,000 members. It had purchased 37 estates costing over £200,000 and, of the £230,000 invested in freehold societies as a whole between 1851 and 1852, *The National* had received £96,137.[66] By 1851 it had purchased estates in many areas in and around London, including 32 acres in Stoke Newington, 204 acres in Romford and 220 acres in Barnet. Its popularity led it to publish a monthly circular, 'for the guidance of its members', which contained financial advice and a forum for discussion on the orientation of the movement and the various problems members encountered. In the first edition of *The Freeholder's Circular*, the objects of the National were stated as to 'facilitate the acquisition of freehold land, and the erection of houses thereon, to enable such of its members as are eligible, to obtain the county franchise, and to afford to all of them a secure and profitable investment for money'.[67]

Freehold land societies functioned as ordinary mutual building societies in that they were established under the Benefit Building Society Act of 1836 'for the purpose of raising a fund, out of which every Member shall receive the amount or value of his share to erect or purchase a dwelling-house, or dwelling houses, or other real or leasehold estate'.[68] However, they distinguished themselves by virtue of the fact that they dealt solely in the distribution of freehold land that had not been previously built upon. Mutuality of rights between members was scrupulously attended to, both as a virtue and as a point of marketing. The National's circular was keen to emphasise the equal opportunity of members in the acquisition of plots stating that. 'lots are after a time offered, on the same terms, to all the members'.[69] Furthermore, it emphasised the right of the members to choose the plots that were most suited to their needs, saying, 'members are enabled in a great measure to select their lots in the situations most convenient to themselves'.[70]

By the end of 1852 there were 130 societies, with 85,000 members subscribing to 120,000 shares. An estimated 310 estates had been purchased divided into 19,500 allotments with paid up subscriptions of £750,000. Politically, it

65 Ibid.
66 Reported in the Freeholder's Circular, 1st edn, 1852, p 11.
67 Ibid, p 3.
68 Benefit Building Society Act 1836.
69 Op. cit., Freeholder's Circular.
70 Ibid.

represented a highly successful allegiance between Liberal politicians and building societies and in the 1852 election Liberal candidates won decisive victories in the previously Conservative strongholds of Middlesex and East Surrey. Perhaps ironically, the movement was bolstered by the adoption of its own tactics by the Conservative Party, who set up the Conservative Land Society. The experience of this society was that within four years 1,803 shares had been taken up of which £218,158 had been paid up and it had allotted 22 estates sold into plots worth £150,000.

As a politically expedient tool, the land society movement formally ceased to be functional following the Reform Act of 1868. However, as one commentator noted, as early as 1853, 'the political idea has almost vanished from the societies; members enter without any declaration of political opinion, and not one in 500 cares a rush about the franchise at all'.[71] Land societies had become successful economic organisations that were easily subsumed into the building society movement. So, for instance, marrying the status of both building society and land society, the Birkbeck Freehold Land Society and the Birkbeck Building Society, although legally separate organisations, operated from the same building and under the same management.

The freehold land society movement graphically joined politics and property under the organisational tool of the building society, yet, significantly, the success of freehold land societies served to undermine the original conception of mutuality. Compared to the early building societies with memberships of around 50, freehold land societies were huge, with some, like The National, numbering tens of thousands in their membership. The numbers involved meant that many freehold land societies offered extra shares to those with the means and desire to finance them. Different levels of investment by members meant the acquisition of more property, thus making them attractive propositions for the more moneyed classes.[72]

The effect of the freehold land movement on the building society movement as a whole had been transformative. For 70 years building societies had been small in size and number, never exceeding 80. But, by 1850, 2,000 societies had registered under the 1836 Act.[73] In addition to this they attracted large sums of money. By 1850 the entire movement was estimated to hold a total annual income of £2,400,000.[74] This meant that the traditional terminating societies had become increasingly inappropriate, designed as they were for a small, non-fluctuating group of saver/borrower members.

However, the most important factor in reconceptualising mutuality lay in

---

71 Editorial from Chambers' Edinburgh Journal, 10 December 1853.
72 Evidence by Table: 'Subscriptions of Members form Commencement of Society to Present Time', op. cit., Freeholder's Circular.
73 Scratchley, A, *Industrial Investment and Emigration*, 2nd edn, 1858, London: John W Parker, p 50.
74 Ibid.

the reorganisation of the mutual society. A particular problem with terminating societies was that individuals who wished to join some time after a society had been founded were often unable to do so due to the high costs of joining late and, effectively, having to 'catch up' with other members' savings.

The solution to this organisational problem was presented and published by the actuary Arthur Scratchley, who argued for a society that did not terminate in a fixed period, but existed indefinitely. These he called 'permanent societies'. Under this organisational form, members would have an individual contract with the society designating them as either investors receiving interest or borrowers paying interest. Investors would be able to withdraw their investment with relative ease, while borrowers would make periodic repayments (usually monthly) over a fixed period, making their loan arrangement 'terminating' rather than the society itself. In this way the society could extend its borrowing according the amount invested in it and borrowers could join without 'making up' the payments made by founder members.

Scratchley highlighted two attributes of terminating building societies that made it imperative to adopt the permanent principle of organisation. The first of these attributes was the general popularity of building societies, the second being the inadequacies of members' actuary skills. On the first point, he argued, 'no benefit building society has ever been started, however ridiculous its pretensions, which has not speedily succeeded in drawing together a number of shareholders'.[75] On the second point, he noted a general inability to calculate compound interest that led many building societies to misrepresent the financial benefits of membership. In his words, 'not one in twenty, or even a greater number can possibly realise for its members, whether investors or borrowers, the advantageous results originally promised'.[76] This problem, exacerbated by an uncritical enthusiasm for building societies, could be resolved by the use of a permanent system. Scratchley argued that the benefits of a permanent over a terminating society were, in the main, that 'the difficulty of funding borrowers, at any time in the course of the existence of a society is removed . . . members don't pay arrears if they join later and the numbers of share holders increase rather than diminish in the life of a building society'.[77] In contrast, a terminating society was founded upon a fixed number of subscribers who paid a monthly subscription until all members had received housing and had paid off outstanding loans undertaken for that purpose, housing, in the main, being allocated by a lottery scheme. Members who wished to join after the founder members were required to pay higher premiums in order to equalise with the payments of earlier

75 Ibid, p 7.
76 Ibid, p 50.
77 Ibid, p 52.

subscribers, that is, individual subscriptions were determined in line with the finite life of a terminating society. This meant that if a member joined half way through the life of the terminating society he would be required to pay double the premium of that paid by founding members, a sum that would obviously increase the later a member joined. This inhibited the desirability of late entry and, as a result, terminating societies would tend to have only a small number of members. In contrast, in a permanent society, the large number of members would mean that the administrative costs of setting up and running the society could be more equitably spread. Furthermore, members could withdraw their investment more readily and the duration of investment could be more easily ascertained.

These stated advantages notwithstanding, it appears to be the case that, in practice, the development of permanent societies was not the result of conscious planning. In the 1874 Royal Commission Report it was noted that it was probable that permanent societies grew organically from the tendency of larger terminating societies to incorporate members throughout their existence, creating indefinitely existing terminating societies.[78] Thus the terminating aspect of these societies more correctly described the relationship of individual members to the society, rather than the organisation *per se*. Put another way, 'a permanent society is a terminating society to every individual from the date at which he enters'.[79]

Terminating societies operating with an increasingly unwieldy membership were experiencing organisational problems that the permanent system could easily accommodate. For example, larger terminating societies tended to engage in periods of great economic activity followed by more fallow periods. As the Commission noted,

> it is a pretty general feature amongst terminating societies that all their activity is concentrated within the first few years of their existence. During these first few years, again, it is almost invariably the case that they resort very largely to loans, in order to obtain as much money as they can for the placing out; advances being made either on the principle of ballot, or of sale to the highest bidder ... during the latter years of their existence, as repayments come in more and more, terminating societies have generally a plethora of money.[80]

In contrast, permanent societies operated on the more regular basis of supply and demand. Investments determined the capital available for the making of

---

78 The Royal Commission Friendly Societies was set up in 1870 and soon after concerned itself with Building Societies and the problems of the 1836 Act.
79 Op. cit., Royal Commission, p 14.
80 Ibid, pp 13–14.

loans, capital obtained either through deposits or through paid up shares. Thus the Commission concluded, 'there be no alternation of energy and stagnation: the money has not all to be put out in the first few years: the demand for it increases steadily with the progress of the society'.[81]

Crucially, as Scratchley had noted some years before, this was facilitated by the separation of members into two separate classes, borrowers and lenders, each class maintaining entirely distinct roles and benefits. A borrower would receive a full advance, secured on a mortgage, itself supported by fixed monthly repayments. Thus 'the members, who become borrowers, at once cease to be investors in respect of the shares on which they obtain advances'; this means that they 'do not participate in any of the subsequent liabilities, or expenses of the society, nor consequently in its profits'.[82] In contrast, investor members do participate in the profits made by the society, and this is the sole motivation to becoming members (although in practice individuals may be both borrowers and investors).

The absolute mutual character of terminating societies that derived from members' equal engagement, commitment and benefit in the organisation was necessarily undermined by the organisation of the permanent principle. In a terminating society members invested in order to borrow. Collective participation enabled them to do as a group what they could not do as individuals. This collective solution was embraced precisely because of the economic status of members who, as we have seen, were largely composed of the better-off working class. In contrast, permanent societies distilled the two functions performed by members into two distinct roles, investor and borrower, thereby drawing a distinction between the benefits and responsibilities attributed to each. In the words of the Royal Commission, 'instead of all the members being expectant borrowers, as appears to have been first the case, and is still the case in some groups, the two classes of investors and borrowers are now distinct, the former usually outnumbering the latter and monopolising the profits'.[83]

Investing members were drawn into the society by the prospect of expanding their own private capital by lending money, secured by a mortgage on property, to individuals who could only finance such purchases by monthly payments over a number of years and who paid interest on these advances. Investing members, therefore, were induced to invest by two main factors. First, the degree to which borrowing members would pay additional moneys on their advancement and, second, upon the security of the investment; in short, the character of the borrower and that of the property held on a mortgage.

---

81 Ibid.
82 Op. cit., Scratchley, p 64.
83 Op. cit., Royal Commission, p 13.

Mutuality remained, to the extent that all members were economically interdependent, but was undermined to the extent that the self-interest of investing members and borrowing members conflicted, as the role of the former had become usurious in character. To be sure, some societies chose to limit this tendency. For example, the Leeds Permanent Society followed a strategy of minimising the difference between the interest paid to its investors and the interest charged to its borrowers thereby circumventing the permanent's tendency to divide mutuality between members. Thus, as the Commission reported, 'the borrowing member stands absolutely on the same footing as the investing member, as respects the sharing of profits, the right of voting, &c'.[84]

However, it was more frequently the case that the separation of the two classes of members led to the charging of high interest rates to borrowers: 'the mere fact that the usual recommendation which building societies put forth for themselves is the large rate of profit they give to investors, is clear proof of the high rate which the borrower has to pay for his money.'[85] Furthermore, the emerging oligargic tendencies of building societies meant that the borrower had little choice but to accept the high rates charged. In evidence to the Commission, James Taylor, founder of the freehold land movement, stated that 'people would not come to our society if they could get their money elsewhere. If a man could get the money in any other way besides belonging to our society, he would never pay a £50 premium for £500'.[86]

As a result of the usurious character of the investor member under the permanents' method of organisation, the social class of participating members shifted from the 'industrious classes' to the middle classes, the latter being particularly represented in the investing class. Furthermore, witnesses to the Commission testified to the corrupt character of the growing domination of middle-class membership in permanent societies, evidence which, on the face of it, the Commission clearly disapproved:

> It is indeed startling to hear of single advances, not only of thousands but of twenty or thirty thousands of pounds being made by building societies, sometimes on the security of mills and factories; and it is roundly alleged by some witnesses that the working classes, by whom and for whose benefit the system was primarily devised, are discounted and kept away.[87]

However, the use of building society funds for these purposes seemed more the exception than the rule. Evidence from the Building Society Protection

84 Ibid, p 15.
85 Ibid.
86 Ibid, Q 3802, p 15.
87 Ibid, p 16.

Society (BSPS)[88] indicated that advances tended to be small and non-commercial. Its statistics drawn from 251 societies indicated that 69,879 advances were made on the 'lower rate' (set at £300), while only 9,393 were made on the higher rate (advances over £300). The proportion of lower rate advances to higher rates, about nine to one, was however lower in London at about six to one. The BSPS nevertheless concluded that building societies still maintained their roots within the 'industrious classes'.

It was, however, less difficult to ignore the class divisions between the terminating system and the permanent system. The Commission observed that 'whilst the smaller terminating societies remain very often still under the management of the working classes, or of persons very near to them in point of station, the larger permanent societies at least are almost invariably under the direction of the middle class'.[89] Furthermore, this division tended to be reflected in the class composition of the membership, particularly in the metropolis where 'working men seem generally to form only a minority in the permanent societies as compared with the middle classes'.[90]

Thus the growth of the permanent system, emerging as a practical response to the general popularity of building societies, brought with it certain characteristics that undermined the principle of mutuality. It separated the role of borrowing from investing member, which inevitably separated their interests. Investing members required high returns from a secure investment. Borrowing members would thus inevitably pay higher interest rates and would be subject to assessment of their personal suitability as borrowers. This more complex process, exacerbated by the growing size of building societies, necessitated the growth of professional arbiters of members' conflicting interests. Assessments as to the security of an investment, that is the character and financial status of a proposed borrower, operated under the ambit and determination of a wealthy, managerial stratum utilising increasingly homogenised and discriminatory criteria. As it tended to be the middle class that were investor members and the working class that were borrower members, by favouring the interests of the investor, societies were favouring the interests of the middle class. This class division was exacerbated by the fact that the required qualified actuaries and managers were drawn from the middle class, particularly in respect of the largest of the building societies, which were permanent societies. So, as the permanent system quickly replaced the terminating system it increasingly sidelined the interests of less wealthy members.

This system, however, was highly successful and was concretised in the Building Societies Act 1874. It remains the method of organising societies today. The separation between borrower member and investing member and

---

88 A group representative of building societies. It is discussed in more detail later in this chapter.
89 Op. cit., Second Report, p 16.
90 Ibid, p 17.

the individual agreements members would have with the society rather than between each other was legally expressed in s 9 of the Building Societies Act 1874. This section determined that registration of a society automatically created a corporate entity, distinct from its members and possessing perpetual succession.

> Every society now subsisting or hereafter established shall, upon receiving a certificate of incorporation under this Act, become a body corporate by its registered name, having perpetual succession, until terminated or dissolved in manner herein provided, and a common seal.[91]

Individualised members now had a legal relationship with a distinct entity, the building society. The new societies were no longer made up of members and indistinguishable from the membership. They were distinct entities responsible for mediating the financial interests between borrowing and investing members.

The new rules were enforced by personal responsibility of members. With the exception of those societies already in existence,[92] members of societies that failed to register would be personally liable for 'every day business is carried on'. Officers of registered societies that exceeded amounts in loans and deposits prescribed by the Act would be personally liable for the amount loaned in excess of this sum.[93] Furthermore, the falsification of accounts could result in a summary conviction upon complaint by the registrar.

However, provided that societies were established for purposes prescribed by s 13 and the rules of the society were set out in the terms prescribed by s 16 (pertaining to the way in which funds were raised, withdrawn, the alteration of rules, auditing, members meetings, powers of directors, penalties for members and the procedure for termination of the society), the registrar was obliged to register them. This set aside the discretion that previous registrars had exercised.

The Act provided a code of regulation of societies' finances. Under s 15, societies could borrow money not exceeding two-thirds of the amount secured by mortgages. Officers in charge of money were required to give security to the society, 'in such sums as the society require, conditioned for rendering a just and true account of all moneys received and paid by him on account of the society'.[94] Under s 31, persons receiving funds by false representation would be liable on summary conviction to a fine of up to £20. Amalgamations of societies were permitted under s 33 if three-quarters of the members

91 Building Societies Act 1874, s 9.
92 Ibid, s 8.
93 Ibid, s 46.
94 Ibid, s 23.

holding two-thirds of the shares voted in favour, the same number being required for the dissolution of a society.[95] Under s 34, disputes were to be resolved by arbitration and the decision of the arbitrator was to be final.[96] Societies were required to compile accurate annual accounts for its members under s 40 while under s 44, the state held the right to check these accounts, 'make regulations respecting the fees, if any, to be paid for the transmission, registration, and inspection of documents under this Act, and generally for carrying this Act into effect'.

The broad aim of the Act appears to have been the provision of a framework for the regulation of building societies as distinct financial institutions and to facilitate the monitoring of their activities while allowing them certain freedoms in their internal organisation. However, legislation was quite clearly intended to maintain building societies as socially useful organisations that facilitated the respectable activities of working people. Thus, unlike the commercial company, whose activities had been extensively liberated in legislation such as the Limited Liability Act 1855 and the Companies Act 1862, the activities of building societies were heavily prescribed.

FACTORS WHICH CAUSED A RETREAT FROM MUTUALITY

In 1836, the law had at last recognised building societies as a distinct, allowable, and regulated form of mutual economic organisation. But at this same moment, historical processes that were to lead eventually to the demise of that central principle of mutuality established themselves. As previously shown, the emergence of the permanent society form had already undermined many of the fundamental principles of mutuality. The processes in addition to this are those that dominate the remaining history of the building society movement, which we now discuss. The first of these processes is the increasing dominance and control of the sector as a whole by the largest societies, centrally through the medium of the Building Societies Association. The second was the legal structures successive governments put in place in order to preserve building societies as institutions which helped the industrious classes. Such structures limited business opportunities for building societies which later made it difficult for societies to compete with banks. Furthermore, these confines frustrated the ambitions of many managers who sought the freedoms offered by the corporate form which was further exacerbated by the more onerous legal requirements put upon building society managers in contrast to company directors. The third process emanated from the prudential

95 Ibid, s 32.
96 Ibid, s 36.

policies of building societies and the uncompetitive practices they engaged in. These processes were internally generated but rendered building societies subject to criticism from outside bodies which eventually filtered through to the government. The criticisms were mainly from the political left and the Labour Party. The fourth process was the legislation which enabled building societies to shed their mutual status. This legislation reflected the pro-free-market approach which characterised the ideology, although not always the practice, of Margaret Thatcher's Neo-Liberal Conservative administration. This new ideology valued free-market institutions rather than the more socially based organisation of mutual societies. The fifth process was the ambition of the building society managers who sought to persuade the membership to demutualise through rhetoric and financial rewards and a membership whose massive support of the demutualisation or conversion of their society made it clear that mutuality gave them no benefits that they could identify.

The Building Societies Association

By the 1870s the building society movement had ceased to be a small number of intimate groupings underpinned by little or no legislation and had, instead, become popular financial institutions worth millions of pounds and under-pinned by detailed legislation and regulatory oversight. And, in addition to the hierarchies forming within societies, hierarchies between societies further distanced mutuality from its origins in equality. This latter development had much to do with the tendency for capital within the industry to become centralised. In 1890, 2,286 societies were registered with total assets of £60 million. By 1988, total assets had increased to £188 bn but the number of building societies had decreased to 131.[97] Furthermore, a series of amalgamations had left a handful of societies, such as the Halifax and the Abbey National, with a huge proportion of the total assets.

The power of the larger societies over the entire building society movement was largely exercised through the Building Societies Association (BSA). The BSA operated as a trade association producing publications that gave general advice and providing a forum for sharing the views of individuals involved in the industry. However, its powers increased immeasurably following the economic slump in the 1930s when the BSA began its policy of determining building society strategy with particular reference to 'advising' interest rates.[98] Furthermore, as the executive board of the BSA was made up from the top management of the wealthiest societies, the small, and already powerful, elite of the industry effectively determined advice.

97 Successive Annual Reports of the Chief Registrar of the Friendly Societies of BSC.
98 This is placed in inverted commas as this advice was taken as a unquestionable by all members of the BSA.

Historically, the emergence of one single organisation representing the estimated 4,000 building societies (of hugely varying sizes) in 1869 derived from the campaigning activities of Liverpool- and London-based societies. In 1869, after 14 years of sporadic activity from the these societies, the Liverpool Association and the London group agreed to form a single permanent organisation that would eventually represent the whole of the building society movement. Thus the Building Societies Protection Association (BSPA) was born. Its rise to being the *de facto* central organisation of building societies derived initially from its activity in the movement for reform of building society legislation, activity that resulted in the passage of the Building Society Act 1874. In this, it was aided by its journal and mouthpiece, *The Building Society Gazette*, which began publication in 1870 and provided a central, popular forum and mode of communication to those in the building society movement.

From its inception the *Gazette* testified to the unashamed elitism of the BSPA. Whether discussing building society management or the manner in which poorer members should be treated, it readily displayed just how far the building society movement was removed from the 'industrious classes' that made up the majority of its membership. In a discussion on the policies to be adopted when a survey was conducted for the purpose of securing an advance, the sensibilities of richer members were considered to be of greater importance than poorer members:

> So long as the operations of a Building Society are confined to the making of advances upon inferior property it may be a matter of little moment whether the privacy of the tenants is invaded by one or two, eight or ten persons, visiting for the purpose of a survey but the case is very different when proposals are received upon a better class of property . . . It need hardly be contended that as Building Societies advance to a higher class of business than was originally contemplated, it is important to avoid everything in their working arrangements that may prove offensive or annoying.[99]

On the issue of the management of societies, views varied from an attempt to justify elitism on sound business grounds to undisguised snobbery. On the first point:

> As the society grew older a large proportion of such men would, in the natural order of things, be eliminated from its membership, and thus the management would fall more and more into the hands of men who lacked the necessary knowledge and judgment for the safe conduct of its affairs and who belong exclusively to the borrowing class, had nothing to

99 Building Societies' Gazette No 15, p 36.

lose, and to their own sanguine expectations, everything to gain, by a policy which appeared at one state, to cancel shares standing as claims against the society and to increase the assets available for bringing it to an early termination.[100]

And on the second:

In some few cases it is true that the rules appear to be formed upon the assumption that all men are equally qualified for the responsibilities and equally entitled to the dignities of office. And every shareholder is consequently permitted or compelled in turn to act as committee man or director; but, excepting societies of the smallest class, assuming rather the character of local clubs than of important financial institutions, any such haphazard theory of management must be dismissed as unworthy of serious discussion. The member selected for this responsible office should a man of good business character, of good practical common sense and of sound and calm judgement.[101]

Or more succinctly:

It is unquestionably desirable to have men of commanding social position, and of extensive financial resource.[102]

With the social bias of BSPA policy in place, it only remained for it to consolidate and centralise its power to spread these policies throughout the whole of the building society movement. This was achieved most notably in the interventionist decades between 1939 and 1980, after the BSPA had reformed with new enhanced powers as the BSA.

During the economic depression of the 1930s the lack of demand for money led to increasingly low interest rates. This increased competition between building societies for the borrowing members on whom they relied in order to pay interest to lending members. The BSA responded to the impending economic ruin of many of the less competitive societies by annihilating competition itself. This was achieved by a policy of recommending interest rates, to which all member societies were obliged to adhere. This policy and power continued unabated for many decades and it was not until the late 1970s that the BSA found itself under much scrutiny. Following two major government reviews, the BSA found itself criticised for centralising power and for engaging in anti-competitive policies.

100 Directory and Handbook of Building and Freehold Land Societies (1873) London Office of 'The Building Societies' Gazette', Chancery Lane, p 8.
101 The Building Societies' Gazette No 18, 1870.
102 Building Societies' Gazette, No 17, Vol 9, 1 May 1870.

On the first point, the constitution of the BSA was highly undemocratic. In 1983 the membership of its ruling council consisted of representatives from the 10 largest societies. The five largest societies held 50 per cent of all the capital of the entire industry and the two largest held 33 per cent of the whole.[103] The chairman of the BSA and head of the Council was (and still is) drawn from the largest building society. In other words the largest societies controlled policy in respect of all the others.[104]

On the second point, the BSA's policy of 'advising' societies on interest rates, adopted in 1939, created an informal cartel. As Barnes put it, 'firms will collude to fix prices – whether in the sense of a formally constructed cartel, through an informed agreement in a smoke-filled room or simply by a tacit agreement to follow the leader'.[105] And, as an earlier government committee testified, the artificial rate of interest created by the BSA had the effect of supporting inefficient firms and allowing larger, more efficient firms to reap super-profits.[106]

Furthermore, the BSA was highly protective of its powers, dealing harshly with members that took business decisions that it (the BSA) had not pre-scribed. The enforced closure of the New Cross Building Society in 1984, following a decision by the Chief Registrar of Friendly Societies, is a case in point. In 1974, Ted Roland became New Cross's chief executive and embarked on some radical departures from the standard practices 'advised' by the BSA. First, the New Cross operated with low management costs, employing just 90 people although during the period between 1975 and 1983 its assets rose from £6 m to £120 m.[107] Second, three-quarters of the society's funds were raised outside their small number of branches. Instead, sales of mortgages were undertaken by a mortgage marketing team and by insurance salesmen. Third, and perhaps most significantly, in March 1993 it took advan-tage of the generally sluggish nature of processing mortgage applications to put up interest rates by 2 per cent for its larger and longer-term investors. This meant that it was able to increase inflows of investment and offer quick and easy mortgages at albeit greatly increased interest. It made this move, to its great corporate advantage, outside the 'advice' of the BSA on the appropriate rate of interest. Fourth, and as a result of the products it was able to offer, its customer base was not that of the traditional building societies. As the *Financial Times* reported,

103 Barnes, P, *The Myth of Mutuality*, 1984, Pluto Press, p 44.
104 All but 0.1 per cent of building societies' assets were affiliated to the BSA.
105 Op. cit., Barnes, p 34. Barnes was reflecting the view of the 1966 command paper cited below.
106 Cmd 3136, 1966, HMSO.
107 Clive Wolman, 'Downfall of a heretic: behind the New Cross closure', 21 January 1984, *Financial Times*, p 24.

Few struggling first-time buyers or any other favourites of building society folklore appeared on their mortgage books. Their borrowers included, they claim, international footballers, entertainers and two MPs who were lent amounts of up to £100,000 each, often on properties they already owned.[108]

The BSA responded in this way. A member of the BSA council contacted the auditors of New Cross, Dearden Farrow, and advised them to scrutinise the 1992–93 accounts more carefully. On doing so they found certain discrepancies relating to 'special advances'. Under the Building Societies Act 1962 only 10 per cent of advances may fall under this category, defined as advances to commercial mortgages or mortgages over £37,500. In the New Cross's audits it became clear that this sum had been slightly exceeded. This circumstance arose because a number of mortgages of £37,500 had fallen into arrears thus increasing the amounts owed, technically putting such loans into the 'special advances' category. Although this discrepancy arose through a grey area of law and although there was no evidence of deliberately flouting building society regulations, the Chief Registrar, Mr Bridgeton, took the unprecedented step of issuing orders to close the New Cross. Furthermore, he took this decision despite recent precedent to the contrary. For, as the *Financial Times* reported, when, 'in 1980, the Peckham Mutual Building Society made special advances of nearly double the permitted level, it was let off with a warning'.[109]

The political construction of a social-commercial organisation

The second process leading towards the death of mutuality has its origins, paradoxically, in the distinctly social course that regulation of building societies took, compared with that of companies. The very fact that legislation – and the judiciary – recognised building societies as organisations having a distinct social content had a number of effects. First, over time, large surpluses accrued which, when the time became ripe, could be raided to pay for agreement to demutualise. Second, directors were under stricter duties to their organisation than company directors and third societies were limited in the kind of business they could undertake which resulted in their later lack of competitiveness compared with banks. While over the period in question the company was treated with greater and greater latitude, the building society was treated as a quasi-social institution rather than a purely commercial enterprise. At the same time that building society legislation was being

108 Ibid, p 24.
109 Ibid.

tightened in respect of the increased powers given to its overseer, the Registrar of Building Societies, the limited liability company was enjoying increased freedoms.[110] Corporate identity was recognised upon the minimum of formalities and in respect of a company that was, in essence, a one-man business.[111] In addition to this, although the judiciary often described the general duties owed by directors of companies in the same terms as those of building society directors, in many important aspects they were treated differently. For example, in respect of maintaining company assets, the judiciary adopted a very liberal attitude to that which a company should maintain before declaring dividends, a practice that remained until the passage of the Companies Act 1981. In contrast, a building society manager was expected to recompense members for a negligently declared dividend.[112] Furthermore, although the objects of a building society were statutorily determined in each new piece of relevant legislation, the strict interpretation of the *ultra vires* rule in respect to early registered companies was gradually loosened and nearly abandoned by the judiciary.[113]

Thus it can be seen that while the government and the judiciary, in particular, placed commercial expediency at the heart of their policy for the company, the building society operated under much tighter controls. While investors in companies were protected, for the most part, by limited liability, they risked the loss of their original investment. In contrast, investors in building societies could expect a greater degree of protection.

However, it was the additional constraints placed on building societies for the protection of investors that produced the ultimate lure for the shedding of mutual status. Societies were required to maintain an annual reserve in order to protect its members from the fluctuations of the market. Over the years, these accumulated into substantial sums that could be used to provide cash or 'free' shares to members upon conversion.[114]

Statutory restraints were on occasion introduced as a result of events. For example, in 1892 one of the largest building societies, The Liberator, collapsed as a result of the fraudulent activities of its directors, causing huge economic instability and moral crisis within the building society movement. The Liberator's crash is popularly understood to have prompted the passage of the 1894 Act, which prohibited the granting of second mortgages and strengthened the powers of the registrar. It empowered the registrar to have the books of a society inspected in a number of different circumstances,

---

110 Building Societies Act 1892.
111 *Salomon v Salomon* (1897) AC 55.
112 *Leeds Estate Building Society v Shepherd* [1936] 36 Ch D 787.
113 Contrast *Ashbury Ry v Riche* (1875) LR 7HL 653 with *Bell Houses Ltd v City Wall Properties Ltd* [1966] 1 QB 2071.
114 For example the 1981 Building Societies (Authorisation) Regulations required 2.5 per cent of assets to be held as reserves.

254   Critical company law

either if the society failed to make a statutory return, or on the initiative of the membership, expressed in various different ways.[115]

If it appeared, after investigation, that the society would be unable to meet its obligations to its members and that 'it would be in their benefit that it should be dissolved', the registrar could 'award that the society be dissolved'.[116] Furthermore, the registrar could cancel the registration of the society if he was

> satisfied that a certificate of incorporation had been obtained for a society under the Building Societies Acts by fraud or mistake, or that any such society exists for an illegal purpose, or has willfully after notice from the registrar violated any of the provisions of Building Societies Acts, or has ceased to exist.[117]

Section 13 of the Act specifically prohibited advances on second mortgages and contravention of this prohibition would render the responsible directors jointly and severally liable for any loss arising from the advance. More generally, the Act provided for a series of fines for officers of the society who did not conform to any rules on the returning of documentation.[118] In addition, it provided that false information in any society document wilfully made would render those officers responsible liable for a fine of up to £50.[119] Finally it stated that any official who received

> any gift, bonus, commission, or benefit, shall be liable on summary conviction to a fine not exceeding fifty pounds, and, in default of payment, to be imprisoned with or without hard labour for any time not exceeding six months.[120]

However, while these measures might seen an entirely sensible response to the Liberator's collapse, it was not the typical governmental response to financial collapse generally. Indeed, the commercial world had been in crisis for over two decades before the passage of this Act without being subject to similarly prescriptive legislation.

This approach to building societies was also reflected in the judiciary's attitude to building societies and their officers. For example, in respect of liability for the payment of non-existent profits to members by directors, the directors of building societies operated under a much more stringent regime

---

115 Building Societies Act 1894, s 5(5)(c).
116 Ibid, s 7(2).
117 Ibid, s 6(1).
118 Ibid, s 21.
119 Ibid, s 22.
120 Ibid, s 23.

than that of companies. In a case bought by the Leeds Estate Building Society against one of its directors, it was held that directors who pay dividends to themselves and shareholders out of illusory profits, on the basis of inaccurate balance sheets which they did not properly examine, were personally liable for the sums paid out and were required to recompense the society accordingly.[121] Building society managers had little flexibility in their accounting practice as they were obliged to show an equal balance between liabilities and assets in order to adhere to the mutual principle.

Further responsibilities placed upon building society managers included a statutory requirement to give security to the society for the monies they managed with their own personal funds.

> Every officer having receipt or charge of any money belonging to the society must, before taking upon himself the execution of his office, become bound with one sufficient surety at the least, in a bond according to the form below or give the security of a guarantee society, or such other security of a guarantee society, or such security as the society direct, in such sum as the society require, conditioned for rendering a just and true account of all moneys received and paid by him on account of the society, at such times as its rules appoint, or as the society require him to do.[122]

Failure to comply would make directors, 'clearly liable for any loss resulting from its non-performance'.[123] As Wurtzburg noted, upon demand, all officers were to account to the board and pay over 'all moneys remaining in his hands; deliver all securities and effects, books, papers, and property of the society in his hands or custody, to such person as the society appoint'.[124] An officer who failed to comply with such a request could be sued by the society upon the bond or it could apply to the county court to make an order against him, against which there was no appeal. Furthermore, a dismissed officer could be ordered to return any society property regardless of whether the dismissal was wrongful and against which there was no appeal. Internal to the building society movement, as previously noted, the BSA expected managers to be men of upstanding social position and to be of financial substance.

Other extrinsic influences which contributed to the greater controls placed over building society directors included the strict application of the *ultra vires* rule. For instance, the statutory object of a building society, that of making advances to members secured upon freehold or leasehold from funds raised from investing members, remained unchanged for over 100 years. A society

---

121 *Leeds Estate Building and Investment Co v Shepherd* (1887), 36 Ch D 787.
122 Building Societies Act 1874, s 23.
123 *Evans v Coventry* 8 De G M & G 835; LJ Ch 400.
124 Wurtzburg (1893) 'The Law Relating to Building Societies', 2nd edition, p 88.

was bound to these objects and was prohibited from extending its business by making changes to its own rules or by any other method.[125] In *Portsea Island Building Society v Barclay*,[126] the society's directors made a further advance to an existing mortgagee by applying to an insurance company for a loan and then paying this sum to the borrowing member in consideration for the conveyance of the mortgaged property to the society. The society agreed to postpone its own mortgage to the insurance company's rights and the deeds to the mortgaged property were deposited with the insurance company as security for the loan. The member then used the loan to repay part of the original mortgage. The rules of the society forbade any advance on an equity of redemption but authorised the directors to release part of any mortgaged property if they were satisfied that the remainder was sufficient security for the loan. The court held the transaction to be *ultra vires* and void. Any departure from the objects of a society instigated or allowed by the directors would be a breach of duty and would render them liable for any loss that might result.[127]

Much later these restrictions on building activity meant that they were under severe pressure in competing for mortgage business with the clearing banks who, by the 1970s, were free from restrictions inhibiting them from competing for savings and mortgage business. Clearing banks could offer mortgages as well as unsecured loans and overdraft facilities all under one roof. Indeed, by the late 1970s Lloyds Bank was offering a complete in-house service to housebuyers. In response, the BSA established the Nature of a Building Society Working Group, chaired by John Spalding, the Chief General Manager of the Halifax Building Society. In 1983 it published a report, 'The Future Constitution and Powers of Building Societies', which proposed that new legislation was required to enable building societies to compete with other financial institutions. It further proposed that future legislation should allow building societies to convert into a corporate body if the membership agreed. Thus the legal restrictions imposed on building societies pushed the movement directly toward demutualisation.

In all other areas of commercialism, *laissez-faire* was the *modus operandi*. As Eric Hobsbawn noted, 'the formation of business companies now became both considerably easier and independent of bureaucratic control . . . Commercial law was adapted to the prevailing atmosphere of buoyant business expansion.'[128] In order to further enhance business expansionism the stringent laws against usury were dropped in Britain, Holland, Belgium and North Germany between the years of 1854 and 1867. Likewise, 'the strict control which governments exercised over mining – including actual operations of mines – was virtually withdrawn . . . so that . . . any entrepreneur could claim

125 *Murray v Scott* (1884) 9 App Cas 519.
126 (1894) 3 Ch 861.
127 *Cullerne v London and Suburban General Permanent Building Society* (1890) 25 QBD 485.
128 Hobsbawn, E, *The Age of Capital 1848–1875*, 1975, p 36.

the right to exploit any minerals he found'.[129] In order to enhance a freer market in labour, the Master and Servant Acts were repealed in 1875, as was the 'annual bond' of the North[130] so that 'in between 1867 and 1875 all significant legal obstacles to trade unions and the right to strike were abolished with remarkably little fuss'.[131]

In contrast, the political and judicial attitude to building societies was quite distinctly not *laissez-faire*. This was partly due, as has been argued, to the desire to maintain and control institutions that so readily attracted the independent 'industrious classes', and incorporate them into mainstream society, a view consistently evidenced by the Commissioners in the 1870s. Integral to this approach has been ensuring the security of investments in societies and much of the emphasis of building society legislation has attempted to achieve this. So, for example, the Building Societies Act 1939 prohibited advances made on securities that were not of a class specified in Part 1 of the Schedule to the Act, that is, advances made on freehold or leasehold land.[132] Directors were under a duty to ensure that adequate measures had been taken to ascertain the proper valuation of property upon which a mortgage would be advanced and the test of competency in this case was objective. A director should ensure that

> the arrangements made for assessing the adequacy of a security to be taken in respect of advances to be made by the society are such as may reasonably be expected to ensure the adequacy of any security to be so taken will be assessed by a competent and prudent person, experienced in matters relevant to the determination of the valuation of that security.[133]

Directors were additionally required to keep prescribed records of advances, including records of a competent valuation.[134] Failure to do this would constitute a summary offence, resulting in a fine.

Another area of security assurance included provisions for maintaining minimum reserves. Larger, permanent building societies had routinely held surplus profits as reserves for the purpose of enhancing financial security. Ultimately these were held on trust for the owner-members (creditors had priority over this fund). In 1947 the BSA recommended a 5 per cent reserve

---

129 Ibid, p 37.
130 Applicable to miners in the North. This was replaced by a standard employment contract, terminable on both sides.
131 Ibid, p 37.
132 Building Societies Act 1939, s 2(1). The basic advance was set at 75 per cent of the value of the property (s 2(4)).
133 Building Societies Act 1939, s 12(1).
134 Building Societies Act 1939, s 12(3).

ratio and four years later a 7.5 per cent minimum liquidity ratio.[135] In 1959, the House Purchase and Housing Act introduced a minimum reserve ratio of 2.5 per cent and a minimum of 7.5 per cent liquidity ratio (assets were required to be a minimum of £0.5 m). The Building Societies Act 1962 removed the requirement for minimum liquid assets (still necessary to achieve trustee status) but stated that:

> A building society shall not invest any part of the surplus funds of a society except in a manner authorised by an order made under this section by the chief registrar with the consent of the treasury.[136]

In 1981, the Building Societies (Authorisation) Regulations made authorisation for the raising of funds dependant on the holding of reserves. This was compulsory for all societies, but the level of reserves would depend on the size of the society. All societies were obliged to hold at least £50,000 as reserves and those with up to £100 m of assets were required to keep 2.5 per cent of this as reserves. A society with between £100 m and £500 m in assets was required to keep 2 per cent of its assets as reserves. This percentage went down to 1.5 per cent for societies with assets worth between £500 m and £1,000 m, with a further reduction of 0.25 per cent for those societies with assets exceeding £1,000 m.[137]

The aim of all the above measures was to achieve one objective, the production of a prudential framework. However, the hoarding of reserves ultimately enabled the argument against maintaining mutual status to be submerged under the benefits of the short-term gains provided by windfall shares.

Prudence and prejudice

The emergence of a commercial institution, the mutual society, that was unique in collecting additional controls over its activities throughout a historical period of liberalisation or *laissez-faire*, was due as much to external political control as to factors internal to the building society movement itself. Early building societies ensured their insulation from the government's draconian anti-collectives policies by adhering to strict internal controls and a non-provocative attitude. Success and expansion in the mid-nineteenth century led to the introduction of an organisational form, the permanent society, that required both responsibility and expertise from its officers, and those active in the movement sought controls to ensure that this happened.

---

135 Boleat, M, The Building Society Industry, 2nd edn, 1986, London: Allen & Unwin, p 146.
136 Building Societies Act 1962, s 58(1).
137 Although the Wilson Report, below, showed that building societies were building higher reserves than this for business reasons.

Furthermore, the permanent societies' reliance on investors, who might have no stake as a borrower, meant that legislative controls were sought to ensure the security of the lender-member's investment. Significantly, this put borrower members under scrutiny and led to building societies introducing rigid lending criteria with a borrower profile that tended to exclude all but white middle-class men. In addition to this, as noted above, reserves designed to protect investors created a fund which could and would be used by ambitious building society directors in order to effect a conversion.

Building societies began to come under scrutiny for their prudential policies which had resulted in indirectly prejudicial lending practices and an overly empowered and unaccountable management. Many of the growing criticisms of building societies were contained in the Wilson Report: Committee to Review the Functioning of Financial Institutions.[138]

The committee, which started work in 1977, presented its report to Parliament in June 1980. The Wilson Report began by assessing the economic significance of the building society movement. It noted that building societies held a significant proportion of investments, second only to banks. Total building society assets by the end of 1978 exceeded £39.9 bn, held predominantly as loans secured by mortgages.

The orientation of building societies to this form of investment, with its incumbent 'lend long borrow short' policy, meant that they were highly susceptible to the volatile nature of both interest rates and inflation. To counterbalance this, the Wilson Committee reported that building societies relied on two dominant strategies. First, building societies had increased the level of reserves in order to subsidise the granting of lower interest rates to borrowers when interest rates were high and savers were seeking higher returns. Second, the BSA operated a price-setting policy for all its members. On the first point, building societies built up reserves through surplus created from the lending and borrowing part of the business (after the deduction of running costs and tax) together with any profits earned from their liquid assets. The reserves were on average 3.5 per cent of the total assets of building societies as a whole. Table 20 of the Wilson Report showed that in 1968 £29 m was held as reserves or 3.8 per cent of total building society assets, in 1972 this had risen to £76 m or 3.64 per cent and by 1978 reserves stood at £212 m or 3.73 per cent of the total building society assets. This policy was one that was to have a very significant effect on the success of demutualisation.

These strategies, argued the report, were not sufficient to immunise building societies from the sharp rises in interest rates at the end of the 1970s. In 1979 the BSA decided to raise its recommended mortgage rate to 15 per cent. This, coupled with the prudential policy of lending only a percentage of the purchase price, had the effect of excluding less wealthy first-time buyers.

138 1980 Cmnd 7937.

The problem was exacerbated by the societies' policy of reducing this proportion of the purchase price on which they would lend when trying to ration funds.

The Wilson Committee concluded that this policy 'discriminates against those who find it difficult to raise the necessary deposit'.[139] And, 'because of their tradition of encouraging self-help and thrift, they have frowned upon the concept of "low start" mortgages, believing that those who feel that the initial payments impose too great a burden should defer house purchase until such time as they can afford it, rather than be financed for a period by the societies' depositors'.[140] And, even more controversially, 'some have argued that it is more sensible for the costs to be loaded in the earlier, rather than the later, years of the loan because in this period it is common for both husband and wife to be employed full-time'.[141]

Instead, proposed the report, building societies should increase the flow of capital available for loans and offer more attractive rates of interest. This could be achieved by abandoning the policy of protecting weaker societies through the BSA's recommended rates system (set at a rate all societies could afford) and subjecting all societies to a competitive market.

> The only sure way of providing a competitive spur to building societies is in our view to end the recommended rate system, that is, to allow societies to set their own rates according to their circumstances and to break the present automatic link between the rates paid to depositors and those charged to borrowers.[142]
> ... The dismantling of the recommended rate system would give building societies greater freedom to compete with other deposit taking institutions as well as with themselves.[143]

Equally, the introduction of market criteria could force building societies to abandon their costly policy of opening branches. The report showed that while in 1968 there were 1,662 building society branches, by 1978 this number had risen to 4,595 while the average number of accounts per branch had only risen from 4,921 to 5,440 in the same period.[144]

> Greater competition between societies would cause them to examine the viability of their branch networks with some care, with the probable effects of promoting mergers – and thus reducing the number of large

139 Ibid, p 85, para 289.
140 Ibid.
141 Ibid.
142 Ibid, p 113, para 380.
143 Ibid, para 384.
144 Ibid, p 110, Table 25.

societies providing facilities nation-wide – or encouraging some degree of regional specialisation, perhaps through an exchange of obligations or amalgamations involving smaller, regionally based societies.[145]

These recommendations later found voice in the growing criticism of management practices which many thought operated with no regard to the interests of members and in an unchecked and self-serving fashion. For example, in Paul Barnes's book *The Myth of Mutuality*, he argued that building society managers were dominated by managerial goals like personal prestige, job security, status symbols and empire building. He argued that managers tended to focus upon 'the non-profit goals of interest groups', and made 'investments beyond those required for the normal operation of the firm'.[146] Indeed, he argued, far from being concerned with profit maximisation, managers viewed profit as 'the basic constraint subject to which other goals may be followed'.[147]

Barnes argued that a clear example of 'non-profit goals' was the empire-building practice of establishing unnecessarily large numbers of building society branches. In analysing the unjustifiably high operational costs of building societies he concluded that in opening branches, managers were not motivated by rational business concerns unless financially constrained to do so.

For example, he argued, in 1978, smaller building societies[148] on average spent 76.7p per £100 of assets on operational costs compared to the operational costs of medium-sized societies,[149] which on average spent 100.8p per £100 of assets on such costs, the former working under tighter budgetary constraints. Furthermore, Barnes argued that the lack of uniformity in spending on operational costs, across the board, indicated the high degree of discretionary power allowed to managers.

Concurring with this view, Christopher Hird argued that there was little inducement for managers to encourage members' intervention as the former enjoyed enormous power over large financial institutions.[150] Furthermore, he argued, if a member's intervention became noticeable or effective, he or she was quickly co-opted onto the board.

The solution was therefore clear, and heralded the forthcoming Thatcher administration:

> External pressure on the cartel results from the queue for mortgages and the expansion of the building societies' branch networks, both of which have become matters of grave concern. We believe that these problems

145 Ibid, p 111, para 376.
146 Op. cit., Barnes, p 45.
147 Ibid.
148 Defined as those with less than £3,711 m of assets.
149 Defined as those with less than £14,278 m of assets.
150 Hird, C, 'Stakeholding and Building Societies', New Left Review, 1977.

could be alleviated by greater competition among the societies . . . we
recommend that the recommended rate system should be abolished.[151]

Recommendations for the prudential regulation of building societies therefore
derived from the desire to subject societies to the market. Changes in prudential regulation were deemed essential to oversee the changes recommended to
increase competition and move away from the situation where 'the weaker and
more inefficient societies have to a large extent been cushioned from normal
commercial pressures by the recommended rate system, which limits price
competition for deposits, and by excess demand for mortgages'.[152]

The system of prudential control at this time was formally based in statute,
the provisions of which were overseen by the Chief Registrar of Friendly
Societies and informally by the BSA. The pertinent legislation was by now the
Building Societies Act 1962, which prescribed the kind of business a society
may undertake, rules of governance and rules pertaining to capital reserves
and liquid assets. Before the Registrar registered the society and therefore
before it could take deposits, he must have been satisfied that it met the
1962 Act's criteria. After that point, however, the Registrar's powers were
considered by the Report to be limited.

The Wilson Report recommended that the requirements for building society registration and designation should be increased and that the Registrar's
powers should be extended. They favoured the introduction of minimum
liquidity or reserve ratios for those societies seeking designation. In respect of
the Registrar's powers they recommended that 'the Registrar should be given
powers to promote mergers or to enforce the winding up of a society for
prudential reasons subject to an appropriate right of appeal'.[153]

The collapse of a reasonably prominent society prompted the Wilson Report
to recommend a strengthening of accountancy procedures. In 1978 Grays
Building Society collapsed losing £7 m of assets. Grays was a medium-sized,
designated society whose accounts falsely showed assets of £11.5 m. The
Registrar's method of monitoring societies was through their annual accounts.
In this case, that fell far short of an adequate method of control. In order to
counteract the problem of a society manager falsifying accounts in order to
disguise fraudulent activity the committee recommended that there be a substantial increase in the number of visits to building societies made by the
registry and that the voluntary cash flow statements should be made compulsory. To facilitate this extended supervision, the Wilson Report recommended
that a separate organisation should be developed in the registry dealing solely
with building society issues. Finally, it recommended a statutory scheme of

151 Op. cit., Wilson Report, p 114.
152 Ibid, p 327.
153 Ibid, p 332, para 1250.

investor protection so that the protection afforded to depositors of societies who were members of the Building Societies Association would be afforded to those outside the Association (at that point, around 100 small societies, accounting for just under 1 per cent of the total of building society assets).

As a generalised approach to reforming building societies, the report recommended that they should operate under the discipline of a competitive market and stricter statutory controls that would further empower the Chief Registrar. This was the report that the Neo-Liberal government of Margaret Thatcher inherited, and, in the context of its much vaunted political orientation it should have provided an ideal base on which to introduce even more far-reaching measures toward *laissez-faire* market strategies.

Thus, the 1980s represented a period when particular factors combined to leave mutuality devoid of any supporters outside a small number within the building society industry itself.

Neo-liberalism and the making of the 1986 Act

According to Thatcherite ideology, the welfare state had, through over-taxation, served to disappropriate individuals from the money they earned and had created a culture of dependency among those that did not, or could not, work. Drawing on, in particular, Hayek's post-war writing, Thatcherism associated welfarism with state intrusion, and state intrusion with the oppression of individualism and entrepreneurialism.[154] It concluded that individual creativity and productivity could only evolve in a market economy that was free from state interference. And, in the same manner that Thatcherism proved the efficacy of its ideology through the sale of council houses into the private ownership of the tenants, so it sought to draw building societies from the shackles of state policy and into the norms of market control.

The Thatcher administration achieved these aims on a number of different levels and with very little opposition. The Labour Party had already criticised the anti-competitive organisation of building societies. The Wilson Report into building societies, which was eventually published in 1980, recommended the abandonment of the BSA's 'recommended' interest rate system, which had been introduced in order to protect the weaker societies and hence the building society industry as a whole. And it did so according to market criteria, introducing market control over the industry by encouraging 'greater competition among the societies'.[155]

By the early part of the Thatcher administration Labour and Liberal MPs were already putting forward the argument that building societies should be subject to the same market criteria as other financial institutions. The initial

154 Hayek, FA, *The Road to Serfdom* 1944/1976, Routledge and Kegan Paul.
155 Cmnd 7937, p 114.

response from the Conservative front benches was, at this time, less than sympathetic to this view. Labour and the Liberal MPs complained about the BSA's 'cartel', the tax privileges enjoyed by building societies, the wasteful number of branches and the problem of making directors accountable. In the House of Commons oral answer session of 22 May 1980, Nigel Lawson was required to answer on all four issues.[156]

On the first point, Mr Budgen stated that the BSA operated as a cartel on interest rates which, he argued, had the effect of reducing the interest of investors and encouraging the growth of the largest societies. Nigel Lawson, far from condemning such non-market practices, disagreed that these strategies aided larger societies; on the contrary, he argued that the suppression of competition provided the public mortgage interest rates at 'lower rates than might be expected'.[157] The issues of director accountability in respect of building society lending strategies, raised by Mr Grimond and, in respect of the unnecessarily large number of branches, raised by Mr Weetch, were dismissed by the Chancellor as issues that shouldn't concern government or legislation. The possible problems of managers pursuing their own self-interest by engaging in mergers was deemed to be a matter for the Registry of Friendly Societies.

At the height of the New Right's free-market policy, the government set into motion extensive legislation on building societies. The government green paper on the subject, *Building Societies: A New Framework*, was presented to Parliament in July 1984. In the context of the New Right's liberalism this report should have been expected to outstrip the 1980 report in its emphasis on competition and deregulation. Instead, however, in all but one important respect, this paper favoured increased structural control and accountability while offering some facility for building societies to offer some additional financial services.

Nigel Lawson's foreword to the paper clearly demonstrated the government's intention to effect a compromise between free-market disciplines and the traditional institutional role of building societies. The latter consideration, echoing the 1871 Royal Commission's intentions to encourage thrift and home ownership in the 'industrious classes', was expressed thus:

> Our purpose is to ensure that the building societies continue primarily in their traditional roles – holding people's savings securely and lending for house purchase – while loosening the legal restraints under which they have operated for a century or more so that they can develop in other fields.[158]

156 Hansard, oral answer session, 22 May 1980.
157 Ibid, p 690.
158 'Building societies: a new framework', July 1984, p 2.

And, later:

> Their primary role as specializing in the housing finance and personal savings markets, and their mutual constitution should remain.[159]

The former consideration was expressed thus:

> So, by allowing the societies new powers, we can both further encourage home ownership and look forward to fuller and freer competition for financial services to the great benefit of all.[160]

and later:

> It is important that building societies should be competitive in attracting savings. Major structural changes are now taking place in the financial services sector . . . building societies will probably need to respond to a trend toward 'one stop' centres for financial and investment services.[161]

However, this paper made clear that any change to building societies would be limited and, to the extent that the organisation was liberalised, it would be subject to extra scrutiny. *Laissez-faire* was not to be the policy underlining much of the proposed legislation.

> The scope for diversification should therefore be limited and subject to proper prudential control. Nor should it create significant conflicts of interest.[162]

The 1984 Paper noted that the statutory limits on the activities of building societies and their financial strategies generally had meant that societies had provided a very safe source of investment for their members. This had allowed building societies to enjoy a certain latitude in their internal organisation. Generally, building societies held 80 per cent of their assets as loans secured on a mortgage, 17–20 per cent in liquid assets and about 1.25 per cent in fixed assets, usually land and offices, while its liabilities were drawn almost entirely from the deposits of individual members. This meant that in the absence of fraud from a borrower, or the liquid assets being translated as fixed assets that fell in value, a building society's assets were very safe. The green paper also noted that 'societies have been able to afford to keep the interest rates paid to their investors in line with market rates, despite large

159 Ibid, para 1.07.
160 Ibid, p 2.
161 Ibid, p 4, para 1.10.
162 Ibid, para 1.11.

fluctuations, by lending on terms under which they can vary at short notice the rates they charge their borrowers'.[163]

As a gentle nod toward liberalism, the green paper proposed that the old s 1 of the Building Societies Act, which restricted building society activities to 'raising, by the subscriptions of the members, a stock or fund for making advances to members out of the funds of the society upon security by way of mortgage of freehold or leasehold',[164] should be replaced by a new section. This section would now state that 'the primary purpose of a building society is to raise funds from individual members for lending on security by mortgage of owner-occupied residential property'.[165]

This would allow building societies to engage in related business such as estate agency and automatic telling machines. Prior to the passage of this Act, building societies had had a problem with certain money transmissions because of a technical point. It could not guarantee payment, on for example cheque guarantee cards, because it would be agreeing to pay funds to a third party regardless as to whether there were sufficient funds in the account in question. This problem would be overcome by dint of the new powers to offer unsecured loans, a facility that would also enable the use of automatic telling machines.

The green paper also proposed that building societies should be empowered to offer an integrated house buying service, 'a package of service to house buyers, including estate agency, conveyancing and structural surveys', subject to any conflict of interests that may arise.[166]

Other services proposed included agency services for building societies' 'under-utilised branches' and collecting 'local authority rent and rates, and bills for public utilities, insurance broking and financial services such as arranging share purchases and general investment advice'.[167]

However, the green paper consistently emphasised that any liberalisation would be accompanied by enhanced prudential control. Thus, the green paper proposed that 90 per cent of assets (other than liquid assets) should be used for residential, first mortgages. Liquid assets should be kept to a maximum of 33.3 per cent and at least 80 per cent of funds should be raised by members. The paper argued that all assets should be classed according to their risks.

In respect of the Chief Registrar's powers the paper proposed that the main statutory powers of the Chief Registrar would be in relation to granting, withholding and revoking authorisation. In order for a building society to be authorised, the Chief Registrar would have to be satisfied that all the requirements on the board of directors could be complied with and that it

---

163 Ibid, para 2.03(b).
164 Ibid, para 2.05.
165 Building Societies Act 1962, s 1(1).
166 Op. cit., 'New framework', para 4.00.
167 Ibid, para 4.05.

would, in general, be capable of safeguarding its investors' interests. In order to clarify precisely the criteria by which a director's duty would be judged and that which he must achieve in order to protect investors' interests, the paper set out a director's statutory duties.[168]

By prescribing very specific duties the paper hoped to provide an immediate response to a director's failure to meet these obligations. Explicitly, the paper noted that 'failure of the board of a society to meet one or more of these requirements would be recognised as a ground for the Chief Registrar to exercise one of his discretionary powers'. In addition to this the paper considered raising the minimum capital required from its existing level of £50,000, in order to provide a more secure fund for investors.

Encapsulating the contradictions inherent in the prevailing political climate, the green paper presented its antithesis to the basic thesis of a restrictive approach to governance. It made a number of proposals deliberately intended to introduce free market criteria. For example, building societies had been specifically exempted from Restrictive Trading Practices legislation so that the BSA's policy of recommending interest rates was not challenged. In response to the abolition of 'corset' controls in 1980 which led to banks taking (by 1985) 25 per cent of new mortgage business, the BSA reformulated its interest rate policy. The original policy, noted above, consisted of two different agreements described by the green paper thus:

(a) The recommendation of basic rates of interest to be paid on building society investments and charged on mortgages; and
(b) An undertaking by participating societies to give 28 days' notice of variations from the recommended rates.[169]

On 21 October 1983, in response to the criticism of the Wilson Report, the BSA had announced new arrangements whereby the recommended rates would be replaced by advised rates for ordinary shares and mortgage loans. There would be no requirement to give notice of changes, although there would be an informal agreement under which societies may be notified of each other's rates. These changes, argued the green paper, had introduced competition between building societies and it could no longer be 'assumed that the prime objective of building societies should be to keep mortgage rates down'.[170] This meant that 'the original rationale for exempting the building societies from the legislation'[171] was removed. And, reasoned the report, if this exemption was removed it would allow the Director General of Fair Trading to legally challenge even the 'advisory' function of the BSA on the

168 Ibid, p 40.
169 Ibid, para 6.06.
170 Ibid, para 6.04.
171 Ibid, para 6.08.

basis that it was contrary to the public interest. A successful challenge on
these grounds would result in building societies setting their own interest rates
without reference to the BSA, entirely subjecting rates to market criteria and,
in the green paper's view, providing 'a greater range of choice and a better
service to building society members'.[172] In order to further this desirable
effect, the green paper proposed that the exemption from the Restrictive
Trade Practices Act 1976 should occur simultaneously with the new building
societies legislation.

The second arm of the introduction of market criteria had already taken
place through other legislation, which homogenised rules relating to taxation
of banks and building societies. Tax-paying investors in building societies had
previously paid a lower rate because they were paid interest net of a compos-
ite rate of tax. This privilege, the report stated, was already now extended to
bank investors (from April 1985). In addition, the 1984 budget had already
brought corporate tax down to 35 per cent for both banks and building
societies, the previous position being corporate tax at 52 per cent for banks
and 40 per cent for building societies. The Lawson Report approved of this
approach.

The third arm of the financial liberalisation of building societies was by far
the most controversial. It proposed to allow building societies to change their
legal status from that of a mutual society to that of an incorporated company. Originally recommended by the Spalding Report, it was not a proposal
that the green paper seemed to embrace with much enthusiasm.[173] Indeed,
it stated that although a 'compulsory change to company status has been
advocated by some in the past' the government 'does not accept that such a
change is needed'.[174] In respect of the increase in competitiveness mooted by
the Spalding Report as a reason for enabling conversion, the green paper
argued that societies had already faced a great deal of competition from other
societies and various financial institutions. This competition, it argued, had
resulted in the acceleration of innovative service for customers and restricted
the costs of management. However, whilst arguing that conversion was
unnecessary, it took the view that

> [i]t is wrong that a society cannot turn itself into a company if its members
> wish. The Government therefore intends to provide for this in new legis-
> lation. Although there are no signs that many societies will wish to become
> companies in the near future, this will provide greater flexibility.[175]

If societies chose the conversion route, the resulting business would then be
subject to the Companies Act 1985 and its directors would owe a fiduciary

172 Ibid, para 6.09.
173 'The future constitution and powers of building societies', 1983, Chairman John Spalding.
174 Ibid, para 5.29.
175 Ibid, para 5.30.

duty to the company. In addition, the new company would require a licence from the Bank of England under the Banking Act 1979. Conversion could only take place following a vote of its members.

The Building Societies Bill was published in June 1985, received its second reading in the House of Commons and was committed to Standing Committee on January 1986 and was passed later that year. The ensuing legislation evidenced both the desire to make building societies more competitive, by granting them more powers, and the view of the larger societies that the building society movement was not homogenous and, for some, conversion was appropriate. The majority of the Act is concerned with the creation of new powers and freedoms for societies coupled with the extended prudential supervision discussed in the green paper. The 'principal purpose' of building societies is stated as the raising of funds to lend on the security of land. Reinforcing this principle, the 1986 Act, in contrast to the 1962 Act, determines that 90 per cent of a building society's business must be for this purpose and furthermore that this business must relate to land for residential use.

The Act, however, widened the areas where building societies could borrow. In addition to raising funds from investing members they could also raise moneys from non-retail funds, such as financial markets. However, only 20 per cent of building society liabilities could be raised in this way.

In general, the Act gave new powers for societies to deal in financial products. In banking, they could provide money transmissions, foreign exchange, overdraft facilities, credit cards, cheque guarantee cards and personal loans. A society could also dispense funds through automatic telling machines. In the area of investment, societies could act as broking agents, and provide personal equity plans and insurance services. As an adjunct to their primary purpose, societies could now offer a range of services relating to property. These included powers to operate estate agencies, offer conveyancing and property valuation services and to directly develop land and housing.

The above liberties were limited, in that no unsecured loan could be above £10,000, ownership of insurance companies was limited to 15 per cent, land development could only be for residential uses, societies could not trade in equities and no business could be conducted with non-EC countries. In other words, the role of building societies as financial institutions for the industrious classes engaged in savings and house purchase was underlined, while the increased expectations of its members in respect of financial products such as debit and credit cards, overdrafts and 'one stop shopping' was realised.

In themselves these measures were a sensible and pragmatic response to modern financial demands and could have enhanced the building society movement while it continued to operate under mutual status. However, these extensive provisions would be overshadowed by a handful of sections whose aim was to achieve the opposite result, not to maintain mutuality but to transfer the business of a mutual society to a commercial company.

These sections operate in this way. Sections 97–103 in conjunction with Schedules 2 and 17 of the 1986 Act provide for the power of members to convert to plc status from mutual status. Section 97(1) states: 'A building society in accordance with this section and other applicable provisions of this Act, may transfer the whole of its business to a company'.[176]

As a constraint on conversion the Act provides that there must be an investors' special resolution and a borrowing members' resolution. In order to convert, 20 per cent of investing members entitled to vote must vote and, of that, 75 per cent of investors and 50 per cent of borrowers entitled to vote must vote in favour of conversion. When the transfer is to an existing company, as opposed to one specially created for the purpose, then the percentage is 50 per cent of those eligible to vote on the special resolution, or the holders of 90 per cent of share capital must vote in favour.

Under s 100 'the terms of a transfer of business by a building society to a company which is to be its successor may include provision for part of the funds of the society or its successor to be distributed among, or other rights in relation to shares in the successor conferred on, members of the society, in consideration of the transfer'. This payment, however, would only be made to 'those members who held shares in the society throughout the period of two years which expired with the qualifying day'.[177] Characterised earlier as 'bribes', these payments would only be paid to those members qualified to vote on a motion on conversion.

Following a vote in favour of conversion, application is made to the Commission for confirmation of transfer, which will be given unless any of the criteria in sub-section 3 of s 98 applies. These provisions include when the Commission considers that:

(a) some information material to the members' vote was not available to all the members eligible to vote; or
(b) the vote on any resolution approving the transfer does not represent the views of the members eligible to vote; or
(c) there is a substantial risk that the successor will not become or, as the case may be, remain (an authorised institution for the purposes of the Banking Act 1987); or
(d) some relevant requirement of this Act or the rules of the society was not complied with.

However, all the above may be disregarded by the Commission if it feels that they were not material factors in the members' decision.[178]

---

176 Building Societies Act 1986, s 97.
177 Building Societies Act 1986, s 100.
178 Building Societies Act 1986, s 98(4).

Following confirmation, the stock is floated, with a percentage of free shares being given to members entitled to vote for conversion. All property, rights and liabilities of the building society pass on to the successor company on the vesting date specified in the transfer agreement.

In specially formed companies, no one person will be allowed to hold more than 15 per cent of the issued share capital or debentures for a period of five years, although the Bank of England held a discretionary right to waive this requirement. The Bank of England played this role as the regulatory supervisor of a public limited company dealing in financial products like the converted or demutualised building societies and would consider an application for a licence under the Banking Act 1979.[179] The newly converted society would also be subject to the Companies Act 1985 and would no longer operate under the Building Societies Acts.

The unwillingness of the legislature to make conversion a simple process, thus annihilating mutuality with some rapidity, may be explained as the result of the contrary norms of conservative thinking. Conservative ideology, reflected in the Building Societies Act 1986, contained a combination of free market liberalism and Burkean social order through social engineering. Thus, part of Conservative thinking desired preservation of building societies for the role they played in the incorporation of working members of society into the norms of ownership which helped ensure a deference and commitment to a society that protected private ownership. The privileges enjoyed by building societies were a small price to pay for the retention of their important social function. Thus, we find that most of the 1986 Act was orientated around reforming controls on building society activities to enable them to compete with other parts of the financial sector without the necessity of changing their legal form. Much of the legislation attempted to preserve mutuality by enhancing the desirability of operating as a mutual. So, were it not for the desires of society managers and society members, ss 97–103 of the Building Societies Act 1986 would have been a dead letter.

However, these sections have been greatly utilised and the management of a number of societies have been extremely proactive in the conversion process, as indeed were a small number of members. In addition to this, in almost all cases members have voted in favour of conversion by a huge majority. As a result, ss 97–103 have transformed the building society movement, taking more than 80 per cent of assets out of the mutual sector. In the words of Mr Weetch, Labour MP for Ipswich and major critic of building societies in the 1970s, 'The Government has created a new competitive world in financial

---

179 The regulatory role for both converted and mutual societies is now played by the Financial Services Association.

institutions. I am glad to see it, because it could have done with more competition, goodness knows.'[180]

Demutualisation, managers and membership

Despite the government's assertion that it would be unlikely that building societies would avail themselves of the facility to demutualise, societies began to explore the possibilities almost immediately after the publication of the Statutory Instrument setting out the practical arrangements for conversion, the Building Societies (Transfer of Business) Regulations 1988.[181] In January 1988 the Halifax began to explore the possibilities *before* the regulations were made, and appointed the merchant banker NM Rothschild to study the possibility of converting into a public company. In the words of a *Financial Times* survey, 'the Halifax is adamant that at this stage, it is only reviewing options, and that conversion is only one of them. Nonetheless there is a strong inference that the days of mutual status, at least as it has been known until now, are numbered'.[182]

In respect to the large proportion of members required to approve demutualisation, the survey argued that although this used to be considered an 'insuperable hurdle', 'most now seem to believe that they probably will be able to do it, even if voters have to be given some sort of sweetener to approve the change'.[183] It argued that the main obstacle to demutualisation was the fear that the market may become swamped by building society shares or that mergers would have to be completed before conversion, as legislation protected the new entity in its entirety for the first five years of existence. Any general hesitation by societies were based purely on the attempt to learn about possible pitfalls from converting societies, and not a heartfelt desire to preserve the traditions of mutuality; 'second tier societies that say that they see no immediate need to shed mutuality are assumed by others to be biding their time, perhaps in the expectation that, once the first wave of conversion is over, building society flotations will be quite normal'.[184]

A similar report to the Halifax's was commissioned by the Woolwich Building Society from Prima Europe, a policy research group based in London, which was published on 15 November 1988. This report concluded that although building societies were under increasing pressure from banks, even without the defensive armoury of being able to raise capital through the sale of equities or the ability to trade in diverse financial products, mutuality

---

180 Hansard 1985, Debate on Building Societies Bill, p 984.
181 SI 1988/1153.
182 Barchard, D, Survey of Building Societies, March 1988, *Financial Times*.
183 Ibid.
184 Ibid.

could still remain a feasible option. It argued that 'the healthy rate of capital generation by societies appears sufficient to pursue a successful development strategy which opens up new prospects of income to counter any squeeze on mortgage margins'.[185] The predominant view among building societies was that wide-scale mergers would help preserve mutuality. Reflecting this view, the chief executive of the Woolwich Building Society was reported as arguing that 'the remaining societies would evolve into mutually owned retail banks competing with the main banks but insulating customers from risks such as developing-country debt'.[186] However, as the article cynically remarked, any new-found allegiance to mutuality was probably driven by the desire for managers to retain their status by avoiding the consequences of take-over to which societies would be vulnerable in the event of conversion.

The Leeds Permanent Building Society commissioned a similar study from Hambros but decided against conversion, subject to review, in 1990. In addition, the National and Provincial appointed JP Morgan, the US Bank, to advise it in February 1989, although a previous poll had already suggested that its members were in favour of conversion. And, as a general assessment on mutual societies, Morgan Grenfell, the London merchant bank, published a report arguing that 'the best long-term future of many big building societies may lie in shedding mutual status and joining a financial services group offering a wide range of products to its clients . . . many of the top 20 societies will find it increasingly difficult to survive alone in an increasingly competitive financial services market in the next decade.'[187]

In short, at this time, the general view of the larger societies and that of their advisors was that mutual status was just one method of organising business among many, and that any decision to shed mutual status, or retain it, would be based on pragmatism. In the context of the market-based understanding of socio-political relations in the 1980s and 1990s and the facilitating aspects of the Building Societies Act 1986, mutuality was understood as either a hindrance or an opportunity and, above all, as something that could be dispensed with.

Most vociferous in demanding greater freedoms for mutual societies were the larger societies, in particular the Abbey National Building Society, which was among the largest financial institutions in the UK. The Abbey National was the first society to demutualise, a process that was instigated and secured by a motivated and self-confessedly pro-conversion management. Under the

185 Quoted in 'Mutual dilemma for building societies: the pressures to seek banking status by flotation, 16 November 1988, *Financial Times*.
186 Ibid.
187 Barchard, D, 'Building societies "may have to alter status to survive" ', 3 April 1989, *Financial Times*.

chief executive, Peter Birch, the Abbey forcefully put the argument in favour of demutualisation to its membership and, some argued, forcefully suppressed alternative views.

The Building Societies Act 1986 provided for the ultimate freedom desired by the Abbey, the ability to shed mutual status and convert into a public limited company. And, although the opportunity for members to gain financial reward through the process of demutualisation was anticipated prior to the passage of the Act, as commentators had already seen the speculative nature of demutualisations in the US, it was the demutualisation of the Abbey National that first showed how this process could bring financial benefits to building society members in the UK. The possibility of financial reward encouraged 'entrepreneurial' individuals to become members of societies with the sole aim of putting forward a motion to convert. A successful motion would ultimately award them personal compensation following the sale of the society to a company. These individuals, outwardly despised by the building society industry, became known in the late 1990s as 'carpetbaggers'.

In the Abbey's case, as soon as was legislatively possible, the society's management began a process that ended with the first building society conversion. In March 1988, the management announced its plan to shed mutual status and a transfer agreement was drafted and put forward to the Abbey's membership for approval. In September 1988 a new company, Abbey National plc, was registered. As a wholly owned subsidiary of Abbey National Building Society, it was created with the express purpose of facilitating the conversion of the building society into a public limited company.

In the event, and with far-reaching results, the transfer agreement drawn up by the Abbey's management was questioned by the Building Societies Commission on a number of points. This led to a resolution in court that served to smooth the path to conversion and encourage the practice of 'carpetbagging'. In attempting to concretise some of the legislation that the Commission assumed existed to preserve the integrity of mutuality, it confronted a judiciary who interpreted the legislation in a more liberal and effectively pro-conversion manner.

The proposals in the transfer agreement that were problematic related to s 100 of the 1986 Act. The first related to the kind of arrangement to which s 100(8) related; the second as to whether or not the offer of shares to members who were not two-year members was contrary to s 100, which provided for the giving of the right to subscribe for additional shares, 'in priority to other subscribers', to two-year members only; while the third question related to the issue of which members were entitled to cash distributions.

On the issue of who qualified for cash distributions, the court held that members who were investors or borrowers 'on the qualifying day and qualified to vote on the requisite shareholder's resolution and each borrowing member entitled to vote on the borrowing member's resolution'[188] would be entitled, free of charge, to an allocation of fully paid up shares in the successor company'.[189] Thus membership, for the purpose of qualifying for a cash distribution, was defined by the court in accordance with s 100(4) as somebody who was a member on the qualifying day and who remained a member continuously until the vesting day.

In respect to the second point, the Commission submitted that the offer of additional shares should be limited to two-year members only and to offer such shares to other members was unlawful under s 100(8). The transfer proposal, it argued, was contrary to the provision of that section in that 'the member's rights to free shares are to be granted in priority to the rights to subscribe for the new shares conferred on *other subscribers*'.[190]

The court held that s 100(8) did cover those situations where there is a subscription for shares in the successor company and '(1) there is a subscription for shares in the successor company, and (2) the subscriber is bound by an obligation imposed by the transfer agreement itself to vest the shares so subscribed for free of charge in the members' and that 'such right is enforceable by each member under s 97(5)'.[191] However, it maintained that the mischief that the section was designed to counter was the attainment by members (other than two-year members) of priority rights in respect of a shares issue. Thus the section would be infringed if 'members other than two-year members are by the transfer agreement given the right to acquire any shares in the successor company, and such right is given to the exclusion of or in priority to persons who are given by the transfer agreement rights to subscribe for those or any other shares in the successor company'.[192] There was no such contravention, the court concluded, if the same class of members is entitled to free shares and to subscribe to the new shares, as no priority right is conferred.

The overall outcome of this decision was that short-term membership was no bar to gaining the same personal benefits afforded to long-term membership unless long-term members were themselves excluded from these benefits. There was now an open door for potential carpetbaggers. Conversion was approved by members on 11 April 1989 and confirmed by the Building Societies Commission on 6 July 1989. Given the proportion of members' votes in favour, it seems to have had little choice but to confirm. As the *Financial Times* argued, 'The Commission seems to

188 *Abbey National Building Society v Building Societies Commission* (1989) 5 BCC 259, 261.
189 Ibid.
190 Ibid, p 264.
191 Ibid, for both quotations.
192 Ibid, p 265.

have decided at the outset that the size of the pro-flotation vote – around 90 per cent of members on a 60 per cent turnout – meant the conversion had to go ahead'.[193] Thus, upon the admission of the share capital onto the Official List of the Stock Exchange and upon authorisation from the Bank of England, conversion was complete and trading of shares in Abbey National plc began.

Demutualisation could not have taken place without the consent of the members and, as previously noted, the Building Societies Commission might have refused confirmation if the vote had not been so overwhelmingly in favour of conversion. However, in the case of the Abbey National, there is evidence to suggest that the conversion process was designed and driven by the management to such an extent that members were unable to make an objective judgment. In other words, the retention of mutuality as something that was still beneficial for members was a view that was either ignored or – some claimed – suppressed.

The benefits for members of the demutualised building society were formally expressed thus:

> every qualifying saver, every qualifying borrower and every qualifying employee who makes a valid application for shares will be subject to the terms and conditions set out in Part XIV, will receive at least 100 shares, whatever the demand for shares.[194]

And, second:

> every qualifying member and qualifying employee will receive 100 free shares and any member who is eligible as both a saver and borrower will receive 200 shares.[195]

However, a number of Abbey National members, in their campaign to stop the demutualisation of the Abbey, argued that these benefits had been distorted and the management was engaged in an attempt to misrepresent the consequences of conversion. Organised as the Abbey National Members Against Flotations (AMAF), a number of pro-mutuality members claimed that the Abbey's directors had undermined their members' volition and control over the procedure for demutualisation by giving one-sided information on its effects and benefits and by suppressing alternative interpretations. They argued that the management had failed to heed the words of the Building

193 Barchard, D, 'Abbey National flotation survives tide of criticism: a regulator's report into the building society's conversion procedures', 7 June 1989, *Financial Times*.
194 Part 1 Key Information, registered at Companies House 14/7/89.
195 Ibid.

Societies Commission when it warned the society that it had the power to cancel conversion procedures if it found partiality in the ballot. In the words of Michael Bridgeman, '[i]t is important that the board explains to the membership the potential consequences of conversion, favourable or unfavourable, as objectively as possible . . . it is not a marketing exercise'.[196]

AMAF argued that the directors were unable to be sufficiently objective as they were all in favour of conversion. To counter this bias AMAF suggested that they (AMAF) should bring the case to members. In pursuance of this AMAF sought to requisition a Special General Meeting. They obtained the signatures of 110 qualified members and provided the cheque for £5,000 necessary to accord with Rule 32(3) of the society's rules. The requisition stated that the purpose of the meeting was to discuss certain resolutions relating to the impartiality of the board and information on demutualisation. In addition to this the requisition stated:

> . . . that this meeting *instructs* the Directors to provide facilities to AMAF to enable it to inform all members of the society of the reasons why the Society should remain a mutual building society existing for the benefit of its members.[197]

The requisition was rejected by the Abbey's management on the technical point that a resolution to 'instruct the director' would be contrary to the Rules of the society, which 'confer on the board the power to direct and manage the business of the Society and the right to exercise all powers of the Society which are not, by statute or by the Society's Rules, required to be exercised in general meeting'.[198]

In short, members could not instruct directors under the rules of the society. In acting within the letter of the rules, the management opened themselves up to the criticism that they were evading the spirit of a mutual society.

This approach continued in the directors' subsequent actions. RW Perks, member of AMAF, reported that following the failure to convene a Special General Meeting, AMAF nominated seven candidates for election on the board in order that they might present the views against demutualisation at the Annual General Meeting.[199] This might have been effective action, for, as the *Financial Times* noted, 'putting up candidates will mean that AMAF can circulate its views to all Abbey's members in the election statement,

---

196 Speech at BSA conference 1988, quoted in Perks, RW, *The fight to stay mutual*, 1991, University of Aberdeen Departments of Accountancy and Economics.
197 Ibid.
198 Ibid.
199 Ibid.

something it has been unable to do so far'.[200] However, Perks argued that in direct response to the nominations, the directors took the unusual step of postponing the AGM to the latest legally permissible date, 26 April 1989. At the same time they set the date for the SGM, the meeting in which flotation was to voted upon, for 11 April, two weeks before the AGM. In addition to the timing of the meeting, the AGM notices that contained the pro-mutual views of the AMAF candidates were not sent out until the latest legally permissible date, in this case 1 April. In contrast, the floatation vote papers were sent out from the middle of March 1989, with instructions to vote 'immediately'.[201] It is therefore likely, as Perks suggests, that 'most of those intending to vote would have done so before receiving the AGM papers'.[202]

Although the AMAF failed to halt the vote on demutualisation in the case of the Abbey National, their actions highlighted the problems of protecting mutuality generally. They showed that a partial management could, within its given powers, control discussions and access to information on a proposed conversion. Second, they showed that the body empowered to oversee conversions, the Building Societies Commission, effectively disempowered itself by a tautology. The 1986 Act conferred on the Commission the power to refuse to confirm a transfer if a society failed to properly inform its membership.

Schedule 17 of the 1986 Act imposed 'an obligation to issue statements (or summaries) to its members in relation to the proposed transfer'.[203] And, under s 98(3), outlined above the Commission could refuse to confirm a transfer.

On considering these criteria in respect of the Abbey's flotation application, the Commission reported among other criticisms that the Abbey had failed to keep its members properly informed. The Commission argued that 'Members could reasonably have expected to find a fair and balanced assessment of the consequences of the proposal . . . It did not measure up to that standard'.[204] The same article described the Commission's report on the Abbey conversion as 'stinging' in its criticism of the bias and dissembling of Abbey's board.

However, the Commission did not conclude that the misleading nature of the information given to members was instrumental in their voting choice.

---

200 Barchard, D, 'Finance and the family: a change of habits at the Abbey' 17 December 1988, *Financial Times*.
201 Op. cit. Perks, p 415.
202 Ibid.
203 Section 98: Transfers of business: supplementary provisions, (1).
204 'Abbey National survives tide of criticism: a regulator's report into the building society's conversion procedures', 7 June 1989, *Financial Times*.

Paradoxically, the Commission allowed the conversion to go ahead because of the enormity of the vote, although the vote was, according to the Commission itself, based on misleading information. As the *Financial Times* commented, this decision seemed even more contrary given that the Commissioner himself had 'warned specifically that he would not grant permission for conversion if it emerged that members had not been fully informed of the disadvantages as well as the advantages'.[205]

This decision came as no surprise to financial commentators. Two months prior to the confirmation the *Financial Times* commented that 'it would be a revolutionary move, however, for the Commission to overrule the results of such a large ballot, and most city analysts believe that is unlikely'.[206]

The particular reasons for the Abbey's conversion may have included self-interest. At least one prominent member of AMAF thought that the personal prospects of the directors played a part:

> The motivations of the professional managers may have included their own remuneration. The total remuneration of Abbey National directors increased from £0.4 m in 1986 to £0.7 m in 1988, prior to flotation; post flotation it increased to £1.2 m, and employee share schemes were introduced.[207]

However, what was clear by the end of 1989 was that a motivated board of directors could persuade a sufficient number of members to vote in favour of demutualisation. And as subsequent cases were to show, a motivated board was easily a match for a Commission with a limited stomach for court action and a judiciary committed to commercialism. The factors were in place for a building society that wished to demutualise to do so, and with greater ease than had been apparently been envisaged when the 1986 Act was drafted.

While the amalgamation of the Cheltenham and Gloucester Building Society with Lloyds plc in 1995 led to a court decision which limited the payment of cash to two-year members only, new members could still be offered free shares as a 'reward' for conversion.[208] Furthermore, the court held that the benefits that the directors might acquire from the transfer agreement did not preclude them from voting on the resolution, provided that the members were properly acquainted with their personal interest benefits before voting.

This decision clarified the law in this respect: in the words of David O'Brien, Chief Executive of National Provincial, 'it leaves us exactly where

---

205 Ibid.
206 Barchard, D, 'Building societies may follow Abbey's lead: the implications of Tuesday's vote for stock market flotation, 13 April 1989, *Financial Times*.
207 Op. cit., Perks, p 425.
208 *Cheltenham and Gloucester Building Society v Building Societies Commission* [1994] Ch 65.

we were before, but it gives us a little more confidence that we do not have to fight in a legal environment with an obvious flaw'.[209] However, the court's bar on cash payments to members of less than two years effectively precluded 27 per cent of existing investors. So, as the above article concluded:

> societies with similar proportions of new members – such as Britannia and Woolwich – will also find take-over difficult. This appears to lessen considerably the worst fear raised by the Lloyds/C&G deal: that it would expose other societies to a form of blackmail. Although boards of societies have no legal obligation to put offers to their members, they would be vulnerable to public debate of an offer.[210]

There followed a reasonably long period between the conversion of the Abbey National in 1989 and the subsequent conversion of the larger societies, the Halifax, the Leeds, the Alliance and Leicester, the Woolwich, and the Northern Rock in 1997. The process of demutualisation was further encouraged by the merger activities of pro-conversion societies who had spent the years following the passage of the 1986 Act taking over the business of smaller societies, and thus removed an even larger proportion of societies from the mutual sector when they eventually converted. This was an ironic outcome, since mergers were suggested as a means to protect against corporate competition by following the 'safety in numbers' principle. Over the same period, the Building Societies Association displayed a remarkable apathy to the protection of mutuality, given the determination of the pro-convertors. However, eventually galvanised by the massive conversion activity in 1997, the remaining mutual members of the BSA (or rather their representatives in the form of chief executive and chairman delegates) resolved to be more proactive in promoting the benefits of mutuality.

CONCLUSION

Mutuality originated as an organic expression of members' equality and control but became something that was controlled and defined by the elite: the Building Societies Association, the government and the judiciary. Mutuality was not a quality that a member would recognise or consider a benefit – it appeared only as a legal term expressing a remnant of the past. By the 1980s, mutuality had already come under heavy criticism. For the political right it represented 'bucking the market', while for the left it represented 'elitist control'. The failure of mutuality to appeal to the entire political spectrum

---

209 Gappre, J, 'Building societies shake off fear of "blackmail" ', 10 June 1994, *Financial Times*.
210 Ibid.

or to the members of building societies led first to the legislative facility to shed mutual status and second to the desire of members to make use of that facility. However, later developments have shown that a new awareness of mutuality by members and a robust pro-mutuality position by management can thwart attempts to convert, as the Nationwide Building Society found on many occasions. Thus an ideological commitment to a business form can ensure its continuance.

Companies and formation

Sections 1–111

COMPANIES ACT 2006

2006 Chapter 46

An Act to reform company law and restate the greater part of the enactments relating to companies; to make other provision relating to companies and other forms of business organisation; to make provision about directors' disqualification, business names, auditors and actuaries; to amend Part 9 of the Enterprise Act 2002; and for connected purposes.   [8th November 2006]

Be it enacted by the Queen's most Excellent Majesty, by and with the advice and consent of the Lords Spiritual and Temporal, and Commons, in this present Parliament assembled, and by the authority of the same, as follows: –

PART 1

GENERAL INTRODUCTORY PROVISIONS

Companies and Companies Acts

1   Companies
  (1) In the Companies Acts, unless the context otherwise requires –
      "company" means a company formed and registered under this Act, that is –
        (a) a company so formed and registered after the commencement of this Part, or
        (b) a company that immediately before the commencement of this Part –
            (i) was formed and registered under the Companies Act 1985 (c. 6) or the Companies (Northern Ireland) Order 1986 (S.I. 1986/1032 (N.I. 6)), or
            (ii) was an existing company for the purposes of that Act or that Order,

(which is to be treated on commencement as if formed and registered under this Act).

(2) Certain provisions of the Companies Acts apply to –

    (a) companies registered, but not formed, under this Act (see Chapter 1 of Part 33), and

    (b) bodies incorporated in the United Kingdom but not registered under this Act (see Chapter 2 of that Part).

(3) For provisions applying to companies incorporated outside the United Kingdom, see Part 34 (overseas companies).

2 The Companies Acts

(1) In this Act "the Companies Acts" means –

    (a) the company law provisions of this Act,

    (b) Part 2 of the Companies (Audit, Investigations and Community Enterprise) Act 2004 (c. 27) (community interest companies), and

    (c) the provisions of the Companies Act 1985 (c. 6) and the Companies Consolidation (Consequential Provisions) Act 1985 (c. 9) that remain in force.

(2) The company law provisions of this Act are –

    (a) the provisions of Parts 1 to 39 of this Act, and

    (b) the provisions of Parts 45 to 47 of this Act so far as they apply for the purposes of those Parts.

Types of company

3 Limited and unlimited companies

(1) A company is a "limited company" if the liability of its members is limited by its constitution.

It may be limited by shares or limited by guarantee.

(2) If their liability is limited to the amount, if any, unpaid on the shares held by them, the company is "limited by shares".

(3) If their liability is limited to such amount as the members undertake to contribute to the assets of the company in the event of its being wound up, the company is "limited by guarantee".

(4) If there is no limit on the liability of its members, the company is an "unlimited company".

4 Private and public companies

(1) A "private company" is any company that is not a public company.

(2) A "public company" is a company limited by shares or limited by guarantee and having a share capital –

    (a) whose certificate of incorporation states that it is a public company, and

    (b) in relation to which the requirements of this Act, or the former Companies Acts, as to registration or re-registration as a public company have been complied with on or after the relevant date.

(3) For the purposes of subsection (2)(b) the relevant date is –

    (a)   in relation to registration or re-registration in Great Britain,
          22nd December 1980;
    (b)   in relation to registration or re-registration in Northern Ireland,
          1st July 1983.
(4) For the two major differences between private and public companies, see
     Part 20.

5   Companies limited by guarantee and having share capital

(1) A company cannot be formed as, or become, a company limited by guarantee
     with a share capital.
(2) Provision to this effect has been in force –
    (a)   in Great Britain since 22nd December 1980, and
    (b)   in Northern Ireland since 1st July 1983.
(3) Any provision in the constitution of a company limited by guarantee that
     purports to divide the company's undertaking into shares or interests is a
     provision for a share capital.
     This applies whether or not the nominal value or number of the shares or
     interests is specified by the provision.

6   Community interest companies

(1) In accordance with Part 2 of the Companies (Audit, Investigations and
     Community Enterprise) Act 2004 (c. 27) –
    (a)   a company limited by shares or a company limited by guarantee and
          not having a share capital may be formed as or become a community
          interest company, and
    (b)   a company limited by guarantee and having a share capital may
          become a community interest company.
(2) The other provisions of the Companies Acts have effect subject to that Part.

PART 2

COMPANY FORMATION

General

7   Method of forming company

(1) A company is formed under this Act by one or more persons –
    (a)   subscribing their names to a memorandum of association (see section
          8), and
    (b)   complying with the requirements of this Act as to registration (see
          sections 9 to 13).
(2) A company may not be so formed for an unlawful purpose.

8   Memorandum of association

(1) A memorandum of association is a memorandum stating that the sub-
     scribers –

  (a)   wish to form a company under this Act, and
  (b)   agree to become members of the company and, in the case of a
        company that is to have a share capital, to take at least one share
        each.
  (2)   The memorandum must be in the prescribed form and must be authenticated
        by each subscriber.

Requirements for registration

9   Registration documents

  (1)   The memorandum of association must be delivered to the registrar together
        with an application for registration of the company, the documents required
        by this section and a statement of compliance.
  (2)   The application for registration must state –
        (a)   the company's proposed name,
        (b)   whether the company's registered office is to be situated in England
              and Wales (or in Wales), in Scotland or in Northern Ireland,
        (c)   whether the liability of the members of the company is to be limited,
              and if so whether it is to be limited by shares or by guarantee, and
        (d)   whether the company is to be a private or a public company.
  (3)   If the application is delivered by a person as agent for the subscribers to the
        memorandum of association, it must state his name and address.
  (4)   The application must contain –
        (a)   in the case of a company that is to have a share capital, a statement of
              capital and initial shareholdings (see section 10);
        (b)   in the case of a company that is to be limited by guarantee, a statement
              of guarantee (see section 11);
        (c)   a statement of the company's proposed officers (see section 12).
  (5)   The application must also contain –
        (a)   a statement of the intended address of the company's registered office;
              and
        (b)   a copy of any proposed articles of association (to the extent that these
              are not supplied by the default application of model articles: see
              section 20).
  (6)   The application must be delivered –
        (a)   to the registrar of companies for England and Wales, if the registered
              office of the company is to be situated in England and Wales (or in
              Wales);
        (b)   to the registrar of companies for Scotland, if the registered office of
              the company is to be situated in Scotland;
        (c)   to the registrar of companies for Northern Ireland, if the registered
              office of the company is to be situated in Northern Ireland.

10   Statement of capital and initial shareholdings

  (1)   The statement of capital and initial shareholdings required to be delivered in
        the case of a company that is to have a share capital must comply with this
        section.

  (2)   It must state –
- (a) the total number of shares of the company to be taken on formation by the subscribers to the memorandum of association,
- (b) the aggregate nominal value of those shares,
- (c) for each class of shares –
  - (i) prescribed particulars of the rights attached to the shares,
  - (ii) the total number of shares of that class, and
  - (iii) the aggregate nominal value of shares of that class, and
- (d) the amount to be paid up and the amount (if any) to be unpaid on each share (whether on account of the nominal value of the share or by way of premium).

  (3)   It must contain such information as may be prescribed for the purpose of identifying the subscribers to the memorandum of association.

  (4)   It must state, with respect to each subscriber to the memorandum –
- (a) the number, nominal value (of each share) and class of shares to be taken by him on formation, and
- (b) the amount to be paid up and the amount (if any) to be unpaid on each share (whether on account of the nominal value of the share or by way of premium).

  (5)   Where a subscriber to the memorandum is to take shares of more than one class, the information required under subsection (4)(a) is required for each class.

11   Statement of guarantee

  (1)   The statement of guarantee required to be delivered in the case of a company that is to be limited by guarantee must comply with this section.

  (2)   It must contain such information as may be prescribed for the purpose of identifying the subscribers to the memorandum of association.

  (3)   It must state that each member undertakes that, if the company is wound up while he is a member, or within one year after he ceases to be a member, he will contribute to the assets of the company such amount as may be required for –
- (a) payment of the debts and liabilities of the company contracted before he ceases to be a member,
- (b) payment of the costs, charges and expenses of winding up, and
- (c) adjustment of the rights of the contributories among themselves,

not exceeding a specified amount.

12   Statement of proposed officers

  (1)   The statement of the company's proposed officers required to be delivered to the registrar must contain the required particulars of –
- (a) the person who is, or persons who are, to be the first director or directors of the company;
- (b) in the case of a company that is to be a private company, any person who is (or any persons who are) to be the first secretary (or joint secretaries) of the company;
- (c) in the case of a company that is to be a public company, the person who is (or the persons who are) to be the first secretary (or joint secretaries) of the company.

(2)   The required particulars are the particulars that will be required to be stated –

    (a)   in the case of a director, in the company's register of directors and register of directors' residential addresses (see sections 162 to 166);

    (b)   in the case of a secretary, in the company's register of secretaries (see sections 277 to 279).

(3)   The statement must also contain a consent by each of the persons named as a director, as secretary or as one of joint secretaries, to act in the relevant capacity.

If all the partners in a firm are to be joint secretaries, consent may be given by one partner on behalf of all of them.

13   Statement of compliance

(1)   The statement of compliance required to be delivered to the registrar is a statement that the requirements of this Act as to registration have been complied with.

(2)   The registrar may accept the statement of compliance as sufficient evidence of compliance.

Registration and its effect

14   Registration

If the registrar is satisfied that the requirements of this Act as to registration are complied with, he shall register the documents delivered to him.

15   Issue of certificate of incorporation

(1)   On the registration of a company, the registrar of companies shall give a certificate that the company is incorporated.

(2)   The certificate must state –

    (a)   the name and registered number of the company,

    (b)   the date of its incorporation,

    (c)   whether it is a limited or unlimited company, and if it is limited whether it is limited by shares or limited by guarantee,

    (d)   whether it is a private or a public company, and

    (e)   whether the company's registered office is situated in England and Wales (or in Wales), in Scotland or in Northern Ireland.

(3)   The certificate must be signed by the registrar or authenticated by the registrar's official seal.

(4)   The certificate is conclusive evidence that the requirements of this Act as to registration have been complied with and that the company is duly registered under this Act.

16   Effect of registration

(1)   The registration of a company has the following effects as from the date of incorporation.

(2)   The subscribers to the memorandum, together with such other persons as may from time to time become members of the company, are a body corporate by the name stated in the certificate of incorporation.

(3)   That body corporate is capable of exercising all the functions of an incorporated company.

(4)   The status and registered office of the company are as stated in, or in connection with, the application for registration.

(5)   In the case of a company having a share capital, the subscribers to the memorandum become holders of the shares specified in the statement of capital and initial shareholdings.

(6)   The persons named in the statement of proposed officers –
    (a)   as director, or
    (b)   as secretary or joint secretary of the company,
are deemed to have been appointed to that office.

PART 3

A COMPANY'S CONSTITUTION

CHAPTER 1

INTRODUCTORY

17   A company's constitution

Unless the context otherwise requires, references in the Companies Acts to a company's constitution include –
    (a)   the company's articles, and
    (b)   any resolutions and agreements to which Chapter 3 applies (see section 29).

CHAPTER 2

ARTICLES OF ASSOCIATION

General

18   Articles of association

(1)   A company must have articles of association prescribing regulations for the company.

(2)   Unless it is a company to which model articles apply by virtue of section 20 (default application of model articles in case of limited company), it must register articles of association.

(3)   Articles of association registered by a company must –
    (a)   be contained in a single document, and
    (b)   be divided into paragraphs numbered consecutively.

(4)   References in the Companies Acts to a company's "articles" are to its articles of association.

19   Power of Secretary of State to prescribe model articles
(1)   The Secretary of State may by regulations prescribe model articles of association for companies.
(2)   Different model articles may be prescribed for different descriptions of company.
(3)   A company may adopt all or any of the provisions of model articles.
(4)   Any amendment of model articles by regulations under this section does not affect a company registered before the amendment takes effect.
"Amendment" here includes addition, alteration or repeal.
(5)   Regulations under this section are subject to negative resolution procedure.

20   Default application of model articles
(1)   On the formation of a limited company –
    (a)   if articles are not registered, or
    (b)   if articles are registered, in so far as they do not exclude or modify the relevant model articles,
the relevant model articles (so far as applicable) form part of the company's articles in the same manner and to the same extent as if articles in the form of those articles had been duly registered.
(2)   The "relevant model articles" means the model articles prescribed for a company of that description as in force at the date on which the company is registered.

Alteration of articles

21   Amendment of articles
(1)   A company may amend its articles by special resolution.
(2)   In the case of a company that is a charity, this is subject to –
    (a)   in England and Wales, section 64 of the Charities Act 1993 (c. 10);
    (b)   in Northern Ireland, Article 9 of the Charities (Northern Ireland) Order 1987 (S.I. 1987/2048 (N.I. 19)).
(3)   In the case of a company that is registered in the Scottish Charity Register, this is subject to –
    (a)   section 112 of the Companies Act 1989 (c. 40), and
    (b)   section 16 of the Charities and Trustee Investment (Scotland) Act 2005 (asp 10).

22   Entrenched provisions of the articles
(1)   A company's articles may contain provision ("provision for entrenchment") to the effect that specified provisions of the articles may be amended or repealed only if conditions are met, or procedures are complied with, that are more restrictive than those applicable in the case of a special resolution.
(2)   Provision for entrenchment may only be made –
    (a)   in the company's articles on formation, or
    (b)   by an amendment of the company's articles agreed to by all the members of the company.

(3)   Provision for entrenchment does not prevent amendment of the company's articles –
- (a)   by agreement of all the members of the company, or
- (b)   by order of a court or other authority having power to alter the company's articles.

(4)   Nothing in this section affects any power of a court or other authority to alter a company's articles.

23   Notice to registrar of existence of restriction on amendment of articles

(1)   Where a company's articles –
- (a)   on formation contain provision for entrenchment,
- (b)   are amended so as to include such provision, or
- (c)   are altered by order of a court or other authority so as to restrict or exclude the power of the company to amend its articles,

the company must give notice of that fact to the registrar.

(2)   Where a company's articles –
- (a)   are amended so as to remove provision for entrenchment, or
- (b)   are altered by order of a court or other authority –
  - (i)   so as to remove such provision, or
  - (ii)   so as to remove any other restriction on, or any exclusion of, the power of the company to amend its articles,

the company must give notice of that fact to the registrar.

24   Statement of compliance where amendment of articles restricted

(1)   This section applies where a company's articles are subject –
- (a)   to provision for entrenchment, or
- (b)   to an order of a court or other authority restricting or excluding the company's power to amend the articles.

(2)   If the company –
- (a)   amends its articles, and
- (b)   is required to send to the registrar a document making or evidencing the amendment,

the company must deliver with that document a statement of compliance.

(3)   The statement of compliance required is a statement certifying that the amendment has been made in accordance with the company's articles and, where relevant, any applicable order of a court or other authority.

(4)   The registrar may rely on the statement of compliance as sufficient evidence of the matters stated in it.

25   Effect of alteration of articles on company's members

(1)   A member of a company is not bound by an alteration to its articles after the date on which he became a member, if and so far as the alteration –
- (a)   requires him to take or subscribe for more shares than the number held by him at the date on which the alteration is made, or
- (b)   in any way increases his liability as at that date to contribute to the company's share capital or otherwise to pay money to the company.

(2)   Subsection (1) does not apply in a case where the member agrees in writing, either before or after the alteration is made, to be bound by the alteration.

26   Registrar to be sent copy of amended articles
  (1)   Where a company amends its articles it must send to the registrar a copy of the articles as amended not later than 15 days after the amendment takes effect.
  (2)   This section does not require a company to set out in its articles any provisions of model articles that –
      (a)   are applied by the articles, or
      (b)   apply by virtue of section 20 (default application of model articles).
  (3)   If a company fails to comply with this section an offence is committed by –
      (a)   the company, and
      (b)   every officer of the company who is in default.
  (4)   A person guilty of an offence under this section is liable on summary conviction to a fine not exceeding level 3 on the standard scale and, for continued contravention, a daily default fine not exceeding one-tenth of level 3 on the standard scale.

27   Registrar's notice to comply in case of failure with respect to amended articles
  (1)   If it appears to the registrar that a company has failed to comply with any enactment requiring it –
      (a)   to send to the registrar a document making or evidencing an alteration in the company's articles, or
      (b)   to send to the registrar a copy of the company's articles as amended,
     the registrar may give notice to the company requiring it to comply.
  (2)   The notice must –
      (a)   state the date on which it is issued, and
      (b)   require the company to comply within 28 days from that date.
  (3)   If the company complies with the notice within the specified time, no criminal proceedings may be brought in respect of the failure to comply with the enactment mentioned in subsection (1).
  (4)   If the company does not comply with the notice within the specified time, it is liable to a civil penalty of £200.
     This is in addition to any liability to criminal proceedings in respect of the failure mentioned in subsection (1).
  (5)   The penalty may be recovered by the registrar and is to be paid into the Consolidated Fund.

Supplementary

28   Existing companies: provisions of memorandum treated as provisions of articles
  (1)   Provisions that immediately before the commencement of this Part were contained in a company's memorandum but are not provisions of the kind mentioned in section 8 (provisions of new-style memorandum) are to be treated after the commencement of this Part as provisions of the company's articles.
  (2)   This applies not only to substantive provisions but also to provision for entrenchment (as defined in section 22).
  (3)   The provisions of this Part about provision for entrenchment apply to such

provision as they apply to provision made on the company's formation, except that the duty under section 23(1)(a) to give notice to the registrar does not apply.

CHAPTER 3

RESOLUTIONS AND AGREEMENTS AFFECTING A COMPANY'S CONSTITUTION

29   Resolutions and agreements affecting a company's constitution
   (1)   This Chapter applies to –
      (a)   any special resolution;
      (b)   any resolution or agreement agreed to by all the members of a company that, if not so agreed to, would not have been effective for its purpose unless passed as a special resolution;
      (c)   any resolution or agreement agreed to by all the members of a class of shareholders that, if not so agreed to, would not have been effective for its purpose unless passed by some particular majority or otherwise in some particular manner;
      (d)   any resolution or agreement that effectively binds all members of a class of shareholders though not agreed to by all those members;
      (e)   any other resolution or agreement to which this Chapter applies by virtue of any enactment.
   (2)   References in subsection (1) to a member of a company, or of a class of members of a company, do not include the company itself where it is such a member by virtue only of its holding shares as treasury shares.

30   Copies of resolutions or agreements to be forwarded to registrar
   (1)   A copy of every resolution or agreement to which this Chapter applies, or (in the case of a resolution or agreement that is not in writing) a written memorandum setting out its terms, must be forwarded to the registrar within 15 days after it is passed or made.
   (2)   If a company fails to comply with this section, an offence is committed by –
      (a)   the company, and
      (b)   every officer of it who is in default.
   (3)   A person guilty of an offence under this section is liable on summary conviction to a fine not exceeding level 3 on the standard scale and, for continued contravention, a daily default fine not exceeding one-tenth of level 3 on the standard scale.
   (4)   For the purposes of this section, a liquidator of the company is treated as an officer of it.

CHAPTER 4

MISCELLANEOUS AND SUPPLEMENTARY PROVISIONS

Statement of company's objects

31 Statement of company's objects

(1) Unless a company's articles specifically restrict the objects of the company, its objects are unrestricted.

(2) Where a company amends its articles so as to add, remove or alter a statement of the company's objects –

   (a) it must give notice to the registrar,

   (b) on receipt of the notice, the registrar shall register it, and

   (c) the amendment is not effective until entry of that notice on the register.

(3) Any such amendment does not affect any rights or obligations of the company or render defective any legal proceedings by or against it.

(4) In the case of a company that is a charity, the provisions of this section have effect subject to –

   (a) in England and Wales, section 64 of the Charities Act 1993 (c. 10);

   (b) in Northern Ireland, Article 9 of the Charities (Northern Ireland) Order 1987 (S.I. 1987/2048 (N.I. 19)).

(5) In the case of a company that is entered in the Scottish Charity Register, the provisions of this section have effect subject to the provisions of the Charities and Trustee Investment (Scotland) Act 2005 (asp 10).

Other provisions with respect to a company's constitution

32 Constitutional documents to be provided to members

(1) A company must, on request by any member, send to him the following documents –

   (a) an up-to-date copy of the company's articles;

   (b) a copy of any resolution or agreement relating to the company to which Chapter 3 applies (resolutions and agreements affecting a company's constitution) and that is for the time being in force;

   (c) a copy of any document required to be sent to the registrar under –

      (i) section 34(2) (notice where company's constitution altered by enactment), or

      (ii) section 35(2)(a) (notice where order of court or other authority alters company's constitution);

   (d) a copy of any court order under section 899 (order sanctioning compromise or arrangement) or section 900 (order facilitating reconstruction or amalgamation);

   (e) a copy of any court order under section 996 (protection of members against unfair prejudice: powers of the court) that alters the company's constitution;

  (f) a copy of the company's current certificate of incorporation, and of any past certificates of incorporation;

  (g) in the case of a company with a share capital, a current statement of capital;

  (h) in the case of a company limited by guarantee, a copy of the statement of guarantee.

(2) The statement of capital required by subsection (1)(g) is a statement of –

  (a) the total number of shares of the company,

  (b) the aggregate nominal value of those shares,

  (c) for each class of shares –

    (i) prescribed particulars of the rights attached to the shares,

    (ii) the total number of shares of that class, and

    (iii) the aggregate nominal value of shares of that class, and

  (d) the amount paid up and the amount (if any) unpaid on each share (whether on account of the nominal value of the share or by way of premium).

(3) If a company makes default in complying with this section, an offence is committed by every officer of the company who is in default.

(4) A person guilty of an offence under this section is liable on summary conviction to a fine not exceeding level 3 on the standard scale.

33 Effect of company's constitution

(1) The provisions of a company's constitution bind the company and its members to the same extent as if there were covenants on the part of the company and of each member to observe those provisions.

(2) Money payable by a member to the company under its constitution is a debt due from him to the company.

In England and Wales and Northern Ireland it is of the nature of an ordinary contract debt.

34 Notice to registrar where company's constitution altered by enactment

(1) This section applies where a company's constitution is altered by an enactment, other than an enactment amending the general law.

(2) The company must give notice of the alteration to the registrar, specifying the enactment, not later than 15 days after the enactment comes into force.

In the case of a special enactment the notice must be accompanied by a copy of the enactment.

(3) If the enactment amends –

  (a) the company's articles, or

  (b) a resolution or agreement to which Chapter 3 applies (resolutions and agreements affecting a company's constitution),

the notice must be accompanied by a copy of the company's articles, or the resolution or agreement in question, as amended.

(4) A "special enactment" means an enactment that is not a public general enactment, and includes –

  (a) an Act for confirming a provisional order,

  (b) any provision of a public general Act in relation to the passing of which any of the standing orders of the House of Lords or the House of Commons relating to Private Business applied, or

(c)   any enactment to the extent that it is incorporated in or applied for the purposes of a special enactment.

(5)   If a company fails to comply with this section an offence is committed by –
(a)   the company, and
(b)   every officer of the company who is in default.

(6)   A person guilty of an offence under this section is liable on summary conviction to a fine not exceeding level 3 on the standard scale and, for continued contravention, a daily default fine not exceeding one-tenth of level 3 on the standard scale.

35   Notice to registrar where company's constitution altered by order

(1)   Where a company's constitution is altered by an order of a court or other authority, the company must give notice to the registrar of the alteration not later than 15 days after the alteration takes effect.

(2)   The notice must be accompanied by –
(a)   a copy of the order, and
(b)   if the order amends –
(i)   the company's articles, or
(ii)   a resolution or agreement to which Chapter 3 applies (resolutions and agreements affecting the company's constitution),
a copy of the company's articles, or the resolution or agreement in question, as amended.

(3)   If a company fails to comply with this section an offence is committed by –
(a)   the company, and
(b)   every officer of the company who is in default.

(4)   A person guilty of an offence under this section is liable on summary conviction to a fine not exceeding level 3 on the standard scale and, for continued contravention, a daily default fine not exceeding one-tenth of level 3 on the standard scale.

(5)   This section does not apply where provision is made by another enactment for the delivery to the registrar of a copy of the order in question.

36   Documents to be incorporated in or accompany copies of articles issued by company

(1)   Every copy of a company's articles issued by the company must be accompanied by –
(a)   a copy of any resolution or agreement relating to the company to which Chapter 3 applies (resolutions and agreements affecting a company's constitution),
(b)   where the company has been required to give notice to the registrar under section 34(2) (notice where company's constitution altered by enactment), a statement that the enactment in question alters the effect of the company's constitution,
(c)   where the company's constitution is altered by a special enactment (see section 34(4)), a copy of the enactment, and
(d)   a copy of any order required to be sent to the registrar under section

35(2)(a) (order of court or other authority altering company's constitution).

(2) This does not require the articles to be accompanied by a copy of a document or by a statement if –
   (a) the effect of the resolution, agreement, enactment or order (as the case may be) on the company's constitution has been incorporated into the articles by amendment, or
   (b) the resolution, agreement, enactment or order (as the case may be) is not for the time being in force.
(3) If the company fails to comply with this section, an offence is committed by every officer of the company who is in default.
(4) A person guilty of an offence under this section is liable on summary conviction to a fine not exceeding level 3 on the standard scale for each occasion on which copies are issued, or, as the case may be, requested.
(5) For the purposes of this section, a liquidator of the company is treated as an officer of it.

Supplementary provisions

37   Right to participate in profits otherwise than as member void
In the case of a company limited by guarantee and not having a share capital any provision in the company's articles, or in any resolution of the company, purporting to give a person a right to participate in the divisible profits of the company otherwise than as a member is void.

38   Application to single member companies of enactments and rules of law
Any enactment or rule of law applicable to companies formed by two or more persons or having two or more members applies with any necessary modification in relation to a company formed by one person or having only one person as a member.

PART 4

A COMPANY'S CAPACITY AND RELATED MATTERS

Capacity of company and power of directors to bind it

39   A company's capacity
(1) The validity of an act done by a company shall not be called into question on the ground of lack of capacity by reason of anything in the company's constitution.
(2) This section has effect subject to section 42 (companies that are charities).

40   Power of directors to bind the company
(1) In favour of a person dealing with a company in good faith, the power of the

directors to bind the company, or authorise others to do so, is deemed to be free of any limitation under the company's constitution.

(2)   For this purpose –

    (a)   a person "deals with" a company if he is a party to any transaction or other act to which the company is a party,

    (b)   a person dealing with a company –

        (i)   is not bound to enquire as to any limitation on the powers of the directors to bind the company or authorise others to do so,

        (ii)   is presumed to have acted in good faith unless the contrary is proved, and

        (iii)   is not to be regarded as acting in bad faith by reason only of his knowing that an act is beyond the powers of the directors under the company's constitution.

(3)   The references above to limitations on the directors' powers under the company's constitution include limitations deriving –

    (a)   from a resolution of the company or of any class of shareholders, or

    (b)   from any agreement between the members of the company or of any class of shareholders.

(4)   This section does not affect any right of a member of the company to bring proceedings to restrain the doing of an action that is beyond the powers of the directors.

But no such proceedings lie in respect of an act to be done in fulfilment of a legal obligation arising from a previous act of the company.

(5)   This section does not affect any liability incurred by the directors, or any other person, by reason of the directors' exceeding their powers.

(6)   This section has effect subject to –

section 41 (transactions with directors or their associates), and

section 42 (companies that are charities).

41   Constitutional limitations: transactions involving directors or their associates

(1)   This section applies to a transaction if or to the extent that its validity depends on section 40 (power of directors deemed to be free of limitations under company's constitution in favour of person dealing with company in good faith).

Nothing in this section shall be read as excluding the operation of any other enactment or rule of law by virtue of which the transaction may be called in question or any liability to the company may arise.

(2)   Where –

    (a)   a company enters into such a transaction, and

    (b)   the parties to the transaction include –

        (i)   a director of the company or of its holding company, or

        (ii)   a person connected with any such director,

the transaction is voidable at the instance of the company.

(3)   Whether or not it is avoided, any such party to the transaction as is mentioned in subsection (2)(b)(i) or (ii), and any director of the company who authorised the transaction, is liable –

    (a)   to account to the company for any gain he has made directly or indirectly by the transaction, and

      (b)   to indemnify the company for any loss or damage resulting from the transaction.

(4)   The transaction ceases to be voidable if –

      (a)   restitution of any money or other asset which was the subject matter of the transaction is no longer possible, or

      (b)   the company is indemnified for any loss or damage resulting from the transaction, or

      (c)   rights acquired bona fide for value and without actual notice of the directors' exceeding their powers by a person who is not party to the transaction would be affected by the avoidance, or

      (d)   the transaction is affirmed by the company.

(5)   A person other than a director of the company is not liable under subsection (3) if he shows that at the time the transaction was entered into he did not know that the directors were exceeding their powers.

(6)   Nothing in the preceding provisions of this section affects the rights of any party to the transaction not within subsection (2)(b)(i) or (ii). But the court may, on the application of the company or any such party, make an order affirming, severing or setting aside the transaction on such terms as appear to the court to be just.

(7)   In this section –

      (a)   "transaction" includes any act; and

      (b)   the reference to a person connected with a director has the same meaning as in Part 10 (company directors).

42 Constitutional limitations: companies that are charities

(1)   Sections 39 and 40 (company's capacity and power of directors to bind company) do not apply to the acts of a company that is a charity except in favour of a person who –

      (a)   does not know at the time the act is done that the company is a charity, or

      (b)   gives full consideration in money or money's worth in relation to the act in question and does not know (as the case may be) –

            (i)   that the act is not permitted by the company's constitution, or

            (ii)   that the act is beyond the powers of the directors.

(2)   Where a company that is a charity purports to transfer or grant an interest in property, the fact that (as the case may be) –

      (a)   the act was not permitted by the company's constitution, or

      (b)   the directors in connection with the act exceeded any limitation on their powers under the company's constitution,

does not affect the title of a person who subsequently acquires the property or any interest in it for full consideration without actual notice of any such circumstances affecting the validity of the company's act.

(3)   In any proceedings arising out of subsection (1) or (2) the burden of proving –

      (a)   that a person knew that the company was a charity, or

      (b)   that a person knew that an act was not permitted by the company's constitution or was beyond the powers of the directors,

lies on the person asserting that fact.

(4)   In the case of a company that is a charity the affirmation of a transaction to

which section 41 applies (transactions with directors or their associates) is
ineffective without the prior written consent of –

    (a)   in England and Wales, the Charity Commission;

    (b)   in Northern Ireland, the Department for Social Development.

(5)   This section does not extend to Scotland (but see section 112 of the
Companies Act 1989 (c. 40)).

Formalities of doing business under the law of England and Wales or Northern Ireland

43   Company contracts

(1)   Under the law of England and Wales or Northern Ireland a contract may be
made –

    (a)   by a company, by writing under its common seal, or

    (b)   on behalf of a company, by a person acting under its authority,
express or implied.

(2)   Any formalities required by law in the case of a contract made by an individual also apply, unless a contrary intention appears, to a contract made by
or on behalf of a company.

44   Execution of documents

(1)   Under the law of England and Wales or Northern Ireland a document is
executed by a company –

    (a)   by the affixing of its common seal, or

    (b)   by signature in accordance with the following provisions.

(2)   A document is validly executed by a company if it is signed on behalf of the
company –

    (a)   by two authorised signatories, or

    (b)   by a director of the company in the presence of a witness who attests
the signature.

(3)   The following are "authorised signatories" for the purposes of subsection
(2) –

    (a)   every director of the company, and

    (b)   in the case of a private company with a secretary or a public company,
the secretary (or any joint secretary) of the company.

(4)   A document signed in accordance with subsection (2) and expressed, in whatever words, to be executed by the company has the same effect as if executed
under the common seal of the company.

(5)   In favour of a purchaser a document is deemed to have been duly executed by
a company if it purports to be signed in accordance with subsection (2). A
"purchaser" means a purchaser in good faith for valuable consideration and
includes a lessee, mortgagee or other person who for valuable consideration
acquires an interest in property.

(6)   Where a document is to be signed by a person on behalf of more than one
company, it is not duly signed by that person for the purposes of this section
unless he signs it separately in each capacity.

(7)   References in this section to a document being (or purporting to be) signed by
a director or secretary are to be read, in a case where that office is held by a

firm, as references to its being (or purporting to be) signed by an individual authorised by the firm to sign on its behalf.

(8)   This section applies to a document that is (or purports to be) executed by a company in the name of or on behalf of another person whether or not that person is also a company.

45   Common seal

(1)   A company may have a common seal, but need not have one.

(2)   A company which has a common seal shall have its name engraved in legible characters on the seal.

(3)   If a company fails to comply with subsection (2) an offence is committed by –
      (a)   the company, and
      (b)   every officer of the company who is in default.

(4)   An officer of a company, or a person acting on behalf of a company, commits an offence if he uses, or authorises the use of, a seal purporting to be a seal of the company on which its name is not engraved as required by subsection (2).

(5)   A person guilty of an offence under this section is liable on summary conviction to a fine not exceeding level 3 on the standard scale.

(6)   This section does not form part of the law of Scotland.

46   Execution of deeds

(1)   A document is validly executed by a company as a deed for the purposes of section 1(2)(b) of the Law of Property (Miscellaneous Provisions) Act 1989 (c. 34) and for the purposes of the law of Northern Ireland if, and only if –
      (a)   it is duly executed by the company, and
      (b)   it is delivered as a deed.

(2)   For the purposes of subsection (1)(b) a document is presumed to be delivered upon its being executed, unless a contrary intention is proved.

47   Execution of deeds or other documents by attorney

(1)   Under the law of England and Wales or Northern Ireland a company may, by instrument executed as a deed, empower a person, either generally or in respect of specified matters, as its attorney to execute deeds or other documents on its behalf.

(2)   A deed or other document so executed, whether in the United Kingdom or elsewhere, has effect as if executed by the company.

Formalities of doing business under the law of Scotland

48   Execution of documents by companies

(1)   The following provisions form part of the law of Scotland only.

(2)   Notwithstanding the provisions of any enactment, a company need not have a company seal.

(3)   For the purposes of any enactment –
      (a)   providing for a document to be executed by a company by affixing its common seal, or
      (b)   referring (in whatever terms) to a document so executed,

a document signed or subscribed by or on behalf of the company in accordance with the provisions of the Requirements of Writing (Scotland) Act 1995 (c. 7) has effect as if so executed.

Other matters

49   Official seal for use abroad
(1)   A company that has a common seal may have an official seal for use outside the United Kingdom.
(2)   The official seal must be a facsimile of the company's common seal, with the addition on its face of the place or places where it is to be used.
(3)   The official seal when duly affixed to a document has the same effect as the company's common seal.
   This subsection does not extend to Scotland.
(4)   A company having an official seal for use outside the United Kingdom may –
   (a)   by writing under its common seal, or
   (b)   as respects Scotland, by writing subscribed in accordance with the Requirements of Writing (Scotland) Act 1995,
   authorise any person appointed for the purpose to affix the official seal to any deed or other document to which the company is party.
(5)   As between the company and a person dealing with such an agent, the agent's authority continues –
   (a)   during the period mentioned in the instrument conferring the authority, or
   (b)   if no period is mentioned, until notice of the revocation or termination of the agent's authority has been given to the person dealing with him.
(6)   The person affixing the official seal must certify in writing on the deed or other document to which the seal is affixed the date on which, and place at which, it is affixed.

50   Official seal for share certificates etc
(1)   A company that has a common seal may have an official seal for use –
   (a)   for sealing securities issued by the company, or
   (b)   for sealing documents creating or evidencing securities so issued.
(2)   The official seal –
   (a)   must be a facsimile of the company's common seal, with the addition on its face of the word "Securities", and
   (b)   when duly affixed to the document has the same effect as the company's common seal.

51   Pre-incorporation contracts, deeds and obligations
(1)   A contract that purports to be made by or on behalf of a company at a time when the company has not been formed has effect, subject to any agreement to the contrary, as one made with the person purporting to act for the company or as agent for it, and he is personally liable on the contract accordingly.
(2)   Subsection (1) applies –

(a) to the making of a deed under the law of England and Wales or Northern Ireland, and

(b) to the undertaking of an obligation under the law of Scotland,

as it applies to the making of a contract.

52 Bills of exchange and promissory notes

A bill of exchange or promissory note is deemed to have been made, accepted or endorsed on behalf of a company if made, accepted or endorsed in the name of, or by or on behalf or on account of, the company by a person acting under its authority.

PART 5

A COMPANY'S NAME

CHAPTER 1

GENERAL REQUIREMENTS

Prohibited names

53 Prohibited names

A company must not be registered under this Act by a name if, in the opinion of the Secretary of State –

(a) its use by the company would constitute an offence, or

(b) it is offensive.

Sensitive words and expressions

54 Names suggesting connection with government or public authority

(1) The approval of the Secretary of State is required for a company to be registered under this Act by a name that would be likely to give the impression that the company is connected with –

(a) Her Majesty's Government, any part of the Scottish administration or Her Majesty's Government in Northern Ireland,

(b) a local authority, or

(c) any public authority specified for the purposes of this section by regulations made by the Secretary of State.

(2) For the purposes of this section –

"local authority" means –

(a) a local authority within the meaning of the Local Government Act 1972 (c. 70), the Common Council of the City of London or the Council of the Isles of Scilly,

(b) a council constituted under section 2 of the Local Government etc. (Scotland) Act 1994 (c. 39), or

(c) a district council in Northern Ireland;

"public authority" includes any person or body having functions of a public nature.
(3)   Regulations under this section are subject to affirmative resolution procedure.

55 Other sensitive words or expressions
(1)   The approval of the Secretary of State is required for a company to be registered under this Act by a name that includes a word or expression for the time being specified in regulations made by the Secretary of State under this section.
(2)   Regulations under this section are subject to approval after being made.

56 Duty to seek comments of government department or other specified body
(1)   The Secretary of State may by regulations under –
   (a)   section 54 (name suggesting connection with government or public authority), or
   (b)   section 55 (other sensitive words or expressions),
require that, in connection with an application for the approval of the Secretary of State under that section, the applicant must seek the view of a specified Government department or other body.
(2)   Where such a requirement applies, the applicant must request the specified department or other body (in writing) to indicate whether (and if so why) it has any objections to the proposed name.
(3)   Where a request under this section is made in connection with an application for the registration of a company under this Act, the application must –
   (a)   include a statement that a request under this section has been made, and
   (b)   be accompanied by a copy of any response received.
(4)   Where a request under this section is made in connection with a change in a company's name, the notice of the change sent to the registrar must be accompanied by –
   (a)   a statement by a director or secretary of the company that a request under this section has been made, and
   (b)   a copy of any response received.
(5)   In this section "specified" means specified in the regulations.

Permitted characters etc

57 Permitted characters etc
(1)   The Secretary of State may make provision by regulations –
   (a)   as to the letters or other characters, signs or symbols (including accents and other diacritical marks) and punctuation that may be used in the name of a company registered under this Act; and
   (b)   specifying a standard style or format for the name of a company for the purposes of registration.
(2)   The regulations may prohibit the use of specified characters, signs or symbols when appearing in a specified position (in particular, at the beginning of a name).

(3)   A company may not be registered under this Act by a name that consists of or includes anything that is not permitted in accordance with regulations under this section.

(4)   Regulations under this section are subject to negative resolution procedure.

(5)   In this section "specified" means specified in the regulations.

CHAPTER 2

INDICATIONS OF COMPANY TYPE OR LEGAL FORM

Required indications for limited companies

58   Public limited companies

(1)   The name of a limited company that is a public company must end with "public limited company" or "p.l.c.".

(2)   In the case of a Welsh company, its name may instead end with "cwmni cyfyngedig cyhoeddus" or "c.c.c.".

(3)   This section does not apply to community interest companies (but see section 33(3) and (4) of the Companies (Audit, Investigations and Community Enterprise) Act 2004 (c. 27)).

59   Private limited companies

(1)   The name of a limited company that is a private company must end with "limited" or "ltd.".

(2)   In the case of a Welsh company, its name may instead end with "cyfyngedig" or "cyf.".

(3)   Certain companies are exempt from this requirement (see section 60).

(4)   This section does not apply to community interest companies (but see section 33(1) and (2) of the Companies (Audit, Investigations and Community Enterprise) Act 2004).

60   Exemption from requirement as to use of "limited"

(1)   A private company is exempt from section 59 (requirement to have name ending with "limited" or permitted alternative) if –

  (a)   it is a charity,

  (b)   it is exempted from the requirement of that section by regulations made by the Secretary of State, or

  (c)   it meets the conditions specified in –

         section 61 (continuation of existing exemption: companies limited by shares), or

         section 62 (continuation of existing exemption: companies limited by guarantee).

(2)   The registrar may refuse to register a private limited company by a name that does not include the word "limited" (or a permitted alternative) unless a statement has been delivered to him that the company meets the conditions for exemption.

(3)   The registrar may accept the statement as sufficient evidence of the matters stated in it.

(4)   Regulations under this section are subject to negative resolution procedure.

61   Continuation of existing exemption: companies limited by shares

(1)   This section applies to a private company limited by shares –

   (a)   that on 25th February 1982 –

      (i)   was registered in Great Britain, and

      (ii)   had a name that, by virtue of a licence under section 19 of the Companies Act 1948 (c. 38) (or corresponding earlier legislation), did not include the word "limited" or any of the permitted alternatives, or

   (b)   that on 30th June 1983 –

      (i)   was registered in Northern Ireland, and

      (ii)   had a name that, by virtue of a licence under section 19 of the Companies Act (Northern Ireland) 1960 (c. 22 (N.I.)) (or corresponding earlier legislation), did not include the word "limited" or any of the permitted alternatives.

(2)   A company to which this section applies is exempt from section 59 (requirement to have name ending with "limited" or permitted alternative) so long as –

   (a)   it continues to meet the following two conditions, and

   (b)   it does not change its name.

(3)   The first condition is that the objects of the company are the promotion of commerce, art, science, education, religion, charity or any profession, and anything incidental or conducive to any of those objects.

(4)   The second condition is that the company's articles –

   (a)   require its income to be applied in promoting its objects,

   (b)   prohibit the payment of dividends, or any return of capital, to its members, and

   (c)   require all the assets that would otherwise be available to its members generally to be transferred on its winding up either –

      (i)   to another body with objects similar to its own, or

      (ii)   to another body the objects of which are the promotion of charity and anything incidental or conducive thereto,

   (whether or not the body is a member of the company).

62   Continuation of existing exemption: companies limited by guarantee

(1)   A private company limited by guarantee that immediately before the commencement of this Part –

   (a)   was exempt by virtue of section 30 of the Companies Act 1985 (c. 6) or Article 40 of the Companies (Northern Ireland) Order 1986 (S.I. 1986/1032 (N.I. 6)) from the requirement to have a name including the word "limited" or a permitted alternative, and

   (b)   had a name that did not include the word "limited" or any of the permitted alternatives,

   is exempt from section 59 (requirement to have name ending with "limited" or permitted alternative) so long as it continues to meet the following two conditions and does not change its name.

(2)   The first condition is that the objects of the company are the promotion of commerce, art, science, education, religion, charity or any profession, and anything incidental or conducive to any of those objects.

(3)   The second condition is that the company's articles –
    (a)   require its income to be applied in promoting its objects,
    (b)   prohibit the payment of dividends to its members, and
    (c)   require all the assets that would otherwise be available to its members generally to be transferred on its winding up either –
        (i)   to another body with objects similar to its own, or
        (ii)   to another body the objects of which are the promotion of charity and anything incidental or conducive thereto,
    (whether or not the body is a member of the company).

63   Exempt company: restriction on amendment of articles

(1)   A private company –
    (a)   that is exempt under section 61 or 62 from the requirement to use "limited" (or a permitted alternative) as part of its name, and
    (b)   whose name does not include "limited" or any of the permitted alternatives,
    must not amend its articles so that it ceases to comply with the conditions for exemption under that section.

(2)   If subsection (1) above is contravened an offence is committed by –
    (a)   the company, and
    (b)   every officer of the company who is in default.
    For this purpose a shadow director is treated as an officer of the company.

(3)   A person guilty of an offence under this section is liable on summary conviction to a fine not exceeding level 5 on the standard scale and, for continued contravention, a daily default fine not exceeding one-tenth of level 5 on the standard scale.

(4)   Where immediately before the commencement of this section –
    (a)   a company was exempt by virtue of section 30 of the Companies Act 1985 (c. 6) or Article 40 of the Companies (Northern Ireland) Order 1986 (S.I. 1986/1032 (N.I. 6)) from the requirement to have a name including the word "limited" (or a permitted alternative), and
    (b)   the company's memorandum or articles contained provision preventing an alteration of them without the approval of –
        (i)   the Board of Trade or a Northern Ireland department (or any other department or Minister), or
        (ii)   the Charity Commission,
    that provision, and any condition of any such licence as is mentioned in section 61(1)(a)(ii) or (b)(ii) requiring such provision, shall cease to have effect. This does not apply if, or to the extent that, the provision is required by or under any other enactment.

(5)   It is hereby declared that any such provision as is mentioned in subsection (4)(b) formerly contained in a company's memorandum was at all material times capable, with the appropriate approval, of being altered or removed under section 17 of the Companies Act 1985 or Article 28 of the Companies

(Northern Ireland) Order 1986 (S.I. 1986/1032 (N.I. 6)) (or corresponding earlier enactments).

64   Power to direct change of name in case of company ceasing to be entitled to exemption

(1)   If it appears to the Secretary of State that a company whose name does not include "limited" or any of the permitted alternatives –

(a)   has ceased to be entitled to exemption under section 60(1)(a) or (b), or

(b)   in the case of a company within section 61 or 62 (which impose conditions as to the objects and articles of the company)–

(i)   has carried on any business other than the promotion of any of the objects mentioned in subsection (3) of section 61 or, as the case may be, subsection (2) of section 62, or

(ii)   has acted inconsistently with the provision required by subsection (4)(a) or (b) of section 61 or, as the case may be, subsection (3)(a) or (b) of section 62,

the Secretary of State may direct the company to change its name so that it ends with "limited" or one of the permitted alternatives.

(2)   The direction must be in writing and must specify the period within which the company is to change its name.

(3)   A change of name in order to comply with a direction under this section may be made by resolution of the directors.
This is without prejudice to any other method of changing the company's name.

(4)   Where a resolution of the directors is passed in accordance with subsection (3), the company must give notice to the registrar of the change.
Sections 80 and 81 apply as regards the registration and effect of the change.

(5)   If the company fails to comply with a direction under this section an offence is committed by –

(a)   the company, and

(b)   every officer of the company who is in default.

(6)   A person guilty of an offence under this section is liable on summary conviction to a fine not exceeding level 5 on the standard scale and, for continued contravention, a daily default fine not exceeding one-tenth of level 5 on the standard scale.

(7)   A company that has been directed to change its name under this section may not, without the approval of the Secretary of State, subsequently change its name so that it does not include "limited" or one of the permitted alternatives.
This does not apply to a change of name on re-registration or on conversion to a community interest company.

Inappropriate use of indications of company type or legal form

65   Inappropriate use of indications of company type or legal form

(1)   The Secretary of State may make provision by regulations prohibiting the use in a company name of specified words, expressions or other indications –

(a)   that are associated with a particular type of company or form of organisation, or

(b)   that are similar to words, expressions or other indications associated with a particular type of company or form of organisation.

(2)   The regulations may prohibit the use of words, expressions or other indications –

    (a)   in a specified part, or otherwise than in a specified part, of a company's name;

    (b)   in conjunction with, or otherwise than in conjunction with, such other words, expressions or indications as may be specified.

(3)   A company must not be registered under this Act by a name that consists of or includes anything prohibited by regulations under this section.

(4)   In this section "specified" means specified in the regulations.

(5)   Regulations under this section are subject to negative resolution procedure.

CHAPTER 3

SIMILARITY TO OTHER NAMES

Similarity to other name on registrar's index

66   Name not to be the same as another in the index

(1)   A company must not be registered under this Act by a name that is the same as another name appearing in the registrar's index of company names.

(2)   The Secretary of State may make provision by regulations supplementing this section.

(3)   The regulations may make provision –

    (a)   as to matters that are to be disregarded, and

    (b)   as to words, expressions, signs or symbols that are, or are not, to be regarded as the same,

for the purposes of this section.

(4)   The regulations may provide –

    (a)   that registration by a name that would otherwise be prohibited under this section is permitted –

        (i)   in specified circumstances, or

        (ii)   with specified consent, and

    (b)   that if those circumstances obtain or that consent is given at the time a company is registered by a name, a subsequent change of circumstances or withdrawal of consent does not affect the registration.

(5)   Regulations under this section are subject to negative resolution procedure.

(6)   In this section "specified" means specified in the regulations.

67   Power to direct change of name in case of similarity to existing name

(1)   The Secretary of State may direct a company to change its name if it has been registered in a name that is the same as or, in the opinion of the Secretary of State, too like –

    (a)   a name appearing at the time of the registration in the registrar's index of company names, or

     (b)   a name that should have appeared in that index at that time.

(2)   The Secretary of State may make provision by regulations supplementing this section.

(3)   The regulations may make provision –

     (a)   as to matters that are to be disregarded, and

     (b)   as to words, expressions, signs or symbols that are, or are not, to be regarded as the same,

for the purposes of this section.

(4)   The regulations may provide –

     (a)   that no direction is to be given under this section in respect of a name –

         (i)   in specified circumstances, or

         (ii) if specified consent is given, and

     (b)   that a subsequent change of circumstances or withdrawal of consent does not give rise to grounds for a direction under this section.

(5)   Regulations under this section are subject to negative resolution procedure.

(6)   In this section "specified" means specified in the regulations.

68   Direction to change name: supplementary provisions

(1)   The following provisions have effect in relation to a direction under section 67 (power to direct change of name in case of similarity to existing name).

(2)   Any such direction –

     (a)   must be given within twelve months of the company's registration by the name in question, and

     (b)   must specify the period within which the company is to change its name.

(3)   The Secretary of State may by a further direction extend that period.

Any such direction must be given before the end of the period for the time being specified.

(4)   A direction under section 67 or this section must be in writing.

(5)   If a company fails to comply with the direction, an offence is committed by –

     (a)   the company, and

     (b)   every officer of the company who is in default.

For this purpose a shadow director is treated as an officer of the company.

(6)   A person guilty of an offence under this section is liable on summary conviction to a fine not exceeding level 3 on the standard scale and, for continued contravention, a daily default fine not exceeding one-tenth of level 3 on the standard scale.

Similarity to other name in which person has goodwill

69   Objection to company's registered name

(1)   A person ("the applicant") may object to a company's registered name on the ground –

     (a)   that it is the same as a name associated with the applicant in which he has goodwill, or

     (b)   that it is sufficiently similar to such a name that its use in the United

Kingdom would be likely to mislead by suggesting a connection between the company and the applicant.

(2)   The objection must be made by application to a company names adjudicator (see section 70).

(3)   The company concerned shall be the primary respondent to the application. Any of its members or directors may be joined as respondents.

(4)   If the ground specified in subsection (1)(a) or (b) is established, it is for the respondents to show –

    (a)   that the name was registered before the commencement of the activities on which the applicant relies to show goodwill; or

    (b)   that the company –

        (i)   is operating under the name, or

        (ii)   is proposing to do so and has incurred substantial start-up costs in preparation, or

        (iii)   was formerly operating under the name and is now dormant; or

    (c)   that the name was registered in the ordinary course of a company formation business and the company is available for sale to the applicant on the standard terms of that business; or

    (d)   that the name was adopted in good faith; or

    (e)   that the interests of the applicant are not adversely affected to any significant extent.

If none of those is shown, the objection shall be upheld.

(5)   If the facts mentioned in subsection (4)(a), (b) or (c) are established, the objection shall nevertheless be upheld if the applicant shows that the main purpose of the respondents (or any of them) in registering the name was to obtain money (or other consideration) from the applicant or prevent him from registering the name.

(6)   If the objection is not upheld under subsection (4) or (5), it shall be dismissed.

(7)   In this section "goodwill" includes reputation of any description.

70   Company names adjudicators

(1)   The Secretary of State shall appoint persons to be company names adjudicators.

(2)   The persons appointed must have such legal or other experience as, in the Secretary of State's opinion, makes them suitable for appointment.

(3)   An adjudicator –

    (a)   holds office in accordance with the terms of his appointment,

    (b)   is eligible for re-appointment when his term of office ends,

    (c)   may resign at any time by notice in writing given to the Secretary of State, and

    (d)   may be dismissed by the Secretary of State on the ground of incapacity or misconduct.

(4)   One of the adjudicators shall be appointed Chief Adjudicator.

He shall perform such functions as the Secretary of State may assign to him.

(5)   The other adjudicators shall undertake such duties as the Chief Adjudicator may determine.

(6)   The Secretary of State may –

(a)   appoint staff for the adjudicators;
(b)   pay remuneration and expenses to the adjudicators and their staff;
(c)   defray other costs arising in relation to the performance by the adjudicators of their functions;
(d)   compensate persons for ceasing to be adjudicators.

71   Procedural rules

(1)   The Secretary of State may make rules about proceedings before a company names adjudicator.
(2)   The rules may, in particular, make provision –
  (a)   as to how an application is to be made and the form and content of an application or other documents;
  (b)   for fees to be charged;
  (c)   about the service of documents and the consequences of failure to serve them;
  (d)   as to the form and manner in which evidence is to be given;
  (e)   for circumstances in which hearings are required and those in which they are not;
  (f)   for cases to be heard by more than one adjudicator;
  (g)   setting time limits for anything required to be done in connection with the proceedings (and allowing for such limits to be extended, even if they have expired);
  (h)   enabling the adjudicator to strike out an application, or any defence, in whole or in part –
    (i)   on the ground that it is vexatious, has no reasonable prospect of success or is otherwise misconceived, or
    (ii)   for failure to comply with the requirements of the rules;
  (i)   conferring power to order security for costs (in Scotland, caution for expenses);
  (j)   as to how far proceedings are to be held in public;
  (k)   requiring one party to bear the costs (in Scotland, expenses) of another and as to the taxing (or settling) the amount of such costs (or expenses).
(3)   The rules may confer on the Chief Adjudicator power to determine any matter that could be the subject of provision in the rules.
(4)   Rules under this section shall be made by statutory instrument which shall be subject to annulment in pursuance of a resolution of either House of Parliament.

72   Decision of adjudicator to be made available to public

(1)   A company names adjudicator must, within 90 days of determining an application under section 69, make his decision and his reasons for it available to the public.
(2)   He may do so by means of a website or by such other means as appear to him to be appropriate.

73   Order requiring name to be changed

(1)   If an application under section 69 is upheld, the adjudicator shall make an order –

     (a)   requiring the respondent company to change its name to one that is not an offending name, and

     (b)   requiring all the respondents –

        (i)   to take all such steps as are within their power to make, or facilitate the making, of that change, and

        (ii)   not to cause or permit any steps to be taken calculated to result in another company being registered with a name that is an offending name.

(2)   An "offending name" means a name that, by reason of its similarity to the name associated with the applicant in which he claims goodwill, would be likely –

     (a)   to be the subject of a direction under section 67 (power of Secretary of State to direct change of name), or

     (b)   to give rise to a further application under section 69.

(3)   The order must specify a date by which the respondent company's name is to be changed and may be enforced –

     (a)   in England and Wales or Northern Ireland, in the same way as an order of the High Court;

     (b)   in Scotland, in the same way as a decree of the Court of Session.

(4)   If the respondent company's name is not changed in accordance with the order by the specified date, the adjudicator may determine a new name for the company.

(5)   If the adjudicator determines a new name for the respondent company he must give notice of his determination –

     (a)   to the applicant,

     (b)   to the respondents, and

     (c)   to the registrar.

(6)   For the purposes of this section a company's name is changed when the change takes effect in accordance with section 81(1) (on the issue of the new certification of incorporation).

74 Appeal from adjudicator's decision

(1)   An appeal lies to the court from any decision of a company names adjudicator to uphold or dismiss an application under section 69.

(2)   Notice of appeal against a decision upholding an application must be given before the date specified in the adjudicator's order by which the respondent company's name is to be changed.

(3)   If notice of appeal is given against a decision upholding an application, the effect of the adjudicator's order is suspended.

(4)   If on appeal the court –

     (a)   affirms the decision of the adjudicator to uphold the application, or

     (b)   reverses the decision of the adjudicator to dismiss the application,

the court may (as the case may require) specify the date by which the adjudicator's order is to be complied with, remit the matter to the adjudicator or make any order or determination that the adjudicator might have made.

(5)   If the court determines a new name for the company it must give notice of the determination –

     (a)   to the parties to the appeal, and

     (b)   to the registrar.

CHAPTER 4

OTHER POWERS OF THE SECRETARY OF STATE

75   Provision of misleading information etc

(1)   If it appears to the Secretary of State –
- (a)   that misleading information has been given for the purposes of a company's registration by a particular name, or
- (b)   that an undertaking or assurance has been given for that purpose and has not been fulfilled,

the Secretary of State may direct the company to change its name.

(2)   Any such direction –
- (a)   must be given within five years of the company's registration by that name, and
- (b)   must specify the period within which the company is to change its name.

(3)   The Secretary of State may by a further direction extend the period within which the company is to change its name.

Any such direction must be given before the end of the period for the time being specified.

(4)   A direction under this section must be in writing.

(5)   If a company fails to comply with a direction under this section, an offence is committed by –
- (a)   the company, and
- (b)   every officer of the company who is in default.

For this purpose a shadow director is treated as an officer of the company.

(6)   A person guilty of an offence under this section is liable on summary conviction to a fine not exceeding level 3 on the standard scale and, for continued contravention, a daily default fine not exceeding one-tenth of level 3 on the standard scale.

76   Misleading indication of activities

(1)   If in the opinion of the Secretary of State the name by which a company is registered gives so misleading an indication of the nature of its activities as to be likely to cause harm to the public, the Secretary of State may direct the company to change its name.

(2)   The direction must be in writing.

(3)   The direction must be complied with within a period of six weeks from the date of the direction or such longer period as the Secretary of State may think fit to allow.

This does not apply if an application is duly made to the court under the following provisions.

(4)   The company may apply to the court to set the direction aside.

The application must be made within the period of three weeks from the date of the direction.

(5)   The court may set the direction aside or confirm it.

If the direction is confirmed, the court shall specify the period within which the direction is to be complied with.

(6) If a company fails to comply with a direction under this section, an offence is committed by –
   (a) the company, and
   (b) every officer of the company who is in default.
   For this purpose a shadow director is treated as an officer of the company.
(7) A person guilty of an offence under this section is liable on summary conviction to a fine not exceeding level 3 on the standard scale and, for continued contravention, a daily default fine not exceeding one-tenth of level 3 on the standard scale.

CHAPTER 5

CHANGE OF NAME

77 Change of name
   (1) A company may change its name –
      (a) by special resolution (see section 78), or
      (b) by other means provided for by the company's articles (see section 79).
   (2) The name of a company may also be changed –
      (a) by resolution of the directors acting under section 64 (change of name to comply with direction of Secretary of State under that section);
      (b) on the determination of a new name by a company names adjudicator under section 73 (powers of adjudicator on upholding objection to company name);
      (c) on the determination of a new name by the court under section 74 (appeal against decision of company names adjudicator);
      (d) under section 1033 (company's name on restoration to the register).

78 Change of name by special resolution
   (1) Where a change of name has been agreed to by a company by special resolution, the company must give notice to the registrar.
   This is in addition to the obligation to forward a copy of the resolution to the registrar.
   (2) Where a change of name by special resolution is conditional on the occurrence of an event, the notice given to the registrar of the change must –
      (a) specify that the change is conditional, and
      (b) state whether the event has occurred.
   (3) If the notice states that the event has not occurred –
      (a) the registrar is not required to act under section 80 (registration and issue of new certificate of incorporation) until further notice,
      (b) when the event occurs, the company must give notice to the registrar stating that it has occurred, and
      (c) the registrar may rely on the statement as sufficient evidence of the matters stated in it.

79   Change of name by means provided for in company's articles

(1)   Where a change of a company's name has been made by other means provided for by its articles –

    (a)   the company must give notice to the registrar, and

    (b)   the notice must be accompanied by a statement that the change of name has been made by means provided for by the company's articles.

(2)   The registrar may rely on the statement as sufficient evidence of the matters stated in it.

80   Change of name: registration and issue of new certificate of incorporation

(1)   This section applies where the registrar receives notice of a change of a company's name.

(2)   If the registrar is satisfied –

    (a)   that the new name complies with the requirements of this Part, and

    (b)   that the requirements of the Companies Acts, and any relevant requirements of the company's articles, with respect to a change of name are complied with,

the registrar must enter the new name on the register in place of the former name.

(3)   On the registration of the new name, the registrar must issue a certificate of incorporation altered to meet the circumstances of the case.

81   Change of name: effect

(1)   A change of a company's name has effect from the date on which the new certificate of incorporation is issued.

(2)   The change does not affect any rights or obligations of the company or render defective any legal proceedings by or against it.

(3)   Any legal proceedings that might have been continued or commenced against it by its former name may be continued or commenced against it by its new name.

CHAPTER 6

TRADING DISCLOSURES

82   Requirement to disclose company name etc

(1)   The Secretary of State may by regulations make provision requiring companies –

    (a)   to display specified information in specified locations,

    (b)   to state specified information in specified descriptions of document or communication, and

    (c)   to provide specified information on request to those they deal with in the course of their business.

(2)   The regulations –

    (a)   must in every case require disclosure of the name of the company, and

    (b)   may make provision as to the manner in which any specified information is to be displayed, stated or provided.

(3)   The regulations may provide that, for the purposes of any requirement to disclose a company's name, any variation between a word or words required to be part of the name and a permitted abbreviation of that word or those words (or vice versa) shall be disregarded.

(4)   In this section "specified" means specified in the regulations.

(5)   Regulations under this section are subject to affirmative resolution procedure.

83   Civil consequences of failure to make required disclosure

(1)   This section applies to any legal proceedings brought by a company to which section 82 applies (requirement to disclose company name etc) to enforce a right arising out of a contract made in the course of a business in respect of which the company was, at the time the contract was made, in breach of regulations under that section.

(2)   The proceedings shall be dismissed if the defendant (in Scotland, the defender) to the proceedings shows –
  (a)   that he has a claim against the claimant (pursuer) arising out of the contract that he has been unable to pursue by reason of the latter's breach of the regulations, or
  (b)   that he has suffered some financial loss in connection with the contract by reason of the claimant's (pursuer's) breach of the regulations,
  unless the court before which the proceedings are brought is satisfied that it is just and equitable to permit the proceedings to continue.

(3)   This section does not affect the right of any person to enforce such rights as he may have against another person in any proceedings brought by that person.

84   Criminal consequences of failure to make required disclosures

(1)   Regulations under section 82 may provide –
  (a)   that where a company fails, without reasonable excuse, to comply with any specified requirement of regulations under that section an offence is committed by –
    (i)   the company, and
    (ii)   every officer of the company who is in default;
  (b)   that a person guilty of such an offence is liable on summary conviction to a fine not exceeding level 3 on the standard scale and, for continued contravention, a daily default fine not exceeding one-tenth of level 3 on the standard scale.

(2)   The regulations may provide that, for the purposes of any provision made under subsection (1), a shadow director of the company is to be treated as an officer of the company.

(3)   In subsection (1)(a) "specified" means specified in the regulations.

85   Minor variations in form of name to be left out of account

(1)   For the purposes of this Chapter, in considering a company's name no account is to be taken of –
  (a)   whether upper or lower case characters (or a combination of the two) are used,
  (b)   whether diacritical marks or punctuation are present or absent,

     (c) whether the name is in the same format or style as is specified under section 57(1)(b) for the purposes of registration,

provided there is no real likelihood of names differing only in those respects being taken to be different names.

(2) This does not affect the operation of regulations under section 57(1)(a) permitting only specified characters, diacritical marks or punctuation.

PART 6

A COMPANY'S REGISTERED OFFICE

General

86 A company's registered office

A company must at all times have a registered office to which all communications and notices may be addressed.

87 Change of address of registered office

(1) A company may change the address of its registered office by giving notice to the registrar.

(2) The change takes effect upon the notice being registered by the registrar, but until the end of the period of 14 days beginning with the date on which it is registered a person may validly serve any document on the company at the address previously registered.

(3) For the purposes of any duty of a company –

    (a) to keep available for inspection at its registered office any register, index or other document, or

    (b) to mention the address of its registered office in any document,

a company that has given notice to the registrar of a change in the address of its registered office may act on the change as from such date, not more than 14 days after the notice is given, as it may determine.

(4) Where a company unavoidably ceases to perform at its registered office any such duty as is mentioned in subsection (3)(a) in circumstances in which it was not practicable to give prior notice to the registrar of a change in the address of its registered office, but –

    (a) resumes performance of that duty at other premises as soon as practicable, and

    (b) gives notice accordingly to the registrar of a change in the situation of its registered office within 14 days of doing so,

it is not to be treated as having failed to comply with that duty.

Welsh companies

88 Welsh companies

(1) In the Companies Acts a "Welsh company" means a company as to which it is stated in the register that its registered office is to be situated in Wales.

(2)   A company –
  (a)   whose registered office is in Wales, and
  (b)   as to which it is stated in the register that its registered office is to be situated in England and Wales,
  may by special resolution require the register to be amended so that it states that the company's registered office is to be situated in Wales.

(3)   A company –
  (a)   whose registered office is in Wales, and
  (b)   as to which it is stated in the register that its registered office is to be situated in Wales,
  may by special resolution require the register to be amended so that it states that the company's registered office is to be situated in England and Wales.

(4)   Where a company passes a resolution under this section it must give notice to the registrar, who shall –
  (a)   amend the register accordingly, and
  (b)   issue a new certificate of incorporation altered to meet the circumstances of the case.

PART 7

RE-REGISTRATION AS A MEANS OF ALTERING A COMPANY'S STATUS

Introductory

89   Alteration of status by re-registration
  A company may by re-registration under this Part alter its status –
  (a)   from a private company to a public company (see sections 90 to 96);
  (b)   from a public company to a private company (see sections 97 to 101);
  (c)   from a private limited company to an unlimited company (see sections 102 to 104);
  (d)   from an unlimited private company to a limited company (see sections 105 to 108);
  (e)   from a public company to an unlimited private company (see sections 109 to 111).

Private company becoming public

90   Re-registration of private company as public
  (1)   A private company (whether limited or unlimited) may be re-registered as a public company limited by shares if –
  (a)   a special resolution that it should be so re-registered is passed,
  (b)   the conditions specified below are met, and
  (c)   an application for re-registration is delivered to the registrar in accordance with section 94, together with –

          (i)   the other documents required by that section, and

          (ii)   a statement of compliance.

(2)   The conditions are –

       (a)   that the company has a share capital;

       (b)   that the requirements of section 91 are met as regards its share capital;

       (c)   that the requirements of section 92 are met as regards its net assets;

       (d)   if section 93 applies (recent allotment of shares for non-cash consideration), that the requirements of that section are met; and

       (e)   that the company has not previously been re-registered as unlimited.

(3)   The company must make such changes –

       (a)   in its name, and

       (b)   in its articles,

as are necessary in connection with its becoming a public company.

(4)   If the company is unlimited it must also make such changes in its articles as are necessary in connection with its becoming a company limited by shares.

91 Requirements as to share capital

(1)   The following requirements must be met at the time the special resolution is passed that the company should be re-registered as a public company –

       (a)   the nominal value of the company's allotted share capital must be not less than the authorised minimum;

       (b)   each of the company's allotted shares must be paid up at least as to one-quarter of the nominal value of that share and the whole of any premium on it;

       (c)   if any shares in the company or any premium on them have been fully or partly paid up by an undertaking given by any person that he or another should do work or perform services (whether for the company or any other person), the undertaking must have been performed or otherwise discharged;

       (d)   if shares have been allotted as fully or partly paid up as to their nominal value or any premium on them otherwise than in cash, and the consideration for the allotment consists of or includes an undertaking to the company (other than one to which paragraph (c) applies), then either –

          (i)   the undertaking must have been performed or otherwise discharged, or

          (ii)   there must be a contract between the company and some person pursuant to which the undertaking is to be performed within five years from the time the special resolution is passed.

(2)   For the purpose of determining whether the requirements in subsection (1)(b), (c) and (d) are met, the following may be disregarded –

       (a)   shares allotted –

          (i)   before 22nd June 1982 in the case of a company then registered in Great Britain, or

          (ii)   before 31st December 1984 in the case of a company then registered in Northern Ireland;

       (b)   shares allotted in pursuance of an employees' share scheme by reason of which the company would, but for this subsection, be precluded under subsection (1)(b) (but not otherwise) from being re-registered as a public company.

(3)   No more than one-tenth of the nominal value of the company's allotted share capital is to be disregarded under subsection (2)(a).

For this purpose the allotted share capital is treated as not including shares disregarded under subsection (2)(b).

(4)   Shares disregarded under subsection (2) are treated as not forming part of the allotted share capital for the purposes of subsection (1)(a).

(5)   A company must not be re-registered as a public company if it appears to the registrar that –
    (a)   the company has resolved to reduce its share capital,
    (b)   the reduction –
        (i)   is made under section 626 (reduction in connection with redenomination of share capital),
        (ii)   is supported by a solvency statement in accordance with section 643, or
        (iii)   has been confirmed by an order of the court under section 648, and
    (c)   the effect of the reduction is, or will be, that the nominal value of the company's allotted share capital is below the authorised minimum.

92   Requirements as to net assets

(1)   A company applying to re-register as a public company must obtain –
    (a)   a balance sheet prepared as at a date not more than seven months before the date on which the application is delivered to the registrar,
    (b)   an unqualified report by the company's auditor on that balance sheet, and
    (c)   a written statement by the company's auditor that in his opinion at the balance sheet date the amount of the company's net assets was not less than the aggregate of its called-up share capital and undistributable reserves.

(2)   Between the balance sheet date and the date on which the application for re-registration is delivered to the registrar, there must be no change in the company's financial position that results in the amount of its net assets becoming less than the aggregate of its called-up share capital and undistributable reserves.

(3)   In subsection (1)(b) an "unqualified report" means –
    (a)   if the balance sheet was prepared for a financial year of the company, a report stating without material qualification the auditor's opinion that the balance sheet has been properly prepared in accordance with the requirements of this Act;
    (b)   if the balance sheet was not prepared for a financial year of the company, a report stating without material qualification the auditor's opinion that the balance sheet has been properly prepared in accordance with the provisions of this Act which would have applied if it had been prepared for a financial year of the company.

(4)   For the purposes of an auditor's report on a balance sheet that was not

prepared for a financial year of the company, the provisions of this Act apply with such modifications as are necessary by reason of that fact.

(5) For the purposes of subsection (3) a qualification is material unless the auditor states in his report that the matter giving rise to the qualification is not material for the purpose of determining (by reference to the company's balance sheet) whether at the balance sheet date the amount of the company's net assets was not less than the aggregate of its called-up share capital and undistributable reserves.

(6) In this Part "net assets" and "undistributable reserves" have the same meaning as in section 831 (net asset restriction on distributions by public companies).

93 Recent allotment of shares for non-cash consideration

(1) This section applies where –
- (a) shares are allotted by the company in the period between the date as at which the balance sheet required by section 92 is prepared and the passing of the resolution that the company should re-register as a public company, and
- (b) the shares are allotted as fully or partly paid up as to their nominal value or any premium on them otherwise than in cash.

(2) The registrar shall not entertain an application by the company for re-registration as a public company unless –
- (a) the requirements of section 593(1)(a) and (b) have been complied with (independent valuation of non-cash consideration; valuer's report to company not more than six months before allotment), or
- (b) the allotment is in connection with –
  - (i) a share exchange (see subsections (3) to (5) below), or
  - (ii) a proposed merger with another company (see subsection (6) below).

(3) An allotment is in connection with a share exchange if –
- (a) the shares are allotted in connection with an arrangement under which the whole or part of the consideration for the shares allotted is provided by –
  - (i) the transfer to the company allotting the shares of shares (or shares of a particular class) in another company, or
  - (ii) the cancellation of shares (or shares of a particular class) in another company; and
- (b) the allotment is open to all the holders of the shares of the other company in question (or, where the arrangement applies only to shares of a particular class, to all the holders of the company's shares of that class) to take part in the arrangement in connection with which the shares are allotted.

(4) In determining whether a person is a holder of shares for the purposes of subsection (3), there shall be disregarded –
- (a) shares held by, or by a nominee of, the company allotting the shares;
- (b) shares held by, or by a nominee of –
  - (i) the holding company of the company allotting the shares,
  - (ii) a subsidiary of the company allotting the shares, or

       (iii)   a subsidiary of the holding company of the company allotting the shares.

(5)   It is immaterial, for the purposes of deciding whether an allotment is in connection with a share exchange, whether or not the arrangement in connection with which the shares are allotted involves the issue to the company allotting the shares of shares (or shares of a particular class) in the other company.

(6)   There is a proposed merger with another company if one of the companies concerned proposes to acquire all the assets and liabilities of the other in exchange for the issue of its shares or other securities to shareholders of the other (whether or not accompanied by a cash payment).

    "Another company" includes any body corporate.

(7)   For the purposes of this section –

    (a)   the consideration for an allotment does not include any amount standing to the credit of any of the company's reserve accounts, or of its profit and loss account, that has been applied in paying up (to any extent) any of the shares allotted or any premium on those shares; and

    (b)   "arrangement" means any agreement, scheme or arrangement, (including an arrangement sanctioned in accordance with –

       (i)   Part 26 of this Act (arrangements and reconstructions), or

       (ii)   section 110 of the Insolvency Act 1986 (c. 45) or Article 96 of the Insolvency (Northern Ireland) Order 1989 (S.I. 1989/2405 (N.I. 19)) (liquidator in winding up accepting shares as consideration for sale of company's property)).

94   Application and accompanying documents

(1)   An application for re-registration as a public company must contain –

    (a)   a statement of the company's proposed name on re-registration; and

    (b)   in the case of a company without a secretary, a statement of the company's proposed secretary (see section 95).

(2)   The application must be accompanied by –

    (a)   a copy of the special resolution that the company should re-register as a public company (unless a copy has already been forwarded to the registrar under Chapter 3 of Part 3);

    (b)   a copy of the company's articles as proposed to be amended;

    (c)   a copy of the balance sheet and other documents referred to in section 92(1); and

    (d)   if section 93 applies (recent allotment of shares for non-cash consideration), a copy of the valuation report (if any) under subsection (2)(a) of that section.

(3)   The statement of compliance required to be delivered together with the application is a statement that the requirements of this Part as to re-registration as a public company have been complied with.

(4)   The registrar may accept the statement of compliance as sufficient evidence that the company is entitled to be re-registered as a public company.

95   Statement of proposed secretary

(1)   The statement of the company's proposed secretary must contain the required

particulars of the person who is or the persons who are to be the secretary or joint secretaries of the company.

(2)   The required particulars are the particulars that will be required to be stated in the company's register of secretaries (see sections 277 to 279).

(3)   The statement must also contain a consent by the person named as secretary, or each of the persons named as joint secretaries, to act in the relevant capacity. If all the partners in a firm are to be joint secretaries, consent may be given by one partner on behalf of all of them.

96   Issue of certificate of incorporation on re-registration

(1)   If on an application for re-registration as a public company the registrar is satisfied that the company is entitled to be so re-registered, the company shall be re-registered accordingly.

(2)   The registrar must issue a certificate of incorporation altered to meet the circumstances of the case.

(3)   The certificate must state that it is issued on re-registration and the date on which it is issued.

(4)   On the issue of the certificate –
  (a)   the company by virtue of the issue of the certificate becomes a public company,
  (b)   the changes in the company's name and articles take effect, and
  (c)   where the application contained a statement under section 95 (statement of proposed secretary), the person or persons named in the statement as secretary or joint secretary of the company are deemed to have been appointed to that office.

(5)   The certificate is conclusive evidence that the requirements of this Act as to re-registration have been complied with.

Public company becoming private

97   Re-registration of public company as private limited company

(1)   A public company may be re-registered as a private limited company if –
  (a)   a special resolution that it should be so re-registered is passed,
  (b)   the conditions specified below are met, and
  (c)   an application for re-registration is delivered to the registrar in accordance with section 100, together with –
    (i)   the other documents required by that section, and
    (ii)   a statement of compliance.

(2)   The conditions are that –
  (a)   where no application under section 98 for cancellation of the resolution has been made –
    (i)   having regard to the number of members who consented to or voted in favour of the resolution, no such application may be made, or
    (ii)   the period within which such an application could be made has expired, or
  (b)   where such an application has been made –

          (i)   the application has been withdrawn, or
          (ii)   an order has been made confirming the resolution and a copy of that order has been delivered to the registrar.

(3)   The company must make such changes –
      (a)   in its name, and
      (b)   in its articles,

as are necessary in connection with its becoming a private company limited by shares or, as the case may be, by guarantee.

98 Application to court to cancel resolution

(1)   Where a special resolution by a public company to be re-registered as a private limited company has been passed, an application to the court for the cancellation of the resolution may be made –
      (a)   by the holders of not less in the aggregate than 5% in nominal value of the company's issued share capital or any class of the company's issued share capital (disregarding any shares held by the company as treasury shares);
      (b)   if the company is not limited by shares, by not less than 5% of its members; or
      (c)   by not less than 50 of the company's members;

but not by a person who has consented to or voted in favour of the resolution.

(2)   The application must be made within 28 days after the passing of the resolution and may be made on behalf of the persons entitled to make it by such one or more of their number as they may appoint for the purpose.

(3)   On the hearing of the application the court shall make an order either cancelling or confirming the resolution.

(4)   The court may –
      (a)   make that order on such terms and conditions as it thinks fit,
      (b)   if it thinks fit adjourn the proceedings in order that an arrangement may be made to the satisfaction of the court for the purchase of the interests of dissentient members, and
      (c)   give such directions, and make such orders, as it thinks expedient for facilitating or carrying into effect any such arrangement.

(5)   The court's order may, if the court thinks fit –
      (a)   provide for the purchase by the company of the shares of any of its members and for the reduction accordingly of the company's capital; and
      (b)   make such alteration in the company's articles as may be required in consequence of that provision.

(6)   The court's order may, if the court thinks fit, require the company not to make any, or any specified, amendments to its articles without the leave of the court.

99 Notice to registrar of court application or order

(1)   On making an application under section 98 (application to court to cancel resolution) the applicants, or the person making the application on their behalf, must immediately give notice to the registrar.

This is without prejudice to any provision of rules of court as to service of notice of the application.

(2)   On being served with notice of any such application, the company must immediately give notice to the registrar.

(3)   Within 15 days of the making of the court's order on the application, or such longer period as the court may at any time direct, the company must deliver to the registrar a copy of the order.

(4)   If a company fails to comply with subsection (2) or (3) an offence is committed by –

    (a)   the company, and

    (b)   every officer of the company who is in default.

(5)   A person guilty of an offence under this section is liable on summary conviction to a fine not exceeding level 3 on the standard scale and, for continued contravention, a daily default fine not exceeding one-tenth of level 3 on the standard scale.

100   Application and accompanying documents

(1)   An application for re-registration as a private limited company must contain a statement of the company's proposed name on re-registration.

(2)   The application must be accompanied by –

    (a)   a copy of the resolution that the company should re-register as a private limited company (unless a copy has already been forwarded to the registrar under Chapter 3 of Part 3); and

    (b)   a copy of the company's articles as proposed to be amended.

(3)   The statement of compliance required to be delivered together with the application is a statement that the requirements of this Part as to re-registration as a private limited company have been complied with.

(4)   The registrar may accept the statement of compliance as sufficient evidence that the company is entitled to be re-registered as a private limited company.

101   Issue of certificate of incorporation on re-registration

(1)   If on an application for re-registration as a private limited company the registrar is satisfied that the company is entitled to be so re-registered, the company shall be re-registered accordingly.

(2)   The registrar must issue a certificate of incorporation altered to meet the circumstances of the case.

(3)   The certificate must state that it is issued on re-registration and the date on which it is issued.

(4)   On the issue of the certificate –

    (a)   the company by virtue of the issue of the certificate becomes a private limited company, and

    (b)   the changes in the company's name and articles take effect.

(5)   The certificate is conclusive evidence that the requirements of this Act as to re-registration have been complied with.

Private limited company becoming unlimited

102   Re-registration of private limited company as unlimited

(1)   A private limited company may be re-registered as an unlimited company if –

      (a) all the members of the company have assented to its being so re-registered,

      (b) the condition specified below is met, and

      (c) an application for re-registration is delivered to the registrar in accordance with section 103, together with –

          (i)   the other documents required by that section, and

          (ii) a statement of compliance.

(2)   The condition is that the company has not previously been re-registered as limited.

(3)   The company must make such changes in its name and its articles –

      (a) as are necessary in connection with its becoming an unlimited company; and

      (b) if it is to have a share capital, as are necessary in connection with its becoming an unlimited company having a share capital.

(4)   For the purposes of this section –

      (a) a trustee in bankruptcy of a member of the company is entitled, to the exclusion of the member, to assent to the company's becoming unlimited; and

      (b) the personal representative of a deceased member of the company may assent on behalf of the deceased.

(5)   In subsection (4)(a), "a trustee in bankruptcy of a member of the company" includes –

      (a) a permanent trustee or an interim trustee (within the meaning of the Bankruptcy (Scotland) Act 1985 (c. 66)) on the sequestrated estate of a member of the company;

      (b) a trustee under a protected trustee deed (within the meaning of the Bankruptcy (Scotland) Act 1985) granted by a member of the company.

103　Application and accompanying documents

(1)   An application for re-registration as an unlimited company must contain a statement of the company's proposed name on re-registration.

(2)   The application must be accompanied by –

      (a) the prescribed form of assent to the company's being registered as an unlimited company, authenticated by or on behalf of all the members of the company;

      (b) a copy of the company's articles as proposed to be amended.

(3)   The statement of compliance required to be delivered together with the application is a statement that the requirements of this Part as to re-registration as an unlimited company have been complied with.

(4)   The statement must contain a statement by the directors of the company –

      (a) that the persons by whom or on whose behalf the form of assent is authenticated constitute the whole membership of the company, and

      (b) if any of the members have not authenticated that form themselves, that the directors have taken all reasonable steps to satisfy themselves that each person who authenticated it on behalf of a member was lawfully empowered to do so.

(5)   The registrar may accept the statement of compliance as sufficient evidence that the company is entitled to be re-registered as an unlimited company.

104   Issue of certificate of incorporation on re-registration

(1)   If on an application for re-registration of a private limited company as an unlimited company the registrar is satisfied that the company is entitled to be so re-registered, the company shall be re-registered accordingly.

(2)   The registrar must issue a certificate of incorporation altered to meet the circumstances of the case.

(3)   The certificate must state that it is issued on re-registration and the date on which it is issued.

(4)   On the issue of the certificate –
    (a)   the company by virtue of the issue of the certificate becomes an unlimited company, and
    (b)   the changes in the company's name and articles take effect.

(5)   The certificate is conclusive evidence that the requirements of this Act as to re-registration have been complied with.

Unlimited private company becoming limited

105   Re-registration of unlimited company as limited

(1)   An unlimited company may be re-registered as a private limited company if –
    (a)   a special resolution that it should be so re-registered is passed,
    (b)   the condition specified below is met, and
    (c)   an application for re-registration is delivered to the registrar in accordance with section 106, together with –
        (i)   the other documents required by that section, and
        (ii)   a statement of compliance.

(2)   The condition is that the company has not previously been re-registered as unlimited.

(3)   The special resolution must state whether the company is to be limited by shares or by guarantee.

(4)   The company must make such changes –
    (a)   in its name, and
    (b)   in its articles,
as are necessary in connection with its becoming a company limited by shares or, as the case may be, by guarantee.

106   Application and accompanying documents

(1)   An application for re-registration as a limited company must contain a statement of the company's proposed name on re-registration.

(2)   The application must be accompanied by –
    (a)   a copy of the resolution that the company should re-register as a private limited company (unless a copy has already been forwarded to the registrar under Chapter 3 of Part 3);
    (b)   if the company is to be limited by guarantee, a statement of guarantee;
    (c)   a copy of the company's articles as proposed to be amended.

(3)   The statement of guarantee required to be delivered in the case of a company that is to be limited by guarantee must state that each member undertakes that, if the company is wound up while he is a member, or within one year

after he ceases to be a member, he will contribute to the assets of the company such amount as may be required for –
   (a)   payment of the debts and liabilities of the company contracted before he ceases to be a member,
   (b)   payment of the costs, charges and expenses of winding up, and
   (c)   adjustment of the rights of the contributories among themselves,
not exceeding a specified amount.
(4)   The statement of compliance required to be delivered together with the application is a statement that the requirements of this Part as to re-registration as a limited company have been complied with.
(5)   The registrar may accept the statement of compliance as sufficient evidence that the company is entitled to be re-registered as a limited company.

107   Issue of certificate of incorporation on re-registration
(1)   If on an application for re-registration of an unlimited company as a limited company the registrar is satisfied that the company is entitled to be so re-registered, the company shall be re-registered accordingly.
(2)   The registrar must issue a certificate of incorporation altered to meet the circumstances of the case.
(3)   The certificate must state that it is issued on re-registration and the date on which it is so issued.
(4)   On the issue of the certificate –
   (a)   the company by virtue of the issue of the certificate becomes a limited company, and
   (b)   the changes in the company's name and articles take effect.
(5)   The certificate is conclusive evidence that the requirements of this Act as to re-registration have been complied with.

108   Statement of capital required where company already has share capital
(1)   A company which on re-registration under section 107 already has allotted share capital must within 15 days after the re-registration deliver a statement of capital to the registrar.
(2)   This does not apply if the information which would be included in the statement has already been sent to the registrar in –
   (a)   a statement of capital and initial shareholdings (see section 10), or
   (b)   a statement of capital contained in an annual return (see section 856(2)).
(3)   The statement of capital must state with respect to the company's share capital on re-registration –
   (a)   the total number of shares of the company,
   (b)   the aggregate nominal value of those shares,
   (c)   for each class of shares –
      (i)   prescribed particulars of the rights attached to the shares,
      (ii)   the total number of shares of that class, and
      (iii) the aggregate nominal value of shares of that class, and
   (d)   the amount paid up and the amount (if any) unpaid on each share (whether on account of the nominal value of the share or by way of premium).

(4)   If default is made in complying with this section, an offence is committed by –
    (a)   the company, and
    (b)   every officer of the company who is in default.

(5)   A person guilty of an offence under this section is liable on summary conviction to a fine not exceeding level 3 on the standard scale and, for continued contravention, a daily default fine not exceeding one-tenth of level 3 on the standard scale.

Public company becoming private and unlimited

109   Re-registration of public company as private and unlimited

(1)   A public company limited by shares may be re-registered as an unlimited private company with a share capital if –
    (a)   all the members of the company have assented to its being so re-registered,
    (b)   the condition specified below is met, and
    (c)   an application for re-registration is delivered to the registrar in accordance with section 110, together with –
        (i)   the other documents required by that section, and
        (ii)   a statement of compliance.

(2)   The condition is that the company has not previously been re-registered –
    (a)   as limited, or
    (b)   as unlimited.

(3)   The company must make such changes –
    (a)   in its name, and
    (b)   in its articles,
as are necessary in connection with its becoming an unlimited private company.

(4)   For the purposes of this section –
    (a)   a trustee in bankruptcy of a member of the company is entitled, to the exclusion of the member, to assent to the company's re-registration; and
    (b)   the personal representative of a deceased member of the company may assent on behalf of the deceased.

(5)   In subsection (4)(a), "a trustee in bankruptcy of a member of the company" includes –
    (a)   a permanent trustee or an interim trustee (within the meaning of the Bankruptcy (Scotland) Act 1985 (c. 66)) on the sequestrated estate of a member of the company;
    (b)   a trustee under a protected trustee deed (within the meaning of the Bankruptcy (Scotland) Act 1985) granted by a member of the company.

110   Application and accompanying documents

(1)   An application for re-registration of a public company as an unlimited private company must contain a statement of the company's proposed name on re-registration.

(2) The application must be accompanied by –
  (a) the prescribed form of assent to the company's being registered as an unlimited company, authenticated by or on behalf of all the members of the company, and
  (b) a copy of the company's articles as proposed to be amended.
(3) The statement of compliance required to be delivered together with the application is a statement that the requirements of this Part as to re-registration as an unlimited private company have been complied with.
(4) The statement must contain a statement by the directors of the company –
  (a) that the persons by whom or on whose behalf the form of assent is authenticated constitute the whole membership of the company, and
  (b) if any of the members have not authenticated that form themselves, that the directors have taken all reasonable steps to satisfy themselves that each person who authenticated it on behalf of a member was lawfully empowered to do so.
(5) The registrar may accept the statement of compliance as sufficient evidence that the company is entitled to be re-registered as an unlimited private company.

111 Issue of certificate of incorporation on re-registration
(1) If on an application for re-registration of a public company as an unlimited private company the registrar is satisfied that the company is entitled to be so re-registered, the company shall be re-registered accordingly.
(2) The registrar must issue a certificate of incorporation altered to meet the circumstances of the case.
(3) The certificate must state that it is issued on re-registration and the date on which it is so issued.
(4) On the issue of the certificate –
  (a) the company by virtue of the issue of the certificate becomes an unlimited private company, and
  (b) the changes in the company's name and articles take effect.
(5) The certificate is conclusive evidence that the requirements of this Act as to re-registration have been complied with.

General duties of directors
Sections 170–259

170 Scope and nature of general duties

(1) The general duties specified in sections 171 to 177 are owed by a director of a company to the company.

(2) A person who ceases to be a director continues to be subject –

    (a) to the duty in section 175 (duty to avoid conflicts of interest) as regards the exploitation of any property, information or opportunity of which he became aware at a time when he was a director, and

    (b) to the duty in section 176 (duty not to accept benefits from third parties) as regards things done or omitted by him before he ceased to be a director.

To that extent those duties apply to a former director as to a director, subject to any necessary adaptations.

(3) The general duties are based on certain common law rules and equitable principles as they apply in relation to directors and have effect in place of those rules and principles as regards the duties owed to a company by a director.

(4) The general duties shall be interpreted and applied in the same way as common law rules or equitable principles, and regard shall be had to the corresponding common law rules and equitable principles in interpreting and applying the general duties.

(5) The general duties apply to shadow directors where, and to the extent that, the corresponding common law rules or equitable principles so apply.

The general duties

171 Duty to act within powers

A director of a company must –

    (a)   act in accordance with the company's constitution, and

    (b)   only exercise powers for the purposes for which they are conferred.

172   Duty to promote the success of the company

(1)   A director of a company must act in the way he considers, in good faith, would be most likely to promote the success of the company for the benefit of its members as a whole, and in doing so have regard (amongst other matters) to –

    (a)   the likely consequences of any decision in the long term,

    (b)   the interests of the company's employees,

    (c)   the need to foster the company's business relationships with suppliers, customers and others,

    (d)   the impact of the company's operations on the community and the environment,

    (e)   the desirability of the company maintaining a reputation for high standards of business conduct, and

    (f)   the need to act fairly as between members of the company.

(2)   Where or to the extent that the purposes of the company consist of or include purposes other than the benefit of its members, subsection (1) has effect as if the reference to promoting the success of the company for the benefit of its members were to achieving those purposes.

(3)   The duty imposed by this section has effect subject to any enactment or rule of law requiring directors, in certain circumstances, to consider or act in the interests of creditors of the company.

173   Duty to exercise independent judgment

(1)   A director of a company must exercise independent judgment.

(2)   This duty is not infringed by his acting –

    (a)   in accordance with an agreement duly entered into by the company that restricts the future exercise of discretion by its directors, or

    (b)   in a way authorised by the company's constitution.

174   Duty to exercise reasonable care, skill and diligence

(1)   A director of a company must exercise reasonable care, skill and diligence.

(2)   This means the care, skill and diligence that would be exercised by a reasonably diligent person with –

    (a)   the general knowledge, skill and experience that may reasonably be expected of a person carrying out the functions carried out by the director in relation to the company, and

    (b)   the general knowledge, skill and experience that the director has.

175   Duty to avoid conflicts of interest

(1)   A director of a company must avoid a situation in which he has, or can have, a direct or indirect interest that conflicts, or possibly may conflict, with the interests of the company.

(2)   This applies in particular to the exploitation of any property, information or opportunity (and it is immaterial whether the company could take advantage of the property, information or opportunity).

(3)   This duty does not apply to a conflict of interest arising in relation to a transaction or arrangement with the company.

(4)   This duty is not infringed –
  (a)   if the situation cannot reasonably be regarded as likely to give rise to a conflict of interest; or
  (b)   if the matter has been authorised by the directors.

(5)   Authorisation may be given by the directors –
  (a)   where the company is a private company and nothing in the company's constitution invalidates such authorisation, by the matter being proposed to and authorised by the directors; or
  (b)   where the company is a public company and its constitution includes provision enabling the directors to authorise the matter, by the matter being proposed to and authorised by them in accordance with the constitution.

(6)   The authorisation is effective only if –
  (a)   any requirement as to the quorum at the meeting at which the matter is considered is met without counting the director in question or any other interested director, and
  (b)   the matter was agreed to without their voting or would have been agreed to if their votes had not been counted.

(7)   Any reference in this section to a conflict of interest includes a conflict of interest and duty and a conflict of duties.

176   Duty not to accept benefits from third parties
  (1)   A director of a company must not accept a benefit from a third party conferred by reason of –
    (a)   his being a director, or
    (b)   his doing (or not doing) anything as director.

  (2)   A "third party" means a person other than the company, an associated body corporate or a person acting on behalf of the company or an associated body corporate.

  (3)   Benefits received by a director from a person by whom his services (as a director or otherwise) are provided to the company are not regarded as conferred by a third party.

  (4)   This duty is not infringed if the acceptance of the benefit cannot reasonably be regarded as likely to give rise to a conflict of interest.

  (5)   Any reference in this section to a conflict of interest includes a conflict of interest and duty and a conflict of duties.

177   Duty to declare interest in proposed transaction or arrangement
  (1)   If a director of a company is in any way, directly or indirectly, interested in a proposed transaction or arrangement with the company, he must declare the nature and extent of that interest to the other directors.

  (2)   The declaration may (but need not) be made –
    (a)   at a meeting of the directors, or
    (b)   by notice to the directors in accordance with –
      (i)   section 184 (notice in writing), or
      (ii)   section 185 (general notice).

(3)   If a declaration of interest under this section proves to be, or becomes, inaccurate or incomplete, a further declaration must be made.

(4)   Any declaration required by this section must be made before the company enters into the transaction or arrangement.

(5)   This section does not require a declaration of an interest of which the director is not aware or where the director is not aware of the transaction or arrangement in question.

For this purpose a director is treated as being aware of matters of which he ought reasonably to be aware.

(6)   A director need not declare an interest –

    (a)   if it cannot reasonably be regarded as likely to give rise to a conflict of interest;

    (b)   if, or to the extent that, the other directors are already aware of it (and for this purpose the other directors are treated as aware of anything of which they ought reasonably to be aware); or

    (c)   if, or to the extent that, it concerns terms of his service contract that have been or are to be considered –

        (i)   by a meeting of the directors, or

        (ii)   by a committee of the directors appointed for the purpose under the company's constitution.

Supplementary provisions

178   Civil consequences of breach of general duties

(1)   The consequences of breach (or threatened breach) of sections 171 to 177 are the same as would apply if the corresponding common law rule or equitable principle applied.

(2)   The duties in those sections (with the exception of section 174 (duty to exercise reasonable care, skill and diligence)) are, accordingly, enforceable in the same way as any other fiduciary duty owed to a company by its directors.

179   Cases within more than one of the general duties

Except as otherwise provided, more than one of the general duties may apply in any given case.

180   Consent, approval or authorisation by members

(1)   In a case where –

    (a)   section 175 (duty to avoid conflicts of interest) is complied with by authorisation by the directors, or

    (b)   section 177 (duty to declare interest in proposed transaction or arrangement) is complied with,

the transaction or arrangement is not liable to be set aside by virtue of any common law rule or equitable principle requiring the consent or approval of the members of the company.

This is without prejudice to any enactment, or provision of the company's constitution, requiring such consent or approval.

(2)   The application of the general duties is not affected by the fact that the case

also falls within Chapter 4 (transactions requiring approval of members), except that where that Chapter applies and –

(a)   approval is given under that Chapter, or

(b)   the matter is one as to which it is provided that approval is not needed,

it is not necessary also to comply with section 175 (duty to avoid conflicts of interest) or section 176 (duty not to accept benefits from third parties).

(3)   Compliance with the general duties does not remove the need for approval under any applicable provision of Chapter 4 (transactions requiring approval of members).

(4)   The general duties –

(a)   have effect subject to any rule of law enabling the company to give authority, specifically or generally, for anything to be done (or omitted) by the directors, or any of them, that would otherwise be a breach of duty, and

(b)   where the company's articles contain provisions for dealing with conflicts of interest, are not infringed by anything done (or omitted) by the directors, or any of them, in accordance with those provisions.

(5)   Otherwise, the general duties have effect (except as otherwise provided or the context otherwise requires) notwithstanding any enactment or rule of law.

181   Modification of provisions in relation to charitable companies

(1)   In their application to a company that is a charity, the provisions of this Chapter have effect subject to this section.

(2)   Section 175 (duty to avoid conflicts of interest) has effect as if –

(a)   for subsection (3) (which disapplies the duty to avoid conflicts of interest in the case of a transaction or arrangement with the company) there were substituted –

"(3)   This duty does not apply to a conflict of interest arising in relation to a transaction or arrangement with the company if or to the extent that the company's articles allow that duty to be so disapplied, which they may do only in relation to descriptions of transaction or arrangement specified in the company's articles.";

(b)   for subsection (5) (which specifies how directors of a company may give authority under that section for a transaction or arrangement) there were substituted –

"(5)   Authorisation may be given by the directors where the company's constitution includes provision enabling them to authorise the matter, by the matter being proposed to and authorised by them in accordance with the constitution.".

(3)   Section 180(2)(b) (which disapplies certain duties under this Chapter in relation to cases excepted from requirement to obtain approval by members under Chapter 4) applies only if or to the extent that the company's articles allow those duties to be so disapplied, which they may do only in relation to descriptions of transaction or arrangement specified in the company's articles.

(4)   After section 26(5) of the Charities Act 1993 (c. 10) (power of Charity Commission to authorise dealings with charity property etc) insert –

"(5A)   In the case of a charity that is a company, an order under this section

> may authorise an act notwithstanding that it involves the breach of a duty imposed on a director of the company under Chapter 2 of Part 10 of the Companies Act 2006 (general duties of directors).".

(5)   This section does not extend to Scotland.

CHAPTER 3

DECLARATION OF INTEREST IN EXISTING TRANSACTION OR ARRANGEMENT

182   Declaration of interest in existing transaction or arrangement

(1)   Where a director of a company is in any way, directly or indirectly, interested in a transaction or arrangement that has been entered into by the company, he must declare the nature and extent of the interest to the other directors in accordance with this section.

This section does not apply if or to the extent that the interest has been declared under section 177 (duty to declare interest in proposed transaction or arrangement).

(2)   The declaration must be made –

    (a)   at a meeting of the directors, or

    (b)   by notice in writing (see section 184), or

    (c)   by general notice (see section 185).

(3)   If a declaration of interest under this section proves to be, or becomes, inaccurate or incomplete, a further declaration must be made.

(4)   Any declaration required by this section must be made as soon as is reasonably practicable.

Failure to comply with this requirement does not affect the underlying duty to make the declaration.

(5)   This section does not require a declaration of an interest of which the director is not aware or where the director is not aware of the transaction or arrangement in question.

For this purpose a director is treated as being aware of matters of which he ought reasonably to be aware.

(6)   A director need not declare an interest under this section –

    (a)   if it cannot reasonably be regarded as likely to give rise to a conflict of interest;

    (b)   if, or to the extent that, the other directors are already aware of it (and for this purpose the other directors are treated as aware of anything of which they ought reasonably to be aware); or

    (c)   if, or to the extent that, it concerns terms of his service contract that have been or are to be considered –

        (i)   by a meeting of the directors, or

        (ii)   by a committee of the directors appointed for the purpose under the company's constitution.

183   Offence of failure to declare interest

(1)   A director who fails to comply with the requirements of section 182 (declaration of interest in existing transaction or arrangement) commits an offence.

(2)   A person guilty of an offence under this section is liable –
   (a)   on conviction on indictment, to a fine;
   (b)   on summary conviction, to a fine not exceeding the statutory maximum.

184   Declaration made by notice in writing
(1)   This section applies to a declaration of interest made by notice in writing.
(2)   The director must send the notice to the other directors.
(3)   The notice may be sent in hard copy form or, if the recipient has agreed to receive it in electronic form, in an agreed electronic form.
(4)   The notice may be sent –
   (a)   by hand or by post, or
   (b)   if the recipient has agreed to receive it by electronic means, by agreed electronic means.
(5)   Where a director declares an interest by notice in writing in accordance with this section –
   (a)   the making of the declaration is deemed to form part of the proceedings at the next meeting of the directors after the notice is given, and
   (b)   the provisions of section 248 (minutes of meetings of directors) apply as if the declaration had been made at that meeting.

185   General notice treated as sufficient declaration
(1)   General notice in accordance with this section is a sufficient declaration of interest in relation to the matters to which it relates.
(2)   General notice is notice given to the directors of a company to the effect that the director –
   (a)   has an interest (as member, officer, employee or otherwise) in a specified body corporate or firm and is to be regarded as interested in any transaction or arrangement that may, after the date of the notice, be made with that body corporate or firm, or
   (b)   is connected with a specified person (other than a body corporate or firm) and is to be regarded as interested in any transaction or arrangement that may, after the date of the notice, be made with that person.
(3)   The notice must state the nature and extent of the director's interest in the body corporate or firm or, as the case may be, the nature of his connection with the person.
(4)   General notice is not effective unless –
   (a)   it is given at a meeting of the directors, or
   (b)   the director takes reasonable steps to secure that it is brought up and read at the next meeting of the directors after it is given.

186   Declaration of interest in case of company with sole director
(1)   Where a declaration of interest under section 182 (duty to declare interest in existing transaction or arrangement) is required of a sole director of a company that is required to have more than one director –
   (a)   the declaration must be recorded in writing,
   (b)   the making of the declaration is deemed to form part of the proceedings at the next meeting of the directors after the notice is given, and

(c)   the provisions of section 248 (minutes of meetings of directors) apply as if the declaration had been made at that meeting.

(2)   Nothing in this section affects the operation of section 231 (contract with sole member who is also a director: terms to be set out in writing or recorded in minutes).

187   Declaration of interest in existing transaction by shadow director

(1)   The provisions of this Chapter relating to the duty under section 182 (duty to declare interest in existing transaction or arrangement) apply to a shadow director as to a director, but with the following adaptations.

(2)   Subsection (2)(a) of that section (declaration at meeting of directors) does not apply.

(3)   In section 185 (general notice treated as sufficient declaration), subsection (4) (notice to be given at or brought up and read at meeting of directors) does not apply.

(4)   General notice by a shadow director is not effective unless given by notice in writing in accordance with section 184.

CHAPTER 4

TRANSACTIONS WITH DIRECTORS REQUIRING APPROVAL OF MEMBERS

Service contracts

188   Directors' long-term service contracts: requirement of members' approval

(1)   This section applies to provision under which the guaranteed term of a director's employment –
   (a)   with the company of which he is a director, or
   (b)   where he is the director of a holding company, within the group consisting of that company and its subsidiaries,
   is, or may be, longer than two years.

(2)   A company may not agree to such provision unless it has been approved –
   (a)   by resolution of the members of the company, and
   (b)   in the case of a director of a holding company, by resolution of the members of that company.

(3)   The guaranteed term of a director's employment is –
   (a)   the period (if any) during which the director's employment –
      (i)   is to continue, or may be continued otherwise than at the instance of the company (whether under the original agreement or under a new agreement entered into in pursuance of it), and
      (ii)   cannot be terminated by the company by notice, or can be so terminated only in specified circumstances, or
   (b)   in the case of employment terminable by the company by notice, the period of notice required to be given,
   or, in the case of employment having a period within paragraph (a) and a period within paragraph (b), the aggregate of those periods.

(4)   If more than six months before the end of the guaranteed term of a director's employment the company enters into a further service contract (otherwise than in pursuance of a right conferred, by or under the original contract, on the other party to it), this section applies as if there were added to the guaranteed term of the new contract the unexpired period of the guaranteed term of the original contract.

(5)   A resolution approving provision to which this section applies must not be passed unless a memorandum setting out the proposed contract incorporating the provision is made available to members –

   (a)   in the case of a written resolution, by being sent or submitted to every eligible member at or before the time at which the proposed resolution is sent or submitted to him;

   (b)   in the case of a resolution at a meeting, by being made available for inspection by members of the company both –

      (i)   at the company's registered office for not less than 15 days ending with the date of the meeting, and

      (ii)   at the meeting itself.

(6)   No approval is required under this section on the part of the members of a body corporate that –

   (a)   is not a UK-registered company, or

   (b)   is a wholly-owned subsidiary of another body corporate.

(7)   In this section "employment" means any employment under a director's service contract.

189   Directors' long-term service contracts: civil consequences of contravention

If a company agrees to provision in contravention of section 188 (directors' long-term service contracts: requirement of members' approval) –

   (a)   the provision is void, to the extent of the contravention, and

   (b)   the contract is deemed to contain a term entitling the company to terminate it at any time by the giving of reasonable notice.

Substantial property transactions

190   Substantial property transactions: requirement of members' approval

(1)   A company may not enter into an arrangement under which –

   (a)   a director of the company or of its holding company, or a person connected with such a director, acquires or is to acquire from the company (directly or indirectly) a substantial non-cash asset, or

   (b)   the company acquires or is to acquire a substantial non-cash asset (directly or indirectly) from such a director or a person so connected,

unless the arrangement has been approved by a resolution of the members of the company or is conditional on such approval being obtained.

For the meaning of "substantial non-cash asset" see section 191.

(2)   If the director or connected person is a director of the company's holding company or a person connected with such a director, the arrangement must also have been approved by a resolution of the members of the holding company or be conditional on such approval being obtained.

(3)   A company shall not be subject to any liability by reason of a failure to obtain approval required by this section.

(4)   No approval is required under this section on the part of the members of a body corporate that –

(a)   is not a UK-registered company, or

(b)   is a wholly-owned subsidiary of another body corporate.

(5)   For the purposes of this section –

(a)   an arrangement involving more than one non-cash asset, or

(b)   an arrangement that is one of a series involving non-cash assets,

shall be treated as if they involved a non-cash asset of a value equal to the aggregate value of all the non-cash assets involved in the arrangement or, as the case may be, the series.

(6)   This section does not apply to a transaction so far as it relates –

(a)   to anything to which a director of a company is entitled under his service contract, or

(b)   to payment for loss of office as defined in section 215 (payments requiring members' approval).

191   Meaning of "substantial"

(1)   This section explains what is meant in section 190 (requirement of approval for substantial property transactions) by a "substantial" non-cash asset.

(2)   An asset is a substantial asset in relation to a company if its value –

(a)   exceeds 10% of the company's asset value and is more than £5,000, or

(b)   exceeds £100,000.

(3)   For this purpose a company's "asset value" at any time is –

(a)   the value of the company's net assets determined by reference to its most recent statutory accounts, or

(b)   if no statutory accounts have been prepared, the amount of the company's called-up share capital.

(4)   A company's "statutory accounts" means its annual accounts prepared in accordance with Part 15, and its "most recent" statutory accounts means those in relation to which the time for sending them out to members (see section 424) is most recent.

(5)   Whether an asset is a substantial asset shall be determined as at the time the arrangement is entered into.

192   Exception for transactions with members or other group companies

Approval is not required under section 190 (requirement of members' approval for substantial property transactions) –

(a)   for a transaction between a company and a person in his character as a member of that company, or

(b)   for a transaction between –

(i)   a holding company and its wholly-owned subsidiary, or

(ii)   two wholly-owned subsidiaries of the same holding company.

193   Exception in case of company in winding up or administration

(1)   This section applies to a company –

      (a)   that is being wound up (unless the winding up is a members' voluntary winding up), or

      (b)   that is in administration within the meaning of Schedule B1 to the Insolvency Act 1986 (c. 45) or the Insolvency (Northern Ireland) Order 1989 (S.I. 1989/2405 (N.I. 19)).

(2)   Approval is not required under section 190 (requirement of members' approval for substantial property transactions) –

      (a)   on the part of the members of a company to which this section applies, or

      (b)   for an arrangement entered into by a company to which this section applies.

194   Exception for transactions on recognised investment exchange

(1)   Approval is not required under section 190 (requirement of members' approval for substantial property transactions) for a transaction on a recognised investment exchange effected by a director, or a person connected with him, through the agency of a person who in relation to the transaction acts as an independent broker.

(2)   For this purpose –

      (a)   "independent broker" means a person who, independently of the director or any person connected with him, selects the person with whom the transaction is to be effected; and

      (b)   "recognised investment exchange" has the same meaning as in Part 18 of the Financial Services and Markets Act 2000 (c. 8).

195   Property transactions: civil consequences of contravention

(1)   This section applies where a company enters into an arrangement in contravention of section 190 (requirement of members' approval for substantial property transactions).

(2)   The arrangement, and any transaction entered into in pursuance of the arrangement (whether by the company or any other person), is voidable at the instance of the company, unless –

      (a)   restitution of any money or other asset that was the subject matter of the arrangement or transaction is no longer possible,

      (b)   the company has been indemnified in pursuance of this section by any other persons for the loss or damage suffered by it, or

      (c)   rights acquired in good faith, for value and without actual notice of the contravention by a person who is not a party to the arrangement or transaction would be affected by the avoidance.

(3)   Whether or not the arrangement or any such transaction has been avoided, each of the persons specified in subsection (4) is liable –

      (a)   to account to the company for any gain that he has made directly or indirectly by the arrangement or transaction, and

      (b)   (jointly and severally with any other person so liable under this section) to indemnify the company for any loss or damage resulting from the arrangement or transaction.

(4)   The persons so liable are –

      (a)   any director of the company or of its holding company with whom the company entered into the arrangement in contravention of section 190,

(b)   any person with whom the company entered into the arrangement in contravention of that section who is connected with a director of the company or of its holding company,

(c)   the director of the company or of its holding company with whom any such person is connected, and

(d)   any other director of the company who authorised the arrangement or any transaction entered into in pursuance of such an arrangement.

(5)   Subsections (3) and (4) are subject to the following two subsections.

(6)   In the case of an arrangement entered into by a company in contravention of section 190 with a person connected with a director of the company or of its holding company, that director is not liable by virtue of subsection (4)(c) if he shows that he took all reasonable steps to secure the company's compliance with that section.

(7)   In any case –

(a)   a person so connected is not liable by virtue of subsection (4)(b), and

(b)   a director is not liable by virtue of subsection (4)(d),

if he shows that, at the time the arrangement was entered into, he did not know the relevant circumstances constituting the contravention.

(8)   Nothing in this section shall be read as excluding the operation of any other enactment or rule of law by virtue of which the arrangement or transaction may be called in question or any liability to the company may arise.

196   Property transactions: effect of subsequent affirmation

Where a transaction or arrangement is entered into by a company in contravention of section 190 (requirement of members' approval) but, within a reasonable period, it is affirmed –

(a)   in the case of a contravention of subsection (1) of that section, by resolution of the members of the company, and

(b)   in the case of a contravention of subsection (2) of that section, by resolution of the members of the holding company,

the transaction or arrangement may no longer be avoided under section 195.

Loans, quasi-loans and credit transactions

197   Loans to directors: requirement of members' approval

(1)   A company may not –

(a)   make a loan to a director of the company or of its holding company, or

(b)   give a guarantee or provide security in connection with a loan made by any person to such a director,

unless the transaction has been approved by a resolution of the members of the company.

(2)   If the director is a director of the company's holding company, the transaction must also have been approved by a resolution of the members of the holding company.

(3)   A resolution approving a transaction to which this section applies must not be passed unless a memorandum setting out the matters mentioned in subsection (4) is made available to members –

    (a)   in the case of a written resolution, by being sent or submitted to every eligible member at or before the time at which the proposed resolution is sent or submitted to him;

    (b)   in the case of a resolution at a meeting, by being made available for inspection by members of the company both –

        (i)   at the company's registered office for not less than 15 days ending with the date of the meeting, and

        (ii)   at the meeting itself.

(4)   The matters to be disclosed are –

    (a)   the nature of the transaction,

    (b)   the amount of the loan and the purpose for which it is required, and

    (c)   the extent of the company's liability under any transaction connected with the loan.

(5)   No approval is required under this section on the part of the members of a body corporate that –

    (a)   is not a UK-registered company, or

    (b)   is a wholly-owned subsidiary of another body corporate.

198   Quasi-loans to directors: requirement of members' approval

(1)   This section applies to a company if it is –

    (a)   a public company, or

    (b)   a company associated with a public company.

(2)   A company to which this section applies may not –

    (a)   make a quasi-loan to a director of the company or of its holding company, or

    (b)   give a guarantee or provide security in connection with a quasi-loan made by any person to such a director,

unless the transaction has been approved by a resolution of the members of the company.

(3)   If the director is a director of the company's holding company, the transaction must also have been approved by a resolution of the members of the holding company.

(4)   A resolution approving a transaction to which this section applies must not be passed unless a memorandum setting out the matters mentioned in subsection (5) is made available to members –

    (a)   in the case of a written resolution, by being sent or submitted to every eligible member at or before the time at which the proposed resolution is sent or submitted to him;

    (b)   in the case of a resolution at a meeting, by being made available for inspection by members of the company both –

        (i)   at the company's registered office for not less than 15 days ending with the date of the meeting, and

        (ii)   at the meeting itself.

(5)   The matters to be disclosed are –

    (a)   the nature of the transaction,

      (b)   the amount of the quasi-loan and the purpose for which it is required, and

      (c)   the extent of the company's liability under any transaction connected with the quasi-loan.

(6)   No approval is required under this section on the part of the members of a body corporate that –

      (a)   is not a UK-registered company, or

      (b)   is a wholly-owned subsidiary of another body corporate.

199   Meaning of "quasi-loan" and related expressions

(1)   A "quasi-loan" is a transaction under which one party ("the creditor") agrees to pay, or pays otherwise than in pursuance of an agreement, a sum for another ("the borrower") or agrees to reimburse, or reimburses otherwise than in pursuance of an agreement, expenditure incurred by another party for another ("the borrower") –

      (a)   on terms that the borrower (or a person on his behalf) will reimburse the creditor; or

      (b)   in circumstances giving rise to a liability on the borrower to reimburse the creditor.

(2)   Any reference to the person to whom a quasi-loan is made is a reference to the borrower.

(3)   The liabilities of the borrower under a quasi-loan include the liabilities of any person who has agreed to reimburse the creditor on behalf of the borrower.

200   Loans or quasi-loans to persons connected with directors: requirement of members' approval

(1)   This section applies to a company if it is –

      (a)   a public company, or

      (b)   a company associated with a public company.

(2)   A company to which this section applies may not –

      (a)   make a loan or quasi-loan to a person connected with a director of the company or of its holding company, or

      (b)   give a guarantee or provide security in connection with a loan or quasi-loan made by any person to a person connected with such a director,

unless the transaction has been approved by a resolution of the members of the company.

(3)   If the connected person is a person connected with a director of the company's holding company, the transaction must also have been approved by a resolution of the members of the holding company.

(4)   A resolution approving a transaction to which this section applies must not be passed unless a memorandum setting out the matters mentioned in subsection (5) is made available to members –

      (a)   in the case of a written resolution, by being sent or submitted to every eligible member at or before the time at which the proposed resolution is sent or submitted to him;

      (b)   in the case of a resolution at a meeting, by being made available for inspection by members of the company both –

  (i)   at the company's registered office for not less than 15 days ending with the date of the meeting, and
  (ii) at the meeting itself.
(5) The matters to be disclosed are –
  (a) the nature of the transaction,
  (b) the amount of the loan or quasi-loan and the purpose for which it is required, and
  (c) the extent of the company's liability under any transaction connected with the loan or quasi-loan.
(6) No approval is required under this section on the part of the members of a body corporate that –
  (a) is not a UK-registered company, or
  (b) is a wholly-owned subsidiary of another body corporate.

201   Credit transactions: requirement of members' approval
(1) This section applies to a company if it is –
  (a) a public company, or
  (b) a company associated with a public company.
(2) A company to which this section applies may not –
  (a) enter into a credit transaction as creditor for the benefit of a director of the company or of its holding company, or a person connected with such a director, or
  (b) give a guarantee or provide security in connection with a credit transaction entered into by any person for the benefit of such a director, or a person connected with such a director,
  unless the transaction (that is, the credit transaction, the giving of the guarantee or the provision of security, as the case may be) has been approved by a resolution of the members of the company.
(3) If the director or connected person is a director of its holding company or a person connected with such a director, the transaction must also have been approved by a resolution of the members of the holding company.
(4) A resolution approving a transaction to which this section applies must not be passed unless a memorandum setting out the matters mentioned in subsection (5) is made available to members –
  (a) in the case of a written resolution, by being sent or submitted to every eligible member at or before the time at which the proposed resolution is sent or submitted to him;
  (b) in the case of a resolution at a meeting, by being made available for inspection by members of the company both –
    (i)   at the company's registered office for not less than 15 days ending with the date of the meeting, and
    (ii) at the meeting itself.
(5) The matters to be disclosed are –
  (a) the nature of the transaction,
  (b) the value of the credit transaction and the purpose for which the land, goods or services sold or otherwise disposed of, leased, hired or supplied under the credit transaction are required, and

       (c)   the extent of the company's liability under any transaction connected with the credit transaction.

(6)   No approval is required under this section on the part of the members of a body corporate that –

       (a)   is not a UK-registered company, or

       (b)   is a wholly-owned subsidiary of another body corporate.

202   Meaning of "credit transaction"

(1)   A "credit transaction" is a transaction under which one party ("the creditor") –

       (a)   supplies any goods or sells any land under a hire-purchase agreement or a conditional sale agreement,

       (b)   leases or hires any land or goods in return for periodical payments, or

       (c)   otherwise disposes of land or supplies goods or services on the understanding that payment (whether in a lump sum or instalments or by way of periodical payments or otherwise) is to be deferred.

(2)   Any reference to the person for whose benefit a credit transaction is entered into is to the person to whom goods, land or services are supplied, sold, leased, hired or otherwise disposed of under the transaction.

(3)   In this section –

          "conditional sale agreement" has the same meaning as in the Consumer Credit Act 1974 (c. 39); and

          "services" means anything other than goods or land.

203   Related arrangements: requirement of members' approval

(1)   A company may not –

       (a)   take part in an arrangement under which –

            (i)   another person enters into a transaction that, if it had been entered into by the company, would have required approval under section 197, 198, 200 or 201, and

            (ii)   that person, in pursuance of the arrangement, obtains a benefit from the company or a body corporate associated with it, or

       (b)   arrange for the assignment to it, or assumption by it, of any rights, obligations or liabilities under a transaction that, if it had been entered into by the company, would have required such approval,

unless the arrangement in question has been approved by a resolution of the members of the company.

(2)   If the director or connected person for whom the transaction is entered into is a director of its holding company or a person connected with such a director, the arrangement must also have been approved by a resolution of the members of the holding company.

(3)   A resolution approving an arrangement to which this section applies must not be passed unless a memorandum setting out the matters mentioned in subsection (4) is made available to members –

       (a)   in the case of a written resolution, by being sent or submitted to every eligible member at or before the time at which the proposed resolution is sent or submitted to him;

       (b)   in the case of a resolution at a meeting, by being made available for inspection by members of the company both –

        (i)   at the company's registered office for not less than 15 days ending with the date of the meeting, and

        (ii)   at the meeting itself.

(4)   The matters to be disclosed are –

    (a)   the matters that would have to be disclosed if the company were seeking approval of the transaction to which the arrangement relates,

    (b)   the nature of the arrangement, and

    (c)   the extent of the company's liability under the arrangement or any transaction connected with it.

(5)   No approval is required under this section on the part of the members of a body corporate that –

    (a)   is not a UK-registered company, or

    (b)   is a wholly-owned subsidiary of another body corporate.

(6)   In determining for the purposes of this section whether a transaction is one that would have required approval under section 197, 198, 200 or 201 if it had been entered into by the company, the transaction shall be treated as having been entered into on the date of the arrangement.

204   Exception for expenditure on company business

(1)   Approval is not required under section 197, 198, 200 or 201 (requirement of members' approval for loans etc) for anything done by a company –

    (a)   to provide a director of the company or of its holding company, or a person connected with any such director, with funds to meet expenditure incurred or to be incurred by him –

        (i)   for the purposes of the company, or

        (ii)   for the purpose of enabling him properly to perform his duties as an officer of the company, or

    (b)   to enable any such person to avoid incurring such expenditure.

(2)   This section does not authorise a company to enter into a transaction if the aggregate of –

    (a)   the value of the transaction in question, and

    (b)   the value of any other relevant transactions or arrangements,

exceeds £50,000.

205   Exception for expenditure on defending proceedings etc

(1)   Approval is not required under section 197, 198, 200 or 201 (requirement of members' approval for loans etc) for anything done by a company –

    (a)   to provide a director of the company or of its holding company with funds to meet expenditure incurred or to be incurred by him –

        (i)   in defending any criminal or civil proceedings in connection with any alleged negligence, default, breach of duty or breach of trust by him in relation to the company or an associated company, or

        (ii)   in connection with an application for relief (see subsection (5)), or

    (b)   to enable any such director to avoid incurring such expenditure, if it is done on the following terms.

(2)   The terms are –

(a) that the loan is to be repaid, or (as the case may be) any liability of the company incurred under any transaction connected with the thing done is to be discharged, in the event of –

    (i) the director being convicted in the proceedings,

    (ii) judgment being given against him in the proceedings, or

    (iii) the court refusing to grant him relief on the application; and

(b) that it is to be so repaid or discharged not later than –

    (i) the date when the conviction becomes final,

    (ii) the date when the judgment becomes final, or

    (iii) the date when the refusal of relief becomes final.

(3) For this purpose a conviction, judgment or refusal of relief becomes final –

    (a) if not appealed against, at the end of the period for bringing an appeal;

    (b) if appealed against, when the appeal (or any further appeal) is disposed of.

(4) An appeal is disposed of –

    (a) if it is determined and the period for bringing any further appeal has ended, or

    (b) if it is abandoned or otherwise ceases to have effect.

(5) The reference in subsection (1)(a)(ii) to an application for relief is to an application for relief under –

    section 661(3) or (4) (power of court to grant relief in case of acquisition of shares by innocent nominee), or

    section 1157 (general power of court to grant relief in case of honest and reasonable conduct).

206   Exception for expenditure in connection with regulatory action or investigation

Approval is not required under section 197, 198, 200 or 201 (requirement of members' approval for loans etc) for anything done by a company –

(a) to provide a director of the company or of its holding company with funds to meet expenditure incurred or to be incurred by him in defending himself –

    (i) in an investigation by a regulatory authority, or

    (ii) against action proposed to be taken by a regulatory authority,

in connection with any alleged negligence, default, breach of duty or breach of trust by him in relation to the company or an associated company, or

(b) to enable any such director to avoid incurring such expenditure.

207   Exceptions for minor and business transactions

(1) Approval is not required under section 197, 198 or 200 for a company to make a loan or quasi-loan, or to give a guarantee or provide security in connection with a loan or quasi-loan, if the aggregate of –

    (a) the value of the transaction, and

    (b) the value of any other relevant transactions or arrangements,

does not exceed £10,000.

(2) Approval is not required under section 201 for a company to enter into a

credit transaction, or to give a guarantee or provide security in connection with a credit transaction, if the aggregate of –
  (a) the value of the transaction (that is, of the credit transaction, guarantee or security), and
  (b) the value of any other relevant transactions or arrangements
does not exceed £15,000.

(3) Approval is not required under section 201 for a company to enter into a credit transaction, or to give a guarantee or provide security in connection with a credit transaction, if –
  (a) the transaction is entered into by the company in the ordinary course of the company's business, and
  (b) the value of the transaction is not greater, and the terms on which it is entered into are not more favourable, than it is reasonable to expect the company would have offered to, or in respect of, a person of the same financial standing but unconnected with the company.

208   Exceptions for intra-group transactions

(1) Approval is not required under section 197, 198 or 200 for –
  (a) the making of a loan or quasi-loan to an associated body corporate, or
  (b) the giving of a guarantee or provision of security in connection with a loan or quasi-loan made to an associated body corporate.
(2) Approval is not required under section 201 –
  (a) to enter into a credit transaction as creditor for the benefit of an associated body corporate, or
  (b) to give a guarantee or provide security in connection with a credit transaction entered into by any person for the benefit of an associated body corporate.

209   Exceptions for money-lending companies

(1) Approval is not required under section 197, 198 or 200 for the making of a loan or quasi-loan, or the giving of a guarantee or provision of security in connection with a loan or quasi-loan, by a money-lending company if –
  (a) the transaction (that is, the loan, quasi-loan, guarantee or security) is entered into by the company in the ordinary course of the company's business, and
  (b) the value of the transaction is not greater, and its terms are not more favourable, than it is reasonable to expect the company would have offered to a person of the same financial standing but unconnected with the company.
(2) A "money-lending company" means a company whose ordinary business includes the making of loans or quasi-loans, or the giving of guarantees or provision of security in connection with loans or quasi-loans.
(3) The condition specified in subsection (1)(b) does not of itself prevent a company from making a home loan –
  (a) to a director of the company or of its holding company, or
  (b) to an employee of the company,
if loans of that description are ordinarily made by the company to its

employees and the terms of the loan in question are no more favourable than those on which such loans are ordinarily made.

(4)   For the purposes of subsection (3) a "home loan" means a loan –

    (a)   for the purpose of facilitating the purchase, for use as the only or main residence of the person to whom the loan is made, of the whole or part of any dwelling-house together with any land to be occupied and enjoyed with it,

    (b)   for the purpose of improving a dwelling-house or part of a dwelling-house so used or any land occupied and enjoyed with it, or

    (c)   in substitution for any loan made by any person and falling within paragraph (a) or (b).

210   Other relevant transactions or arrangements

(1)   This section has effect for determining what are "other relevant transactions or arrangements" for the purposes of any exception to section 197, 198, 200 or 201. In the following provisions "the relevant exception" means the exception for the purposes of which that falls to be determined.

(2)   Other relevant transactions or arrangements are those previously entered into, or entered into at the same time as the transaction or arrangement in question in relation to which the following conditions are met.

(3)   Where the transaction or arrangement in question is entered into –

    (a)   for a director of the company entering into it, or

    (b)   for a person connected with such a director,

the conditions are that the transaction or arrangement was (or is) entered into for that director, or a person connected with him, by virtue of the relevant exception by that company or by any of its subsidiaries.

(4)   Where the transaction or arrangement in question is entered into –

    (a)   for a director of the holding company of the company entering into it, or

    (b)   for a person connected with such a director,

the conditions are that the transaction or arrangement was (or is) entered into for that director, or a person connected with him, by virtue of the relevant exception by the holding company or by any of its subsidiaries.

(5)   A transaction or arrangement entered into by a company that at the time it was entered into –

    (a)   was a subsidiary of the company entering into the transaction or arrangement in question, or

    (b)   was a subsidiary of that company's holding company,

is not a relevant transaction or arrangement if, at the time the question arises whether the transaction or arrangement in question falls within a relevant exception, it is no longer such a subsidiary.

211   The value of transactions and arrangements

(1)   For the purposes of sections 197 to 214 (loans etc) –

    (a)   the value of a transaction or arrangement is determined as follows, and

    (b)   the value of any other relevant transaction or arrangement is taken to be the value so determined reduced by any amount by which the liabilities of the person for whom the transaction or arrangement was made have been reduced.

(2)   The value of a loan is the amount of its principal.

(3)   The value of a quasi-loan is the amount, or maximum amount, that the person to whom the quasi-loan is made is liable to reimburse the creditor.

(4)   The value of a credit transaction is the price that it is reasonable to expect could be obtained for the goods, services or land to which the transaction relates if they had been supplied (at the time the transaction is entered into) in the ordinary course of business and on the same terms (apart from price) as they have been supplied, or are to be supplied, under the transaction in question.

(5)   The value of a guarantee or security is the amount guaranteed or secured.

(6)   The value of an arrangement to which section 203 (related arrangements) applies is the value of the transaction to which the arrangement relates.

(7)   If the value of a transaction or arrangement is not capable of being expressed as a specific sum of money –

(a)   whether because the amount of any liability arising under the transaction or arrangement is unascertainable, or for any other reason, and

(b)   whether or not any liability under the transaction or arrangement has been reduced,

its value is deemed to exceed £50,000.

212   The person for whom a transaction or arrangement is entered into

For the purposes of sections 197 to 214 (loans etc) the person for whom a transaction or arrangement is entered into is –

(a)   in the case of a loan or quasi-loan, the person to whom it is made;

(b)   in the case of a credit transaction, the person to whom goods, land or services are supplied, sold, hired, leased or otherwise disposed of under the transaction;

(c)   in the case of a guarantee or security, the person for whom the transaction is made in connection with which the guarantee or security is entered into;

(d)   in the case of an arrangement within section 203 (related arrangements), the person for whom the transaction is made to which the arrangement relates.

213   Loans etc: civil consequences of contravention

(1)   This section applies where a company enters into a transaction or arrangement in contravention of section 197, 198, 200, 201 or 203 (requirement of members' approval for loans etc).

(2)   The transaction or arrangement is voidable at the instance of the company, unless –

(a)   restitution of any money or other asset that was the subject matter of the transaction or arrangement is no longer possible,

(b)   the company has been indemnified for any loss or damage resulting from the transaction or arrangement, or

(c)   rights acquired in good faith, for value and without actual notice of the contravention by a person who is not a party to the transaction or arrangement would be affected by the avoidance.

(3)   Whether or not the transaction or arrangement has been avoided, each of the persons specified in subsection (4) is liable –
    (a)   to account to the company for any gain that he has made directly or indirectly by the transaction or arrangement, and
    (b)   (jointly and severally with any other person so liable under this section) to indemnify the company for any loss or damage resulting from the transaction or arrangement.

(4)   The persons so liable are –
    (a)   any director of the company or of its holding company with whom the company entered into the transaction or arrangement in contravention of section 197, 198, 201 or 203,
    (b)   any person with whom the company entered into the transaction or arrangement in contravention of any of those sections who is connected with a director of the company or of its holding company,
    (c)   the director of the company or of its holding company with whom any such person is connected, and
    (d)   any other director of the company who authorised the transaction or arrangement.

(5)   Subsections (3) and (4) are subject to the following two subsections.

(6)   In the case of a transaction or arrangement entered into by a company in contravention of section 200, 201 or 203 with a person connected with a director of the company or of its holding company, that director is not liable by virtue of subsection (4)(c) if he shows that he took all reasonable steps to secure the company's compliance with the section concerned.

(7)   In any case –
    (a)   a person so connected is not liable by virtue of subsection (4)(b), and
    (b)   a director is not liable by virtue of subsection (4)(d),
if he shows that, at the time the transaction or arrangement was entered into, he did not know the relevant circumstances constituting the contravention.

(8)   Nothing in this section shall be read as excluding the operation of any other enactment or rule of law by virtue of which the transaction or arrangement may be called in question or any liability to the company may arise.

214   Loans etc: effect of subsequent affirmation

Where a transaction or arrangement is entered into by a company in contravention of section 197, 198, 200, 201 or 203 (requirement of members' approval for loans etc) but, within a reasonable period, it is affirmed –
    (a)   in the case of a contravention of the requirement for a resolution of the members of the company, by a resolution of the members of the company, and
    (b)   in the case of a contravention of the requirement for a resolution of the members of the company's holding company, by a resolution of the members of the holding company,
the transaction or arrangement may no longer be avoided under section 213.

Payments for loss of office

215   Payments for loss of office

(1)   In this Chapter a "payment for loss of office" means a payment made to a director or past director of a company –

   (a)   by way of compensation for loss of office as director of the company,

   (b)   by way of compensation for loss, while director of the company or in connection with his ceasing to be a director of it, of –

      (i)   any other office or employment in connection with the management of the affairs of the company, or

      (ii)   any office (as director or otherwise) or employment in connection with the management of the affairs of any subsidiary undertaking of the company,

   (c)   as consideration for or in connection with his retirement from his office as director of the company, or

   (d)   as consideration for or in connection with his retirement, while director of the company or in connection with his ceasing to be a director of it, from –

      (i)   any other office or employment in connection with the management of the affairs of the company, or

      (ii)   any office (as director or otherwise) or employment in connection with the management of the affairs of any subsidiary undertaking of the company.

(2)   The references to compensation and consideration include benefits otherwise than in cash and references in this Chapter to payment have a corresponding meaning.

(3)   For the purposes of sections 217 to 221 (payments requiring members' approval) –

   (a)   payment to a person connected with a director, or

   (b)   payment to any person at the direction of, or for the benefit of, a director or a person connected with him,

is treated as payment to the director.

(4)   References in those sections to payment by a person include payment by another person at the direction of, or on behalf of, the person referred to.

216   Amounts taken to be payments for loss of office

(1)   This section applies where in connection with any such transfer as is mentioned in section 218 or 219 (payment in connection with transfer of undertaking, property or shares) a director of the company –

   (a)   is to cease to hold office, or

   (b)   is to cease to be the holder of –

      (i)   any other office or employment in connection with the management of the affairs of the company, or

      (ii)   any office (as director or otherwise) or employment in connection with the management of the affairs of any subsidiary undertaking of the company.

(2)   If in connection with any such transfer –

(a) the price to be paid to the director for any shares in the company held by him is in excess of the price which could at the time have been obtained by other holders of like shares, or

(b) any valuable consideration is given to the director by a person other than the company,

the excess or, as the case may be, the money value of the consideration is taken for the purposes of those sections to have been a payment for loss of office.

217   Payment by company: requirement of members' approval

(1) A company may not make a payment for loss of office to a director of the company unless the payment has been approved by a resolution of the members of the company.

(2) A company may not make a payment for loss of office to a director of its holding company unless the payment has been approved by a resolution of the members of each of those companies.

(3) A resolution approving a payment to which this section applies must not be passed unless a memorandum setting out particulars of the proposed payment (including its amount) is made available to the members of the company whose approval is sought –

(a) in the case of a written resolution, by being sent or submitted to every eligible member at or before the time at which the proposed resolution is sent or submitted to him;

(b) in the case of a resolution at a meeting, by being made available for inspection by the members both –

(i) at the company's registered office for not less than 15 days ending with the date of the meeting, and

(ii) at the meeting itself.

(4) No approval is required under this section on the part of the members of a body corporate that –

(a) is not a UK-registered company, or

(b) is a wholly-owned subsidiary of another body corporate.

218   Payment in connection with transfer of undertaking etc: requirement of members' approval

(1) No payment for loss of office may be made by any person to a director of a company in connection with the transfer of the whole or any part of the undertaking or property of the company unless the payment has been approved by a resolution of the members of the company.

(2) No payment for loss of office may be made by any person to a director of a company in connection with the transfer of the whole or any part of the undertaking or property of a subsidiary of the company unless the payment has been approved by a resolution of the members of each of the companies.

(3) A resolution approving a payment to which this section applies must not be passed unless a memorandum setting out particulars of the proposed payment (including its amount) is made available to the members of the company whose approval is sought –

(a) in the case of a written resolution, by being sent or submitted to every eligible member at or before the time at which the proposed resolution is sent or submitted to him;

   (b)   in the case of a resolution at a meeting, by being made available for inspection by the members both –

      (i)   at the company's registered office for not less than 15 days ending with the date of the meeting, and

      (ii)   at the meeting itself.

(4)   No approval is required under this section on the part of the members of a body corporate that –

   (a)   is not a UK-registered company, or

   (b)   is a wholly-owned subsidiary of another body corporate.

(5)   A payment made in pursuance of an arrangement –

   (a)   entered into as part of the agreement for the transfer in question, or within one year before or two years after that agreement, and

   (b)   to which the company whose undertaking or property is transferred, or any person to whom the transfer is made, is privy,

is presumed, except in so far as the contrary is shown, to be a payment to which this section applies.

219   Payment in connection with share transfer: requirement of members' approval

(1)   No payment for loss of office may be made by any person to a director of a company in connection with a transfer of shares in the company, or in a subsidiary of the company, resulting from a takeover bid unless the payment has been approved by a resolution of the relevant shareholders.

(2)   The relevant shareholders are the holders of the shares to which the bid relates and any holders of shares of the same class as any of those shares.

(3)   A resolution approving a payment to which this section applies must not be passed unless a memorandum setting out particulars of the proposed payment (including its amount) is made available to the members of the company whose approval is sought –

   (a)   in the case of a written resolution, by being sent or submitted to every eligible member at or before the time at which the proposed resolution is sent or submitted to him;

   (b)   in the case of a resolution at a meeting, by being made available for inspection by the members both –

      (i)   at the company's registered office for not less than 15 days ending with the date of the meeting, and

      (ii)   at the meeting itself.

(4)   Neither the person making the offer, nor any associate of his (as defined in section 988), is entitled to vote on the resolution, but –

   (a)   where the resolution is proposed as a written resolution, they are entitled (if they would otherwise be so entitled) to be sent a copy of it, and

   (b)   at any meeting to consider the resolution they are entitled (if they would otherwise be so entitled) to be given notice of the meeting, to attend and speak and if present (in person or by proxy) to count towards the quorum.

(5)   If at a meeting to consider the resolution a quorum is not present, and after

the meeting has been adjourned to a later date a quorum is again not present, the payment is (for the purposes of this section) deemed to have been approved.

(6) No approval is required under this section on the part of shareholders in a body corporate that –
   (a) is not a UK-registered company, or
   (b) is a wholly-owned subsidiary of another body corporate.

(7) A payment made in pursuance of an arrangement –
   (a) entered into as part of the agreement for the transfer in question, or within one year before or two years after that agreement, and
   (b) to which the company whose shares are the subject of the bid, or any person to whom the transfer is made, is privy,

is presumed, except in so far as the contrary is shown, to be a payment to which this section applies.

220 Exception for payments in discharge of legal obligations etc

(1) Approval is not required under section 217, 218 or 219 (payments requiring members' approval) for a payment made in good faith –
   (a) in discharge of an existing legal obligation (as defined below),
   (b) by way of damages for breach of such an obligation,
   (c) by way of settlement or compromise of any claim arising in connection with the termination of a person's office or employment, or
   (d) by way of pension in respect of past services.

(2) In relation to a payment within section 217 (payment by company) an existing legal obligation means an obligation of the company, or any body corporate associated with it, that was not entered into in connection with, or in consequence of, the event giving rise to the payment for loss of office.

(3) In relation to a payment within section 218 or 219 (payment in connection with transfer of undertaking, property or shares) an existing legal obligation means an obligation of the person making the payment that was not entered into for the purposes of, in connection with or in consequence of, the transfer in question.

(4) In the case of a payment within both section 217 and section 218, or within both section 217 and section 219, subsection (2) above applies and not subsection (3).

(5) A payment part of which falls within subsection (1) above and part of which does not is treated as if the parts were separate payments.

221 Exception for small payments

(1) Approval is not required under section 217, 218 or 219 (payments requiring members' approval) if –
   (a) the payment in question is made by the company or any of its subsidiaries, and
   (b) the amount or value of the payment, together with the amount or value of any other relevant payments, does not exceed £200.

(2) For this purpose "other relevant payments" are payments for loss of office in relation to which the following conditions are met.

(3) Where the payment in question is one to which section 217 (payment by company) applies, the conditions are that the other payment was or is paid –

- (a)   by the company making the payment in question or any of its subsidiaries,
- (b)   to the director to whom that payment is made, and
- (c)   in connection with the same event.
- (4)   Where the payment in question is one to which section 218 or 219 applies (payment in connection with transfer of undertaking, property or shares), the conditions are that the other payment was (or is) paid in connection with the same transfer –
  - (a)   to the director to whom the payment in question was made, and
  - (b)   by the company making the payment or any of its subsidiaries.

222   Payments made without approval: civil consequences

- (1)   If a payment is made in contravention of section 217 (payment by company) –
  - (a)   it is held by the recipient on trust for the company making the payment, and
  - (b)   any director who authorised the payment is jointly and severally liable to indemnify the company that made the payment for any loss resulting from it.
- (2)   If a payment is made in contravention of section 218 (payment in connection with transfer of undertaking etc), it is held by the recipient on trust for the company whose undertaking or property is or is proposed to be transferred.
- (3)   If a payment is made in contravention of section 219 (payment in connection with share transfer) –
  - (a)   it is held by the recipient on trust for persons who have sold their shares as a result of the offer made, and
  - (b)   the expenses incurred by the recipient in distributing that sum amongst those persons shall be borne by him and not retained out of that sum.
- (4)   If a payment is in contravention of section 217 and section 218, subsection (2) of this section applies rather than subsection (1).
- (5)   If a payment is in contravention of section 217 and section 219, subsection (3) of this section applies rather than subsection (1), unless the court directs otherwise.

Supplementary

223   Transactions requiring members' approval: application of provisions to shadow directors

- (1)   For the purposes of –
  - (a)   sections 188 and 189 (directors' service contracts),
  - (b)   sections 190 to 196 (property transactions),
  - (c)   sections 197 to 214 (loans etc), and
  - (d)   sections 215 to 222 (payments for loss of office),
  a shadow director is treated as a director.
- (2)   Any reference in those provisions to loss of office as a director does not apply in relation to loss of a person's status as a shadow director.

224   Approval by written resolution: accidental failure to send memorandum
(1)   Where –
   (a)   approval under this Chapter is sought by written resolution, and
   (b)   a memorandum is required under this Chapter to be sent or submitted to every eligible member before the resolution is passed, any accidental failure to send or submit the memorandum to one or more members shall be disregarded for the purpose of determining whether the requirement has been met.
(2)   Subsection (1) has effect subject to any provision of the company's articles.

225   Cases where approval is required under more than one provision
(1)   Approval may be required under more than one provision of this Chapter.
(2)   If so, the requirements of each applicable provision must be met.
(3)   This does not require a separate resolution for the purposes of each provision.

226   Requirement of consent of Charity Commission: companies that are charities
   For section 66 of the Charities Act 1993 (c. 10) substitute –
   "66   Consent of Commission required for approval etc by members of charitable companies
   (1)   Where a company is a charity –
      (a)   any approval given by the members of the company under any provision of Chapter 4 of Part 10 of the Companies Act 2006 (transactions with directors requiring approval by members) listed in subsection (2) below, and
      (b)   any affirmation given by members of the company under section 196 or 214 of that Act (affirmation of unapproved property transactions and loans),
      is ineffective without the prior written consent of the Commission.
   (2)   The provisions are –
      (a)   section 188 (directors' long-term service contracts);
      (b)   section 190 (substantial property transactions with directors etc);
      (c)   section 197, 198 or 200 (loans and quasi-loans to directors etc);
      (d)   section 201 (credit transactions for benefit of directors etc);
      (e)   section 203 (related arrangements);
      (f)   section 217 (payments to directors for loss of office);
      (g)   section 218 (payments to directors for loss of office: transfer of undertaking etc).
   66A   Consent of Commission required for certain acts of charitable company
   (1)   A company that is a charity may not do an act to which this section applies without the prior written consent of the Commission.
   (2)   This section applies to an act that –
      (a)   does not require approval under a listed provision of Chapter 4 of Part 10 of the Companies Act 2006 (transactions with directors) by the members of the company, but
      (b)   would require such approval but for an exemption in the provision in question that disapplies the need for approval on the

part of the members of a body corporate which is a wholly-owned subsidiary of another body corporate.

(3) The reference to a listed provision is a reference to a provision listed in section 66(2) above.

(4) If a company acts in contravention of this section, the exemption referred to in subsection (2)(b) shall be treated as of no effect in relation to the act.".

CHAPTER 5

DIRECTORS' SERVICE CONTRACTS

227 Directors' service contracts

(1) For the purposes of this Part a director's "service contract", in relation to a company, means a contract under which –

    (a) a director of the company undertakes personally to perform services (as director or otherwise) for the company, or for a subsidiary of the company, or

    (b) services (as director or otherwise) that a director of the company undertakes personally to perform are made available by a third party to the company, or to a subsidiary of the company.

(2) The provisions of this Part relating to directors' service contracts apply to the terms of a person's appointment as a director of a company.

They are not restricted to contracts for the performance of services outside the scope of the ordinary duties of a director.

228 Copy of contract or memorandum of terms to be available for inspection

(1) A company must keep available for inspection –

    (a) a copy of every director's service contract with the company or with a subsidiary of the company, or

    (b) if the contract is not in writing, a written memorandum setting out the terms of the contract.

(2) All the copies and memoranda must be kept available for inspection at –

    (a) the company's registered office, or

    (b) a place specified in regulations under section 1136.

(3) The copies and memoranda must be retained by the company for at least one year from the date of termination or expiry of the contract and must be kept available for inspection during that time.

(4) The company must give notice to the registrar –

    (a) of the place at which the copies and memoranda are kept available for inspection, and

    (b) of any change in that place,

unless they have at all times been kept at the company's registered office.

(5) If default is made in complying with subsection (1), (2) or (3), or default is made for 14 days in complying with subsection (4), an offence is committed by every officer of the company who is in default.

(6) A person guilty of an offence under this section is liable on summary conviction

to a fine not exceeding level 3 on the standard scale and, for continued contravention, a daily default fine not exceeding one-tenth of level 3 on the standard scale.

(7)   The provisions of this section apply to a variation of a director's service contract as they apply to the original contract.

229   Right of member to inspect and request copy

(1)   Every copy or memorandum required to be kept under section 228 must be open to inspection by any member of the company without charge.

(2)   Any member of the company is entitled, on request and on payment of such fee as may be prescribed, to be provided with a copy of any such copy or memorandum.
The copy must be provided within seven days after the request is received by the company.

(3)   If an inspection required under subsection (1) is refused, or default is made in complying with subsection (2), an offence is committed by every officer of the company who is in default.

(4)   A person guilty of an offence under this section is liable on summary conviction to a fine not exceeding level 3 on the standard scale and, for continued contravention, a daily default fine not exceeding one-tenth of level 3 on the standard scale.

(5)   In the case of any such refusal or default the court may by order compel an immediate inspection or, as the case may be, direct that the copy required be sent to the person requiring it.

230   Directors' service contracts: application of provisions to shadow directors

A shadow director is treated as a director for the purposes of the provisions of this Chapter.

CHAPTER 6

CONTRACTS WITH SOLE MEMBERS WHO ARE DIRECTORS

231   Contract with sole member who is also a director

(1)   This section applies where –
   (a)   a limited company having only one member enters into a contract with the sole member,
   (b)   the sole member is also a director of the company, and
   (c)   the contract is not entered into in the ordinary course of the company's business.

(2)   The company must, unless the contract is in writing, ensure that the terms of the contract are either –
   (a)   set out in a written memorandum, or
   (b)   recorded in the minutes of the first meeting of the directors of the company following the making of the contract.

(3)   If a company fails to comply with this section an offence is committed by every officer of the company who is in default.

(4)   A person guilty of an offence under this section is liable on summary conviction to a fine not exceeding level 5 on the standard scale.

(5)   For the purposes of this section a shadow director is treated as a director.

(6)   Failure to comply with this section in relation to a contract does not affect the validity of the contract.

(7)   Nothing in this section shall be read as excluding the operation of any other enactment or rule of law applying to contracts between a company and a director of the company.

CHAPTER 7

DIRECTORS' LIABILITIES

Provision protecting directors from liability

232   Provisions protecting directors from liability

(1)   Any provision that purports to exempt a director of a company (to any extent) from any liability that would otherwise attach to him in connection with any negligence, default, breach of duty or breach of trust in relation to the company is void.

(2)   Any provision by which a company directly or indirectly provides an indemnity (to any extent) for a director of the company, or of an associated company, against any liability attaching to him in connection with any negligence, default, breach of duty or breach of trust in relation to the company of which he is a director is void, except as permitted by –

    (a)   section 233 (provision of insurance),

    (b)   section 234 (qualifying third party indemnity provision), or

    (c)   section 235 (qualifying pension scheme indemnity provision).

(3)   This section applies to any provision, whether contained in a company's articles or in any contract with the company or otherwise.

(4)   Nothing in this section prevents a company's articles from making such provision as has previously been lawful for dealing with conflicts of interest.

233   Provision of insurance

Section 232(2) (voidness of provisions for indemnifying directors) does not prevent a company from purchasing and maintaining for a director of the company, or of an associated company, insurance against any such liability as is mentioned in that subsection.

234   Qualifying third party indemnity provision

(1)   Section 232(2) (voidness of provisions for indemnifying directors) does not apply to qualifying third party indemnity provision.

(2)   Third party indemnity provision means provision for indemnity against liability incurred by the director to a person other than the company or an associated company.

Such provision is qualifying third party indemnity provision if the following requirements are met.

(3)   The provision must not provide any indemnity against –
     (a)   any liability of the director to pay –
         (i)   a fine imposed in criminal proceedings, or
         (ii)   a sum payable to a regulatory authority by way of a penalty in respect of non-compliance with any requirement of a regulatory nature (however arising); or
     (b)   any liability incurred by the director –
         (i)   in defending criminal proceedings in which he is convicted, or
         (ii)   in defending civil proceedings brought by the company, or an associated company, in which judgment is given against him, or
         (iii)   in connection with an application for relief (see subsection (6)) in which the court refuses to grant him relief.

(4)   The references in subsection (3)(b) to a conviction, judgment or refusal of relief are to the final decision in the proceedings.

(5)   For this purpose –
     (a)   a conviction, judgment or refusal of relief becomes final –
         (i)   if not appealed against, at the end of the period for bringing an appeal, or
         (ii)   if appealed against, at the time when the appeal (or any further appeal) is disposed of; and
     (b)   an appeal is disposed of –
         (i)   if it is determined and the period for bringing any further appeal has ended, or
         (ii)   if it is abandoned or otherwise ceases to have effect.

(6)   The reference in subsection (3)(b)(iii) to an application for relief is to an application for relief under –
     section 661(3) or (4) (power of court to grant relief in case of acquisition of shares by innocent nominee), or
     section 1157 (general power of court to grant relief in case of honest and reasonable conduct).

235   Qualifying pension scheme indemnity provision

(1)   Section 232(2) (voidness of provisions for indemnifying directors) does not apply to qualifying pension scheme indemnity provision.

(2)   Pension scheme indemnity provision means provision indemnifying a director of a company that is a trustee of an occupational pension scheme against liability incurred in connection with the company's activities as trustee of the scheme.
Such provision is qualifying pension scheme indemnity provision if the following requirements are met.

(3)   The provision must not provide any indemnity against –
     (a)   any liability of the director to pay –
         (i)   a fine imposed in criminal proceedings, or
         (ii)   a sum payable to a regulatory authority by way of a penalty in respect of non-compliance with any requirement of a regulatory nature (however arising); or
     (b)   any liability incurred by the director in defending criminal proceedings in which he is convicted.

(4)   The reference in subsection (3)(b) to a conviction is to the final decision in the proceedings.

(5)   For this purpose –
   (a)   a conviction becomes final –
      (i)   if not appealed against, at the end of the period for bringing an appeal, or
      (ii)   if appealed against, at the time when the appeal (or any further appeal) is disposed of; and
   (b)   an appeal is disposed of –
      (i)   if it is determined and the period for bringing any further appeal has ended, or
      (ii)   if it is abandoned or otherwise ceases to have effect.

(6)   In this section "occupational pension scheme" means an occupational pension scheme as defined in section 150(5) of the Finance Act 2004 (c. 12) that is established under a trust.

236   Qualifying indemnity provision to be disclosed in directors' report

(1)   This section requires disclosure in the directors' report of –
   (a)   qualifying third party indemnity provision, and
   (b)   qualifying pension scheme indemnity provision.
Such provision is referred to in this section as "qualifying indemnity provision".

(2)   If when a directors' report is approved any qualifying indemnity provision (whether made by the company or otherwise) is in force for the benefit of one or more directors of the company, the report must state that such provision is in force.

(3)   If at any time during the financial year to which a directors' report relates any such provision was in force for the benefit of one or more persons who were then directors of the company, the report must state that such provision was in force.

(4)   If when a directors' report is approved qualifying indemnity provision made by the company is in force for the benefit of one or more directors of an associated company, the report must state that such provision is in force.

(5)   If at any time during the financial year to which a directors' report relates any such provision was in force for the benefit of one or more persons who were then directors of an associated company, the report must state that such provision was in force.

237   Copy of qualifying indemnity provision to be available for inspection

(1)   This section has effect where qualifying indemnity provision is made for a director of a company, and applies –
   (a)   to the company of which he is a director (whether the provision is made by that company or an associated company), and
   (b)   where the provision is made by an associated company, to that company.

(2)   That company or, as the case may be, each of them must keep available for inspection –
   (a)   a copy of the qualifying indemnity provision, or

     (b) if the provision is not in writing, a written memorandum setting out its terms.

(3) The copy or memorandum must be kept available for inspection at –
    (a) the company's registered office, or
    (b) a place specified in regulations under section 1136.

(4) The copy or memorandum must be retained by the company for at least one year from the date of termination or expiry of the provision and must be kept available for inspection during that time.

(5) The company must give notice to the registrar –
    (a) of the place at which the copy or memorandum is kept available for inspection, and
    (b) of any change in that place,
unless it has at all times been kept at the company's registered office.

(6) If default is made in complying with subsection (2), (3) or (4), or default is made for 14 days in complying with subsection (5), an offence is committed by every officer of the company who is in default.

(7) A person guilty of an offence under this section is liable on summary conviction to a fine not exceeding level 3 on the standard scale and, for continued contravention, a daily default fine not exceeding one-tenth of level 3 on the standard scale.

(8) The provisions of this section apply to a variation of a qualifying indemnity provision as they apply to the original provision.

(9) In this section "qualifying indemnity provision" means –
    (a) qualifying third party indemnity provision, and
    (b) qualifying pension scheme indemnity provision.

238   Right of member to inspect and request copy

(1) Every copy or memorandum required to be kept by a company under section 237 must be open to inspection by any member of the company without charge.

(2) Any member of the company is entitled, on request and on payment of such fee as may be prescribed, to be provided with a copy of any such copy or memorandum.
The copy must be provided within seven days after the request is received by the company.

(3) If an inspection required under subsection (1) is refused, or default is made in complying with subsection (2), an offence is committed by every officer of the company who is in default.

(4) A person guilty of an offence under this section is liable on summary conviction to a fine not exceeding level 3 on the standard scale and, for continued contravention, a daily default fine not exceeding one-tenth of level 3 on the standard scale.

(5) In the case of any such refusal or default the court may by order compel an immediate inspection or, as the case may be, direct that the copy required be sent to the person requiring it.

Ratification of acts giving rise to liability

239   Ratification of acts of directors

   (1)   This section applies to the ratification by a company of conduct by a director amounting to negligence, default, breach of duty or breach of trust in relation to the company.

   (2)   The decision of the company to ratify such conduct must be made by resolution of the members of the company.

   (3)   Where the resolution is proposed as a written resolution neither the director (if a member of the company) nor any member connected with him is an eligible member.

   (4)   Where the resolution is proposed at a meeting, it is passed only if the necessary majority is obtained disregarding votes in favour of the resolution by the director (if a member of the company) and any member connected with him.
         This does not prevent the director or any such member from attending, being counted towards the quorum and taking part in the proceedings at any meeting at which the decision is considered.

   (5)   For the purposes of this section –
         (a)   "conduct" includes acts and omissions;
         (b)   "director" includes a former director;
         (c)   a shadow director is treated as a director; and
         (d)   in section 252 (meaning of "connected person"), subsection (3) does not apply (exclusion of person who is himself a director).

   (6)   Nothing in this section affects –
         (a)   the validity of a decision taken by unanimous consent of the members of the company, or
         (b)   any power of the directors to agree not to sue, or to settle or release a claim made by them on behalf of the company.

   (7)   This section does not affect any other enactment or rule of law imposing additional requirements for valid ratification or any rule of law as to acts that are incapable of being ratified by the company.

CHAPTER 8

DIRECTORS' RESIDENTIAL ADDRESSES: PROTECTION FROM DISCLOSURE

240   Protected information

   (1)   This Chapter makes provision for protecting, in the case of a company director who is an individual –
         (a)   information as to his usual residential address;
         (b)   the information that his service address is his usual residential address.

   (2)   That information is referred to in this Chapter as "protected information".

   (3)   Information does not cease to be protected information on the individual ceasing to be a director of the company.
         References in this Chapter to a director include, to that extent, a former director.

241   Protected information: restriction on use or disclosure by company

(1)   A company must not use or disclose protected information about any of its directors, except –
  (a)   for communicating with the director concerned,
  (b)   in order to comply with any requirement of the Companies Acts as to particulars to be sent to the registrar, or
  (c)   in accordance with section 244 (disclosure under court order).

(2)   Subsection (1) does not prohibit any use or disclosure of protected information with the consent of the director concerned.

242   Protected information: restriction on use or disclosure by registrar

(1)   The registrar must omit protected information from the material on the register that is available for inspection where –
  (a)   it is contained in a document delivered to him in which such information is required to be stated, and
  (b)   in the case of a document having more than one part, it is contained in a part of the document in which such information is required to be stated.

(2)   The registrar is not obliged –
  (a)   to check other documents or (as the case may be) other parts of the document to ensure the absence of protected information, or
  (b)   to omit from the material that is available for public inspection anything registered before this Chapter comes into force.

(3)   The registrar must not use or disclose protected information except –
  (a)   as permitted by section 243 (permitted use or disclosure by registrar), or
  (b)   in accordance with section 244 (disclosure under court order).

243   Permitted use or disclosure by the registrar

(1)   The registrar may use protected information for communicating with the director in question.

(2)   The registrar may disclose protected information –
  (a)   to a public authority specified for the purposes of this section by regulations made by the Secretary of State, or
  (b)   to a credit reference agency.

(3)   The Secretary of State may make provision by regulations –
  (a)   specifying conditions for the disclosure of protected information in accordance with this section, and
  (b)   providing for the charging of fees.

(4)   The Secretary of State may make provision by regulations requiring the registrar, on application, to refrain from disclosing protected information relating to a director to a credit reference agency.

(5)   Regulations under subsection (4) may make provision as to –
  (a)   who may make an application,
  (b)   the grounds on which an application may be made,
  (c)   the information to be included in and documents to accompany an application, and
  (d)   how an application is to be determined.

(6)   Provision under subsection (5)(d) may in particular –

    (a)   confer a discretion on the registrar;

    (b)   provide for a question to be referred to a person other than the registrar for the purposes of determining the application.

(7)   In this section –

      "credit reference agency" means a person carrying on a business comprising the furnishing of information relevant to the financial standing of individuals, being information collected by the agency for that purpose; and

      "public authority" includes any person or body having functions of a public nature.

(8)   Regulations under this section are subject to negative resolution procedure.

244 Disclosure under court order

(1)   The court may make an order for the disclosure of protected information by the company or by the registrar if –

    (a)   there is evidence that service of documents at a service address other than the director's usual residential address is not effective to bring them to the notice of the director, or

    (b)   it is necessary or expedient for the information to be provided in connection with the enforcement of an order or decree of the court,

and the court is otherwise satisfied that it is appropriate to make the order.

(2)   An order for disclosure by the registrar is to be made only if the company –

    (a)   does not have the director's usual residential address, or

    (b)   has been dissolved.

(3)   The order may be made on the application of a liquidator, creditor or member of the company, or any other person appearing to the court to have a sufficient interest.

(4)   The order must specify the persons to whom, and purposes for which, disclosure is authorised.

245 Circumstances in which registrar may put address on the public record

(1)   The registrar may put a director's usual residential address on the public record if –

    (a)   communications sent by the registrar to the director and requiring a response within a specified period remain unanswered, or

    (b)   there is evidence that service of documents at a service address provided in place of the director's usual residential address is not effective to bring them to the notice of the director.

(2)   The registrar must give notice of the proposal –

    (a)   to the director, and

    (b)   to every company of which the registrar has been notified that the individual is a director.

(3)   The notice must –

    (a)   state the grounds on which it is proposed to put the director's usual residential address on the public record, and

    (b)   specify a period within which representations may be made before that is done.

(4)   It must be sent to the director at his usual residential address, unless it appears to the registrar that service at that address may be ineffective to bring it to the individual's notice, in which case it may be sent to any service address provided in place of that address.

(5)   The registrar must take account of any representations received within the specified period.

(6)   What is meant by putting the address on the public record is explained in section 246.

246   Putting the address on the public record

(1)   The registrar, on deciding in accordance with section 245 that a director's usual residential address is to be put on the public record, shall proceed as if notice of a change of registered particulars had been given –
  (a)   stating that address as the director's service address, and
  (b)   stating that the director's usual residential address is the same as his service address.

(2)   The registrar must give notice of having done so –
  (a)   to the director, and
  (b)   to the company.

(3)   On receipt of the notice the company must –
  (a)   enter the director's usual residential address in its register of directors as his service address, and
  (b)   state in its register of directors' residential addresses that his usual residential address is the same as his service address.

(4)   If the company has been notified by the director in question of a more recent address as his usual residential address, it must –
  (a)   enter that address in its register of directors as the director's service address, and
  (b)   give notice to the registrar as on a change of registered particulars.

(5)   If a company fails to comply with subsection (3) or (4), an offence is committed by –
  (a)   the company, and
  (b)   every officer of the company who is in default.

(6)   A person guilty of an offence under subsection (5) is liable on summary conviction to a fine not exceeding level 5 on the standard scale and, for continued contravention, a daily default fine not exceeding one-tenth of level 5 on the standard scale.

(7)   A director whose usual residential address has been put on the public record by the registrar under this section may not register a service address other than his usual residential address for a period of five years from the date of the registrar's decision.

CHAPTER 9

SUPPLEMENTARY PROVISIONS

Provision for employees on cessation or transfer of business

247   Power to make provision for employees on cessation or transfer of business

(1)   The powers of the directors of a company include (if they would not otherwise do so) power to make provision for the benefit of persons employed or formerly employed by the company, or any of its subsidiaries, in connection with the cessation or the transfer to any person of the whole or part of the undertaking of the company or that subsidiary.

(2)   This power is exercisable notwithstanding the general duty imposed by section 172 (duty to promote the success of the company).

(3)   In the case of a company that is a charity it is exercisable notwithstanding any restrictions on the directors' powers (or the company's capacity) flowing from the objects of the company.

(4)   The power may only be exercised if sanctioned –
    (a)   by a resolution of the company, or
    (b)   by a resolution of the directors,
in accordance with the following provisions.

(5)   A resolution of the directors –
    (a)   must be authorised by the company's articles, and
    (b)   is not sufficient sanction for payments to or for the benefit of directors, former directors or shadow directors.

(6)   Any other requirements of the company's articles as to the exercise of the power conferred by this section must be complied with.

(7)   Any payment under this section must be made –
    (a)   before the commencement of any winding up of the company, and
    (b)   out of profits of the company that are available for dividend.

Records of meetings of directors

248   Minutes of directors' meetings

(1)   Every company must cause minutes of all proceedings at meetings of its directors to be recorded.

(2)   The records must be kept for at least ten years from the date of the meeting.

(3)   If a company fails to comply with this section, an offence is committed by every officer of the company who is in default.

(4)   A person guilty of an offence under this section is liable on summary conviction to a fine not exceeding level 3 on the standard scale and, for continued contravention, a daily default fine not exceeding one-tenth of level 3 on the standard scale.

249   Minutes as evidence

(1)   Minutes recorded in accordance with section 248, if purporting to be authenticated by the chairman of the meeting or by the chairman of the next

directors' meeting, are evidence (in Scotland, sufficient evidence) of the proceedings at the meeting.

(2) Where minutes have been made in accordance with that section of the proceedings of a meeting of directors, then, until the contrary is proved –
   (a) the meeting is deemed duly held and convened,
   (b) all proceedings at the meeting are deemed to have duly taken place, and
   (c) all appointments at the meeting are deemed valid.

Meaning of "director" and "shadow director"

250 "Director"

In the Companies Acts "director" includes any person occupying the position of director, by whatever name called.

251 "Shadow director"

(1) In the Companies Acts "shadow director", in relation to a company, means a person in accordance with whose directions or instructions the directors of the company are accustomed to act.

(2) A person is not to be regarded as a shadow director by reason only that the directors act on advice given by him in a professional capacity.

(3) A body corporate is not to be regarded as a shadow director of any of its subsidiary companies for the purposes of –
   Chapter 2 (general duties of directors),
   Chapter 4 (transactions requiring members' approval), or
   Chapter 6 (contract with sole member who is also a director),
by reason only that the directors of the subsidiary are accustomed to act in accordance with its directions or instructions.

Other definitions

252 Persons connected with a director

(1) This section defines what is meant by references in this Part to a person being "connected" with a director of a company (or a director being "connected" with a person).

(2) The following persons (and only those persons) are connected with a director of a company –
   (a) members of the director's family (see section 253);
   (b) a body corporate with which the director is connected (as defined in section 254);
   (c) a person acting in his capacity as trustee of a trust –
      (i) the beneficiaries of which include the director or a person who by virtue of paragraph (a) or (b) is connected with him, or
      (ii) the terms of which confer a power on the trustees that may be exercised for the benefit of the director or any such person,
      other than a trust for the purposes of an employees' share scheme or a pension scheme;

    (d)   a person acting in his capacity as partner –
- (i)   of the director, or
- (ii) of a person who, by virtue of paragraph (a), (b) or (c), is connected with that director;

    (e)   a firm that is a legal person under the law by which it is governed and in which –
- (i)   the director is a partner,
- (ii) a partner is a person who, by virtue of paragraph (a), (b) or (c) is connected with the director, or
- (iii) a partner is a firm in which the director is a partner or in which there is a partner who, by virtue of paragraph (a), (b) or (c), is connected with the director.

(3)   References in this Part to a person connected with a director of a company do not include a person who is himself a director of the company.

253 Members of a director's family

(1)   This section defines what is meant by references in this Part to members of a director's family.

(2)   For the purposes of this Part the members of a director's family are –
- (a)   the director's spouse or civil partner;
- (b)   any other person (whether of a different sex or the same sex) with whom the director lives as partner in an enduring family relationship;
- (c)   the director's children or step-children;
- (d)   any children or step-children of a person within paragraph (b) (and who are not children or step-children of the director) who live with the director and have not attained the age of 18;
- (e)   the director's parents.

(3)   Subsection (2)(b) does not apply if the other person is the director's grandparent or grandchild, sister, brother, aunt or uncle, or nephew or niece.

254 Director "connected with" a body corporate

(1)   This section defines what is meant by references in this Part to a director being "connected with" a body corporate.

(2)   A director is connected with a body corporate if, but only if, he and the persons connected with him together –
- (a)   are interested in shares comprised in the equity share capital of that body corporate of a nominal value equal to at least 20% of that share capital, or
- (b)   are entitled to exercise or control the exercise of more than 20% of the voting power at any general meeting of that body.

(3)   The rules set out in Schedule 1 (references to interest in shares or debentures) apply for the purposes of this section.

(4)   References in this section to voting power the exercise of which is controlled by a director include voting power whose exercise is controlled by a body corporate controlled by him.

(5)   Shares in a company held as treasury shares, and any voting rights attached to such shares, are disregarded for the purposes of this section.

(6) For the avoidance of circularity in the application of section 252 (meaning of "connected person") –

    (a) a body corporate with which a director is connected is not treated for the purposes of this section as connected with him unless it is also connected with him by virtue of subsection (2)(c) or (d) of that section (connection as trustee or partner); and

    (b) a trustee of a trust the beneficiaries of which include (or may include) a body corporate with which a director is connected is not treated for the purposes of this section as connected with a director by reason only of that fact.

255 Director "controlling" a body corporate

(1) This section defines what is meant by references in this Part to a director "controlling" a body corporate.

(2) A director of a company is taken to control a body corporate if, but only if –

    (a) he or any person connected with him –

        (i) is interested in any part of the equity share capital of that body, or

        (ii) is entitled to exercise or control the exercise of any part of the voting power at any general meeting of that body, and

    (b) he, the persons connected with him and the other directors of that company, together –

        (i) are interested in more than 50% of that share capital, or

        (ii) are entitled to exercise or control the exercise of more than 50% of that voting power.

(3) The rules set out in Schedule 1 (references to interest in shares or debentures) apply for the purposes of this section.

(4) References in this section to voting power the exercise of which is controlled by a director include voting power whose exercise is controlled by a body corporate controlled by him.

(5) Shares in a company held as treasury shares, and any voting rights attached to such shares, are disregarded for the purposes of this section.

(6) For the avoidance of circularity in the application of section 252 (meaning of "connected person") –

    (a) a body corporate with which a director is connected is not treated for the purposes of this section as connected with him unless it is also connected with him by virtue of subsection (2)(c) or (d) of that section (connection as trustee or partner); and

    (b) a trustee of a trust the beneficiaries of which include (or may include) a body corporate with which a director is connected is not treated for the purposes of this section as connected with a director by reason only of that fact.

256 Associated bodies corporate

For the purposes of this Part –

    (a) bodies corporate are associated if one is a subsidiary of the other or both are subsidiaries of the same body corporate, and

    (b)   companies are associated if one is a subsidiary of the other or both are subsidiaries of the same body corporate.

257   References to company's constitution

  (1)   References in this Part to a company's constitution include –

     (a)   any resolution or other decision come to in accordance with the constitution, and

     (b)   any decision by the members of the company, or a class of members, that is treated by virtue of any enactment or rule of law as equivalent to a decision by the company.

  (2)   This is in addition to the matters mentioned in section 17 (general provision as to matters contained in company's constitution).

General

258   Power to increase financial limits

  (1)   The Secretary of State may by order substitute for any sum of money specified in this Part a larger sum specified in the order.

  (2)   An order under this section is subject to negative resolution procedure.

  (3)   An order does not have effect in relation to anything done or not done before it comes into force.

       Accordingly, proceedings in respect of any liability incurred before that time may be continued or instituted as if the order had not been made.

259   Transactions under foreign law

       For the purposes of this Part it is immaterial whether the law that (apart from this Act) governs an arrangement or transaction is the law of the United Kingdom, or a part of it, or not.

Derivative claims

Sections 260–264

PART 11

DERIVATIVE CLAIMS AND PROCEEDINGS BY MEMBERS

CHAPTER 1

DERIVATIVE CLAIMS IN ENGLAND AND WALES OR NORTHERN IRELAND

260 Derivative claims

 (1) This Chapter applies to proceedings in England and Wales or Northern Ireland by a member of a company –

    (a) in respect of a cause of action vested in the company, and

    (b) seeking relief on behalf of the company.

This is referred to in this Chapter as a "derivative claim".

 (2) A derivative claim may only be brought –

    (a) under this Chapter, or

    (b) in pursuance of an order of the court in proceedings under section 994 (proceedings for protection of members against unfair prejudice).

 (3) A derivative claim under this Chapter may be brought only in respect of a cause of action arising from an actual or proposed act or omission involving negligence, default, breach of duty or breach of trust by a director of the company.

The cause of action may be against the director or another person (or both).

 (4) It is immaterial whether the cause of action arose before or after the person seeking to bring or continue the derivative claim became a member of the company.

 (5) For the purposes of this Chapter –

    (a) "director" includes a former director;

    (b) a shadow director is treated as a director; and

    (c) references to a member of a company include a person who is not a member but to whom shares in the company have been transferred or transmitted by operation of law.

261   Application for permission to continue derivative claim
(1)   A member of a company who brings a derivative claim under this Chapter must apply to the court for permission (in Northern Ireland, leave) to continue it.
(2)   If it appears to the court that the application and the evidence filed by the applicant in support of it do not disclose a prima facie case for giving permission (or leave), the court –
    (a)   must dismiss the application, and
    (b)   may make any consequential order it considers appropriate.
(3)   If the application is not dismissed under subsection (2), the court –
    (a)   may give directions as to the evidence to be provided by the company, and
    (b)   may adjourn the proceedings to enable the evidence to be obtained.
(4)   On hearing the application, the court may –
    (a)   give permission (or leave) to continue the claim on such terms as it thinks fit,
    (b)   refuse permission (or leave) and dismiss the claim, or
    (c)   adjourn the proceedings on the application and give such directions as it thinks fit.

262   Application for permission to continue claim as a derivative claim
(1)   This section applies where –
    (a)   a company has brought a claim, and
    (b)   the cause of action on which the claim is based could be pursued as a derivative claim under this Chapter.
(2)   A member of the company may apply to the court for permission (in Northern Ireland, leave) to continue the claim as a derivative claim on the ground that –
    (a)   the manner in which the company commenced or continued the claim amounts to an abuse of the process of the court,
    (b)   the company has failed to prosecute the claim diligently, and
    (c)   it is appropriate for the member to continue the claim as a derivative claim.
(3)   If it appears to the court that the application and the evidence filed by the applicant in support of it do not disclose a prima facie case for giving permission (or leave), the court –
    (a)   must dismiss the application, and
    (b)   may make any consequential order it considers appropriate.
(4)   If the application is not dismissed under subsection (3), the court –
    (a)   may give directions as to the evidence to be provided by the company, and
    (b)   may adjourn the proceedings to enable the evidence to be obtained.
(5)   On hearing the application, the court may –
    (a)   give permission (or leave) to continue the claim as a derivative claim on such terms as it thinks fit,
    (b)   refuse permission (or leave) and dismiss the application, or
    (c)   adjourn the proceedings on the application and give such directions as it thinks fit.

263 Whether permission to be given

(1)   The following provisions have effect where a member of a company applies for permission (in Northern Ireland, leave) under section 261 or 262.

(2)   Permission (or leave) must be refused if the court is satisfied –

    (a)   that a person acting in accordance with section 172 (duty to promote the success of the company) would not seek to continue the claim, or

    (b)   where the cause of action arises from an act or omission that is yet to occur, that the act or omission has been authorised by the company, or

    (c)   where the cause of action arises from an act or omission that has already occurred, that the act or omission –

        (i)   was authorised by the company before it occurred, or

        (ii) has been ratified by the company since it occurred.

(3)   In considering whether to give permission (or leave) the court must take into account, in particular –

    (a)   whether the member is acting in good faith in seeking to continue the claim;

    (b)   the importance that a person acting in accordance with section 172 (duty to promote the success of the company) would attach to continuing it;

    (c)   where the cause of action results from an act or omission that is yet to occur, whether the act or omission could be, and in the circumstances would be likely to be –

        (i)   authorised by the company before it occurs, or

        (ii) ratified by the company after it occurs;

    (d)   where the cause of action arises from an act or omission that has already occurred, whether the act or omission could be, and in the circumstances would be likely to be, ratified by the company;

    (e)   whether the company has decided not to pursue the claim;

    (f)   whether the act or omission in respect of which the claim is brought gives rise to a cause of action that the member could pursue in his own right rather than on behalf of the company.

(4)   In considering whether to give permission (or leave) the court shall have particular regard to any evidence before it as to the views of members of the company who have no personal interest, direct or indirect, in the matter.

(5)   The Secretary of State may by regulations –

    (a)   amend subsection (2) so as to alter or add to the circumstances in which permission (or leave) is to be refused;

    (b)   amend subsection (3) so as to alter or add to the matters that the court is required to take into account in considering whether to give permission (or leave).

(6)   Before making any such regulations the Secretary of State shall consult such persons as he considers appropriate.

(7)   Regulations under this section are subject to affirmative resolution procedure.

264 Application for permission to continue derivative claim brought by another member

(1)   This section applies where a member of a company ("the claimant") –

    (a)   has brought a derivative claim,

      (b)   has continued as a derivative claim a claim brought by the company, or

      (c)   has continued a derivative claim under this section.

(2)   Another member of the company ("the applicant") may apply to the court for permission (in Northern Ireland, leave) to continue the claim on the ground that –

      (a)   the manner in which the proceedings have been commenced or continued by the claimant amounts to an abuse of the process of the court,

      (b)   the claimant has failed to prosecute the claim diligently, and

      (c)   it is appropriate for the applicant to continue the claim as a derivative claim.

(3)   If it appears to the court that the application and the evidence filed by the applicant in support of it do not disclose a prima facie case for giving permission (or leave), the court –

      (a)   must dismiss the application, and

      (b)   may make any consequential order it considers appropriate.

(4)   If the application is not dismissed under subsection (3), the court –

      (a)   may give directions as to the evidence to be provided by the company, and

      (b)   may adjourn the proceedings to enable the evidence to be obtained.

(5)   On hearing the application, the court may –

      (a)   give permission (or leave) to continue the claim on such terms as it thinks fit,

      (b)   refuse permission (or leave) and dismiss the application, or

      (c)   adjourn the proceedings on the application and give such directions as it thinks fit.

Classes of share and class rights

Sections 629–640

CHAPTER 9

CLASSES OF SHARE AND CLASS RIGHTS

Introductory

629   Classes of shares

(1)   For the purposes of the Companies Acts shares are of one class if the rights attached to them are in all respects uniform.

(2)   For this purpose the rights attached to shares are not regarded as different from those attached to other shares by reason only that they do not carry the same rights to dividends in the twelve months immediately following their allotment.

Variation of class rights

630   Variation of class rights: companies having a share capital

(1)   This section is concerned with the variation of the rights attached to a class of shares in a company having a share capital.

(2)   Rights attached to a class of a company's shares may only be varied –

    (a)   in accordance with provision in the company's articles for the variation of those rights, or

    (b)   where the company's articles contain no such provision, if the holders of shares of that class consent to the variation in accordance with this section.

(3)   This is without prejudice to any other restrictions on the variation of the rights.

(4)   The consent required for the purposes of this section on the part of the holders of a class of a company's shares is –

    (a)   consent in writing from the holders of at least three-quarters in nominal value of the issued shares of that class (excluding any shares held as treasury shares), or

    (b)   a special resolution passed at a separate general meeting of the holders of that class sanctioning the variation.

(5)   Any amendment of a provision contained in a company's articles for the variation of the rights attached to a class of shares, or the insertion of any such provision into the articles, is itself to be treated as a variation of those rights.

(6)   In this section, and (except where the context otherwise requires) in any provision in a company's articles for the variation of the rights attached to a class of shares, references to the variation of those rights include references to their abrogation.

631   Variation of class rights: companies without a share capital

(1)   This section is concerned with the variation of the rights of a class of members of a company where the company does not have a share capital.

(2)   Rights of a class of members may only be varied –
   (a)   in accordance with provision in the company's articles for the variation of those rights, or
   (b)   where the company's articles contain no such provision, if the members of that class consent to the variation in accordance with this section.

(3)   This is without prejudice to any other restrictions on the variation of the rights.

(4)   The consent required for the purposes of this section on the part of the members of a class is –
   (a)   consent in writing from at least three-quarters of the members of the class, or
   (b)   a special resolution passed at a separate general meeting of the members of that class sanctioning the variation.

(5)   Any amendment of a provision contained in a company's articles for the variation of the rights of a class of members, or the insertion of any such provision into the articles, is itself to be treated as a variation of those rights.

(6)   In this section, and (except where the context otherwise requires) in any provision in a company's articles for the variation of the rights of a class of members, references to the variation of those rights include references to their abrogation.

632   Variation of class rights: saving for court's powers under other provisions

Nothing in section 630 or 631 (variation of class rights) affects the power of the court under –
   section 98 (application to cancel resolution for public company to be re-registered as private),
   Part 26 (arrangements and reconstructions), or
   Part 30 (protection of members against unfair prejudice).

633   Right to object to variation: companies having a share capital

(1)   This section applies where the rights attached to any class of shares in a company are varied under section 630 (variation of class rights: companies having a share capital).

(2)   The holders of not less in the aggregate than 15% of the issued shares of the class in question (being persons who did not consent to or vote in favour of

the resolution for the variation) may apply to the court to have the variation cancelled.

For this purpose any of the company's share capital held as treasury shares is disregarded.

(3) If such an application is made, the variation has no effect unless and until it is confirmed by the court.

(4) Application to the court –

    (a) must be made within 21 days after the date on which the consent was given or the resolution was passed (as the case may be), and

    (b) may be made on behalf of the shareholders entitled to make the application by such one or more of their number as they may appoint in writing for the purpose.

(5) The court, after hearing the applicant and any other persons who apply to the court to be heard and appear to the court to be interested in the application, may, if satisfied having regard to all the circumstances of the case that the variation would unfairly prejudice the shareholders of the class represented by the applicant, disallow the variation, and shall if not so satisfied confirm it. The decision of the court on any such application is final.

(6) References in this section to the variation of the rights of holders of a class of shares include references to their abrogation.

634   Right to object to variation: companies without a share capital

(1) This section applies where the rights of any class of members of a company are varied under section 631 (variation of class rights: companies without a share capital).

(2) Members amounting to not less than 15% of the members of the class in question (being persons who did not consent to or vote in favour of the resolution for the variation) may apply to the court to have the variation cancelled.

(3) If such an application is made, the variation has no effect unless and until it is confirmed by the court.

(4) Application to the court must be made within 21 days after the date on which the consent was given or the resolution was passed (as the case may be) and may be made on behalf of the members entitled to make the application by such one or more of their number as they may appoint in writing for the purpose.

(5) The court, after hearing the applicant and any other persons who apply to the court to be heard and appear to the court to be interested in the application, may, if satisfied having regard to all the circumstances of the case that the variation would unfairly prejudice the members of the class represented by the applicant, disallow the variation, and shall if not so satisfied confirm it. The decision of the court on any such application is final.

(6) References in this section to the variation of the rights of a class of members include references to their abrogation.

635   Copy of court order to be forwarded to the registrar

(1) The company must within 15 days after the making of an order by the court on an application under section 633 or 634 (objection to variation of class rights) forward a copy of the order to the registrar.

(2)   If default is made in complying with this section an offence is committed by –
    (a)   the company, and
    (b)   every officer of the company who is in default.

(3)   A person guilty of an offence under this section is liable on summary conviction to a fine not exceeding level 3 on the standard scale and, for continued contravention, a daily default fine not exceeding one-tenth of level 3 on the standard scale.

Matters to be notified to the registrar

636   Notice of name or other designation of class of shares

(1)   Where a company assigns a name or other designation, or a new name or other designation, to any class or description of its shares, it must within one month from doing so deliver to the registrar a notice giving particulars of the name or designation so assigned.

(2)   If default is made in complying with this section, an offence is committed by –
    (a)   the company, and
    (b)   every officer of the company who is in default.

(3)   A person guilty of an offence under this section is liable on summary conviction to a fine not exceeding level 3 on the standard scale and, for continued contravention, a daily default fine not exceeding one-tenth of level 3 on the standard scale.

637   Notice of particulars of variation of rights attached to shares

(1)   Where the rights attached to any shares of a company are varied, the company must within one month from the date on which the variation is made deliver to the registrar a notice giving particulars of the variation.

(2)   If default is made in complying with this section, an offence is committed by –
    (a)   the company, and
    (b)   every officer of the company who is in default.

(3)   A person guilty of an offence under this section is liable on summary conviction to a fine not exceeding level 3 on the standard scale and, for continued contravention, a daily default fine not exceeding one-tenth of level 3 on the standard scale.

638   Notice of new class of members

(1)   If a company not having a share capital creates a new class of members, the company must within one month from the date on which the new class is created deliver to the registrar a notice containing particulars of the rights attached to that class.

(2)   If default is made in complying with this section, an offence is committed by –
    (a)   the company, and
    (b)   every officer of the company who is in default.

(3)   A person guilty of an offence under this section is liable on summary

conviction to a fine not exceeding level 3 on the standard scale and, for continued contravention, a daily default fine not exceeding one-tenth of level 3 on the standard scale.

639   Notice of name or other designation of class of members

(1)   Where a company not having a share capital assigns a name or other designation, or a new name or other designation, to any class of its members, it must within one month from doing so deliver to the registrar a notice giving particulars of the name or designation so assigned.

(2)   If default is made in complying with this section, an offence is committed by –

(a)   the company, and

(b)   every officer of the company who is in default.

(3)   A person guilty of an offence under this section is liable on summary conviction to a fine not exceeding level 3 on the standard scale and, for continued contravention, a daily default fine not exceeding one-tenth of level 3 on the standard scale.

640   Notice of particulars of variation of class rights

(1)   If the rights of any class of members of a company not having a share capital are varied, the company must within one month from the date on which the variation is made deliver to the registrar a notice containing particulars of the variation.

(2)   If default is made in complying with this section, an offence is committed by –

(a)   the company, and

(b)   every officer of the company who is in default.

(3)   A person guilty of an offence under this section is liable on summary conviction to a fine not exceeding level 3 on the standard scale and, for continued contravention, a daily default fine not exceeding one-tenth of level 3 on the standard scale.

Protection of members against unfair prejudice

Sections 994–999

PART 30

PROTECTION OF MEMBERS AGAINST UNFAIR PREJUDICE

Main provisions

994 Petition by company member

(1) A member of a company may apply to the court by petition for an order under this Part on the ground –

    (a) that the company's affairs are being or have been conducted in a manner that is unfairly prejudicial to the interests of members generally or of some part of its members (including at least himself), or

    (b) that an actual or proposed act or omission of the company (including an act or omission on its behalf) is or would be so prejudicial.

(2) The provisions of this Part apply to a person who is not a member of a company but to whom shares in the company have been transferred or transmitted by operation of law as they apply to a member of a company.

(3) In this section, and so far as applicable for the purposes of this section in the other provisions of this Part, "company" means –

    (a) a company within the meaning of this Act, or

    (b) a company that is not such a company but is a statutory water company within the meaning of the Statutory Water Companies Act 1991 (c. 58).

995 Petition by Secretary of State

(1) This section applies to a company in respect of which –

    (a) the Secretary of State has received a report under section 437 of the Companies Act 1985 (c. 6) (inspector's report);

    (b) the Secretary of State has exercised his powers under section 447 or 448 of that Act (powers to require documents and information or to enter and search premises);

    (c) the Secretary of State or the Financial Services Authority has exercised his or its powers under Part 11 of the Financial Services and Markets Act 2000 (c. 8) (information gathering and investigations); or

(d)   the Secretary of State has received a report from an investigator appointed by him or the Financial Services Authority under that Part.

(2)   If it appears to the Secretary of State that in the case of such a company –

    (a)   the company's affairs are being or have been conducted in a manner that is unfairly prejudicial to the interests of members generally or of some part of its members, or

    (b)   an actual or proposed act or omission of the company (including an act or omission on its behalf) is or would be so prejudicial,

he may apply to the court by petition for an order under this Part.

(3)   The Secretary of State may do this in addition to, or instead of, presenting a petition for the winding up of the company.

(4)   In this section, and so far as applicable for the purposes of this section in the other provisions of this Part, "company" means any body corporate that is liable to be wound up under the Insolvency Act 1986 (c. 45) or the Insolvency (Northern Ireland) Order 1989 (S.I. 1989/2405 (N.I. 19)).

996   Powers of the court under this Part

(1)   If the court is satisfied that a petition under this Part is well founded, it may make such order as it thinks fit for giving relief in respect of the matters complained of.

(2)   Without prejudice to the generality of subsection (1), the court's order may –

    (a)   regulate the conduct of the company's affairs in the future;

    (b)   require the company –

        (i)   to refrain from doing or continuing an act complained of, or

        (ii)   to do an act that the petitioner has complained it has omitted to do;

    (c)   authorise civil proceedings to be brought in the name and on behalf of the company by such person or persons and on such terms as the court may direct;

    (d)   require the company not to make any, or any specified, alterations in its articles without the leave of the court;

    (e)   provide for the purchase of the shares of any members of the company by other members or by the company itself and, in the case of a purchase by the company itself, the reduction of the company's capital accordingly.

Supplementary provisions

997   Application of general rule-making powers

The power to make rules under section 411 of the Insolvency Act 1986 (c. 45) or Article 359 of the Insolvency (Northern Ireland) Order 1989 (S.I. 1989/ 2405 (N.I. 19)), so far as relating to a winding-up petition, applies for the purposes of a petition under this Part.

998   Copy of order affecting company's constitution to be delivered to registrar

(1)   Where an order of the court under this Part –

    (a)   alters the company's constitution, or

(b) gives leave for the company to make any, or any specified, alterations to its constitution,

the company must deliver a copy of the order to the registrar.
(2) It must do so within 14 days from the making of the order or such longer period as the court may allow.
(3) If a company makes default in complying with this section, an offence is committed by –
   (a) the company, and
   (b) every officer of the company who is in default.
(4) A person guilty of an offence under this section is liable on summary conviction to a fine not exceeding level 3 on the standard scale and, for continued contravention, a daily default fine not exceeding one-tenth of level 3 on the standard scale.

999 Supplementary provisions where company's constitution altered
(1) This section applies where an order under this Part alters a company's constitution.
(2) If the order amends –
   (a) a company's articles, or
   (b) any resolution or agreement to which Chapter 3 of Part 3 applies (resolution or agreement affecting a company's constitution),

the copy of the order delivered to the registrar by the company under section 998 must be accompanied by a copy of the company's articles, or the resolution or agreement in question, as amended.
(3) Every copy of a company's articles issued by the company after the order is made must be accompanied by a copy of the order, unless the effect of the order has been incorporated into the articles by amendment.
(4) If a company makes default in complying with this section an offence is committed by –
   (a) the company, and
   (b) every officer of the company who is in default.
(5) A person guilty of an offence under this section is liable on summary conviction to a fine not exceeding level 3 on the standard scale.

Index